s for Travel
a Tourism

Interpersonal Skills for Travel and Tourism

Jon and Lisa Burton

 LONGMAN

Addison Wesley Longman Limited
Edinburgh Gate, Harlow
Essex CM20 2JE, England
and Associated Companies throughout the world.

First published by Pitman Publishing 1994
Reprinted by Longman Scientific & Technical 1995
Reprinted by Addison Wesley Longman 1996, 1997 (twice)

British Library Cataloguing in Publication Data
A CIP record for this book is available from the British Library

ISBN 0 – 582 – 27946 – 1

Produced through Longman Malaysia, ACM

Contents

Preface

Good interpersonal skills are the key to success in any job, and in most industries. In a working situation, where employees are in continuous contact with each other and with the public, the ability to interact and communicate well is essential to the outcome of so much of the work they do.

This is especially true of the travel industry, where good interpersonal skills are a major part of everyone's job. Whether selling a holiday, dealing with a complaint, or taking a telephone enquiry, employees will need to demonstrate good communication skills in listening and questioning techniques, and building up rapport with the customer. The standard of service that your customers receive depends ultimately on the training and development of your staff. No training is needed more, and whilst your staff may possess excellent product knowledge and a high degree of technical skills, you will fail to win and keep customers if they do not have the requisite interpersonal skills.

Interpersonal skills though, are not limited just to sales situations. They also play an important part in the development of good working relationships and effective communication in the workplace. To be a really good manager, you will need to develop your interpersonal skills in interviewing, counselling, dealing with staff problems and leading discussions about staff performance. Managers who lack these vital interpersonal skills will be less able to motivate, lead and develop their staff to meet the demands of the business. The degree of interpersonal skill exhibited by management is always reflected in the way that staff are treated, and in the way that staff relate to their customers.

This book aims to provide the reader with the necessary interpersonal skills to enable them to communicate effectively in a variety of working situations. It will also enable the reader to become more familiar with some of the more complex interpersonal theory such as transactional analysis and assertiveness.

The book has been written in line with the requirements of Travel Services NVQ Levels I to IV, and provides candidates with the background information, practical guidelines and assignments necessary for the development of good interpersonal skills. The content of the book, though written mainly for travel agents and tour operators, is nevertheless just as relevant to other sectors of the travel industry such as: transport providers – air, rail, coach and ferry operators; tourist guides and tourist information centres; hotels and overseas resort representatives.

The main objectives of the book are to provide the reader with the knowledge to:

- create a professional impression on the customer – both face to face and over the telephone

- use active selling skills to increase sales of travel- and tourism-related products
- deal with customer complaints in a professional manner which will satisfy all parties
- use both written and verbal communication skills to communicate effectively with both customers and staff
- develop and enhance internal staff relationships through effective use of interpersonal skills.

The book is divided into fifteen chapters, each dealing with a particular aspect of interpersonal skills. The first five chapters of the book; Customer Care; Professional Use of the Telephone; Selling Skills; Handling Customer Complaints; and Written Communication are written in line with the requirements of NVQ Levels I, II and III, and may also be relevant background reading for managers or supervisors responsible for staff undertaking qualifications at this level. The following chapter on presentation skills is aimed at managerial staff – those taking NVQ Levels III and IV – but will be equally relevant to anyone who is expected to undertake a personal or sales presentation. The remaining sections of the book are written for managers and supervisors who intend to undertake NVQ Levels III and IV, although other staff may find specific chapters of the book, such as the Basics Of Assertiveness and Handling Interpersonal Conflict, of particular interest as background reading.

Each chapter of the book is written to stand alone as a subject, but some of the themes and concepts may appear in other chapters to which they are appropriate.

THE AUTHORS

This book was written jointly by husband and wife team, Jon and Lisa Burton who, between them, bring a wealth of knowledge and experience of various aspects of the travel industry.

Lisa Burton began her career in retail travel and has worked as sales consultant and, latterly, as branch manager in independent and multiple travel companies. With a keen interest in staff development and training, she moved into a large training organization in 1988 and has been delivering interpersonal training to all sectors of the travel industry over the last five years. She specialises in customer care, telephone techniques, selling and assertiveness skills.

Jon Burton started his career in travel in 1975, working towards a diploma in travel and tourism at Bournemouth College. Since then he has worked in both the retail and commercial sectors of industry, before moving into a full-time training position with Renwicks Travel in 1981. Jon has been heavily involved in interpersonal skills training and development for the last nine years, and specialises in personal presentations and management skills. In his spare time, Jon is a registered Blue Badge Guide for both the Southern and West Country Tourist Boards.

Illustrations

To our son Oliver

1

....

Customer care

Good customer care means different things to different people. For some, it may be a sympathetic sales person and a friendly and relaxed approach. For others, it may be a slick, quick professional service. The important thing to remember is that customers have many different expectations.

With this in mind, it is important that all sales and service staff are able to understand and use customer contact skills. But, this is only the beginning of providing real customer care, and once the basics have been acquired, the real skill comes with being able to adapt and change personal approach and manner to suit each individual customer. This chapter aims to give you an insight into the importance of providing quality customer care and provides you with practical guidelines to create a friendly, positive and professional image to your customer.

OBJECTIVES

Once you have read this chapter of the book, you should be able to:
- **state the importance of providing good customer care**
- **state guidelines for using an appropriate manner with the customer**
- **use active listening skills to ensure that you are paying full attention to the customer**
- **state guidelines for building a professional relationship with the customer**
- **state how personal levels of motivation affect the standard of service the customer receives**
- **state guidelines for dealing with a variety of 'difficult' customers.**

WHAT IS GOOD CUSTOMER CARE?

Good customer care is whatever the customer believes it to be. If customers are fully satisfied with the service they receive, then their needs as customers have been met. If they are not satisfied, then the care they have received as customers has fallen short of their expectation.

Customer care is more than a standard framework of communication, and it is not possible to quantify it simply in terms of how long the sales person spends with the customer. So, customer care is about much more than spending time with the customer. Providing good customer care is about giving the customer rather more than they expect.

If customers receive service below that expected, then they will normally consider this to be poor service. If, however, they receive the standard of service they expected, they may not consider this as special in any way because it was, after all, no more than they expected. It is only when customers receive more than they expected that they consider the service to be really good. In other words, good customer care is about exceeding the customer's expectations, but remember that different customers may have very different levels of expectation.

....

CASE STUDY

A businessman I used to know travelled quite regularly and used to stay in three-star hotels. Not unnaturally, he expected the staff to be helpful and polite. He expected his hotel room to be clean and comfortable and felt it important to have a television, trouser-press and tea- and coffee-making facilities in his room. He was also quite discerning about the quality of the hotel's catering, and expected the restaurant service to be of a high standard. As a customer, he had clearly defined expectations of every hotel in which he stayed and, one day, he took the time and trouble to explain to me why this was so.

In his early travelling days, he visited one particular town on a number of occasions. At The Raven, the first hotel he stayed at, he was kept waiting at reception for about ten minutes before check-in, with no explanation for the delay. When he ordered dinner in the restaurant, his order arrived incomplete and when he checked out in the morning his bill was incorrect. The hotel was very comfortable, the facilities above average and the staff extremely helpful and polite, nevertheless, he made a mental note not to use the hotel again.

The second hotel in which he stayed, The Marlborough, had all of the facilities he required. The service was prompt, the staff were both helpful and polite and the restaurant of an acceptable standard. He had no complaints about The Marlborough and thought no more about the matter.

It was only sometime later, when he was obliged to stay at another hotel, The Metropole, that he began to reflect on customer service. At the reception he was offered a complimentary glass of sherry. On entering his room, he found a bottle of mineral water and some fruit, with a card offering compliments of the management. When he asked to sign his bill in the restaurant, it was accompanied by a Belgian chocolate, and the next morning he received a complimentary newspaper.

Think carefully about these experiences. To which of the hotels would you have chosen to return?

Well, some weeks later, one of his colleagues was making a trip to the same town and asked him to make a recommendation for a suitable hotel. He looked at his colleague and replied, 'Don't, bother with The Raven – the service was awful! The Marlborough was OK – quite central, and they look after you well, but if you want really good service, go to The Metropole. They were excellent! In fact, while

I was there I picked up a list of the other hotels in their chain'.

You can see from this typical reaction that the hotel which made the most lasting impression on the customer was The Metropole – the only one which exceeded his expectations. Though the Marlborough matched his expectations, it did not make an outstanding impression on him, as the standard of service he received was no more than he expected.

An interesting point to note from the case study is that the customer was very quick to recommend The Metropole as the best in which to stay. When customers are impressed with the service they receive, they will actively promote the provider of that service to other people. Equally, if customers receive what they consider to be poor service, they will actively discourage friends and colleagues from making the same mistake.

If you provide poor service:

- **95 per cent of dissatisfied customers will never complain . . . but, they will tell nine other people how bad your service is.**
- **13 per cent of those will tell at least twenty other people they meet . . . and 90 per cent of those originally dissatisfied customers will never return.**

Why is good customer care so important?

Good customer care is important because, quite simply, it is what makes one organisation stand out from another. If a customer receives the same service at the same price from a number of different suppliers, the one more likely to obtain the customer's repeat business is the supplier providing the best and most consistently good service.

But, customers don't just buy products or services. They also buy the many intangible things which go with the selling of a product or service – friendliness, goodwill, a caring attitude, and a whole range of other behaviours and emotions which go to create the package called 'Good Customer Care'. In fact, it can truly be said about really good customer care that the whole effect is greater than the sum of the separate parts.

CASE STUDY

Ridgeway Tours has always had a reputation for having well-trained staff but, following expansion of the company's main tour programme, they had taken on a number of very inexperienced staff, not all of whom had been properly inducted into the company's operations. One of the new sales staff, Jane, took on a telesales job as a temporary measure, and had no intention of staying more than two months – just long enough to save enough money to go off on an extended summer holiday. Jane's problem was that her intention to leave the job as soon as she could reflected in the way she worked and her attitude to the job. She failed to record details of bookings, was sometimes rude to customers phoning in and, for most of the time, adopted an attitude of take-it-or-leave-it. Jane had very little interest in the job, and made this fact quite obvious. Unfortunately for Ridgeway Tours, their rather inadequate staff training programme meant that the effects of Jane's indifferent attitude to the job were not immediately recognised.

ABC Travel had dealt with Ridgeway Tours for a number of years, and most of the counter sales staff were on very good speaking terms with all of the tour operations staff. When the assistant manager telephoned through with a booking, and got Jane on the end of the line, she very quickly realised that the level of service was not up to Ridgeway's usual standard. The good standing between the two companies, however, meant that the matter was easily resolved at supervisor level. Jane quite rightly received a ticking off from the reservations supervisor, the agency received an apology, and confidence was restored once more.

Inter-World Travel had never used Ridgeway Tours before but, due to a number of difficulties finding a suitable holiday for a large group, the manager telephoned Ridgeway to make a reservation on their new programme. Unfortunately for the tour operator, the very person who answered the call was Jane and, true to form, she treated the agent in her usual manner, failing to show any real interest in the booking and ringing off before the agent had properly finished the call. The agent was neither pleased with Jane's attitude, nor the service he received but, unlike ABC Travel, the agency had had no previous dealings with Ridgeway Tours and did not realise that Jane's attitude was in no way typical of the attitude of the whole company. The manager of Inter-World Travel urgently needed to find a suitable holiday for his clients, but also felt it important to entrust the booking to a reliable tour operator.

What sort of impression would Jane's attitude have made on you, if you found yourself in a similar situation?

The manager of Inter-World Travel thought back on his conversation with Jane. 'If she's typical of the whole company, then I'm not impressed. I just can't afford to take a chance with this booking.' He then walked from his office into the agency, and spoke to his staff:

'Can I just have your attention for a minute, . . . Ridgeway Tours . . . no one's to make a booking with them under any circumstances . . . OK!'

Jane's poor attitude to the job had not only caused an upset, but had lost the company a potentially lucrative booking and a future client.

....

Every single employee makes an impression on the customer on behalf of the whole company. If a customer feels they have been poorly treated by just one employee, then the poor impression will often be of the whole company. It does not matter how good the other staff are at their jobs, or how much money the company spends on training and marketing their services. The customer's perception will be that the company does not know how to treat its customers. Remember that when you are dealing with a customer, you represent the entire company, and whatever impression you give to the customer will be the impression he or she has of the whole company.

....

Assignment   1 Think about your own experiences as a customer.

2 Make a note of service that you have received which you would consider to be above average.

3 Now make a note of service that you have received which you consider to be poor.

4 What was it about the service that made you form these impressions?

5 How likely are you return to these establishments in the future?

....

As you have seen, good customer care means different things to different people, and poor service by one employee gives an unfavourable impression of the whole company. You will learn later how your own approach to customers can be adapted to suit the individual needs of your customers. The rest of this chapter deals with some of the key areas of customer care provision.

The customer environment

....

CASE
STUDY

Some years ago, before motorway service stations became popular, and when most traffic travelled across Britain via trunk routes, the place to stop and take a break was the roadside café. They were used mostly by heavy goods vehicle drivers, where the pull-in was a lay-by and where a meal could be bought relatively cheaply at any time of the day or night. Tea came in a mug, the menu was posted up on a blackboard and meals were usually cooked to order. Roadside pull-ins were extremely popular with lorry and van drivers who were able to buy a good, cheap meal. No fuss, no frills – these were simply not necessary.

However, the development of a fast motorway system, and the arrival of the motoring family and increased leisure time brought about a revolution in catering for the travelling public. Heavy goods traffic, too, turned to the motorways, and trade on the trunk roads began to diminish. A new network of motorway service stops was built, with both the professional and the private motorist in mind. The once rough-and-ready tea-stops gradually disappeared from the map, as the idea of steamy, smoke-filled cafés, with limited menus and choice had less appeal. Catering for the motoring family meant the provision of a wide-ranging menu, and cleaner and more comfortable surroundings. A revolution in service had begun.

Strangely enough, in more recent times, the old roadside cafés have been revived in the form of the caravan or trailer tea-stop, catering for the professional trunk road users who generally pull up in Britain's lay-bys. The motorway restaurant service, regarded once as so revolutionary, has received less than favourable criticism. Bright, clean and modern surroundings are no substitute for the provision of friendly and personal attention.

....

Assignment   1 Think about your own experiences when dining out, especially in the new, popular restaurants of today – the local pubs.

2 Do you always manage to sit down to a clear table, in a smoke-free environment, or do you have to clear away the empty glasses first? What sort of impression is created in your mind?

3 Write a list of the good and poor service you have received when eating out at a pub.

....

Bright, clean and tidy surroundings also play an important part in the customer's perception of your agency. Few customers will fail to make an immediate judgment when they first walk in. Dirty coffee cups on desks or counters, fading window displays and piles of unpacked brochures in the gangways give a poor impression of efficiency and professionalism. Bright, clean and tidy surroundings in an agency make a much more favourable impression on the customer. Most customers will seek, if only at a subconscious level, real confirmation that yours is a businesslike and efficient company. First impressions really do count.

As you can see from the last case study, and perhaps as you yourself have found from past personal experiences, the working environment seen by customers will nearly always influence their feelings about both the attitude of the staff and the quality of service that those staff are likely to provide. If a customer enters a shop or an agency which looks untidy and disorganised, the message conveyed to that customer is clear: staff who pay little attention to the tidiness and cleanliness of their working environment are unlikely to pay much attention to the needs of their customers. For this reason it is important that the business environment should always be clean and tidy, brochure racks should be well stocked, and all newly delivered brochures kept away from the customer area. Remember, too, that there is also the question of a safe working environment –

for you, and for your customers.

Many companies now insist on the customer area being a no-smoking area for staff. Apart from the more obviously professional objection to seeing staff smoking, it is also extremely unpleasant for a non-smoking customer to conduct business in close proximity to someone who is smoking. Most agencies operate a no-smoking business area, but if your company policy permits customers to smoke at the counter, then you should ensure that clean ashtrays are always available for customers' use. This does mean, however, that every dirty ashtray needs to be cleaned when customers leave so as not to cause offence to non-smoking customers.

It is most likely that your company will also have rules about eating and drinking at the counter. It certainly looks unprofessional to be seen eating in full view of your customers and, even if you are busy and short staffed, time should always be set aside for taking lunch away from your work area. Even snacks need to be very discreetly eaten – the sight of a half-eaten bar of chocolate or apple sitting in front of the customer is not quite the picture of professional efficiency your customers will wish to see. It is also advisable to avoid eating certain strongly odorous foods such as onions or garlic, which usually stay on the breath and which are likely to be noticed by customers. Similarly, if you bring hot food into the agency, be aware of the lingering smell left by many fast foods. Imagine how it must appear to customers who open the door of your agency to the smell of fish and chips.

Liquid refreshments taken in a cup rarely cause any offence. Most people who work in a busy agency or office atmosphere soon become used to grabbing a quick cup of tea or coffee. Remember though, that strong smelling liquids such as soups can cause offence. If your company allows you to drink tea or coffee at the counter, or if you normally offer a drink to favoured clients, try to ensure that all used cups are removed from the customer area as soon as the customer has gone or, at least before you serve the next customer.

If you have no appointed office cleaner for your office or agency, the onus for maintaining a clean working environment may rest with you and your colleagues. Try to draw up a daily rota for hoovering and dusting. Customers soon notice if carpets are dirty or counters and desks look in need of a polish. If possible, first thing in the morning, remove any street rubbish which has accumulated outside the agency overnight. Every effort should be made to ensure that the outside of your office remains attractive to the customer.

Finally, remember that many new customers will be drawn into your agency by what they see in the window. People will stop as they walk by, and take a look at your latest offers board or the promotional display which you may have in your window, so these need to be both interesting and up to date in order to attract clients' attention. Window displays and latest offers should, therefore, always be kept right up to date and in good decorative order. If your displays are left to go out of date and fade in the sun, then they will be a poor advertisement for your company, so try to ensure that time-sensitive displays are removed as soon as the offer date has expired. Customer care always begins at the first point of contact.

Staff appearance

Many travel companies realise the importance of smartly turned out staff and many of these have policies which set out guidelines for all staff, not only what they must wear in the workplace, but also how they should present themselves personally so as to project a good company image.

....

CASE STUDY

Becky joined one such company about six months ago as a sales assistant. The company provides her with a very smart uniform, which has to be kept cleaned and pressed at all times, but there are also rules about Becky's personal appearance – her hair, the length of her nails, the type of shoes, stockings and even the sorts of jewellery she is allowed to wear. Some of Becky's friends, who have other kinds of jobs, find the restrictions imposed by Becky's firm rather harsh and dictatorial. Becky does not mind, however, as she has an extremely good job in a good working environment. The type of customers her agency attracts usually demand a very high level of service, but the work that Becky does in finding all the different sorts of holidays, offers the kind of challenge that keeps her interested in the work, and keeps the customers interested in her.

Sean joined a different travel company at about the same time as Becky. His company, too, has a staff uniform, though there are no rules as to how staff should otherwise dress and present themselves. Sean wears his hair slicked back and sports a double earring. Sometimes, like many of the other staff, he leaves off part of his uniform or wears a jumper over the top. As he says, 'Nobody seems to mind our appearance, really.'

Sean and Becky often meet at evening presentations. They talk about the travel business and the sort of work they do. Sean thinks that Becky's company is too fussy about her everyday appearance. He rather likes the sort of freedom he gets. One thing always puzzles Sean, though, and that is why Becky always seems to be involved in such interesting bookings. 'Of course, we don't get the sort of customers your company gets. I just can't understand why . . . after all, we offer exactly the same services as you, don't we?'

Becky smiled. 'Yes,' she agreed, 'but your staff never seem to look quite as smart as us, do they?'

'Rubbish!' said Sean. 'What does that matter? It's not us the customers come to see, is it.'

'No, perhaps not,' replied Becky, 'but they still have to look at you, don't they, and many of our customers admit that they only decided to come into the agency because they thought we always looked well turned out. To lots of clients, that's quite important.'

....

Assignment   1 Consider which of the two agencies shown in the case study above would make a better first impression on you. Then, think about all the shops you have been in where, through their smart appearance, the staff have made a favourable impression on you.

2 Make a list of these, then consider the shops whose staff have failed to make a good impression on you.

3 Did you find that more shops than not ensure that staff turn out smartly dressed before the public?

....

The way that staff appear before their customers usually says much about the company and the attitude of its staff. Those staff who take a pride in their appearance usually also take a pride in their work. Similarly, those who take less pride in their appearance, are more likely to adopt a less ordered approach to their work. Even where this does not strictly follow, many customers still make judgments about the quality of service they are likely to receive from what they observe in the overall dress and demeanour of staff.

Some companies lay down rules about all aspects of dress where they have a proper customer care policy. Most employees working directly with the public in the travel industry do wear a uniform. Not only does this save obvious wear and tear on one's own clothes, but it usually looks smart, makes employees readily identifiable and promotes a corporate image of the company. If uniforms are not available, then try to choose clothes which are suitable for working in a business environment and which create an image of professionalism.

Ideally, men should wear a suit or a smart pair of trousers and a shirt and tie, and ladies should wear either a suit, or smart dress, or skirt or trousers and a blouse. Whatever you choose, do ensure that your clothes are regularly cleaned and pressed. Footwear should also be in keeping with a business environment; smart, polished and without scuff marks. If your job does not involve you coming face to face with customers, you may be able to wear what you like to work. However, do bear in mind the advantages of having a separate set of clothes for work, as it is not always easy to adopt a professional and businesslike attitude if you feel no differently dressed for work than you do socially.

Finally, remember that personal grooming is also very important. Working in close proximity to customers across a desk or counter means that all aspects of your personal appearance will be on show: customers will soon notice unkempt and untidy hair, dirty or chipped fingernails, men who fail to shave, and women who wear excessive make-up. Try to make sure that you always look your best in front of customers. That way you will ensure that people are pleased to see you, happy to talk to you and always keen to approach you.

Body language

Body language, or non-verbal communication, is a very subtle aspect of communication between people. The 'language' consists of the infinitely variable modes of expression and bodily movement which make a statement about how we feel and what we truly think about those people with whom we interact and the situations in which we find ourselves. By watching a person's body language it is possible to tell quite a lot about what he or she feels and thinks without a single spoken word being exchanged.

In all situations where you have to interact with the public, it is very important that you are aware of the signals given out by your own body language and the effect these have on those persons with whom you are interacting. Unfortunately for us, our body language often seems to run counter to what we are saying. We may well be saying all the right things but, at the same time, showing distinct signs of irritation and impatience. Those who are astute 'people-watchers' will always recognise these signals and, if the message of our indifference or impatience is sufficiently strong, even the least astute customer will realise its significance. Of course, as we all know through meeting people, body language can also show the positive side of our feelings – happiness, joy and pleasure – as it shows when we meet with friends, or when we meet for the first time someone to whom we are obviously attracted.

So what exactly does the term 'body language' cover? The answer is that body language covers all of those physical moods and movements which are reactions to feelings; facial expressions, eye contact, eye movements, posture and stance, hand gestures, body movements, distance from others (called 'proxemics') and nervous habits.

Perhaps, the first lesson for students of body language is to build up an awareness of those more reactive signals – especially those which convey the not-so-pleasant side of our nature. Facial expressions such as nodding, attentive eye movement, and smiles, usually convey that we are genuinely interested in what the customer is saying, or that we have some empathy with the customer. However, facial expressions can also give away those less pleasant thoughts you may have, and many of these body signals have their roots in the moods and expressions of childhood:

- pouting with the lower lip – worry or nervousness
- pursed lips or pouting – annoyance or irritation
- sucking of lips – puzzlement
- curled lip – dislike or distaste
- knitted brows – puzzlement
- pulling a face – indifference or annoyance
- raised eyebrows – surprise or disagreement
- one raised eyebrow – displeasure.

A smile is the most positive form of facial expression you can use. It shows warmth, friendliness and approachability. Smiles are infectious, and people often smile back in response to a genuine sunny smile, but if you don't smile at all the customer may consider you to be sullen and indifferent. There are, of course, those smiles which are given purely for temporary effect, such as the 'rubber band' smile, where a person's facial expression quickly returns to a pout or tight-lipped position. This, together with the smirk or leer, are nearly always seen by others as disingenuous or insincere.

Eye movements convey much about your thoughts. When you are dealing with a customer you should try to maintain good eye contact, for it shows that you are interested in what is going on and that you are confident in what you do. If you studiously avoid eye contact with your customer, he or she may feel that you are disinterested, or that you lack confidence or are very nervous. If your customer sees that your gaze is elsewhere whilst they are speaking, this will immediately convey a lack of interest, or show that your attention has another focus. The only way to show your customers that you are genuinely interested is to give them your full attention at all times. Maintaining good eye contact is very important, but be careful not to stare.

Body movements

Leaning forwards slightly towards your customer, whether you happen to be seated or standing, shows that you are listening and concentrating on what is being said. Nodding occasionally whilst you are listening also indicates that you are paying attention.

Leaning back with your head resting on the back of your chair shows that you are totally disinterested in the whole thing, and clasping your hands behind your head shows a hint of arrogance. Slouching in a chair always looks generally unprofessional, and will normally indicate to the customer that you do not have a very conscientious approach to work.

Fidgeting movements are generally very irritating to the other person, whether you are playing with a pen or pencil, wringing your hands or shuffling continuously from one foot to another. Always try to sit or stand in a good, upright position – it shows that you are interested, attentive and keen to interact with your customers.

Hand gestures

Hand gestures are a very expressive form of body language, and they say quite a lot about our confidence – or lack of confidence. Open hands, like most open gestures, demonstrate warmth and confidence, and show the customer that you are interested and attentive.

However, hand movements also give away many nervous habits of which you may not even be aware. These nervous movements can be very irritating to the customer, especially wringing of hands and fiddling with clothes, jewellery or objects on the counter or desk. Other distractions may be equally irritating: doodling, playing with your hair, chewing the end of a pen, all detract from the most powerful of all non-verbal signals – eye contact with the customer.

Assignment   1 Think about your own body language. Are any of these habits yours?

2 If you know that your hands seem to have a life of their own when you are nervous or in a stressful situation, then make a note of your particular distraction and pull yourself up whenever it happens.

3 If you really do not know whether you fiddle with objects or play with your hands, ask a colleague to watch you next time you serve a customer and let you know if any bad habits are obvious. It is not necessarily a major problem if you do, but it could be if it were very obvious to the customer, and you may need to make an effort to control hand movements if they are particularly distracting.

Personal space

Respect for other people's personal space is one of the fundamentals of life. We all need a certain amount of personal space in which to stand, sit or move about, and when someone else invades that space it sometimes feels as if we are being threatened. If you have ever experienced this at any time when someone – especially someone unfamiliar to you – tries to stand or sit too close to you for comfort, you will know precisely how this feels. Our normal, and immediate instinct, is to step or lean back, or to move away from the 'intruder'. This is a normal reaction in any social situation. Closeness, togetherness, and physical contact such as touching is very much a sign of familiarity or friendliness, and the best way to show friendliness to your customers is with direct, warm eye contact – and a smile! So, try to bear this in mind when you come into contact with your customers. You may find that some customers have a tendency to invade your space, as well, so keep a businesslike distance and leave your smile to say that you wish to be welcoming and friendly.

CASE STUDY

If you have ever been into a shop or office premises where you have felt unwelcome, you will know that sometimes, whether intentional or not, some staff make it plain by way of their body language that they do not wish to serve you.

An old friend, Penny, visited her local information centre to get some information on local places to visit during the summer holidays. There were no other customers in the office when she arrived, though there were three staff standing behind the counter on duty. So, Penny went straight up to the counter and waited to be served.

The man behind the counter kept his head down and refused to look up and acknowledge her presence. He suddenly threw down his pencil and yawned. Next, he leaned back in his chair with his hands clasped behind his head and exhaled deeply. Finally, he got up and wandered through a door into the back office. He had steadfastly refused to look at Penny.

The young girl next to the man was speaking over the telephone, with the receiver tucked between her ear and shoulder. She looked extremely fed up and was idly drawing on the corner of a brochure. Again, there was not the slightest sign of acknowledgement of Penny's presence.

Penny looked lastly towards the third member of staff in the hope of receiving a more favourable reception. The third member of staff, a lady in her mid-thirties was sitting at the far end of the counter – head down and engrossed in paperwork. Penny went over and stood in front of her to draw the woman's attention, but she also failed to look up, and just continued with her paperwork. After a minute or so, she glanced up at my friend, showed her irritation with a stony glare and looked over towards the young girl who was still on the telephone. She then sighed loudly and called out to the man who had walked off smartly when Penny had come into the office. She then went back to her paperwork with no further acknowledgement of Penny's presence. The door then opened and the young man appeared in the doorway, holding a lighted cigarette behind him.

'Can I help?' he said.

'Yes,' said Penny. 'You can give me the name of your manager!'

Penny felt that her need for information had been, by this time, rather overtaken by this amazing display of indifference. In similar circumstances, according to statistics and studies, 95 per cent of customers would have walked out, never to come back. Indeed, many may also have been minded to say something less than pleasant to the staff. Penny was one who always complained, and went straight home to write a letter of complaint to the manager.

In this rather extreme example of indifference, each of the three staff had communicated their clear intention to ignore the customer, and had used very strong body language to demonstrate this. The first had deliberately absented himself from the scene and, worse still, had been very resolute in ignoring the customer's presence. The young girl had also failed to acknowledge the customer, though perhaps she did have the excuse of being engaged on the telephone. The older woman showed a three-way irritation: first, with the customer, for standing right in front of her; secondly, with the young girl, for being unavailable; and finally, with the man at whom she shouted – her exasperation obviously getting the better of her impatience.

We do not know the underlying reasons for the behaviour of these three people. Perhaps they were simply ill-mannered, and just did not know how to relate to the customer. Perhaps they had had a bad day, or maybe their working environment denied their rights as people. Whatever the reasons, it was clear that each one, without any vocal contact with the customer, showed by their actions alone that they were disinterested, indifferent and uncaring about the customer. Whatever the reasons, it was evident that these three staff were untrained in simple interpersonal skills, and indifferent to the fact that, without a word to the customer, the unspoken language of non-verbal communication had said all there was to say.

USING AN APPROPRIATE MANNER WITH YOUR CUSTOMER

One of the requirements of the NVQ award is that you deal with your customers in an appropriate manner. But what is appropriate? Is the same manner appropriate to all of your customers, and is it appropriate to deal with the same customer in the same manner on every occasion regardless of the circumstances?

Later in this book you are given some guidelines on how to deal with particular types of difficult customer. Before you read that section, however, it might be a sound idea to lay down the ground rules. First of all, it will be necessary to agree what exactly is inappropriate.

CASE
STUDY

A number of years ago I was working in a retail travel agency, where one of the employees, a young woman of sixteen, was coming to the end of her first week at work. She was well dressed and well groomed, made good eye contact with those who entered the agency, and looked in every way, a pleasant trainee travel agent.

At this time, she was not expected to sell travel products, but had been instructed to carry out a few simple administration tasks and to sit with the assistant manager to observe how the customers were dealt with, and how the paperwork was processed. At this early stage in her career she was not expected to deal with any customers herself.

On one particular afternoon, a regular customer came in to pay a balance. He was a valued customer who would book several fairly expensive tours in the course of a year. He was a very pleasant man who was quite friendly, but who liked to feel special, in that he was always treated well and received the best service from staff. He talked with the assistant manager for some time, and then asked a few questions of the new travel assistant – how she liked the job and how she was getting on etc. He then turned his attention back to the assistant manager and started to write out a cheque for his holiday balance.

'What is the date today?' he asked.

'It's the thirteenth,' replied the assistant manager.

'Oh, Friday the thirteenth,' he said. 'Unlucky for some!'

'Yes,' said the new trainee. 'You never know, your cheque might bounce!'

The customer looked more than a little taken aback, and we were equally astounded and wished the ground to open up and swallow us.

The young assistant, new to this situation, certainly intended no rudeness to the customer. She was attempting to engage in what she thought was friendly conversation with the customer, but her inexperience meant that she did not appreciate that a comment which might be perfectly acceptable in a light-hearted social situation amongst people she knew, was totally inappropriate in a business situation. Fortunately, on this occasion, the company's good standing with the customer was not affected and he continued to use our services. But, perhaps if this had been his first visit to the agency, this very inappropriate and unfortunate remark may have ensured that it was also his last.

....

Once you enter the world of business, you will need to adopt a 'business register'. This is the choice of words and phrases that you use, and a business register will be quite different from a social register.

Social registers are informal, openly friendly and relaxed. For instance, if you were amongst friends, consider how you would greet another friend who joined your group. You might begin the conversation with 'Hi there! How are things with you? Done anything exciting lately?' Such a greeting is perfectly acceptable in this situation – in fact if it were more formal your friends might consider it very odd indeed.

When you speak to a customer, your approach will need to be more formal. A suitable address to a customer entering your office would be, 'Good-morning' or 'Good-afternoon'. If you feel more comfortable, you might even say, 'Good-morning, sir' or 'Good-morning, madam', as appropriate. However, the way you address customers will also depend upon the age of the person, as someone younger may feel embarrassed to be addressed in this manner, whereas an older person will normally consider it polite. It is for you to judge the situation, the person and the appropriateness of the greeting.

If you know the customer fairly well, you may continue the greeting by engaging in further conversation. Socially, 'How is everything with you?' is appropriate, but in a business conversation it should be, 'How are you?', or 'How are you today?'. This particular form of greeting is very British, since it is said only as a matter of politeness, and not because you wish the other person to go into graphic detail about the state of their health. In fact, we would consider it embarrassing and inappropriate if we received such a response. Instead, the normal reply to such a question is expected to be, 'Very well, thank you'. So, if a customer asks how you are, you should simply reply, 'Fine, thank you', even if you are really at death's door.

Whilst it is normally polite to ask a regular customer how they feel, it is not altogether appropriate to ask this of someone you have never met before, or with whom you have had only brief dealings. Such familiarity would be considered as rather embarrassing to the customer.

If you have served the customer before, and you remember the name, then try and use it in your greeting. When, for instance, your customer Mrs Hamilton looks into your agency on return from her holiday, she will probably be impressed and flattered that you remember her if you greet her by name with, 'Hello, Mrs Hamilton. How are you today?' This will indicate to Mrs Hamilton that she is a valued customer, and the fact that she is important to your company, will be important to her.

If the customer is known to you, the way in which you continue the conversation will probably depend on the customer's personality and your standing with him or her. You will constantly need to be judging these things whenever you speak to your customers. Adopting an appropriate manner of speech is very important in business.

If you see a customer after his or her return from holiday, and you are able to remember where they have been, it is usually a nice idea to ask them generally how they enjoyed their trip. Customers will often come into your agency to tell you about their holiday if they particularly enjoyed it, and this gives you the opportunity to build up a relationship with customers. Remember that you can always be friendly to customers, even when maintaining a respectable professional distance.

Be careful when asking customers about aspects of their personal lives. The customer who is always chatty, and tells you all about her husband's job and her daughter's wedding plans, will be pleased that you have remembered to ask how the family are, and will be happy to let you know. But, the businessman who makes it plain that he uses the services of your agency purely to make his business travel arrangements will almost certainly want to maintain his own professional distance. There would normally be no reason for him to mention his private life, and he would certainly consider it inappropriate if you asked.

Never use slang in a business conversation. Your customers will expect you to behave in a professional manner, and the use of slang is most definitely not professional. Avoid phrases like, 'Hang on a second', or 'Ta'. You should say, more politely, 'If you wouldn't mind waiting', and 'Thank you'.

I recently overheard a telephone conversation between a travel agent and a tour operator in which the tour operator used phrases such as, 'We don't just change things willy-nilly, you know' and, 'It sounds to me like you've bitten off more than you can chew'. Understandably, the travel agent was rather annoyed at the high-handed manner adopted by the tour operator, and complained to a supervisor. Not only was this approach very rude, but the language was also totally inappropriate. These were definitely not the sort of phrases to use in a business conversation.

At the other extreme is the use of industry language that the customer would not normally be expected to understand. This is called 'jargon', and in the travel industry, in common with some other industries, we use rather a lot of jargon. Whilst it may demonstrate that you know your job and the terms which go with it, using jargon or technical language is inappropriate where the customer would not normally understand the terms, and where its use would alienate the customer from the conversation.

Customers expect you to speak in a language which they can understand, and may either feel embarrassed at having to ask you to explain what you mean, or annoyed at what might be considered your superior attitude. So, rather than saying, 'That will be TOD at the BA Domestic ticket desk. I've issued an MCO against the booking, so if you give them your locator, that'll be OK', it would be better to say, 'Your ticket will be waiting for you at the British Airways Domestic ticket desk – that is, for flights within the UK. I have issued all the necessary documents and advised British Airways, so they'll know that you've already paid for the ticket. All you have to do is give them your booking reference and they will hand you your ticket.'

Approaching the customer

If you work in a shop or an office where customers visit you in person, you may have noticed that on first coming in through the door they will often do one of two things: some walk straight up to the counter and wait to be served, others start browsing through information and brochures in your display area. All customers visiting your agency ought to be approached at some point, but how and when this is done will depend upon the circumstances.

First, let's deal with a customer who comes straight up to the counter. This is the sort of person who normally expects immediate attention, and who will be unhappy if it is not given. If you are free, then a friendly smile, direct eye contact and, 'Good-morning' or 'How may I help you?' is a good professional approach. However, there may be occasions when you are not able to give immediate attention to the customer. If you are already busy with someone, then any new customer will appreciate that you cannot possibly serve everyone at once, though if you completely ignore a waiting customer, this can sometimes be the cause of some irritation. You should always acknowledge someone's presence, and explain that you will be available shortly – you might even offer a seat if one is available.

Sometimes it is possible to deal with two customers at once, but you need to be sufficiently proficient to retain control and ensure that both customers feel equally important. I was recently in a shop where this might easily have been done, but the sales person missed the opportunity and managed to aggravate other waiting customers.

CASE STUDY

I went into the shop knowing exactly what I wanted, but was unable to find it. I approached one of the staff on the sales floor and explained what it was I was looking for. She directed me to the cash desk, saying that the lady there would be able to help. I went over to the cash desk and, as no one else was there, I was served immediately. However, the cashier had run out of the item I wanted, and had to call for the help of a colleague to get further supplies from the stockroom. Everyone had been helpful and polite, so I was quite happy to wait for the goods to arrive, but a queue was steadily building behind me, and I could sense some irritation from those who were being kept waiting.

The cashier was clearly going to deal with only one thing at a time, and studiously ignored all the other customers, keeping her eyes firmly on the stockroom door. She looked rather uncomfortable – perhaps because she realised she was not paying attention to the other customers. Yet she really did not know how to switch her attention from me to them. Eventually, I urged the cashier to serve the other people while we were waiting. The lady behind me moved forward, looking quite irritated with the cashier, but turned to me and said, 'Thank you', though the look on her face said, 'Thank you for doing what the cashier should have done'.

You will have to use your own judgement if you find yourself in a similar situation, but if an opportunity presents itself, then use it. If one of your customers wishes to read the small print of the insurance policy personally, then your services may not be needed for a few minutes, and you can ask the customer if they mind you serving someone else while they do this. A customer will rarely object in such a case.

If a customer is looking at your displays or reading through brochures, do not be in too much of a hurry to rush over to them. You can always acknowledge the customer's presence, but give some time before you move forward to offer assistance. You may have had your own experiences of the overzealous sales person on occasions, especially if you have just gone into a shop to look around, with no real intention to buy. Within seconds you have been pounced upon by a sales assistant, asking, 'Can I help you?' 'No thanks, I'm really only looking,' you reply. The salesperson has effectively invaded your space a little too early for comfort. If you do the same thing to your customers, you may receive the same rebuff.

As a professional salesperson, you should approach the customer at some time, but do give them a little space and allow them to look around. When you do talk to them, try not to begin with 'Can I help you?' as you are likely to receive the rather brusque 'I'm just looking' response. If the customer has approached you, the best response is often simply 'Can I help you?' or 'How can I help you?'

If you make the first approach, try to put a more direct question, like 'Is it the summer or winter brochure you are looking for?' The customer is then obliged to answer by giving you information, which makes it much easier for you to begin a conversation. If the customer is looking at a particular type of holiday, such as the USA, you might try asking a more specific question, such as which particular part of the United States they wish to visit. At times like this, there may be many opening questions you can ask, but try to avoid the usual 'Can I help you?'

If possible, it is better that you approach the customer in the shop area rather than speaking from behind your desk or counter, as this makes you more remote, and makes it easier for the customer to ignore you. During busy periods, you may not be able to speak to customers until they are at the door and ready to leave. It is never too late to speak, and it is always worth checking that the customers have what they want. 'Did you find what you wanted?' is sufficient to let customers know you were interested. If they did find what they were looking for, you will still have made that important contact. If, however, they were unable to find the brochure they wanted, they could be on their way to the travel agency down the road. If you find out what the customers want, then it is often a simple matter of going to the stockroom or directing them to the correct place on the brochure rack.

In the early part of your career, you will often find that customers ask for something you are unable to deal with. Try not to be embarrassed by this, as everyone has to learn the business. When you can, be honest with customers by saying that you are in training. If you lack a particular specialist knowledge yourself, you will be doing nothing wrong by asking a colleague to deal with the enquiry. If someone is available immediately, then you can hand over to them straightaway. However, if there is no one else available, you will be helping everybody by asking a few basic questions to find out something about the enquiry before your colleague takes over. Questioning skills are covered later in the book but, at this point, remember that you only need to know about the product to answer questions – not to ask them.

If you ask basic questions, you may find that you actually can help the customer. The customer's initial request does not always make clear what he or she wants. For example, if a customer begins by saying, 'I would like some information about India', before you do anything, find out exactly what sort of information the client requires and then decide whether or not you are able to help. If the customer expresses an interest in a type of holiday that you feel you are unable to deal with satisfactorily, then you should pass the enquiry to a more knowledgeable colleague. If the information requested by the customer concerned visa and passport requirements, then you may feel sufficiently confident to deal with this yourself by referring to the relevant manuals. If a customer has a query that you are unsure whether you can answer, always try to find out something about it before you make the decision to hand over to a colleague.

Giving the customer your full attention

If you work in a busy office, there may be many things going on around you when you are trying to serve the customer. However, no matter how busy the agency is, the customer should always feel that you are giving him or her your full attention.

CASE STUDY

A friend and I were shopping in one of the large department stores. It was a Saturday, and the two young women serving at the cash desk were, to judge by their name tags, both Saturday assistants doing part-time weekend work. We came to our turn in the queue and waited patiently while one of the women checked our purchases. This, normally speedy transaction began to take a little time, as the two women – one of whom was standing next to the cash desk – began a conversation about some personal matter.

The fact that they were talking to one another was not in itself a problem. The problem was that the young woman who should have been concentrating on serving my friend and I was continually distracted from her work as she turned to talk to her colleague. She would stop halfway through her checking and, holding the garment in her hand, would then turn away from us and chat to her colleague. We looked on whilst this continued for the third time, before I had finally had enough of these little interruptions to say something in rebuke to the cashier. I told her firmly, but politely, that she could talk with her colleague a little later, but that for the present moment she should concentrate on serving us, as customers.

Afterwards, we sought out the customer services manager to ask whether or not the store possessed a customer care policy and, if so, whether it was known to each member of staff. The customer services manager realised quickly that this enquiry was probably by way of complaint, and turned her attention very quickly to trying to find out details of who these staff were. As my friend and I had both agreed that it was not necessary to get the two assistants into trouble by making a formal complaint, we both made the point that if there were a customer care policy in place, then the customer service department should ensure that every member of staff had read and understood exactly what it meant.

....

Assignment   1 If you had been the customer in this situation, how would you have reacted to being kept waiting, or being totally ignored? Would you recommend this shop as one which gave good service, and where the customer always came first? Of course not. Without realising it, these two young women were extremely rude, and demonstrated a complete disregard for the customer.

2 Now think about this in your own situation. Make sure, no matter how interesting your conversation may be, that it does not distract you from your work and from giving proper attention to the customer. Try not to interrupt colleagues while they are dealing with customers when it is really not that important, and never let your own attention be distracted from the customer by something unconnected going on around you in the office.

3 What about personal telephone calls? Should you continue these while the customer is kept waiting? What sort of an impression of the company do you think it creates when the customer is kept waiting while a member of staff continues chatting with a friend. Remember that no matter what else is going on, the customer always comes first.

4 Over the next few days, make a note of any incident where either you or one of your colleagues shows any signs of not paying full attention to the customer. What sort of impression do you think the customer had of the company on each of these occasions?

....

Listening

Listening is an essential part of your job, and one of the key interpersonal skills. Listening is actually much harder than talking and, as most of us prefer to talk than to listen, it is easy to switch off while we are listening to someone else. You can probably recall a situation where you have been talking to a friend or relative, and you become aware that they are no longer listening to you. The usual reaction when this happens is to draw their attention back to you by saying, 'Are you listening to me?' and the response will usually be, 'Sorry, I was thinking about something else'.

Although somewhat irritating, in a social or family situation it is not so important, but in a business context it is the height of rudeness and the customer will usually be extremely annoyed. Switching off indicates to the customer that you are not interested in what is being said to you, and probably demonstrates that you will not give the necessary care and attention when handling the business. As we saw from the section on body language, it is easy to see from someone's eye contact whether or not they are really paying attention. So, if you have stopped listening, the customer will normally very quickly detect that this is the case.

Switching off through lack of interest is not always the reason why we don't fully take in everything the customer is saying. Listening is a complex mental process, as the model below demonstrates. It shows the process we go through whenever we are listening to someone.

You speak	*I listen*
You continue to speak	*I evaluate what you are saying*
You continue to speak	*I form an opinion*
You continue to speak	*I plan my reply*
You continue to speak	*I rehearse my reply*
You continue to speak	*I start listening again waiting for a gap in the conversation in which to speak*

You can see from this model that I'm not listening to very much of what is being said, but that as soon as the need for a response is triggered, I immediately turn off so that I can concentrate on thinking through and planning a reply of my own. This is a natural process and one of which most people are completely unaware. You will need to train yourself to listen carefully to everything that the customer says to you, and this takes considerable effort and practise. You may find it a little easier if you make a few notes as you are listening to ensure that you haven't missed anything. This will also serve as a memory jogger, should you need to refer back to the conversation at a later time.

....

Assignment   If you would like to improve your listening skills here is an exercise for you to try.

Ask a friend to select a passage from a book or an article from a newspaper and read it to you. Your task is to listen intently and remember as much of what you have heard as possible. You should not take notes, but just listen. When you have heard the passage, tell your friend as much as you can remember about what has been read to you. Once you have repeated everything you can remember check with your friend on how accurate the facts were that you repeated, and what, if anything, you missed out.

....

Verbal mannerisms

Some of us are prone to sprinkle social conversations with a number of verbal mannerisms which we tend to repeat in a business conversation, yet which add nothing to the meaning of what we are saying. Some well-used examples that I have come across are 'sort of thing' and 'know what I mean'. You may have a favourite word that you repeat over and over, such as 'actually' or 'basically'. Many people do not realise that they use such mannerisms in a business conversation. The customer may do, however, and may also find it a particularly irritating habit.

In more formal speech, such as presentations, these simple verbal mannerisms become a distraction to the audience, and some of them may even find themselves unwittingly turning their attention to the number of times a word or phrase occurs in the speech. I once worked for a manager who was fond of the term 'as it were'. This became a standing joke amongst the staff, to the point that whenever office meetings were held, we would take bets on the number of times that our manager would use the phrase, and this meant that although we all listened intently to what he was saying, we did not listen to what was being said. Our only interest was to count the number of 'as it weres', rather than to concentrate on the information we were being given. To ensure that you don't fall into the same trap, ask a colleague to listen to you while you are talking to a customer, and to tell you if you have any well-used verbal mannerisms of your own.

....

Exercise

Before you continue with the text, assess how good you are at creating a good impression on the customer. Grade yourself on a scale of 1 to 10, with 1 being the poorest standard and 10 being the very highest standard.

I always acknowledge the customer	1 2 3 4 5 6 7 8 9 10
I always smile at the customer, even if I don't feel like it.	1 2 3 4 5 6 7 8 9 10
I always take care that I look my best.	1 2 3 4 5 6 7 8 9 10
I never continue a conversation with my friends or colleagues in front of a customer.	1 2 3 4 5 6 7 8 9 10
I always show the customer that I am interested in what they are saying.	1 2 3 4 5 6 7 8 9 10
I always make good eye contact with the customer.	1 2 3 4 5 6 7 8 9 10
I always address the customer in an appropriate manner.	1 2 3 4 5 6 7 8 9 10
I always use the customer's name if I know it.	1 2 3 4 5 6 7 8 9 10
I avoid using jargon with the customer	1 2 3 4 5 6 7 8 9 10

Once you have completed your self-assessment, ask a colleague to watch you with some customers and make their own assessment. If there are any appreciable differences, you can discuss these afterwards. Where you have scored less than eight, try to make a conscious effort to improve those areas over the next few weeks.

CREATING A GOOD RELATIONSHIP WITH A NEW CUSTOMER

A large part of the work we do in our industry involves us in building relationships, and it is important that you are able to create and maintain good relationships with new customers. We have already covered, in some depth, how to approach and greet customers when they come into your office, and how important it is that your appearance conveys professionalism. But, once you become involved in conversation with a customer, there is much more to consider. Let's think about it from the customer's point of view. What is it exactly that the customer expects of you?

If you were to ask your customers to list the qualities in you which were most important to them, the list would probably include the following:

- a professional manner
- a positive attitude
- politeness
- efficiency
- accuracy
- good product knowledge
- taking responsibility as the salesperson.

Every point on the list is important to the customer, but they are all building blocks which enable the customer to hand over responsibility to you as the salesperson. When customers come into your agency to make a booking, they will expect you to take over the responsibility and ensure that everything runs smoothly – that all documents and information are checked for accuracy and passed on accordingly. But, before the customer makes the decision as to whether or not to place the booking with you, they will be looking for signs that, as an efficient salesperson, you are able to fulfil all of their other needs. Even if this does not happen at a conscious level, most customers will certainly be looking subconsciously to confirm the belief that you are competent and businesslike, and that they will be confident in your ability to look after their needs as efficiently as possible. However brief your contact with the customer, it will usually give a good indication of the level of service you provide, and how they are likely to be looked after. If a customer is unsure about your ability from the way in which you talk to them, they may well take their business elsewhere.

What is a professional manner?

We have already discussed in some detail the business register and the appropriate manner in which you should greet the customer, but once you begin to talk in more depth, there are a number of important points which the customer will be looking out for subconsciously as signs of your professional integrity – confidentiality, your trustworthiness, your loyalty to your company and to the industry, and your general conduct.

Confidentiality

All of your customers expect you to treat their business as confidential. You should never divulge any information about the customers' travel arrangements, including dates of travel, destination, travelling companions etc., to any person other than the customer or those nominated by the customer to act on their behalf. Under no circumstances should you ever give out a customer's home address to anyone. There have been more than a few cases of local burglary at a time when the occupants have been known to be away on holiday.

Occasionally, in an emergency, you may be contacted by a member of the customer's family and asked for an overseas contact number. If this happens, you should make absolutely sure that it is a genuine enquiry before passing on such information, and you should certainly always consult your manager before you give out private information of this kind. If you are not sure if the caller is whom they say they are, you could either offer to contact the client yourself (ensuring that you do), or you could check the identity of the caller by asking them to confirm some personal information about the customer – home telephone number, names and initials of any children etc. If you receive an enquiry of this nature before the customer travels, under no circumstances give out any information before you have checked with the customer that you have permission to do so.

Another aspect of confidentiality is the respect your must have for the privacy of your customer. You should never discuss any matter concerning one customer within earshot of another customer, or openly with any of your colleagues. Under no circumstances should you disclose to another customer any unfavourable opinion you may have, nor any knowledge you have of their credit worthiness or financial standing. Not only is this extremely unprofessional, and a breach of confidentiality, but it also demonstrates that you may well talk about all of your customers in the same free manner, and that you cannot be trusted. You should always be guarded about what you say about any of your customers. It is so easy to break a confidence without even realising it.

Loyalty

Your employer will expect you to be loyal to the company for the duration of your employment. This is not simply a matter of protecting business interests and the company's name, but it is highly unprofessional for a member of staff to make derogatory remarks about the company which employs them. There may be times when you feel justified in passing comment, especially if you feel you are having to shoulder the blame for someone else's mistake or because of an internal company error or problem.

CASE STUDY

Tom, a young reservations agent, has received an urgent telephone call for his supervisor, who is out to lunch. Later that lunchtime, Tom picks up the telephone once more to the same enquirer. He is somewhat embarrassed by his supervisor's absence and feels awkward at the urgency of the enquiry, for the supervisor has now been out to lunch for over an hour and a half. He feels irritated at having to make excuses. When the same enquirer telephones for the third time, Tom is unable to contain his irritation any more and tells the caller, 'Looks like she's out for a late lunch, again. Perhaps you ought to call tomorrow morning, because she never seems to be back on time.'

It is perhaps understandable that the reservations agent feels that he is, unfairly, having to make excuses on behalf of his supervisor. There is certainly embarrassment on his part at having to explain away her absence, especially when the caller telephones for the third time. However, awkward though he may feel about the situation and the excuses he feels he has to make to the caller, his last remark was far less than professional. While Tom is not obliged to make 'excuses' for his supervisor, to say in irritation that she always seems to be late – no matter how truthful this statement may be – conveys to the caller a rather poor image of the company and its staff relations. This is potentially damaging to business.

In such cases as this, you should be careful about what you say and just how truthful you really need to be. Did Tom really have to admit that his supervisor was still out to lunch? He could, and should, have simply said that she had not yet returned, or that she was unavailable at that moment, and that the caller's message would be passed on as soon as the supervisor was available. (Note the choice of words: 'not yet returned', 'unavailable at the moment'.) These facts are, after all, quite clear to the caller, who has called three times. It is not for Tom to have to make excuses but, equally, neither is necessary for him to pass damaging personal opinion in the form of comment. The caller will quickly make up their mind about the situation, either accepting the supervisor's non-availability, or forming a personal opinion about the efficiency of the company.

Casual remarks to customers or callers can be damaging to a company's business reputation, especially when these convey the impression that the company is less than efficient. To observe to a client that an invoice is late, and casually remark that 'They're always a bit slow in accounts', does not transmit a favourable company image. Even if it is true, it is wrong to make such a statement to anyone outside the company.

As well as remaining loyal to your company, you should also be loyal to the industry – certainly while you are in front of a customer. Privately, you may hold a particular opinion about some individual or company with whom you trade. There may be commonly held beliefs amongst colleagues that this company or that person is best avoided, or that they are less than effective. However, you must be very careful how opinions like this are put to the customer. You may wish to protect the interests of your customers and offer knowledgeable guidance and advice, but this should never be achieved by giving negative information or opinion about other businesses or organisations. Be careful to avoid phrases such as: 'I wouldn't bother with them', 'I'm not surprised you can't contact that operator', or 'I always have trouble with these people'.

CASE STUDY

When I first started in the travel industry, I worked in a small retail agency which was owned and run by a very pleasant and knowledgeable man who was liked and respected by all of his customers. One day I was listening to him dealing with some customers who wanted flight seats to Malaga at very short notice, and I learned a valuable lesson which has held me in good stead in my dealing with customers. The incident occurred in the days before travel had become fully computerised, and so my boss found himself telephoning a number of companies to check availability for the customer, and this was taking some time.

While he was waiting to get through to operators, he struck up a conversation with the customers which eventually led to their asking his opinion on the merits of the huge choice of charter airlines operating on that route. This happened to be a pet subject of his, and he went into graphic detail about the merits and pitfalls of each carrier. Finally, he said, 'The worst flight I ever had was with B . . . B airlines. The staff were rude, the food was awful and they even ran out of duty-frees.'

The customer thanked him for his advice and then attention was switched back to the call that was being answered by the tour operator. Up to now, no availability had been found, but on this occasion a flight with suitable timings was available. The customer was quite satisfied with the price and decided to book straightaway. As my boss and the tour operator began to process the booking, the customer said, 'Oh, by the way, which airline are we flying with?'

My boss asked the operator, looked very sheepish, then looked up at the customer and quietly said, 'Uhh . . . it's B . . . B Airlines'.

The customer declined the offer, and my boss lost the sale. His opinion had been taken quite literally, and there was no way that he could then reinstate the customer's faith in that company. Careless talk, in this instance, lost valuable business!

Positive attitude

One of the main ingredients of good customer care is a positive attitude. Your company will expect you to have a positive attitude towards your job; customers will expect you to take a positive attitude to their business needs. The travel industry is essentially a 'people' business, and the job tends to attract positive thinkers, who like to meet or converse with people and for whom personal interaction is important. So, how can you make sure that you adopt a good attitude – a positive attitude to all of your customers' needs?

The previous case study demonstrates very clearly that personal experiences tend to colour the way we think about a particular airline, tour operator, car rental firm, or any other company we deal with. It is also true that when it comes to holidays, we have our own personal preferences. Ask any group of travel industry people what type of holiday they prefer, or what they like to do on holiday, and they will give a variety of answers – lying on a hot sunny beach; dancing till the early hours; visiting the local sights; touring in a car; camping; trekking, and so on. The point is that not everybody likes a sun, sand and sea holiday. We each have our personal preferences.

Relating to someone who has the same preference for mode of travel or type of holiday is usually quite easy. If you have been on holiday to Majorca, and you thoroughly enjoyed it, then relating to others who have also enjoyed a holiday in Majorca will be easy. In the same way, you will be likely to sell Majorca enthusiastically as a holiday destination. That is one of the principal benefits of going on an educational visit. If you are a good skier, or you love water sports, or you like pony-trekking, you will almost certainly be positive about selling those sort of activity holidays to your customers. It is easy to adopt a positive attitude and to be enthusiastic about the kinds of things we enjoy, and to share our experiences openly with customers.

It is very much more difficult, though, to relate meaningfully to those kinds of holidays which hold no particular interest for us, and which do not meet our expectations of fun, relaxation and a good time. If the idea of a tour to the classic archaeological sights of the Middle East is as far from your ideal holiday as it is possible to be, then you may not find it quite so easy to express the same commitment and enthusiasm for this kind of holiday. Yet, customers who book a sightseeing tour will expect you to be just as committed, and to be just as positive and enthusiastic about their choice as you would be if you were booking your own holiday. A positive attitude to the customer's needs and personal preferences is an important part of selling. Enthusiasm on your part is more likely to elicit a positive response from the customer.

CASE STUDY

I once witnessed a very telling example of the effects of negative attitude on a sales training course which I ran for a group of second year travel students, which demonstrated well how expressing personal opinion about the customer's choice of holiday can jeopardise a sale. It was the second afternoon of the course, and delegates were practising their newly acquired selling skills in role-play. In this particular instance, a young lady, playing the part of the travel agent, was discussing the needs of a safari holiday with the customer. The safari was a trekking tour which had no set itinerary. Trekkers are accompanied by a guide who takes them into the bush in search of game. During the day they follow the game in a motor-kombi, and every night they pitch camp wherever they happen to be. The young travel agent was selling the tour with some enthusiasm, until the point where the 'customer' mentioned that the safari was to be part of his honeymoon. The agent stopped, looked in disbelief at the customer and said, 'Honeymoon – in a tent?'

Once the role-play had finished and feedback discussions had begun, this point was very quickly raised by the young man who had played the part of the customer. He felt that in a real situation, he would have been much offended by the sales assistant's comment, and may well have decided to book elsewhere. Interestingly, the young travel agent did not recall having made this comment. She did make the point, though, that her own idea of a honeymoon was to stay in a luxury hotel on a tropical island. This was a classic case of letting thoughts become words. Her comment was entirely spontaneous, yet suggested strongly to the customer that she disapproved of his personal choice.

....

Another time that negative attitudes sometimes show themselves to the customer is over the question of price. People have very widely differing views on what constitutes an 'expensive' or a 'cheap' holiday, and you should always guard against any tendency to attach your personal values to the cost of the customer's choice of holiday, hotel or mode of travel. If a customer asks for a product you consider to be 'very expensive', be careful not to express thoughts openly, in a way which might prejudice the sale. What you or I might consider expensive, may be well within the pocket of the customer. Furthermore, chance remarks about the value of a holiday product may offend the customer. If a customer can afford to pay for a high-value product, then remarks about 'expensive holidays' might indicate that you consider the holiday to be beyond the customer's price range. If the customer's pocket is not quite so deep, however, comments about 'cheap holidays' may suggest to the customer that you are looking down on his or her choice. The following two examples illustrate this:

CUSTOMER: We normally travel by charter, but this year we thought we'd go by scheduled airline.

AGENT: Scheduled air is far more expensive than chartered air, and it would add a lot to the holiday cost.

CUSTOMER: Yes, I realise that, but price is not the issue!

The customer is obviously irritated by the agent's attitude, which seems to suggest two things: 'I don't think you realise the difference in cost' and 'I don't think you can afford it'.

CUSTOMER: We want to book the Miramar Hotel in. . . .

AGENT Ah! I've been to that resort, and I thought that hotel was a bit down market.

CUSTOMER: Oh! Well, we've been going there for the last five years. Our friends go there, too. And that's good enough for us!

In the first example the agent is making the assumption that the customer is unaware of the difference in price, and is attaching his or her own values to the holiday and expressing an unwanted opinion as to what the customer should do, i.e. 'I think this is expensive, and I certainly wouldn't pay the extra money.' The agent has actually been rude to the customer, though probably without malice or intention.

In the second example, the agent equates the Miramar Hotel with a cheap-and-cheerful holiday, though the customer's reason for going has little to do with the price, and everything to do with the fact that they have enjoyed their previous visits.

Politeness

We have seen a number of examples of the inappropriate use of opinion – probably, in most cases quite unintentional on the part of the agent – but nevertheless, quite plain to the customer from the choice of words, from the expression in the voice or from the salesperson's body language. Being polite to customers is essential at all times. Any hint of unwanted opinion may be regarded as rudeness and will not endear you to the customer.

As a general rule, always say 'please' and 'thank you', and try not to interrupt the customer when he or she is speaking. Try to find out the customer's name early on in the conversation, and use it when speaking to them. At some point in the conversation – whether face-to-face or over the telephone – give your own name. Not only does this help to build a personal relationship between you and the customer, but it also allows the customer to ask for you by name whenever he or she needs to contact your office. This is especially important with telephone conversations, as you cannot be identified visually. It can be very irritating to try to locate you as 'the person I spoke to yesterday about the Tenerife Sol Hotel'. In terms of customer care, these seemingly insignificant points are very important.

Efficiency

Many customers look for efficiency in sales staff as a way of judging the business efficiency of the company. Being efficient is a combination of your knowledge, skill and attitude. Knowledge is an accumulative part of the process. Few people actually start off in their jobs as superefficient salespersons. First, you have to get to know the job and what is expected of you in that job, and many old hands at the business will tell you that you can never know absolutely everything. Learning is a continuous process, and there is always something new to learn.

Skill comes with practice. It is the degree of deftness and efficiency with which you are able to perform your job. Some jobs demand a high degree of skill, which takes time to acquire. The knowledge you have will underpin the level of competence you reach in any of your skills, which means, generally, that the greater your knowledge the more competent you are likely to be. The skills you require to be able to book, say, a two-week family holiday to the Costa del Sol are the same in principal as those you will need to be able to book an extended South American tour. If you know something about the geography of both places, and something about the cultures, the people, cuisine and nature of tourism within the two areas, you will probably find no difference in the way you need to approach these two holidays. But, if your knowledge of South America is so scant that you know little of its geography, its countries and their respective tourism possibilities, you will lack the underpinning knowledge necessary to enable you to discuss the tour or advise customers in the same way as you would were this a European 'bucket and spade' holiday.

Attitude is the third ingredient for acquiring efficient working skills. Your attitude to work, to learning and to dealing with people should be positive and welcoming. If you see your job as a drudge, then learning new skills will be a long and tedious process, but if you regard work as a challenge and an opportunity to develop, then acquiring further knowledge and greater skill is easier and gives you pleasure and fulfilment. Efficiency is not something you have, it is something you acquire.

....

CASE STUDY

Louise is busy behind her desk. She picks up the phone to a lady who wishes to find out about the visa arrangements necessary for a visit to the Far East. Louise does not have the answer to hand, but promises to look up the information for the customer and says, 'I'll phone back as soon as I've checked for you'.

Some three hours later she telephones the customer with the necessary information. The customer thanks her but, because of the time lapse, believes that Louise is inefficient.

Philip is also working in a busy office. He picks up the telephone to a customer who wants some flight information for a trip to Australia. Like Louise, Philip promises to return the call with the information, but is a little more positive about when he will do this.

'I'll phone you back in half an hour, Mr J. . . .'

He telephones the customer after two hours, apologising for the delay, and explaining that things have been very busy in the agency and that this has been the first opportunity he has had during the morning. The customer thanks him for his trouble. He too, looks on the agent as being inefficient, and is rather irritated at having to wait around in anticipation of an answer.

Alison works in a city agency, where people are constantly coming and going. She picks up the telephone just after ten o'clock to a customer who wants some general advice on holiday destinations and a few ideas for a family holiday She promises to call back, though she lets the customer know that things are rather busy.

'We're very busy at the moment, so I can't really say that I can phone you back straight away, but I will promise to ring back by twelve o'clock.'

In fact, Alison telephones the customer just before eleven o'clock with the required information. The customer thanks her very much. He is very impressed by her efficiency, as he was not expecting a return call until about midday.

....

These short case studies demonstrate that customers tend, among other things, to judge your efficiency by the level at which their expectations have been met. Louise set no expectations at all, so the customer really had no idea when she would return the call, but you will remember that she did promise to do this 'as soon as I've checked for you'. Obviously, her idea of 'as soon as' did not match the customer's, neither did this meet expectations of efficiency if the customer believed that Louise would call back within the hour.

Philip did set the customer's expectations and said he would phone back within half an hour. But, he failed to do this and eventually phoned back an hour and a half after this time. Again, the customer's expectations of an efficient service were not met.

When Alison took the enquiry, she judged how long it would take her to deal with it, then allowed herself additional time should anything else come up which would delay her contacting the customer. Alison suggested a time by which she could be reasonably sure she could contact the customer. Alison set the customer's expectations at a level she knew she could satisfy, then exceeded them by telephoning before the deadline she had agreed.

Efficiency, as Alison sees it, is simply the exceeding of the level of the customer's expectation. By telephoning the customer well before the time she had agreed, Alison had demonstrated her efficiency to the customer. Efficiency can be demonstrated in other ways, too, e.g. by providing additional information to the customer, and generally doing more than is expected of you.

Accuracy

Accuracy is fundamentally important in the world of travel and tourism. Accurate information on published times, latest offers, costings, tariffs and other general information are all important to the customer. No one will be impressed to receive inaccurate information or documentation. Most travel companies have a rule by which all outgoing documentation, letters and tickets are always double-checked by a senior member of staff.

....

CASE STUDY

Mr Jones was buying a holiday from a young and inexperienced travel agent. It was a late booking and the customer had just come in on the off chance that something would be available. The young agent managed to locate a holiday within the customer's stated price and time range. The details were being finalised over the telephone, and the customer was asked if he wished to make the booking firm.

'Yes,' he replied, 'provided, of course, that the resort has a sandy beach.'

The young agent was quite emphatic. 'Oh, yes,' he said.

However, the agent had not checked this information, either with the tour operator or in the brochure. It was some weeks later that an angry customer walked back into the travel agency and approached the young agent. Suddenly, a small bag of pebbles was emptied out on to the desk in front of the young man.

'There!' said the irate customer. 'That's your sandy beach.'

....

This was something which occurred a few years ago, before technology made the booking of holidays so very much easier. However, the lesson is clear – never make an emphatic statement of fact to a customer unless you can verify that it is true, either by checking the latest information or by contacting a known and reliable source.

Product knowledge

Your customers will expect you to have a fair degree of product knowledge, which normally means that they will expect you to know at least as much, if not usually far more about the product than they do. Of course, you cannot know everything, and are not expected to know everything but if you know where you can find the information you want, and can find it quickly and efficiently, you will always gain the customer's respect.

As you progress in your career and gain more experience, so your product knowledge will increase. By taking every opportunity given you during the course of your work, you will quickly increase your knowledge and, in turn, you will find continuously increasing job satisfaction. Some knowledge takes a long time to acquire – especially geographical knowledge of resorts, places and countries. Unfortunately, there is no substitute for looking up this information on a suitable map but, if you make it a rule to locate and memorise the places of every holiday destination you book for your clients, then your geographical knowledge will be the envy of friends and colleagues.

....

Assignment   We have now covered your main responsibilities to the customer, and the sorts of knowledge, skills and attitude by which they will judge your ability. These are: confidentiality, loyalty, a positive attitude, politeness, efficiency, accuracy and product knowledge.

Try to gauge how well you think you perform in each of these areas, and how you might improve your performance. Make a few notes for yourself for each of these headings and discuss them with your manager.

....

PERSONAL MOTIVATION

Levels of motivation always affect standards, and the level of motivation of staff often affects the standard of service given to the customer, and usually the outcome of a sales situation. If the customer is dealing with someone who shows a high degree of self-motivation they will feel fairly confident that their enquiry will be dealt with properly. If a salesperson is not very motivated, this does not instil much confidence in either the salesperson or the company. It is difficult for the customer to have confidence in a member of staff who shows no real commitment.

CASE STUDY

The Soames family are on holiday in Majorca and call in to see their holiday representative, Susan, for some advice on car hire. Susan is normally very outgoing and helpful and is considered by her area manager to be one of the best representatives on the island. Susan has had a very long, hard day and is tired. She has just had to deal with a problem in the resort which occurred as a result of carelessness on the part of the UK-based staff. When Mr and Mrs Soames arrive in her office, she really doesn't feel like talking with them, and does the barest minimum, sending them away with a leaflet and telling them to come back when they have made a decision on the type of car they would like. Susan is aware that the service she gave fell below her normal standard but, after a difficult and trying day, she just wants to be able to take a break from problems.

Mr and Mrs Soames are rather puzzled by the service they have received and feel that they should have received better treatment. They feel that Susan was rather dismissive of their needs and that they were perhaps an irritation to her.

'I thought that was a bit off, didn't you, Jim?'

'Hmm,' replies Mr Soames, 'I don't know whether we'll be using this tour company next year.'

'Well, she didn't seem in the slightest bit interested in us, did she?' says Mrs Soames.

The problem for Susan was that her normally high level of motivation had dropped because of a previous problem she had to deal with. When Mr and Mrs Soames arrived she was still feeling demotivated and this affected her performance. Not unreasonably, Mr and Mrs Soames were unhappy about the way they were dealt with and, as a result, may be tempted to use another company for their holiday next year.

Demotivated staff = unhappy customers

In this particular case study Susan was demotivated by an operational problem caused by someone else but she was the person who had had to deal with it. Susan was irritated at the lack of competence of the UK staff, and felt that she had had little support in dealing with the matter. In this case, Susan's demotivation was directly attributable to the incompetence of others, yet, difficult though it may have been, she should have guarded against any drop in her own professional standards. There are many such daily irritations and obstructions which may have the effect of lowering a normally high level of self-motivation. For example:

- relationship problems with colleagues
- boredom, due to lack of variety or challenge
- lack of necessary knowledge and skill to do the job
- an angry customer.

We all have different levels of self-motivation at which we normally operate, but our level of motivation can alter, up or down, depending on the living or working environment, how we feel in ourselves, or outside influences such as the ones listed above. Susan allowed the frustrations of a problem to affect her work, and this was passed on to Mr and Mrs Soames. Had Susan just received a note of appreciation, or praise from one of her customers, her mood would certainly have been very different. Her level of motivation would have been far higher, and this would have affected the way in which she handled the Soames's enquiry.

Having discussed the poor service which Susan gave, let's now look at motivation a little more closely to examine its direct effect on levels of service provided by sales people to their customers. Figure 1.1 shows a simplified model of motivational levels. Three levels of motivation are identified, and whilst most of us move up and down the motivation scale according to our moods and the way we feel, in a sales situation, where our moods affect the level of service we give to the customer, it is important to try to maintain a consistently high level of motivation whenever we interact with the customer.

People who continually operate at the lowest level – **must** – show the minimum of personal motivation. This is the 'have to do it' level, and most who work at this level tend to do a job simply to earn money. They rarely put more than a little effort into work, show no desire to progress and usually never act on their own initiative. Those working at the lowest level of motivation often display boredom and lack of interest in the job. They are never conscious of the effect this has on the customer, neither do they seek opportunities to improve the quality of service they provide. To these people, work is often a drudge – a means to an end – and the little commitment they show means that they put practically nothing into the job and get virtually nothing out of it.

The next highest level of motivation, the **should** level, is the level at which most people are content to operate. Those working at this level do far more than the minimum required of them and generally enjoy their work. They will act on their own initiative, and normally do not mind putting in the occasional extra work when this is necessary. They are often the bright and cheerful sales people who attain good rapport with customers, and who provide a very satisfactory standard of service.

At the **could** level, people are working hard to do just that bit more than the customer expects. To work at this level is a challenge, and usually means that the person is looking for opportunities to widen their scope – to expand their knowledge and develop new skills. Highly motivated people are generally

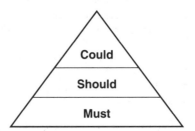

Fig 1.1   Model of personal motivation levels

motivated by their own success and achievements. This is the level at which customer expectations are exceeded.

As individuals, we are motivated or demotivated by a wide range of different stimuli. Whilst one person may be stimulated by statistics and the analysis of data or the challenge of a practical skill, another may only be motivated by interaction with people. Quite obviously then, the best sales people are those sociable types who enjoy the social skills of listening to, talking to, and serving the public.

Assignment

1 Make a list of all of the aspects of your job which you find motivating.

2 Number them in order of importance to you, starting with the most highly motivating factors.

3 Now make a note of anything in your job which you find demotivating, starting with the most demotivating factor.

4 Which list is longer? Does your list of motivators outweigh your list of demotivators? Are you able to balance out those things which demotivate you with those things which you find motivating?

5 At which level of motivation do you feel that you generally operate? Is there anything that you could do to improve your general level of motivation? If you don't feel able to do this on your own, then perhaps you might like to discuss it with your manager.

Behavioural factors in selling

As the travel and tourism industry is so varied, and offers a wide range of challenges, you probably have many different tasks to perform and may find that some stimulate you more than others.

CASE STUDY

Jill works in a very busy telesales office. Many of the enquiries she receives involve her taking notes of customers' needs and then phoning back with the information they require. This can mean that Jill often has a long list of enquiries, through which she must work in the order that they were received. Today she has left two more 'difficult' enquiries in favour of those she considers easier to deal with. Both enquiries are for products which Jill actively dislikes. She knows that she must deal with them at some point, so why has she put them to the bottom of the pile?

Jill has dealt first with all of the enquiries she finds stimulating and personally motivating, and has managed to leave until last those she finds much less motivating. Putting off those tasks we don't want to do is a natural reaction but, at the end of the day, those enquiries will still be waiting in the in-tray and your customers will still be expecting an answer.

....

Selling is about products and the people who buy them. Your motivation may be affected by the way you feel about certain customers and by your knowledge and experience in dealing with them. The standard of service you give very often depends upon your level of motivation. Most of us like to deal with certain types of customer because we get along well with them, but there may be other customers whose personalities do not appeal quite so much and with whom we have no instant rapport. Quite simply, you are more likely to find yourself highly motivated when you deal with a customer you like and less motivated when you have to deal with a customer you do not like. It is exactly the same with products – some products stimulate our interest, and we love to sell them, others have very little appeal. These feelings about our customers and the things we sell usually affect the level of service we are able to give.

So, this mix of customers and products, likes and dislikes, gives us a useful model from which we can examine our attitude and levels of motivation (see Fig. 1.2). The model makes quite clear that the ideal selling situation is where we are selling the product we most like to the customer with whom we have the greatest rapport. We like the product, we like the customer, and this makes us motivated to give a high level of service. The least enjoyable selling situation is where we are selling a product we do not like to a customer with whom we have the least rapport. We do not like the product, we do not feel at ease with the customer, and this affects our attitude and makes us less motivated to provide a good level of service.

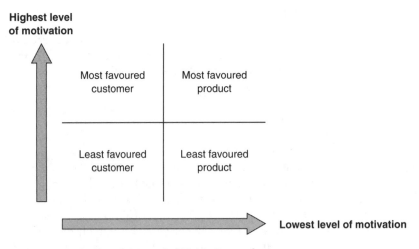

Fig 1.2   The four dimensions of attitude to service

There may be many different reasons why we do not like a particular product or customer. With people it may be a question of personalities, where we find certain customers awkward to deal with, or where we perceive them to be difficult. With products it may be a case of lack of knowledge, and hence a lack of confidence in dealing with the product, or perhaps that the booking arrangements are complex and seen as difficult. All of these bad feelings can be seen as demotivating factors, which affect the level of service we are likely to give. We tend to avoid such situations by making ourselves suddenly unavailable, or by trying to wrap up the sales conversation as quickly as we can, or we give out piles of brochures and urge customers to return when they have made up their minds. When we find ourselves in these situations, it usually takes a great deal of effort to maintain a sufficiently high level of motivation to provide the right level of service.

Sometimes you will find yourself in a half-and-half situation, where you have to sell a product you don't like to a customer with whom you have good rapport, or perhaps a product you do like to a customer you don't get on with. Which of these two situations you find less difficult will depend on your feelings and your personality. Generally though, most sales people are sociable beings and enjoy interaction with others. If we like the person, this usually makes the selling situation so much easier because we can make good use of this relationship to build on rapport, working together with the customer to overcome our lack of knowledge and experience. Good customer relations always helps in the selling situation.

....

CASE STUDY

James works in the reservations department of a tour operator and deals with a variety of different types of holiday to the USA. He likes his job very much and has a good knowledge of the products which his company sells. His personal level of motivation is quite high and he enjoys the challenge of working towards his sales targets, which he rarely fails to meet. James has a good manner on the telephone and goes out of his way to help any callers he deals with, but James's supervisor has noticed that whenever he has to deal with a tour which includes a cruise in the itinerary, his manner changes and he becomes far less helpful than usual. He has a tendency to rush the call, and rarely achieves a satisfactory outcome.

So, why does James's behaviour alter in this way when he has to deal with a cruise?

James is not confident in selling cruises for several reasons:

- His product knowledge is insufficient.
- He doesn't fully understand the booking procedure.
- He is often asked questions to which he doesn't know the answer.
- It is a high-value product and James is concerned at the consequences of making errors due to his lack of product knowledge.

All of these factors are material to James's lack of confidence and loss of motivation when confronted with a cruise itinerary, and result in his reluctance to deal effectively with the enquiry and the subsequently less than satisfactory service he gives to the customer.

What can James do to increase his level of motivation when dealing with this product?

James could start by increasing his general knowledge of cruising, and then progress to increasing his knowledge of the company's particular cruise itinerary. He could speak to his supervisor about the booking procedures and then arrange for further practice in order to gain experience. Once he has done this, he could set himself a personal target for a number of cruise bookings within a given period. He should also attempt to seek out answers to those questions which create a problem for him, and should look on this, not as problem, but as an opportunity to increase his general product knowledge.

Having done this, James should now be able to regard cruise enquiries as a challenge rather than a chore and, once he has increased his personal confidence, he will also succeed in raising his self-esteem, his level of motivation and the level of service he gives to callers.

....

Assignment

1 Think carefully about any particular products you dislike dealing with.

2 Consider why it is that you dislike the product? What level of motivation do you reach when you have to deal with the product, and how does this affect the standard of service you give to the customer?

3 Think about what you can do to improve the situation and increase your personal level of motivation? Make yourself a few notes and then discuss with your manager how this can be achieved.

....

CASE
STUDY

Julia was sent on an educational visit to Kenya last year which included a five-day safari. She really enjoyed the trip and is now the agency's appointed safari expert. She has acquired a good knowledge of safaris as a product, and has made a point of expanding her knowledge since returning to the UK. Her colleagues often refer safari enquiries to her as she has useful firsthand knowledge and experience. Julia is very confident in selling this type of holiday, and is able to give good advice to customers and enjoys the challenge of answering their many questions about what to see and do on safari. Her enthusiasm for safari bookings is obvious, and she has a high success rate for converting enquiries into sales.

Yesterday Mr Lennox called into the agency to enquire about a safari holiday and was referred to Julia. Julia has dealt with Mr Lennox before and doesn't like him. Last year he booked a Far Eastern tour and was very demanding. Julia feels that he has reacted unreasonably on a number of occasions, especially when he accused her of being inefficient when tickets and other documents failed to arrive on time from the tour operator.

Julia was not pleased to see Mr Lennox again, and felt herself very much on edge in his presence. Julia's normal confidence and enthusiasm for safari holiday enquiries rapidly vanished, and she appeared to be less than interested in the booking. When Mr Lennox began to question her about certain details of the holiday, Julia was reluctant to engage in any prolonged conversation and gave only the simplest of answers. She finally managed to free herself from the situation by handing out a few safari holiday brochures to Mr Lennox, inviting him to read these through and make a decision about which holiday would suit him best.

In this situation Julia had to deal with a customer she didn't like, even though she had good knowledge and direct experience of the product. She allowed all of her bad feelings for the customer to cancel out entirely her good feelings about safari holidays. Julia's usually high level of motivation had been affected by her previous experiences with Mr Lennox. Even though he had behaved in a perfectly normal and acceptable way towards Julia, it was the memory of those previous encounters which had affected her feelings for the customer, and her attitude towards him.

How should Julia have dealt with Mr Lennox?

Julia should first have made an effort to suppress her bad feelings based on her previous experiences with Mr Lennox. She should have offered him the same amount of help and attention she would give to any other customer, and tried to use her superior knowledge and enthusiasm to create a better rapport with the customer. If Mr Lennox had really been dissatisfied in his previous dealings with Julia, he would have been unlikely to return to the agency, and it may just be that Julia's fears are somewhat unfounded. Mr Lennox, of course, could be a rather difficult customer and, if he is, he is likely to adopt the same abrupt attitude in every salesperson/customer situation. Difficult though it may be for Julia, she would have done better to have risen above her feelings and concentrated on the real issue – being the agency's expert on safari holidays!

....

Attitude is a very important part of giving good service and, in a selling situation, a poor attitude to the customer will not be compensated by a high degree of competence or superior knowledge and experience of the product.

....

Assignment   Do you have any customers that you dislike dealing with? How does this affect your level of motivation? What can you do to ease these awkward situations? Make a few notes for yourself and make a conscious effort to deal with these customers in a more positive frame of mind when you next see them.

....

Although you may have a particular like or dislike for certain types of people, there are a number of recognisable personality types which can be labelled 'difficult customers'. This next section of the book gives an insight into these personality types and offers some practical guidelines for handling these situations.

HANDLING DIFFICULT CUSTOMERS

Difficult customers are those people perceived as being 'awkward', or 'difficult' to deal with in a service situation. Exactly who you regard as difficult, though, really depends on the sort of person you are. For example, if you are the chatty sort who enjoys talking to other people in a social context, then you may never have a great problem with the type of customer who never stops talking. But if you do not enjoy small talk, you may regard a very chatty customer as rather difficult to deal with – if only because you find it distracting while you are trying to concentrate.

Sometimes, too, things can work the other way when a perfectly reasonable customer becomes difficult as a reaction to the way they are treated. This is often the case where a customer feels he or she has reasonable grounds for complaint, then becomes aggrieved or dissatisfied with the response from the other party, or the way in which the complaint is handled. You will see how to deal with customer complaints later in the book.

To help you recognise and deal effectively with difficult customers, there are some practical guidelines on the next few pages. It should be said that there are no hard and fast rules for handling awkward customers except to remain polite at all times and show no sign of anger or irritation, no matter what the temptation.

The talker

Incessant talkers are normally very pleasant people. The point is that they never stop talking. It usually doesn't matter to them what they talk about and they often just slip from one topic to another without a break. They are generally of a happy disposition – the sort of people who will gladly tell you all about family and friends, holidays, a new shop they've seen or anything else that comes to mind. The only problem with talkers is how to stop them talking. Dealing effectively and politely with a talker takes time. A reservation or enquiry which would normally take minutes to deal with can turn into a marathon if the customer also wants to keep a conversation going.

The positive side of talkers is that, where they feel they have received good service, and that usually includes positive feelings for you, they are very likely to let everyone else know about your service. Talkative types who are treated well can be the best ambassadors for you and your company. This also applies, though, where they have received poor service. The compulsive talker will tell just about everyone they meet – it is a part of their nature.

Talkative types make up some 13 per cent of your customers, who each tell their story to another twenty people. For this reason alone, it is worth cultivating good relations from the start. So how should you treat them?

First, give them your full attention and try not to cut in too abruptly on what they are saying, no matter how disinterested you may be. This does not mean, of course, that you simply stand there and put yourself at the mercy of their endless chatter. It is not really difficult to steer the talkative customer back to the subject – you just listen out for a suitable opportunity to ask a leading question or summarise the conversation. If a customer is telling you all about her husband, and how hard he has been working, and how difficult it is for him to relax, etc., you can easily bring your customer back to the subject by saying, 'Oh dear, well he's certainly in need of this holiday. Shall we look for something relaxing, so that your husband can unwind?'

You will probably find that you need to bring your customer back on track a number of times during the course of the conversation, as the compulsive talker rarely finds listening as easy. If you persevere, though, you will find the situation easy to handle. Talkers will always give you the information you require. You just have to be skilled at listening for the clues and picking out the relevant information from all the other things that are being said. You will need to avoid giving away any signs that you are bored, though, so try to look interested in what the customer is saying.

Possibly the most difficult situation in which to deal with a talker is when they have 'just dropped in for a chat' and you are extremely busy. If you have a queue of customers waiting, most people will appreciate that you are busy and call in another time. But when you are busy with paperwork, with no other customers around, the compulsive talker is likely to settle in and chat. The most polite way to handle the situation is to say, 'I'd love to talk to you, but I've got some very urgent work to deal with at the moment. Why don't you pop in later this afternoon when we can have a proper chat?' This will not normally give offence, the customer is given an opportunity to call in again and you have your own time and space to get on with some very necessary work.

Let's take another look at the guidelines for dealing with talkative customers:

- Try to look interested in what they are saying.
- Bring them back to the subject by asking questions.
- If they just want to chat and you are very busy, make an arrangement for them to call back at a better time.
- Treat them well and let them do your advertising for you.

The show-off

The show-off is the sort of person who always makes a point of letting you know where they have been, what they have done, and what and who they know. Show-offs like to throw out this kind of information everywhere they go, and it often seems they are doing it just to put you down, and to prove their superiority.

Those who go through life with an 'I'm better than you' attitude, usually do so to hide underlying feelings of insecurity. Behaving this way allows them to mask their insecurity, though it can be intensely irritating to those on the receiving end of their constant snubbing. The natural reaction when you meet a show-off is to fight back in a similarly superior fashion, and to snub them, especially where you know that what is being said is incorrect. It is wise to avoid the temptation, though, because if you do succeed in snubbing a show-off, you will only have confirmed their insecurity, and probably find that they will become more determined and much more difficult to deal with.

Since the show-off needs to feel important, the best way to handle the situation is to allow them to feel important by treating them as someone a bit special. If they make a particular point of telling you how widely travelled they are, try to use this information to your own advantage by asking their opinion. Be careful how you do this, though, because in asking questions, you must not make yourself appear grossly ignorant or stupidly inferior. Avoid obvious questions, such as, 'Didn't you find the flight to Hong Kong rather long?'

Try to listen out for clues, and make use of their more discerning knowledge about specific places and experiences. Then you can always pose more searching questions to try to find out the sort of information not published in the brochure or on the database: 'The Hotel Mandarin's got a very good reputation. Do you think it lives up to this?' These more searching questions usually elicit a wealth of inside information which you can always use in the future.

Flattery is essential when dealing with the show-off, but do be subtle about it, and always use lead-ins such as, 'As you would know from your own experience . . .', 'Not many people have your understanding of the situation . . .' or 'That's an interesting point. What do you believe will happen when . . .'. But, you must make absolutely sure that what you say to the customer sounds sincere.

Let's take another look at the guidelines for dealing with show-offs:

- Never be tempted to put them down.
- Avoid showing your anger or irritation.
- Try to make them feel important.
- Ask about their experiences – you might learn something.

The doubter

Doubters have their own irritating way of never quite believing what you say, and often make this obvious by such statements as, 'Ah yes, well they all say that, don't they', 'I'll believe that when I see it' or 'What's the catch, then – there always is one?' Doubters are never quite sure, either about themselves, or about anyone else, which means that every piece of information has to be checked and double-checked. Doubters ask seemingly endless questions and, no matter how much information you give out, it never seems to be enough. Furthermore, they may well check it out by looking for themselves, by asking your colleagues or by checking out the information with several other tour operators or agencies. This endless checking can be very unsettling. One of the doubters's favourite questions is, 'Are you sure about that?'

So, in order to be really effective, you will have to be sure of your subject, sure of your sources and sure of your facts, and you will have to have the courage of your own convictions. If you are in any way unsure of your facts, those endless questions will shake your confidence, and probably make you doubt yourself. If you don't know the answer, never be tempted to guess. Unless you have guessed correctly, you will usually be found out.

Dealing effectively with the doubter takes time, so you will need to be very patient. Answer every question calmly and with conviction, and don't let yourself be ruffled. Above all, never rush this sort of customer, or you are likely to draw suspicion that you are hiding something. The doubter wants to tread carefully and cautiously through every enquiry. You will find, too, that every piece of documentation will have to be thoroughly scrutinised – booking conditions, insurance policies, brochure resorts and hotel descriptions. The doubter will almost certainly want to read every word. All this takes time, but the doubter will not normally be offended if you need to do something in the meantime – whether answering the telephone or checking other work – provided you are polite and come back to the customer when they are ready.

Doubters are always on the lookout for a bargain and, if they think they can get something a few pounds cheaper elsewhere, they will certainly say so. Make sure that you find them the best possible deal, and ensure that you correctly apply all supplements and reductions, and that you explain them fully to the customer. Customers should be made aware of the full costs of what they are buying. If doubters find out that they could have saved money, their naturally suspicious nature may lead them to conclude that you are deliberately trying to overcharge – so beware!

As with every awkward customer, though, there is a positive side. With doubters, it is a fact that friends and family all know how difficult they are to satisfy. They are truly sceptical shoppers and purchasers, and their suspicious nature can make them seem like a one-person quality control. If there's a flaw, they will find it. If something is incorrect, they will point it out. If they have had poor service, you will know about it. So, if this customer praises your services, it will be praise indeed.

Here are the guidelines for dealing with the doubter:

- Know your subject. Know your facts.
- Don't let the doubter undermine your confidence.
- Remain firm but be polite in your replies.
- If they want to read a document from start to finish, let them. They won't be offended if you do something else until they are ready.
- Always ensure that you have given out accurate and correct information, especially when it comes to money.

The impatient customer

Impatient customers are constantly in a hurry. Their need to be one step ahead of themselves means that they will expect your service to be fast, efficient and accurate, and they will show great irritation if it is not. Impatient customers want things done fast, and they can get you just as flustered as the last type of customer. Still, they are not particularly difficult to deal with provided you recognise their basic need for speed and efficiency and respond accordingly by making absolutely sure that you have all the necessary facts to enable you to deal effectively with their enquiry.

Since time is all important to the impatient customer, deal quickly and simply with every enquiry. They will have no time to chat, neither will they expect you to waste too much valuable time on pleasantries. Their normal approach is very down-to-earth and businesslike, so if you know it will take time to deal with their enquiry, suggest that they leave all details with you so that you can have an answer when they call back later. If they are in a real hurry, you will do better to telephone them at an agreed time. Remember, though, that because they are busy people, you will need to agree a time by which you can telephone them with the information. If your impatient customer is told that they will have an answer by four o'clock, they will expect one, and will take you to be inefficient if you are not able to provide the promised information by that time.

A good tip for dealing effectively with impatient customers is to use the technique of setting the customer's expectation at a reasonable level and then exceeding those expectations as discussed earlier in the chapter. Time is the driving force of the impatient customer, so try to exceed their expectation that nothing can be done too quickly, by telephoning back long before they realise that time is running short.

Here are the guidelines for dealing with the impatient customer:

- Provide a fast, efficient and accurate service.
- Keep the conversation on a business level.
- Avoid wasting the customer's time at all costs.
- Employ 'underpromise and overdelivery' techniques.

2

....

Professional use of the telephone

The travel industry as a whole is a large user of the telephone, and much of the work that you do will be conducted over the phone. This may be either directly with the customer or with other sectors of the industry, such as travel agents, tour operators, airlines, etc. The previous chapter of this book examined how the contact with one person representing the company can influence a customer's decision on the efficiency and quality of service that the company as a whole provides, and this is especially so when the customer only has contact with the company by telephone. In this case, the customer will base their decision on the efficiency and quality of service provided by the company solely on the way that one telephone call was dealt with. As part of your NVQ assessment, you will be required to demonstrate your knowledge of good telephone practice and your ability to handle both incoming and outgoing calls in an efficient and professional manner. This chapter aims to provide you with the background knowledge you will require and opportunities to practise your skills in the workplace.

Objectives

Once you have read this chapter of the book, you should be able to:
- **state guidelines for creating a good impression on the telephone**
- **state guidelines for good telephone practice**
- **state guidelines for effective operation of a switchboard**
- **use an answerphone in a professional manner**
- **use effective communication skills on the telephone**
- **state guidelines for dealing with difficult calls.**

ADVANTAGES AND DISADVANTAGES OF COMMUNICATING BY TELEPHONE

....

Assignment   Consider the types of telephone calls you make and receive as part of your working day. What are the advantages of conducting business over the phone as opposed to dealing with someone face to face? Make a few notes before you continue reading the text.

....

First, the telephone allows you to conduct business over a very wide geographical area which you might otherwise not be able to reach if it were necessary for you to have face-to-face contact with all of your customers. Telephone is quicker than relying on the postal service and is far more interactive than communicating by fax or letter.

Another point which many consider to be an advantage is that the caller cannot see you. This means that appearance and work surroundings cannot have any influence on the impression the caller may make. You may prefer this as it enables you to save face by putting the call on hold if you need to check information with a colleague, or ask how you should deal with something with which you are not familiar. If you are not visible to the caller, they may not realise that you are somewhat flustered – providing you are able to project an air of confidence in your voice. However, the fact that the caller cannot see you can also be something of a disadvantage, as this can make communication more difficult.

....

Assignment   Now think about other disadvantages of communicating by telephone to the caller. Make a few notes before you continue with the text.

....

A major disadvantage of using the telephone from the caller's point of view is that a telephone call may not be treated with as high a priority as a personal caller to the same office. This may result in calls being left ringing because staff are too busy to answer the phones or, as in the following case study, telephone enquiries not being considered as important as enquiries made in person.

CASE STUDY

Mrs Blake wants some information about holidays to France, and telephones her local travel agency to speak to Judy, the young travel consultant who booked her last holiday. After a little time, Mrs Blake manages to get through, and speaks to another young lady who tells her that the agency is very busy and that Judy is currently with a customer. Mrs Blake asks if it is possible for Judy to phone her as soon as she is free. The young lady says she will pass the message on. Judy's colleague makes a note of the message and puts it on Judy's desk. Judy glances at it and indicates to her colleague that she has acknowledged it. Though very busy with her clients, Judy has every intention of phoning Mrs Blake as soon as she is free, but there is a continual flow of customers, and it is three hours later before Judy is able to find the time to return Mrs Blake's call. Unfortunately by this time, Mrs Blake has gone out.

Judy did not ignore the request from Mrs Blake to phone back. She felt, however, that dealing with the customers in front of her was a higher priority than returning the telephone call. Mrs Blake, who was unable to see the situation in the travel agency, probably did not appreciate the fact that Judy was genuinely very busy, and may have felt that she just did not bother to 'phone her back. If you find yourself in this situation ask a colleague to ring back and apologise on your behalf – perhaps even see whether or not someone else can help. If the customer really does need to speak with you, then employ the tactic discussed in the previous chapter of setting customer expectations at a reasonable level to ensure that you can meet them.

If you work in a very busy office, which deals with both personal callers and telephone enquiries, there may be occasions when the telephone is left ringing because the staff are too busy to take the calls. Whilst other sectors of the industry may appreciate the reason for this, members of the public might assume that you are closed or that you never bother to answer the telephone. If the customer makes one of these assumptions and elects to phone one of your competitors who does answer the phone, they may well obtain business which was originally intended for you.

Some companies adopt a standard that telephones must be answered within a given number of rings. This in itself is very good practice as it puts a more equal emphasis on the service that a telephone enquiry receives as opposed to a personal caller. However, I have telephoned some companies who answer the telephone within the specified number of rings, but tell the caller straightaway that everyone is too busy to deal with their request, and advise that someone will ring back as soon as possible. This is not always good practice, as very often the customer has to wait a considerable amount of time before anyone is available to phone them, and may well regard this as poor service on the part of the agent.

Telephone enquiries should be treated with the same level of professionalism as personal callers, and should receive the same standard of service. Just as with a personal caller, each telephone call waiting to be dealt with should be regarded as a potential booking, and deserves just as much care and attention as the customer standing in front of you.

CREATING A GOOD IMPRESSION

CASE
STUDY

Company A has spent considerable time and money on the training of its staff. Everyone has received telephone techniques training and all staff use the company corporate image. Whenever customers telephone Company A they are greeted courteously and politely by voice-trained staff:

'Good-morning, . . . Corporation. How can I help you, sir?' In a recent survey conducted by Company A to elicit responses from their customers, they received very high scores for the telephone manner and technique employed by the staff.

Company B does practically no training. None of the staff has had any kind of telephone training and, subsequently, no voice training. Staff answer the telephones when they are ready, or if they are not busy, and they certainly have no particular business address to their customers. Company B staff have many different ways of answering the telephone: 'Hello!', 'Morning, who is it?', 'Yeah!', 'Simpson 'ere.', 'Who d'ya want?' Company B has never circulated a survey form to its customers. They have no idea how professional or unprofessional they appear over the telephone, but, like Company A, they are probably quite well known for the way in which they do answer the telephone.

As we have already discussed, when a customer contacts you by telephone, they have nothing visual on which to base their judgement of the standard of service they will receive. Therefore the impression they will form of you and the company is based entirely on the way the call is dealt with. It is therefore vitally important that you make every effort to create a favourable impression which will encourage the customer to do business with you. Over the next few pages we will examine what can be done to help create a good, professional image over the telephone.

Assignment

1 Before continuing with the text, think about telephone calls that you have made to other businesses.

2 Make some notes of things which have caused you to form a poor impression of the company, and things which have given you a good impression of the company.

A number of things will help to create a good, or bad, impression over the telephone. You may have included such things as: the way the call is answered, the manner that was used towards you, the person's voice, how efficiently the call was dealt with, perhaps even how confident and enthusiastic the person sounded. A whole range of influences can affect the impression that a customer forms, and most of these are within the control of the person who answered the phone. In this section of the chapter we will examine how your voice and manner can help you create a good impression on the caller.

The greeting

When a customer telephones your office, the first thing they should hear when the call is answered is the greeting. You may not consider the greeting to be a particularly important part of the call, but the way a call is answered often sets the tone for the rest of the conversation. If the greeting is poor and does not project a businesslike image, the caller may have formed a poor impression of you and the company before the conversation has even started.

Many companies have a standard greeting which all staff are expected to use, this helps to create a good corporate image and ensures that every call is answered to the same high standard. If your company does not have a standard greeting, then you may like to consider the following:

(a) 'Tour Australia, good-morning.'
(b) 'Good-morning. Tour Australia. How may I help you?'

Greeting (a) and greeting (b) are commonly used styles of greetings. If you were telephoning a company, which style would you prefer and why?

Both greetings are polite and give the name of the company. However, greeting (a) may not be as clear to the caller as greeting (b). Imagine that the caller has been waiting for some time, or is not concentrating on listening to the sound of the telephone ringing. When the call is answered, the caller needs time to adjust from the ringing tone to the sound of the voice of the person who answers the call. In this case, they may not be concentrating fully when the company name is given. The caller is even less likely to hear the first few words of the greeting if either party is using a Mercury telephone system, which gives a series of 'pips' as the call is connected.

To ensure that the caller has not missed anything of importance at the beginning of the greeting, it is preferable to begin with 'Good-morning' or 'Good-afternoon', as in greeting (b), before the company name is given. This will enable the caller to tune in properly to what is being said and hear the important part of the greeting, the company name. By including 'How may I help you?' in the greeting, the person answering the phone is starting the conversation with the first question. This is especially important when dealing with members of the public who may not be used to conducting business over the telephone.

Some companies insist that their staff always identify themselves in the greeting, e.g. 'Good-morning, Tour Australia, Amanda speaking. How may I help you?' This does sound very professional and efficient, and may go some way to building a relationship with the caller. If this is not part of your standard greeting you may wish to practise giving your name and see how comfortable you feel with it.

Once you have decided upon your greeting and start to use it, you should consider how you sound. It is all too easy to allow your voice to fall into a familiar pattern, or perhaps to rush things. You should always try to make your greeting sound genuine, rather than sounding like a programmed response that is replayed every time you answer the phone. You may have heard it hundreds of times before, but your caller has not.

Use of the voice

When using the telephone, the voice is a very important instrument which plays a major part in creating an image – professional or otherwise. Even if your telephone technique is excellent, if the voice is not used to good effect, the impression the caller forms of the person to whom they are speaking may not be favourable.

Often when speaking to someone that you have not previously met, you will form a mental image of that person, and that image will be based entirely on the sound of the person's voice. If you regularly listen to the radio, you may have a picture in your mind of how a certain disc jockey or a presenter looks, but it is rare that the image will bear any resemblance to how that person looks in reality. This really doesn't matter as long as the mental picture which is created represents the image that is required. The people you speak to on the telephone will quickly form an image of you, purely on how you sound, and if you make professional use of the telephone and use your voice to good effect, they will probably imagine you to be smart and tidy in appearance. However, if your manner, telephone technique and use of the voice are poor, their image of you will not be so favourable.

To understand how the voice can make such an impression on the caller, we need to examine each component part of the voice. The components are: pace, pitch, volume, emphasis and clarity. Let's take each one in turn.

Pace

This is the speed at which we normally talk. Some people are naturally fast in their speech, others may be slower, but become fast when nervous or excited. If the pace is too fast, the caller may not hear everything that is said and may even become confused. Fast talkers rarely pause, and this can be very tiring to listen to. Pauses are a natural part of speech and need to be used, however briefly, to allow the caller time to take in the information they are being given. The average human brain can only take in between eight to ten words at a time, before a pause is necessary to enable the sorting and storing of the given information, so by adding sufficient pauses to your speach, you will help to ensure that the caller has a clear understanding of what is being said.

Slow talkers can be equally difficult to listen to, as they give the impression of being very dull and, perhaps, a little unsure of themselves. The caller may will them to speed up, and their irritation may cause them to cease listening. How often have you listened to a slow talker? How interesting do they sound? Did you listen intently, or did your mind start to wander?

On the whole, people who use the telephone as part of their job have a tendency to speak too quickly rather than too slowly. Listen to yourself occasionally, and assess the suitability of your own pace.

Pitch

Every voice has a natural pitch, or register. Some voices are naturally very high pitched while others are naturally low, but within that natural register, the voice needs to have a variety of pitch to make the voice sound interesting. A voice which lacks variety, a monotone, sounds very dull and boring and the listener will very quickly switch off. In a selling situation, a monotonous voice will give the impression of disinterest and will certainly lack the enthusiasm that is vital to achieve any level of success in a sales role.

Volume

Volume of the voice should ideally be mid-range and comfortable for the caller to listen to. A voice which is quiet may often give the impression that the speaker is shy and lacks confidence. A voice which is too loud will usually give the impression of someone who is overbearing and is not very pleasant for the caller to listen to. Most people in the travel industry have little problem with volume, but this may sometimes be affected by use of telephone equipment. Correct use of equipment is covered later in this section.

Emphasis

This is a very important aspect of the voice and can be used to good effect, but do be aware that emphasis can also change the whole meaning of a phrase or sentence, e.g. 'This hotel has the *best* appointed rooms in the area', meaning that the rooms are undoubtedly the best appointed. But if the emphasis were changed to another word; 'This *hotel* has the best appointed rooms in the area', the implication is that other types of accommodation have rooms which are better. In fact, the same sentence could be read over and over again, emphasising a different word each time, and thus changing its meaning.

Emphasis can also be used as a way of making certain important words stand out in a sentence, such as, 'You need *full* British passports', 'You need to check in at least *one hour* before departure', 'The train will depart from Platform *four* today' and 'I shouldn't think the main road will cause *too* much noise'.

Overall, emphasis is a useful and important element of the voice which gives additional interest and meaning to what is being said, but if used carelessly, can betray personal opinions, which are best not disclosed.

Clarity

Obviously when speaking over the telephone, special attention should be paid to the clarity of the voice. Whilst the language and phraseology that is used plays an important part in ensuring clarity, the way that the voice is used is equally important, especially when dealing with foreigners or people from different regions of the country where the dialect may be slightly different. Pace and volume play an important part in ensuring the voice is clear, as words may be lost or unclear if the pace is too fast or the volume too low.

Finally, try and smile when you are speaking on the telephone, even though the caller cannot see you, they will certainly hear your smile, and this will make you sound and feel more positive and confident.

Assignment

1 List the component parts of the voice and make some notes on how you think your voice sounds under each of the components.

2 Now ask your supervisor to listen to you when you next deal with a business call, and compare their observations with your own.

3 If either of you are able to identify an area where improvements could be made, draw up an action plan and agree a time at which your supervisor can listen to you again.

Using an appropriate manner

Have you ever heard a colleague or member of your family, answer the phone in one manner, and then immediately switch to another because they recognise the voice of the caller? Most of us have adopted a 'telephone voice' which is used in the business environment and should be used whenever a business conversation is conducted over the phone. However, once a friend or member of the family has been identified, a 'telephone voice' would not be at all appropriate. As well as adopting a particular type of voice, it is necessary to adopt a business manner, and much of the information provided in the chapter on customer care regarding using an appropriate manner with the customer, is equally appropriate to dealing with a customer on the phone as it is to dealing with the customer face to face. If you have not read the chapter, you should refer back to it, but in addition to this there are some specific issues which apply purely to telephone conversations.

In an environment where all work is conducted over the telephone and the staff are out of public view, there is often a high level of interaction and social conversation between the staff while they are not dealing with calls. This is quite natural since we are social beings, and to sit in silence while not dealing with calls would be particularly unpleasant. However, in an environment such as this, the social conversation can sometimes be a hindrance to the call, with staff finding themselves easily distracted and paying more attention to what is going on around them than to what the caller is saying.

CASE STUDY

John works for Seascape Travel and is telephoning a number of tour operators looking for late availability to Florida for one of his regular customers. He is currently phoning ContiTours and is waiting for his call to be answered.

The staff at ContiTours are not particularly busy today, there has been a steady flow of calls, but they have certainly not been rushed off their feet. The four reservations agents currently on duty are positioned around a bank of desks and are discussing a television serial which had its penultimate episode last night. There is a lively discussion about what each of the agents thinks will happen next. Meanwhile a bank of flashing call lights goes unanswered. Finally Lorraine picks up one of the calls as she finishes her contribution to the conversation.

John hears the call being answered and switches his attention from the customer to the call. There is a lot of background noise and laughter and then he hears Lorraine say, 'Hello, ContiTours'.

John starts to explain to Lorraine what he is looking for but has the feeling that she is not really paying attention. He can hear a lot of background conversation and laughter and has the feeling that Lorraine is only half listening to what he is saying, giving the rest of her attention to what is going on around her. Lorraine offers to check availability for him.

'I'll just put you on hold for a minute,' she says.

John waits for Lorraine to check availability. She comes back on the line, 'Hello. Sorry, did you say Gatwick or Manchester?'

'Manchester,' says John.

'And that was two weeks wasn't it?'

'No, three!' says John, by now somewhat irritated by Lorraine's manner, since it appears obvious that she is conducting two conversations at once, and his seems to be coming a very poor second.

'Just a minute,' says Lorraine.

A few minutes later Lorraine comes back to John with several hotels which are available for the dates he has asked for. John makes a note of these, but decides that he will try and find availability with another company before he offers this to the customer. After all, if Lorraine's apparent lack of interest in the call is a reflection of the way the rest of the company runs, he has serious doubts as to the quality of holiday his customer is likely to receive.

John was quite correct in his assumption that Lorraine was not paying full attention to the call. Whilst she was dealing with him, she was still listening to the conversation between her colleagues about the previous night's television programme. As John was making his request for availability, Lorraine was thinking about her next contribution to the conversation between her colleagues as soon as she could put her call on hold. When she did start to check availability, she found that she didn't have all of the information that she needed, so had to go back to John and ask again. All in all, Lorraine's lack of concentration created a very poor image of the company as a whole.

Continuing a personal conversation while dealing with a call is very unprofessional and may cause offence to the caller since it will be obvious that they are not receiving the full attention they deserve. Once you are dealing with a call, all of your attention should be given to the caller, and no matter how hard it may seem, you should block out everything else that is going on around you. To make doubly sure that you don't forget any of the information that the caller is giving, make a few notes when the initial enquiry is given to you. Sometimes personal conversations with other staff can be heard as a call is switched back from being on hold, or even at the end of the conversation; either situation may allow the caller to hear something which they should not.

CASE STUDY

I once made a call to an airline which was handled well, but as the call ended I heard the agent say, 'What an idiot!' as she disconnected the call. As I had the agent's name, I phoned through to the Reservations Supervisor and complained at the agent's conduct, but was surprised when the supervisor said he was expecting my call. The agent in question had been referring to a colleague she had just seen, but had realised that I had probably heard the comment and considered it to be directed at me. She had gone to her supervisor straight away and explained the situation in case I did phone back and complain. Everyone apologised profusely and no offence was taken. However, had I not phoned back, I would have formed a very poor impression of the company and may have tried to avoid using them in the future.

Finally, there is one last thing which can happen in a telesales environment which, although out of the control of the reservations agent who is taking the call, can still affect the quality of service that is provided. All too often, another member of staff, or even a supervisor will try and attract the attention of the reservations agent, to ask them a question or ask them to read something, all while they are dealing with a call. Once this happens, the agent cannot possibly be giving their full attention to what the caller is saying, and sometimes may even find it necessary to put the call on hold so that they can deal with their colleague. It is very rare indeed that a query is so urgent that it cannot wait until the call is finished, yet interruptions of this kind go on day after day. Perhaps no one has stopped to think of the effect this has on the quality of service provided. Are you ever guilty of interrupting someone else while they are on a call? Have you ever tried to communicate with a colleague whilst they are talking to a customer?

When you are not dealing with a call yourself you should respect that your colleagues should not be interrupted. It is all too easy to break their concentration by trying to ask them a question or pass on information while they are dealing with a call. Even just standing close by them, waiting for them to finish, is an invitation to interrupt concentration for some, so use your judgement and think about it from your own and the customer's point of view.

GOOD TELEPHONE PRACTICE

So far we have discussed how manner and voice affect the overall impression that is made on a caller, but in addition to this, telephone practice should also be considered. Telephone practice is the way that calls are managed and equipment is used. Good telephone practice requires skill, and once mastered, will help you to create a good professional image of both yourself and the company. Good telephone practice is something which if present will not be noticed by the caller, but if a caller experiences bad telephone practice, they most certainly will notice, and will probably consider that the service you provide is below par.

Preparing to answer the call

Always ensure that you are fully prepared when answering a call. This means detaching yourself from any other conversation and switching your attention to dealing with the call. Always ensure that you have pen and paper ready, as you will no doubt need to make some notes during the conversation, and it will be very obvious to the caller that you are unprepared if you have to excuse yourself to get a pen to make some notes. If most of the enquiries you receive necessitate checking your computer terminal for information, ensure that you take your screen back to the appropriate starting page at the end of each call, and ensure that you have completed all the necessary paperwork before dealing with the next call. You cannot possibly give the caller your full attention if you are still dealing with work from a previous enquiry.

Try not to work in too much of a mess. If your desk is cluttered up with piles of paper and brochures, you may find yourself hunting through your work to find the information that you need while you are trying to deal with the call. Everyone has daily tasks that they need to work through, but try and keep it in some sort of order so that you can easily locate information as and when you need it.

Your posture

Posture is quite important when speaking on the telephone, even though the caller cannot see you, as the way you are sitting will affect the way you sound. If you are slumped or slouched while you are speaking on the phone, it can affect your breathing, thus altering your voice slightly. In addition to this, a slouched position which may be adopted in moments of low level motivation can sometimes be evident in the voice. Always try to adopt an upright position as you would if you were seen by the customer, as this will make you feel, and therefore sound, more professional.

Sometimes, in moments when you feel your confidence deserting you, standing up may help you to increase your confidence. Even though the caller cannot see you, a standing position is much stronger than a sitting one, and this will help you to feel more positive.

Use of equipment

There is now a huge variety of different types of telephone systems available to businesses, and some of them have very complex and useful functions. When you first started your job you should have been shown how to use all of the functions on your particular telephone system, but you may find it useful to read through the instruction manual again to ensure that you are fully familiar with all of the functions available to you. Your system may have such functions as leaving a message on an internal extension or automatically locating an outside line when one becomes available. All of these functions are designed to save you time, so try to make the best use of them.

You may have the option of using either a headset or a handset in your job, and you should ensure that, whichever one you use, it is positioned correctly. When using a handset ensure that the mouthpiece is in a position to enable the caller to hear what you are saying. Do not tuck the handset between your shoulder and your ear, as this will impare the quality of your speech as heard by the caller.

If your job is in telesales, you may find it more convenient to use a headset, as this will allow you to keep your hands free to operate keyboards and use manuals, etc. Another major advantage of using a headset is that you do not necessarily need to put the call on hold as you check for information. This allows you to hear any additional information from the caller as you check, and will also enable you to keep the caller informed of what you are doing. If you need to check information with a colleague, you can simply switch off the microphone, rather than putting the call on hold. This means that although you can hear the caller, the caller won't be able to hear you. When speaking to a caller on a headset, ensure that the microphone is correctly positioned. If it is too close to the mouth, quality of speech can be distorted.

Putting calls on hold

When you receive a telephone enquiry, it is quite likely that you will need to put the call on hold at some point during the conversation to enable you to check information. If handled properly, the caller will be quite accepting of the fact, but if the call is left on hold for what seems an interminable length of time, with no explanation as to the reason why, this can be very irritating indeed. Although it may seem quite reasonable to you that you need to spend some time locating the information – perhaps asking a colleague or even going into another department – the caller cannot see what you are doing and therefore has no appreciation of why they are being left for so long.

CASE
STUDY

CALLER: Can you tell me what currency I need for the Philippines?
ANDREW: Can you hold the line for a minute and I will find out?
CALLER: Thank you.

Andrew does not know where to look for the information and searches through a few brochures. He then tries to attract the attention of a colleague who is on the phone. She eventually signals to him the guide book he requires, which Stella is using with her customer. Andrew waits very patiently until Stella has finished and then takes the book back to his desk, finds the information he needs and picks up the telephone. His quest for the information has taken him about three minutes.

ANDREW: It's the peso.
CALLER: The what?
ANDREW: The peso
CALLER: Thank you.

The caller rings off before Andrew has the chance to say anything else. Andrew is pleased that he took the time and trouble to find the information for himself, next time he will know where to look. However, the caller thought that the service was appalling, and makes a mental note not to use the agency again.

Although Andrew was very conscientious in his work and took the trouble to find the information for his customer, the customer was unable to see the processes it was necessary for Andrew to follow to locate the information. Perhaps the customer had expected Andrew to know the answer straight away and may have been surprised that any investigation was necessary. Although Andrew did inform the customer that he would need to locate the information, the words he used, 'Can you hold the line for a minute . . .', gave no indication to the customer of how long the wait would be, or the reason for it. To create a more professional image, Andrew should have explained that he needed to consult a directory and that this may take him a few minutes.

When Andrew finally returned to the telephone, he started the conversation straightaway, giving the caller no opportunity to prepare to receive the information. This meant that the customer did not hear the answer properly the first time and had to ask Andrew to repeat himself. Andrew should have apologised to the customer for keeping him waiting before giving him the information. Not only is this common courtesy, but it would also have ensured that the customer was paying full attention when Andrew gave him the information that he required.

In this example, the call was put on hold while information was checked, and while Andrew did not handle this in the best way possible, it is far better to put the call on hold while you check information, than to leave the call live and allow the caller to hear the background conversation. While most people will accept that they might be dealt with by a trainee who may need help from a colleague when they are still learning the job, care should still be taken to ensure that a professional image is maintained. It is far better to explain that you need to ask for advice and put the call on hold in a professional manner, than to allow the caller to hear, 'I've got someone on the phone who wants to know about prepaid car-hire vouchers, I haven't got a clue what he's talking about'.

Guidelines for putting calls on hold

1 When putting a call on hold explain to the caller that you will be putting them on hold and the reason why, e.g. 'I need to speak to my supervisor about this'.
2 Give the caller an indication of how long you are likely to be. Be realistic. 'I won't be a minute' doesn't tell the caller very much. Ensure that you set the caller's expectations at a reasonable level, and don't forget that although a minute may pass very quickly for you, it will seem an age to the caller.
3 Explain what will happen when the call goes on hold. Will the line go dead, or will there be music? If the line does go dead when calls are placed on hold, explain this to the caller so that they don't think that they have been cut off.
4 If you are using a handset, or you are taking off a headset and leaving your desk, ensure that you use the hold facility, or switch your microphone off. The caller will be able to hear background noise and will certainly be able to hear you speaking to your colleagues if this is not done. If using a handset, never place your hand over the receiver to speak to a colleague instead of using the hold facility. The caller will still be able to hear every word that you say.
5 When returning to the call, attract the caller's attention before anything else is said. If the call has been on hold for some time, the caller may be distracted, especially if they themselves are phoning from business premises. Just saying 'Hello' is sufficient. Once they have responded to this, you can continue with the conversation.
6 Always apologise for keeping the caller waiting. If you were gone longer than the time that you initially indicated, then explain the reason why, e.g. 'I'm sorry I took so long, someone else was using the manual I needed to refer to'.
7 If, once the call has been put on hold, you find that you are delayed, then go back to the caller and apologise again for keeping them waiting, and ask if they mind holding again, or would they prefer you to phone them back.

Transferring calls

As part of your normal day-to-day duties you will undoubtedly need to transfer calls to colleagues on other extensions. Care needs to be taken with transferring calls, as if this is not done in a professional manner it can create a very poor impression of the company's efficiency.

....

CASE STUDY

Alan works for a travel agency called Haden Travel. This morning he received an invoice from a tour operator which shows incorrect flight details. He telephones the operator to check the flight details. Wendy answers the calls.

WENDY: Hello, reservations.

ALAN: Can you check something on my invoice please?

WENDY: I'll put you through to accounts.

ALAN: No it's . . . (but Wendy has already transferred the call).

ACCOUNTS: Hello, accounts.

ALAN: I'm sorry. I don't want accounts. Can you transfer me back to reservations please?

ACCOUNTS: I'm sorry, all of their lines are busy. Can you call back later?

In this example, Wendy was in too much of a hurry to transfer the call to someone else and assumed, quite wrongly, that Alan's query was an accounts query. Wendy failed to establish exactly what the nature of the query was. Had she done so, she may have been able to help Alan herself, if not she could have explained who he needed to speak to before he was transferred. When Wendy told Alan she was going to transfer him to accounts, he objected, but his objection was ignored. Alan then found himself in the irritating position of being transferred to a department he didn't want to speak to, and then finding that he would have to redial to speak to reservations again.

Alan reflected on his experience. This was not the first time he had been treated in this way by the company. He made a note to speak to the sales representative about it next time she called.

Some months later, Alan phoned the company again and was pleasantly surprised by the way his call was handled.

WENDY: Good morning, reservations. How may I help you?

ALAN: Can you clarify something on my invoice please?

WENDY: I'll certainly try. What is your query?

ALAN: We've sent you a cheque for £328, but your invoice shows that you have received £250.

WENDY: I'll see what the computer says. May I take your booking number?

ALAN: It's Y23X94AD

WENDY: You're Haden Travel of Berwick on Tweed.

ALAN: Yes that's right.

WENDY: And who am I speaking to?

ALAN: Alan.

WENDY: I have your booking here Alan. My screen is showing a collection of £250. The difference appears to be the insurance of £78. It's probably best if I transfer you to our accounts department. They'll be able to tell you exactly what has happened. Is that alright?

ALAN: Yes, of course.

WENDY: If you wouldn't mind waiting for a few minutes, I'll find someone who will be able to help you.

ALAN: Thank you.

WENDY: ('Phones through to the accounts department) Hello Sue. I've got Alan from Haden Travel on the line. He has a query on the collection amount shown on his invoice. He's sent us a cheque for £338, but the invoice only shows that we've received £250. Would you speak to him and sort it out.

SUE: Yes sure. Have you got the booking number there?

WENDY: Yes, it's Y23X94AD.

SUE: Yes, I've got that. Put him through then.

WENDY: (Going back to Alan) Hello Alan, I'm putting you through to Sue in our accounts department. She'll be able to help you.

ALAN: Thank you.

SUE: Hello Alan. I understand there's a discrepancy of £78 on our collection advice. Let's see if we can sort this out. When did you send us your cheque?

In this case study, Wendy has made a professional job of transferring the call. She first found out what the query was, and looked into the details. Having found that she was not able to help, she then located a colleague in accounts and informed her of the details. When Alan was transferred to Sue, she had all of the necessary information, so Alan had no need to repeat his story again.

Guidelines for transferring calls

1 Establish what the call is regarding by asking a few questions. Even if the caller asks to be transferred to a specific department, by asking a few questions you can ensure that they will be transferred to the right person.
2 Obtain the caller's name and company.
3 Locate the right person to deal with the call. Never transfer a call to a ringing extension and leave it. This is very irritating to the caller, as they will eventually have to phone back to find someone else to deal with their enquiry.
4 Explain to your colleague what the call is regarding, the name of the caller and the company they are phoning from.

Dealing with misdirected calls

You may sometimes answer a call which has been misdirected to your extension. If this happens you should follow the same procedure as you would for transferring calls and ensure that the caller is transferred to the correct person without any further inconvenience. Once this has been done, if it is possible, it may be worth speaking to the person who misdirected the call to clarify any misunderstanding so that the error does not occur again.

Dealing with wrong numbers

From time to time you may receive a call which is a wrong number. However, before you dismiss the call, do ensure that it really is a misdialled number, and not a misunderstanding on behalf of the caller. Many companies operate under several names, their brand name and their company name, e.g. The Bantum Group is the name of the company, but has several brand names; Eagle Tours, Jay Travel, etc. A caller could easily become confused by the different names and think they had misdialled when in fact they had not, so do check exactly what the caller wanted before they ring off.

Taking messages

You will not always be able to transfer calls to your colleagues or manager and you may therefore need to take a message. Taking telephone messages may seem a simple enough task, but all too often messages are incorrect, incomplete or not passed on. At best this is unprofessional, at worst it can have disasterous consequences.

CASE STUDY

Oliver is a sales executive for a medium-sized tour operator. He spends much of his time out on the road visiting agents and running promotional events. He enjoys his job and has made many good business contacts over the years. He has a reputation for being reliable and of going out of his way to help with any problems which travel agencies may experience. He is known within the company as 'The PR Man'.

Last week, Oliver was so busy that he didn't get the opportunity to call into the office at all, but maintained telephone contact and took any telephone messages that had been left for him so that he could deal with anything of particular importance before he was next due in the office. This system seemed to work quite well and he was able to contact and deal with all of his urgent calls, and asked that the non-urgent messages be left in his tray for him to deal with the following week.

When Oliver was next in the office, he looked through his tray for post and telephone messages and found a message which read as follows: Oliver – Sam Banks from Westours rang (Tuesday). He wants to check availability for Portugal next year. Can you phone him back on 071–658–6912. Oliver recalled being given this message over the phone, but since he didn't know any Sam Banks from Westours and thought that a vague enquiry for availability to Portugal next year didn't sound very important, he had left the call to be dealt with once he was back in the office. He picked up the phone.

OLIVER: May I speak to Sam Banks please?
AGENT: Who's calling?
OLIVER: It's Oliver Westwood from Icarus Holidays.
AGENT: Just a moment, I'll see if he's available.

There is a few minutes wait, and then the agent comes back on to the line.

AGENT: Hello Mr Westwood?
OLIVER: Yes.
AGENT: I've spoken to Sam, and he said that he had called you to quote for a group booking of forty golfers to Portugal next year. He explained what he wanted to your secretary and asked that you contact him as soon as possible. But, as its been over a week since he phoned, he's placed the booking with someone else.

Oliver apologised for not being able to return the call any sooner and said he would be glad to be of any assistance in the future. Oliver replaced the phone and stared hard at it. His company had just lost a booking which could have been worth over ten thousand pounds, and all because the telephone message he had been given had been inaccurate and had not explained fully what the caller had wanted. Oliver got up from behind his desk and headed for the Managing Director's office. This was a training need which needed addressing right now.

Accurate message taking and passing the message on within an acceptable time-scale is a very important part of ensuring that the internal communications within the office run smoothly. If a customer leaves a message for a colleague and indicates that it is important, and for some reason you are unable to pass on the message, you need to use your common sense. Will a delay cause further problems? Is the customer expecting a return call within a given time? Has that time now lapsed? If the answer to any of these questions is yes, then it may be appropriate for you to contact the customer yourself and explain the delay. If the person the call is for is out for the day, or away, or unable to return the call for a long period of time for some other reason, then do ensure that the caller is made aware of the time-scale which is likely to pass before their call is returned.

Accuracy is obviously important, so to be sure that you are accurate in your message taking, ensure that you have the following information:

- who the message is for
- the name of the person who called and the company they are from
- the caller's telephone number
- the date and time that the message was taken
- the message
- the action that your colleague is required to take, e.g. phone back etc.
- who took the message.

Always read the message back to the caller to ensure that you have correctly heard and noted the information given. Many companies use standard telephone message pads which prompt you to ask all of the necessary questions. If your company does not use these, any good stationery supplier will stock them.

Sometimes, you may find that a caller gives you a long and complex message which you would need to paraphrase to record on the message pad. If this is the case, make absolutely sure that you understand the message as far as possible, otherwise the message could become distorted when you put it into your own words and may therefore put a different meaning on the message that your colleague finally receives. This may mean that your colleague carries out instructions which were different from what the caller requested, or they may have to contact the caller to ask them to explain the message again. Either of these courses of action will give a poor impression of the company to the caller.

Never commit your colleague to action which you cannot guarantee they will take, e.g. 'She will phone you back within the hour'. This may not be possible, and it is not fair for you to make commitments like this on behalf of your colleague. If they are unable to fulfil the commitment, then they have not satisfied the customers's expectations that you have set.

Assignment

1 What is the policy within your company for taking and passing on telephone messages?

2 Do you have special message pads? If not, what information are you expected to record?

3 What system do you have in place for ensuring that messages are passed on? Is it satisfactory? Can you make any suggestions for its improvement?

4 Discuss these points with your manager.

Ending the call

Ending the call professionally is just as important as starting it well, but, unfortunately, regular users of the telephone seem not to pay as much attention to the way they end the call as they do to the way that they start it.

Guidelines for ending the call

1 If the call was a business enquiry, then ensure that the caller has your name before the call is finished, e.g. 'My name is Katy, if you require any further assistance'. If the caller has your name, it will be much easier for them to continue the enquiry at a later date.
2 Thank the caller for phoning.
3 Wait for the caller to ring off before you terminate the connection. There may be occasions when the caller thinks of something else they would like to ask. If you ring off first, they may find themselves talking to a dialling tone.

If you are not already doing so, then try ending your calls in this way in the future. It may seem a little unnatural at first, but with practise you will soon get used to it and it will certainly sound more professional to your customers.

USING A SWITCHBOARD

Depending on the size and set-up of your company, you may at times be required to operate a switchboard. As well as requiring the technical skills of operating the board, a switchboard operator also needs to have a professional manner and be efficient in dealing with the calls. The switchboard operator plays a very important role in projecting an appropriate company image to the caller as they are often the first point of contact, and no matter how good a service the rest of the company provides, the caller will form a poor impression of the company if the switchboard is not operated properly.

....

CASE STUDY

Leanne is a young trainee who joined Maple Tours a few months ago. She hasn't received any specific job training yet, but one of the duties she has been assigned is to run the switchboard over the lunchtime period. Leanne doesn't mind the task, but she does get a little confused, and quite often finds that she doesn't know where to transfer calls. One day the sales manager telephones the company from a customer's premises, and the call is answered by Leanne. He asks to speak to a Ray Saunders. Leanne has not heard of Ray and sounds vague.

'Um . . . are you sure he works here?' she asks.

'Yes,' says the sales manager. 'He's the marketing manager!'

'Oh! Sorry,' says Leanne. 'I haven't heard of him before, let me see if I can find him.'

There is a long wait, and the sales manager eventually hears an extension ringing. When it is answered, he finds that he has been put through to the accounts manager. Exasperated, he asks to be transferred to Ray. While he is waiting for Ray to answer he reflects on the way Leanne had dealt with the call. If he had been a customer, he would certainly not have a very good impression of the company. He makes a mental note to speak to the training manager about looking into some telephone training for Leanne.

....

In this case study, the switchboard operator was not intentionally unhelpful, but perhaps did not realise the importance of her role and had not received sufficient training to enable her to present an appropriate and professional image of the company. Many of the techniques described in the previous pages are appropriate to switchboard operators, but there are a few other skills which the switchboard operate needs to possess to be really effective in that function.

The greeting

Whenever an incoming call is answered, the switchboard operator should always sound bright and friendly. The greeting is very important, and should sound genuine. A switchboard operator probably answers hundreds of calls a day, but to the caller, it should sound fresh and attentive.

Know the staff

Switchboard operators should ensure that they know who the staff are and where they can be contacted. As you saw from the case study, if the person answering the call is not familiar with the staff who work for the company, the caller may not feel very confident in the efficiency of the company as a whole. Whilst you might be forgiven for not knowing the name of the typist who started last week, not knowing the name of the marketing manager is quite a different matter. Most companies have a list of all of the staff and the departments that they work in along with their extension numbers. Make sure that this is made available to you. While it is not necessary to know every extension number by heart, you should at least ensure that you are familiar with the names of the members of staff. If no such list exists in your company, then one of your priorities should be to compile one.

Know the functions of each department

If your company has a number of different departments, then find out what each one does. Not all of the calls you answer will be specific requests for named staff, or even departments, instead the caller may ask you to transfer them to the appropriate department that can help them with a specific request. In this case, knowledge of the functions of each department will help you direct the call to the appropriate extension. If the caller asks for something with which you are not familiar, then if time permits, try to locate the correct person to deal with the enquiry before you put the caller through.

Establish the nature of the call

Use open questions to establish the nature of the call. If the caller says, 'I'd like to speak to someone regarding your brochure', you need to establish exactly what it is they want to discuss. You need not go into great detail, perhaps a question such as 'Did you wish to order some brochures?' or, 'Is it a query on the content?' The response to this question should provide you with enough information to transfer the call to the correct department.

Transferring the call

The way the call is transferred from the switchboard to the internal extension is dependent on the policy of your particular company. In a company where the switchboard is very busy, the policy may be to transfer the calls off the board as quickly as possible in order to cut down the waiting time for outside calls to be answered. On a less busy switchboard, the policy may be for the operator to locate the recipient of the call and inform them who the caller is, before the call is put through. If you are not sure what your own company policy is, then ask your manager to explain.

When the extension is engaged

If the extension the caller requires is busy, the caller should be informed and asked if they wish to hold or if someone else can help them. If the caller indicates that they would prefer to hold, the operator should keep an eye on the waiting call, and periodically intercept the call and apologise for the delay and enquire if the caller still wishes to hold.

When there is no reply from the extension

If possible, it is better not to leave the caller listening to an unanswered extension for very long. Some switchboards are designed to divert the call back to the board after a period of time if the extension is not answered, but if your board does not have this facility, you will need to intercept the call yourself. Whichever is the case, you should apologise to the caller and then offer them one of the following options: phone back later on; take a message; pass the call to someone else; try and locate the recipient either by phoning around the building or by using a public-address system. Let's examine each of these options in turn.

Advising the caller to phone back

Unless company policy instructs that you do this, or the caller indicates a desire to phone back, this is perhaps the least helpful option to offer to the caller. The caller is not being assisted in any way and there is no guarantee that they will be any more successful in reaching the person they wanted to speak to if they phone back at a later time. However, you can be a little more proactive if you are able to advise the caller of a time by which you believe the recipient of the call will be available. For example, you may say: 'He's in a meeting this morning, but he should be finished by twelve o'clock. Perhaps if you phone after that time he might be available.'

Taking a message

Depending on the size and set-up of your organisation it may, or may not, be possible for you to take a message on the switchboard. If you are able to, then follow the instructions given for message taking in the previous pages. Assure the caller that you will pass the message on as soon as the recipient becomes available, and make sure that you do. Some switchboard operators use a message book in which they record all telephone messages that are taken, and then log the time at which the message was passed on. In a large organisation this is a good way of keeping track of messages, and enables the operator to advise the caller whether or not the message has been passed on if they should happen to call again.

Passing the call to someone else

If the recipient of the call has a secretary, you may suggest to the caller that you put them through. The secretary will then be able to take a message, or in some cases act on the manager's behalf. If no secretary is available, you might elect to pass the call to a colleague of the recipient instead. If this is the case, advise the colleague that this is what you intend to do before you put the call through to them.

Locating the recipient

If you choose to try and find the recipient, then advise the caller of your intention so that they understand why they are being kept waiting. If you are using a public-address system, then ensure that your voice is clear and that the message is concise. It is a good idea to repeat the message, or at least part of it, to ensure that the recipient has heard it, e.g. 'Mr Leonard to contact switchboard. Mr Leonard to contact switchboard. We have a call waiting for you.' Before using the public-address system, make sure that the call warrants it, as you may be interrupting a meeting or something else of importance for a call which does not warrant such an interruption.

Companies who wish to provide an efficient service through their switchboard, often have established systems for recording staff attendance. This is usually a simple system, whereby the switchboard operator receives a list every morning of those staff who are absent due to sickness, leave or business reasons. When calls come through for these people the operator is able to advise the caller of the absence, so eliminating time wasted on trying to find the employee, and avoiding taking messages for people who will not be available to receive them.

CASE STUDY

Joanne works as a switchboard operator and receptionist for a large organisation which employs over two hundred staff. She does not know all of the people who work in the building, but has a comprehensive list of all of the names and extension numbers of the people who work there and in the other building across town. This morning she received a call for a Jackie Wainwright. Joanne didn't know Jackie, but she found her extension number on the list and tried to put the call through. There was no reply. Joanne went back to the caller and asked if anyone else could help, but the caller explained that it was Jackie that he needed to speak to. Joanne offered to take a message and pass it on to Jackie as soon as she was able to locate her.

Some time later in the day, the caller phoned back and asked again to speak to Jackie Wainwright. Joanne explained that she hadn't been able to pass the mesage on to Jackie, so offered to page her instead. Joanne put out a call for Jackie on the public-address system and very quickly Jackie's extension rang through to the switchboard.

'Hello, this is Jan Humphries. Jackie's been off sick since yesterday and she's not expected back before next week. Do you want me to take the call?'

Joanne explained the situation to the caller and put him through to Jan. Joanne felt that she must have appeared quite inefficient to the caller, as she should have been able to tell him the first time he called that Jackie was off sick. She decided to speak to her manager about what could be done to ensure that she had this information to hand in the future.

Had the switchboard operator in the case study been aware that Jackie was on sick leave, and advised the caller, she would have appeared much more efficient.

In a small company, it is likely that the operator would have been aware of people's movements, but in a larger company, an attendance record is the only really effective way of keeping track of the whereabouts of the staff.

....

Assignment

1 Does your company have a method of notifying switchboard of the staff who are absent each day?

2 How effective is the system which is currently in place?

3 If no such system exists, make a few suggestions as to the type of system which would enable switchboard to quickly ascertain who is absent each day.

4 Discuss your thoughts with your manager.

....

Combining switchboard with reception duties

Quite often switchboard and reception are run by the same person. If this is the case in your organisation, you will need to combine the management of the switchboard with dealing with personal callers, and at times this may cause a conflict of interests. If your switchboard is full of a bank of flashing lights of calls waiting to be answered and there are people waiting in front of you, what should you do?

....

CASE
STUDY

Pat operates a switchboard, which is in the reception area of a company, and is often on duty on her own. Today has been a particulary stressful day with a number of personal callers and a constant flow of calls coming into the switchboard. At the moment Pat is taking a call, has three others waiting and has two calls on hold waiting for the extensions to answer. She also has a visitor standing in front of her waiting to be seen. Pat hurriedly transfers the call she is dealing with and switches her attention to the visitor. She looks strained and asks the visitor who he has come to see. Before he can answer, a call which was on hold, comes back on to the board Pat sighs and picks it up.

'I'm sorry, there doesn't appear to be anyone on that extension at the moment, would you like to call back later?' She finishes the call, picks up another and says, 'Sorry to keep you waiting' and switches off again before the caller has a chance to answer. She diverts her attention back to the visitor.

'Now who did you say you wanted to see?'

Although working under difficult circumstances Pat did not make a very good impression on any of the people she spoke to. Whilst she obviously did not have all of the time in the world to exchange pleasantries with everyone she dealt with, she should have adopted a more positive attitude and tried to deal with the visitor without any interruptions.

Combining switchboard and reception duties can be difficult at times, and it requires skill to ensure that as well as managing the switchboard, an appropriate manner is maintained with personal callers too. As receptionist, you are the visitor's first point of contact and may be the first glimpse he or she has of the company and its staff. If the visitor is not handled well, this may create a poor impression of the company as a whole.

If you regularly find yourself in the situation described in the previous case study, you need to speak to your manager to see if some relief could be arranged for particularly busy periods. If this is not possible, then try using the following guidelines.

Guidelines for combining switchboard and reception duties

1 Try and deal with each telephone call and personal caller as you would under normal circumstances. Do not try to rush anyone. If a call is waiting for a particularly long time before you are able to answer it, then apologise for the delay.
2 If a personal caller arrives while you are dealing with a telephone call, acknowledge them with a smile and good eye contact. As soon as you are able to, apologise for keeping them waiting.
3 Once you are able to deal with personal callers, establish who they wish to see, and ask them to take a seat until the relevant person is available to see them.
4 Ask your manager what the company policy is regarding the priorities of combined switchboard and reception duties. Is it preferable for you to treat switchboard as a priority over personal callers or vice versa?

If you have not already done so, read Chapter 1 on customer care as this will provide you with more detailed information on how to deal with personal callers.

USING AN ANSWERPHONE

Retrieving messages from an answerphone

As part of your daily duties, you will probably be expected to retrieve messages from the office answerphone and then pass them on to the appropriate people. The principles are very much the same as taking a telephone message, except that in the case of a very long message it may be necessary to paraphrase, so it is important that although the message is brief, it is still meaningful to the person for whom it is intended.

....

CASE STUDY

'Hello, this is Alan Baker. I'm ringing about my flights to Glasgow next week, that's the 23rd. I've been speaking to our office up there and they've changed the meeting, so I now need to be in Glasgow on the 24th instead. Now that's a Saturday, so I thought I may as well make a weekend of it and take my wife. So could you change the flights to leave from Heathrow after four on the 23rd and add my wife to the booking, that's Sandra Baker, and book us a double room at the Crest Hotel for the nights of the 23rd and 24th. We'll need a flight back at about three on Sunday afternoon. Oh, and I think we'd better have a car. Can you arrange for me to pick something up at the airport when we arrive. Something like an Escort will be fine.

I've had an invoice from you for the original flights which I don't believe we've paid for yet, so perhaps you could let me know the difference in the cost and whether you'll be sending me a new invoice for the total or just for the additional cost of taking my wife. I'm in the Reading office tomorrow, perhaps you could give me a call. Thanks.'

Although this message is fairly detailed and Mr Baker has made his instructions quite clear, it is obviously far too long a message to pass on to a colleague in its present form, so it needs to be abbreviated, but must still contain all of the information necessary to effect the changes Mr Baker requires.

....

Exercise

On a sheet of paper, rewrite the message into a form which would be suitable to pass on to a colleague, but which contains all of the relevant information.

Your message may have read something like this:

Mr Baker rang re his flights to Glasgow. Please change to flight departing after 16.00 from Heathrow to Glasgow and add Mrs S. Baker. Return flight required for both at approximately 15.00 on the 25th. Please book Escort or similar to be collected at Glasgow airport on arrival. Also required: one double room at the Crest Hotel for nights of 23rd and 24th. Please phone him at his Reading office and advise of new costs and invoice details.

The abbreviated message contains all of the information that a colleague would need to change Mr Baker's reservation, and is much easier to decipher than the original message left on the answerphone. When you write a message of this kind, it is a good idea to listen to the message again after you have made your notes to ensure that what you have written is accurate.

....

Leaving messages on an answerphone

People who attend telephone training courses often highlight leaving messages on an answerphone as the least popular aspect of using the telephone, and many people admit to avoid leaving messages as soon as they hear one, preferring to phone back another time when they can speak to someone instead. The main reasons given for the dislike of using answerphones are: it is impersonal; a feeling of self-conciousness when speaking to a machine; not knowing what to say; not knowing how to end the message. However, most people find that once they have a framework from which to work, leaving a message on an answerphone is a relatively simple process.

Guidelines for leaving a message on an answerphone

Whenever you leave a message on an answerphone you should try and include the following information:

1 The time and date of the message. If you are phoning a private householder, it is possible that messages will not be retrieved every day. If the householder has been away, it will be useful to them to know when the message was left. Even if messages are retrieved every day, you should always give the time at which you left your message as this may have same bearing on the message itself, e.g. if a message is received stating, 'If you're home within the next hour can you phone me back?' it will mean nothing to the recipient if the time of the call was not given.

2 Your name and the company you are phoning from. Even if you have regular contact with the person you are telephoning, it is good practise to leave these details. Voices can sometimes sound distorted on an answerphone, and a voice which is normally quite distinctive, may sound different. There is of course also the chance that the message will be retrieved by someone else, who would not be expected to recognise your voice under any circumstances. Always leave a telephone number where you can be contacted. Even if the recipient has your number, if it is on the answer phone, it makes it easier for them to respond.

3 The message. Try and keep your message clear and concise. As we saw from the previous example of Mr Baker's message, there can be a tendency to have a long and unnecessary conversation with an answerphone which can make it hard for the recipient to decipher the message when it is retrieved. Try and sound positive and avoid any 'ums' or 'ers'. At the end of the message, include any action that you require the recipient to take, e.g. 'Please telephone us tomorrow and advise us if these flight timings are suitable.' If there is a time limit attached to the action, then you should mention that too, e.g. 'If you are home before five o'clock this afternoon, you can contact me at the Manchester office, if not, I can be reached at home after six-thirty on 061–563–3274' or 'Can you send the documents by datapost tomorrow. If this is not possible, please let me know by lunchtime and we'll arrange for a courier to collect them.'

4 Ending the call. People often find this the hardest part of talking to an answerphone, and feel very awkward about it. Once you have given your

message you need say no more, but if you do want to round off the message, you can end it just by saying 'Thank you'.

If you know that you will have to leave a message on an answerphone, then you may prefer to prepare the message before you make the call. If, however, you are taken unawares by an answerphone, and really don't feel confident enough to leave a message, then ring off, prepare your message and then ring back. Once you have done this a few times you will feel quite confident enough to leave a message whenever you hear an answerphone.

Assignment   You will need the help of a colleague for this assignment.

1 Imagine that you are telephoning a customer to advise them that their original choice of holiday is not available for the dates they require. Other comparable hotels are available, but you would like to know if they would prefer to change their dates and go to the hotel of their original choice and, if so, how flexible are they with their dates? If their holiday dates are fixed, which of the other hotels would they be prepared to accept. You can make up the details of the hotels for the purpose of this exercise.

2 Prepare your message.

3 Now sit back to back with your colleague and role-play leaving the message on an answerphone. Ask your colleague to make a note of the message and then discuss the following with you:
   (a) How clear was the message?
   (b) What action do they understand that they must take?
   (c) How professional and confident did you sound?

MAKING OUTGOING CALLS

As well as receiving incoming calls you may also need to make outgoing business calls, and these need to be handled with an equal level of professionalism. Depending on the sector of the industry that you work in, your calls might be to customers, or to other parts of the industry. Whichever types of calls you make, however, the basic principles will be the same.

Cost-effective use of the telephone

As part of your NVQ assessment you will be required to demonstrate cost-effective use of the telephone. The next few pages aim to provide you with some background information on call rates to help you achieve this.

Telephone call charges are based on the time of day that the call is made and the distance of the call. Calls made at weekends or after 18.00 on weekdays are charged as off-peak calls.

Some companies may provide a choice of telephone numbers on which they can be contacted, e.g. airlines or tour operators may have regional offices with different telephone numbers. If you have a choice of numbers, remember that calls made within a thirty-five mile radius are charged as local calls and are cheaper than anything outside of this radius which is charged as a long distance call. Some companies have '0345' numbers. These are specially dedicated numbers which begin with the prefix 0345 and are charged as local calls no matter where in the country you are phoning from. So a call made to Glasgow from London on an 0345 number would be charged as a local call. Telephone numbers beginning with 0800 are entirely free to the caller.

However, some prefixes indicate that the call will be at a higher charge, e.g. a number beginning with either 0836 or 0860 is a mobile phone which can cost considerably more to call than other telephone numbers. Other numbers advertised as information services with a prefix of 08 are usually charged at premium rate, which is a very high charge. Advertisements for such information services usually carry a notice indicating the charge per minute made for such calls. Full details of call rates can be obtained from British Telecommunications plc.

Making a reservations call to an industry provider

If you are phoning a tour operator to make a reservation on behalf of a customer, you need to prepare your enquiry beforehand to ensure that your call is both efficient and cost-effective. If you were booking a package holiday you would need to advise the operator of the following:

- numbers of passengers travelling
- ages of any children travelling
- departure date and the duration of the holiday
- travel details including departure and arrival points and any flight codes or flight numbers
- name of the accommodation and any accommodation codes
- types and numbers of rooms required
- names of the passengers.

If you are unable to find any of the information in the brochure, then the reservations agent will help you, but if you are able to locate the information yourself, the call will be more efficient and you will appear to be more professional to the customer who is sitting in front of you.

When your call is answered, it is polite to begin the conversation by introducing yourself and your company; the reservations agent will often use your name during the conversation if you give it to them. Tell the agent that you wish to check some availability, and then allow them to ask you for the information they require. This is because if they are using a computer reservations system, they will need to enter the requirements in a specific order on to their screen. If you reel off the entire enquiry as soon as they answer the call, you may have to repeat parts of it again which wastes time for both of you.

EFFECTIVE COMMUNICATION SKILLS

By relying entirely on conversation as a means of communication on the telephone, you are not able to communicate anything with the use of visual aids. Initially, this may not appear to be a problem, but just imagine how difficult it is to explain to a caller what a hotel looks like, or how you might describe a particular document, rather than being able to show it to someone. It is said that a picture paints a thousand words, but without the ability to use any form of visuals to support what you are saying, you need to be very good at communication to make your points clear.

When conducting business over the phone, the need for good communication skills is especially important. Not only are you relying solely on the spoken word as a form of communication, but misunderstandings are more likely to occur over the phone than through any other medium of communication.

One of the first things you will need to learn to aid your communication skills is the phonetic alphabet. This is a list of words which are recognised as indicating certain letters of the alphabet, and serves to ensure that they are not confused with any other, e.g. the letter 'S' and 'F' are easily confused as are 'M' and 'N'. If you are not already familiar with the phonetic alphabet, it is listed below.

A	– Alpha	J	– Juliet	S	– Sierra
B	– Bravo	K	– Kilo	T	– Tango
C	– Charlie	L	– Lima	U	– Uniform
D	– Delta	M	– Mike	V	– Victor
E	– Echo	N	– November	W	– Whisky
F	– Foxtrot	O	– Oscar	X	– X Ray
G	– Golf	P	– Peter	Y	– Yankey
H	– Hotel	Q	– Quebec	Z	– Zulu
I	– India	R	– Romeo		

The phonetic alphabet is particularly useful when checking the spellings of names or initials and is widely used to give booking references, or locators, e.g. locator T3SMNQ98 becomes Tango, number three, Sierra, Mike, November, Quebec, number nine, number eight. If you are not yet able to recite the phonetic alphabet, then make a point of learning it and ask a colleague to test you.

As part of your job, you will also need to give clear instructions over the phone, and without the use of visual aids. A high degree of communication skills is required to ensure that your message is clear and there are no misunderstandings.

Assignment   To test your own communication skills, you may like to try the following exercise. You will need the help of a colleague who will require a piece of paper and a pen or pencil.

1 Study the diagram in Fig. 2.1. Do not show it to your colleague.

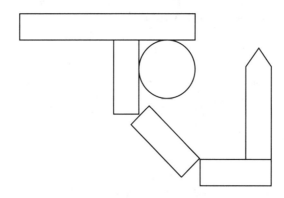

2.1 Verbal communication assignment diagram

2 Now sit back to back with your colleague so that you cannot see each other. Your task is to describe the diagram to your colleague and ask them to draw it. Your colleague may ask you questions to clarify your instructions, but neither of you may have visual contact.

3 Once your colleague has finished drawing, show them your diagram. You can assess the level of your communication skills by how closely their drawing matches the one in the book. If their drawing is a close match to the diagram, then you have done very well. If the drawing looks nothing like the diagram in the book, then you may need to improve your communication skills.

Giving costings

You may sometimes need to give complex costings over the phone, and it is important that you make these very clear to the caller, so that there can be no misunderstanding which could damage business relationships in the future. It is all too easy for misunderstandings to arise over supplements and reductions, so you should make certain that the caller understands exactly what you mean.

CASE
STUDY

Martin works for a tour operator, and spends a great deal of his time giving costings over the phone, an aspect of his job which he dislikes, as callers never seem to pay enough attention and then get things wrong. One day his supervisor who had noticed that there had been a number of queries on the costings given by Martin, listened in to some of his calls to ensure that the costings Martin was giving were correct and clear to the caller. This is what she heard.

'That's £350 basic plus £5.50 sea-view supplement plus £7 underoccupancy supplement – they're both per person per night – plus £29 by two flight supplement.'

Martin's supervisor was horrified, it was not surprising that misunderstandings had occurred over costings if this was the way the staff were giving them. When the call was finished she spoke to Martin about the way he had given the costing and asked him whether he thought that the way he communicated with the caller might be partly the reason why misunderstandings occurred. He agreed that it was possible, and asked how he should give costings in the future. His supervisor demonstrated:

'The basic cost is £350 per person, so for two passengers that's £700. The sea-view supplement is £5.50 per person per night, so for fourteen nights that's another £154. There is an underoccupancy supplement of £7 per person per night, making an additional supplement of £196, and finally a flight supplement of £29 per person, making a subtotal of £58. As a grand total, I make that £1108.'

Martin adopted this method of giving costing from then on and found that he had far fewer problems with callers misunderstanding what he was saying.

When giving costings over the phone take extreme care. If the caller is not familiar with pricing structures within the industry or for a particular product, it is all too easy for misunderstandings to occur. Always be methodical with costings and double check that the caller has correctly understood you. The supervisor in the case study gave a complete breakdown, including subtotals and totals. This is the best way to avoid confusion. If it is possible, ask the caller to check the costing with you so that there can be no room for error or misunderstandings.

Assignment

1 Select a holiday from a brochure and calculate a full costing.

2 Now give the costing to a friend who is not in the travel industry. How clear did they think your explanation of the costing was? Would they agree with the total amount shown on the invoice when it arrives?

Another aspect of your job which you may have to deal with frequently over the phone, is providing customers with travel itineraries. In this situation it is especially important that the caller has a clear understanding of the routes, dates, times of arrival and departure, and the check-in times. For example, let's assume that you had booked the following journey for a passenger:

London/Paris	23 October	AF921	12.20/14.20
Paris/Brussels	25 October	AF701	09.10/10.20
Brussels/Amsterdam	25 October	KL057	17.30/18.35
Amsterdam/London	27 October	KL022	18.00/18.30

If the itinerary were read to the caller just as it is written here, there may be some confusion. Whilst people who work in the industry would probably be familiar with an itinerary such as this and would understand the flight details, a member of the public most probably would not. It would therefore be necessary to interpret the information for them.

If we take the first item on the itinerary, and interpret it for a non-travel person, it may be expressed as: 'Your flight departs from London Heathrow airport on the 23rd of October on Air France flight number AF921 at 12.30 and arrives at Paris Charles De Gaulle at 14.20 French time. You will need to check in at least one hour before departure.' When giving an itinerary such as this over the phone, try not to go too quickly, and ensure that the caller has properly understood and recorded each item before continuing with the next.

Mixed messages

Occasionally a situation may arise where a misunderstanding has occurred as a result of poor communication over the phone. This could be for a variety of reasons such as poor listening skills, unclear instructions, a request which has not been clarified, or one or both parties making an assumption. In any of these circumstances, it should be remembered that the onus is not on the caller to ensure that they have asked the right question or understood what has been said. The responsibility of ensuring that understanding is clear lies with the provider of the service. If this is not the case, the consequences can be disastrous.

CASE STUDY

Mrs James has bought some airline tickets in order to visit her daughter in Madrid, and further to a conversation with her family, has decided that she may change the date of her outward journey. She telephones the travel agent from where the tickets were purchased to ask if this is possible.

MAGGIE: Good-morning, Rougemont Travel. How can I help you?

MRS JAMES: Oh, good-morning. I bought some airline tickets to Madrid from you. I'm due to travel on the 24th May and I was wondering if it would be possible to change that to the 30th.

MAGGIE: What sort of tickets are they?

MRS JAMES: Um. It's with British Airways.

MAGGIE: Are they economy tickets?

MRS JAMES: Yes I think so.

MAGGIE: That's fine. Just pop into the agency next time you're in town and we'll change those for you.

Mrs James goes to the agency the next day and is served by Chris.

MRS JAMES: I telephoned yesterday about changing my flight tickets to departing on the 30th May, and I was told that if I called in you could do that for me. (She hands the tickets to Chris)

CHRIS: (Studies the tickets) Do you know who you spoke to?

MRS JAMES: It was a young lady. I didn't get her name. Why is there a problem?

CHRIS: This particular type of ticket can't be changed without penalty. The only way you could alter your dates is to cancel the whole ticket and rebook. That would involve you in quite a lot of extra expense.

MRS JAMES: But the young lady I spoke to said it would be no problem. This is really very annoying. I've already changed my plans to travel on the 30th.

CHRIS: Well I'm very sorry, Mrs James, but there does appear to have been a misunderstanding. These tickets definitely can't be altered.

MRS JAMES: Well perhaps you could speak to the young lady concerned and ensure that in future she provides the right information. I'm really not very happy with the service that I've received at all.

Mrs James leaves and Chris goes off to speak to Maggie to see if it was her that spoke to Mrs James. When he explains the situation to her, Maggie replies, 'Well the stupid woman told me she had an economy ticket. If she'd said it was an Apex, of course I would have told her she can't change it. It's not my fault if she doesn't know what she booked.'

This case study demonstrates how easy it is for misunderstandings to occur when dealing with a request of this type over the phone. The agent used industry jargon when questioning the customer, 'Is it an economy ticket?' (a coach-class ticket which carries no restrictions or cancellation penalties) and assumed that the customer understood the meaning of economy in terms of airline tickets. The customer, understandably, took economy to mean the cheapest ticket and replied that this was the type of ticket which had been booked. Although perhaps it could be argued that the customer should have asked the agent to explain exactly what the term meant, the fault lies with the agent who should have made the request clear. It was certainly not the customer's responsibility to know the rules, and the agent should have ensured that both parties were in agreement of the facts so that there was no room for any error due to poor communication skills.

DEALING WITH DIFFICULT CALLS

As part of your NVQ assessment, you will be required to demonstrate your ability to deal with difficult calls. Your assessor will need to see two examples: an emergency call and one other type of difficult call. Although every call you receive which could be termed difficult needs to be handled in the manner most appropriate to the precise nature of the call, the next few pages aim to provide you with some general guidelines for dealing with calls of this type.

Emergency calls

At some point in your career you will be on the receiving end of a call from a customer who has a problem which needs sorting out there and then. It may be anything from lost tickets, forgotton passports or missed departures. But what-ever it is, the problem can't wait until someone else is available or you feel in a better frame of mind to deal with it. The customer is in a state of distress or anxiety and wants action now. This is an emergency call.

CASE
STUDY
(Part One)

Mr Jackson phones his travel agent from Gatwick airport in a state of extreme anxiety. He was due to depart from Gatwick on a charter flight to Tenerife half an hour ago, but missed the flight due to a disruption of rail services, which caused his train to arrive at the airport three hours late. His family are very upset and worried that they might lose their holiday altogether. He wants to travel to Tenerife as soon as possible so that he can continue with his holiday. He doesn't want to incur extra charges in paying for another flight.

Assignment

1 Before reading any further, think about what you would do if you received this call. Make a few notes of the questions you might ask Mr Jackson and the action you would take.

2 What steps would you take to try and calm Mr Jackson?

Guidelines for handling an emergency call

1 Try and remain as calm as possible. No matter what you feel inside, you must convey to the customer that you are fully in control of your own emotions. This in itself may help to calm the customer a little.
2 Question the caller to establish exactly what has happend. In an emergency

situation where emotions run high, it can be difficult for the caller to explain very clearly what has happened. Repeat back to the caller your understanding of the problem if it is not clear.

3 If there is any question of the situation being a result of an error, do not get into an argument with the caller as this will only aggravate the situation. If you have access to information regarding the reservation in your office, such as customer files, or computer records, then check these against what the customer is saying.

4 Don't promise the caller any specific outcome at this stage. It will be very difficult to go back on any promises that you have made if you subsequently find that you cannot fulfil them, and will only serve to increase the caller's anxiety.

5 Explain clearly to the caller what you will do next and how long this will take. Be realistic. If it will take you half an hour to sort out, then say so. If you tell the caller you will phone them back as soon as possible, they will expect to hear from you within the next five minutes. If it is not possible for the you to phone the caller, then arrange for them to phone you back at a specific time. Try and ensure that there is a line free at the appropriate moment so that the call is not delayed.

6 Refer to your manager or a senior colleague for help and advice immediately. If there is no one in authority available, then try and contact someone else in authority within the company for advice, even if they are in a different office.

7 Contact a senior person at the airline or tour operator involved, and ask them for help and advice.

....

CASE STUDY (Part Two)

The travel agent, Judy, who received the call from Mr Jackson, tried to remain as calm as possible while speaking to him. She asked him to explain exactly what happened regarding the rail disruption and the time that he eventually arrived at the airport. She then asked him what happened at check-in and whether he had been given any advice or had seen a representative of the tour operator with whom his holiday was booked. While Mr Jackson was still on the line, she obtained his file and checked the flight details to ensure that there had been no changes.

Mr Jackson told her that he knew there were seats available on a flight leaving later that afternoon, but didn't want to have to pay extra for the seats. Judy told Mr Jackson that she needed to contact the tour operator for their advice, and hoped to have an answer for him within half an hour. She arranged for Mr Jackson to phone her at that time.

When Judy contacted the tour operator, they advised her that they may be able to obtain extra flight seats on the later flight to Tenerife, but that they could not be held responsible for disruption to rail services and would therefore make a charge. The tour operator agreed to phone back within fifteen minutes with an answer.

Judy's manager had now arrived at the office, so she explained the situation to him and outlined what she had done so far. He agreed with the action that she had taken, but was concerned that the agency should not be liable to pay for additional flight seats. He asked Judy to check what insurance cover Mr Jackson had. Judy said that it was the company's own policy. Her manager said that he thought the customer was covered for missed departure and asked her to check. This was indeed the case, meaning that the customer could reclaim any out-of-pocket expenses for purchasing a second set of flight tickets. Judy telephoned the insurance company for specific instructions to give to Mr Jackson when he phoned back. At that moment, the tour operator phoned and confirmed that they could provide seats on a later flight and gave Judy full flight details and instructions for the customer to collect the tickets. They also agreed the additional cost and billing instructions.

By the time Mr Jackson phoned, Judy had the whole situation under control and advised him of his new flight, where to collect his tickets and how to claim for their cost from the insurance company. Mr Jackson was very relieved and expressed his gratitude for Judy's efficiency in dealing with the matter.

Difficult calls

There may be occasions when you will take a call from someone who is unpleasant and very difficult to deal with. The difficult caller is usually someone who is very angry or irritable before they make the call, perhaps for some reason totally unrelated to you or your company. Guidelines for dealing with angry people and people who have cause for complaint are given in Chapter 4, and if the call is of this nature, a satisfactory conclusion can be reached if the caller is dealt with properly.

However, perhaps the most difficult type of call to handle is from someone who does not fall into either of these categories, but is just downright nasty. Nothing will please a caller like this and they are likely to huff and puff and show their irritation and displeasure no matter how well the call is dealt with. They are apt to criticise and put the person dealing with the call under considerable pressure, which can be very upsetting and may cause loss of confidence leading to a hesitancy in the replies that are given, or even cause errors to be made.

Dealing with a caller who behaves in this way is never a pleasant experience. If you do find yourself in this situation, the most important thing to remember is that although you may be on the receiving end, the abuse is not directed at you personally. It may be of some comfort to you to know that whoever had answered the phone would probably have received the same treatment and no doubt the caller will make other calls in the same vein and upset other people as well.

No matter how unpleasant the caller is, you should try and remain calm and refrain from being unpleasant back, no matter how tempted you may feel. You should try to retain a professional manner throughout the call, and avoid sinking to the level of the caller. If you do respond in a rude or unpleasant manner this will simply exacerbate the problem, and may even result in a complaint against you being made to a higher authority. Although you need to remain polite, you may also need to be quite firm with a caller of this nature. If the caller is very aggressive, you may begin to feel your confidence ebb away, and it will be at this point that you may begin to sound a little hesitant or start to make mistakes. This will only serve to give the caller something more to criticise. To be effective you need to strike a delicate balance; remain firm but polite and do not allow yourself to become defensive. For a fuller explanation on assertiveness techniques, you should refer to Chapter 7.

Once you have finished the call, it is probably a good idea to take a break for a few minutes, if this is possible, and allow yourself to calm down a little. Even if you remained calm and appeared confident during the call, the adrenalin will still be pumping, and you will probably feel quite angry that someone should speak to you in that way.

Assignment   1 Consider any emergency or difficult call which you have dealt with in the past.

2 How did you handle the call?

3 In retrospect, how effective do you feel you were?

4 If you were given the opportunity to deal with the call again, what would you do differently?

3

....

Selling skills

Whether you are employed in a travel agency, by a tour operator, or work in a tourist information centre, or even as an overseas representative, a certain amount of your time will be spent on selling products or services. Selling is a skill, and although a successful salesperson requires a friendly and positive manner and needs to employ many of the customer care and telephone techniques tactics outlined in Chapters 1 and 2, to ensure that the customer receives a good quality of service, selling is quite a separate issue which needs skill and practice in order to be proficient.

As part of your NVQ assessment, you will be required to demonstrate an ability to sell a variety of products in a number of different customer situations. This chapter aims to provide you will the background knowledge you will require to become a more proficient salesperson, and to enable you to convert more enquiries into sales.

OBJECTIVES

Once you have read this chapter of the book, you should be able to:
- **state the component parts of the selling equation**
- **state the structure and purpose of the sales conversation**
- **use open questioning techniques to establish the customer's requirements**
- **use benefit statements to present the product to the customer**
- **state guidelines to actively close the sale**
- **state guidelines to overcome customer objections**
- **state guidelines to effectively switch sell from one product to another.**

THE ENERGY OF SELLING

In any sales situation there must be a seller and a buyer. Each has a role to play in the transaction and each gives a certain amount of energy to making the sale, but it is dependent on each situation as to how much of that energy comes from the seller and how much from the buyer. In a situation where the buyer has done

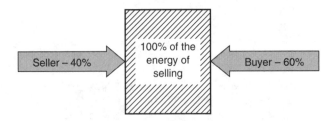

Fig 3.1 The energy of selling

all of the investigative work themselves, then most of the energy has come from the buyer. But when the seller has had to draw on product knowledge and selling skills to persuade the buyer to buy something, then most of the 'energy of selling' has been generated by the seller.

In order to achieve a sale, it doesn't necessarily matter who contributed the most energy to the sale. The buyer will have decided upon the amount of energy they will provide and the success of the transaction will then depend on the seller's ability to gauge the shortfall of the equation and then to make up that shortfall. In Fig. 3.1, the buyer has done a fair amount of investigative work and is aware of some of the options available to them. They have contributed approximately 60 per cent of the energy of selling so they are fairly committed to buying, and have a good idea of what they want to achieve. All they need is for the seller to fill in a few gaps and apply a little specialist knowledge. In this situation the seller needs to contribute another 40 per cent to the energy of selling to make the equation complete. If, however, the seller fails to do this, it is unlikely that he or she will achieve a sale.

In some cases the buyer may contribute very little energy to the sale. For example, the buyer has decided they may be interested in making a purchase and approaches the seller to see what type of product might be on offer, but has no clear idea of what they want or how they can achieve it. In this situation, the buyer has probably contributed less than 10 per cent of the energy, so it is almost entirely up to the seller to provide the energy of selling to complete the equation and achieve a sale. This obviously requires much more skill from the seller than the previous example where the seller only needed to contribute 40 per cent. In this case, if the seller fails to make up the missing 90 per cent of the equation, it is almost certain that a sale will not be made.

The selling equation

The energy of selling is made up of a number of components, the four main ones being:

- time
- knowledge
- skill
- goodwill.

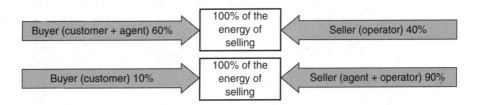

Fig 3.2 A double transaction in the energy of selling

The degree to which each of these components must be employed depends on the individual sales situation and the amount of each component that the buyer has already contributed. Where the buyer has contributed most of the energy of selling, they have probably spent a considerable amount of time gathering information and discussing various options with their travelling companions. They have certainly sold the product to themselves and will probably have sold it to everyone else who will be travelling, so all they need from the seller is goodwill and the skill of processing the booking. But where the buyer has contributed very little time to the equation and has little knowledge of the range of products that are available, the seller needs to contribute time, knowledge, skill and goodwill to make the equation complete.

If a third party is involved, the equation becomes a little more complex. For example, the buyer comes to the seller to purchase a holiday. The seller in this case is the travel agent. The buyer has little or no knowledge of the products available and has contributed less than 10 per cent to the energy of selling. The travel agent has to make up the other 90 per cent of the equation in order to achieve the sale, but this need not all come from the travel agent's own repertoire of knowledge and skill. The travel agent is able to consult reference materials, but is also able to call on the expert knowledge of the supplier – the tour operator, the airline, hotel, etc. In this case there is a double transaction, as the travel agent becomes the buyer and the supplier becomes the seller. In this situation, the equation may be as shown in Fig. 3.2.

The buyer, in this case the customer who will eventually utilise the product, contributed 10 per cent to the equation and requires the seller to provide the other 90 per cent to complete the equation. The agent as an individual, is able to contribute time, goodwill and skill making up 50 per cent, but is unable to provide the necessary knowledge. In this case the agent will refer to the supplier for specialised knowledge. This leads us to the second transaction. The agent, now the buyer, approaches the supplier, the seller with 60 per cent of the equation being made up of a combination of both the agent's and the customer's time, goodwill and skill. The part of the equation which is missing is the knowledge, and if the supplier is able to provide the missing 40 per cent of the equation, then the second transaction will be complete. Once this is done, the agent can then go back to the customer and provide the missing 90 per cent of the equation which is a combination of the agent's goodwill, time and skill and the supplier's knowledge.

This example illustrates that everybody involved in the sale, even if not in direct contact with the end-user, (the person who will eventually utilise the product) must play their part in the energy of selling and identify and then contribute to the missing parts of the equation.

CASE STUDY

Mrs Jones has decided that she would like to take a motoring holiday to Germany this year and has been collecting information from a variety of brochures and from the tourist office. After a few weeks of planning and discussions with her husband, she has selected a go-as-you-please holiday from one of the brochures and chosen all of the hotels she wishes to use. Both she and her husband are very excited about the prospect of their forthcoming holiday and can picture themselves driving through the German countryside and visiting little, unspoilt villages. All that needs to be done now is to make the necessary arrangements. So next time Mrs Jones is in town she visits a newly opened travel agency where she is greeted by Melanie.

Melanie is very friendly and expresses an interest in the holiday that Mrs Jones has selected saying, 'I haven't visited Germany. It does look nice. Have you been there before?'

While they are discussing Mrs Jones' previous visit to Germany, Melanie makes all of the necessary arrangements for the holiday and completes the paperwork. At the end of the conversation, Melanie explains to Mrs Jones when she can can expect to receive invoices and tickets. Mrs Jones leaves the office thinking what a nice girl Melanie was and how different this transaction had been to the way her enquiry had been handled last year.

Last year Mrs Jones visited a long-established travel agent in town who had been recommended by a friend. The holiday that Mrs Jones had chosen was a driving holiday to Vienna with various stops *en route*. Just like this year, she had done a lot of the work herself and visited the agency to make the booking. She was dealt with by Bob, the manager, who has worked in the industry for a number of years and has a reputation for his extensive knowledge of the business. When Mrs Jones approached Bob, she explained what she would like to do and produced the brochure she wanted to book from. Bob listened to Mrs Jones, took a cursory look at the brochure and then said, 'I don't think this company will book the type of arrangement you're asking for.'

Mrs Jones pointed out the text which explained that it was possible and asked him to make the booking. Bob's body language showed that he was a little irritated at being caught out. He asked Mrs Jones a few questions about the arrangements she wanted to make, and when she stated the ferry crossing that she would like to use, Bob said, 'You would be much better off taking a longer ferry crossing and cutting down on the driving time once you arrive in France. The roads are better from the other ports.'

Mrs Jones told him quite firmly that she was well aware of this but had chosen the shorter route as they intended to visit friends near Bologne. Finally, Bob told her that Vienna was probably a lot further than she had imagined and was a very long way to drive in two weeks.

'If you really want to go there, you'd probably be better off taking a weekend break and flying,' he said. 'There are some very good packages available. Do you realise how much this is likely to cost you in petrol?'

Mrs Jones thanked him for his advice and left saying that she might have to reconsider booking the holiday. When she got home she telephoned the tour operator and made the booking herself. What she actually meant when she was talking to Bob was, 'I have reconsidered making this booking with you and have decided that I'm not going to!'

Melanie was successful in dealing with Mrs Jones because she was able to identify the missing part of the sales equation and then provide it. Mrs Jones had contributed most of the energy to this sale by investing her own time to investigate and then evaluate the different products available and had developed her skill in interpreting the information in the brochure. She had obtained the goodwill of her husband and was very happy with the choice herself; all she needed was the goodwill of the seller and the skill required to make the booking. Melanie was able to provide both of these and thus completed the equation.

Bob on the other hand was somewhat dismissive of the time and effort that Mrs Jones had already contributed and showed his irritation that she knew more about the product than he did. Bob failed to provide the missing part of the equation – the goodwill – and therefore lost the sale.

Why did he behave in this way?

Bob is an excellent technician and has a good deal of experience within the industry. He has good product knowledge and has visited a lot of tourist destinations, both in Europe and further afield. What makes Bob feel good is to provide a buyer with the benefit of his experience and expert knowledge that they may not be able to get elsewhere. This makes Bob feel important and he never misses an opportunity of showing the buyer just how much he knows.

In dealing with Mrs Jones, Bob was placed in a position in which he was not comfortable, i.e. the buyer had the superior knowledge and this made Bob feel inferior. Bob tried to correct what he saw as an imbalance by querying Mrs Jones's knowledge. Whether he realised it or not, Bob was quite dismissive of the customer's knowledge and the time and effort that she had already contributed to the sale. All that Bob needed to do was add the goodwill. However, in Bob's mind he must always contribute his knowledge to the equation, even when it is not necessary and in this case Bob exceeded the requirements of one aspect of the equation but at the expense of the goodwill. The result of this was that Bob lost the booking – although he probably doesn't see it that way. In Bob's mind, thanks to his superior knowledge, Mrs Jones now realises that she had made an inappropriate choice of holiday, and will be back to book an alternative once she has talked it over with her husband.

But if Bob has such a good reputation, surely he doesn't treat everyone like this? The answer is, no he doesn't. Bob excels himself in a situation where his undoubted knowledge and experience are required to complete the equation. Bob really prefers buyers like Mr Jacobs.

Mr Jacobs owns a small business in town and needs to take a trip to various cities in Europe. He is a busy man and needs to make the trip at fairly short notice. His secretary has made his appointments for him in Paris, Brussels, Rome and Florence and he now needs someone to take care of all of the travel arrangements, so he visits Bob. Bob takes down all of the details of where and when Mr Jacobs has to be, and then suggests that he telephones Mr Jacobs later on in the day with an itinerary. Once Mr Jacobs has left, Bob is in his element and sets about finding the best way to get Mr Jacobs to all of his appointments on time and books him suitable hotels in each city which are conveniently located for both the airport and the location of the meeting. When Bob telephones Mr Jacobs later on that day, Mr Jacobs is delighted and confirms the reservation thinking how efficient Bob has been. He makes a mental note to use Bob's services in the future.

Why was Bob so much more successful with Mr Jacobs than he was with Mrs Jones?

Mr Jacobs had contributed very little to the equation, allowing Bob maximum opportunity to contribute, giving him practically all of the energy of selling. In this situation Bob needed to use his knowledge, skill and time to produce the itinerary. Mr Jacobs provided the goodwill. This is the balance that Bob always wants to operate with. The danger here is that if Bob's contribution to the equation is not appropriate to the needs of the buyer, he will not always be successful.

Before visiting Bob, Mr Jacobs had been to another agency and seen Debbie. Debbie is very sociable and loves speaking to all of her customers. She enjoys especially dealing with the chatty customers and has a reputation for being very friendly and always having time for people who want to talk. She has quite a number of regular customers and makes a point of remembering little things about them and has found that she gets a good response when she brings them up in the conversation at a later date by asking things like, 'How is your daughter getting on at her new school?'

When Mr Jacobs visited Debbie with his enquiry he was short of time and just wanted a fast and efficient service. Debbie tried to strike up a conversation with Mr Jacobs but was unsuccessful, in fact she thought Mr Jacobs seemed quite irritated with her and indicated several times that he would just like her to get on with making his booking. Debbie decided that she didn't like Mr Jacobs and started to feel on edge. She didn't feel at all confident in this situation and started to show her anxiety through her body language and also made a few mistakes along the way. Mr Jacobs mirrored her anxiety with a further display of irritation and eventually left the shop taking his business with him.

The problem for Debbie was that she wanted to contribute goodwill to the equation and diverted all of her energy to this aspect of it. Mr Jacobs wanted her knowledge and skill but Debbie felt uncomfortable in this situation. This equation was far from complete and no sale was achieved. Debbie's ideal customer would have been Mrs Jones as all Mrs Jones required was goodwill and a small amount of skill to complete the equation. Debbie would have responded in much the same way as Melanie did and Mrs Jones would have been happy with the service that she received.

What would have happened if Mr Jacobs had visited Melanie?

When Melanie dealt with Mrs Jones she completed the equation by providing the goodwill. This was all that Mrs Jones required and she was more than happy with her decision to place her booking with Melanie. But does this mean that like Debbie, Melanie would have found Mr Jacobs difficult to deal with? On the contrary, Melanie would have dealt with Mr Jacobs in a very similar way to Bob, and would have provided the necessary knowledge skill and time to complete the equation.

The difference between Melanie, and Bob and Debbie, is that Melanie is able to see exactly how much energy she needs to contribute to the sale and which particular aspects of the equation need to be provided. She is then able to adapt her style to provide the necessary quantities of time, knowledge, skill and goodwill in order to achieve the sale. She is more successful than Bob or Debbie who generally only achieve sales when the customer requires the parts of the sales equation which they are prepared to give. In Bob's case this is knowledge, skill and time, and in Debbie's case, goodwill and time. Neither Bob nor Debbie realise that they need to adapt their own contributions to different circumstances and until they do, they will continue to make the same mistakes.

Key pointers for success in the energy of selling

- Identify how much energy the buyer has put into the sale and meet the shortfall.
- Identify which parts of the equation are missing: time, knowledge, skill or goodwill.
- Contribute the missing parts of the equation in the correct quantities.
- Remember that it is always the buyer who dictates the missing part of the equation and a good seller will make up the difference.

DEVELOPING YOUR SELLING SKILLS

Whatever your organisation does it will be involved in selling or promoting something. You may sell holidays or ferry tickets or maybe a service such as that of an overseas representative or a tour guide. People are selling all of the time and sometimes don't realise it.

As you saw from the section on the energy of selling there are degrees of selling, from the situation where the customer has made their choice, done all of the groundwork and merely requires the seller to make the necessary arrangements, to the customer who has no clear ideas at all about what is available or what they want to do and relies entirely on the knowledge and skill of the seller in order to make the sale. In each of these cases the seller needs to employ all of the necessary elements of good customer service and telephone practice as appropriate, since no matter what stage the customer is at in the sale they will always want to be treated properly and in an appropriate manner. But as far as selling is concerned, the difference between these two extremes is that one is **order taking** and the other is **selling**.

Order taking

A customer visits a travel agency and asks the agent to book a twin room at the Halcyon Palace Hotel for two weeks departing on the 22nd August. The agent makes the booking, the customer pays a deposit and leaves. In this type of situation the travel agent has made a sale, but did not actually sell anything to the customer – just acted on the customer's instructions. This is order taking.

Selling

Selling is finding out what the customer wants, then finding a product which meets those needs and, finally, creating a desire in the customer to buy the product. Selling only happens when the customer is persuaded to buy something, not when money is taken for something the customer had already decided to buy.

Depending on the part of the industry that you work in, you will probably find that most of the sales that you make are as a result of order taking, and you may find that you are more likely to be order taking at certain times of the year, e.g. when the main summer brochures first come out you might have a very busy few weeks trying to book holidays which customers have chosen for themselves. At other times of the year though, notably around late booking periods, you may find that much of your time is spent searching for late availability and actively selling what you find to your customer.

Characteristics of a good salesperson

In previous chapters we have discussed how important it is to have a suitable and positive attitude to the customer and how if this is missing it may jeopardise the chances of making a sale. Many people are recruited into our industry purely because of their personalities, and you may have heard it said that someone is 'a natural'. However very successful salespeople are not just naturals. Although they probably had the right sort of personality to start with, personality alone will not be enough to carry them through each and every sales situation that they encounter with the same degree of success. People who are consistently high achievers in sales, no matter what it is they are selling, are those who have a positive attitude, but have also learned and practised good selling skills.

....

CASE STUDY

Jenny is full of life and considered by her friends and colleagues to be the life and soul of the party. She always has a story to tell and takes a very light-hearted approach to her job. At work, she is always very well turned out, and takes a pride in her appearance. Jenny is highly motivated and is always full of enthusiasm when she is talking to her customers. She believes that she is able to sell most things with her personality and tends to do most of the talking. She doesn't often ask the customers very much about what kind of holiday they are looking for as she believes that you can tell what sort of people they are and have a fairly good idea of the sort of thing they are looking for just by talking to them. Jenny has a tendency to try and sell places she has been to herself, or the type of holiday she would like to take in the future.

Marcia appears to be quietly self-confident and is by no means as outgoing as Jenny. She too is well turned out and enjoys contact with the customers. But unlike Jenny, Marcia always makes a point of finding out exactly what the customer wants before she makes any recommendations. She takes an interest in learning about new destinations and products and tries to be as objective as possible about places that she would not necessarily want to visit herself. When she does try and sell a holiday to a customer she is a lot calmer than Jenny and checks that the customer is interested before going too far into her sales pitch.

Who do you think achieves the most sales, and for what reason?

While Jenny undoubtedly has the stronger personality and a very positive attitude, she probably, at a subconscious level, limits her sales to the places in which she has a particular interest. Because she doesn't investigate the customer's needs, she may well try and sell something to the customer that they would not be interested in. Jenny relies almost entirely on her own personality to make sales for her.

While Marcia is quieter than Jenny, she still has self-confidence. Marcia's approach is more systematic than Jenny's and by finding out exactly what kind of holiday the customer would be interested in, she stands more chance of selling them a product which matches their needs. Marcia has the added advantage over Jenny in her product knowledge. By making a point of studying new products and destinations she was a wider breadth of product knowledge to draw upon than Jenny. Marcia makes sure once she does begin her sales pitch that the customer is interested. If not, she can double check her understanding of the customer's requirements and respond accordingly. Jenny on the other hand goes blindly on and is often way off target. Marcia has combined her positive and professional attitude with selling skills and good product knowledge and is therefore able to make consistently more sales than Jenny.

This example clearly demonstrates that a good salesperson needs:

- a positive attitude
- good product knowledge
- good selling skills.

THE SALES CONVERSATION

As we have discussed, a good salesperson needs to have good selling skills. Marcia had developed these skills and is able to achieve consistently better sales results than Jenny. Marcia understands the structure of the sales conversation and uses it to her advantage every time she deals with a customer.

The sales conversation is different from a normal social conversation because it has an **objective** – to achieve a sale – and it has a distinct **structure** which always includes the same four elements which follow on from each other in the same sequence. These elements are rapport, questioning, presentation and commitment. Let's expand a little on each of these.

Rapport

Rapport is all about the relationship that is built with the customer. The customer needs to feel at ease in the sales environment and confident that the enquiry will be dealt with properly and in an appropriate manner. Although this is the first stage in the sales conversation, rapport needs to be maintained right through until the close of the sale and beyond this into any subsequent dealings with the customer. If the relationship with the customer should break down at any stage during the sales conversation, the chances of making a sale may be jeopardised. Chapter 1 of this book covers in some depth all aspects of creating an appropriate and professional relationship with the customer.

Questioning

Once a relationship with the customer is established, the next stage of the sales conversation is to establish the customer's needs. Some customers will volunteer this information themselves, especially if they have already made their choice of product they wish to purchase. In this case it may well be the customer who asks most of the questions. But in a real selling situation where you need to find something suitable for the customer, the first stage is to establish exactly what it is they are looking for, and the most effective way of doing this is to employ good questioning skills.

Presentation

Once the customer's needs have been established, the next stage in the sales conversation is to find a product which matches the needs that have been identified. You will then need to present the product to the customer in a manner which creates a desire in them to buy the product. Presentation is quite a skilful part of the sales conversation, since it will be necessary to convince the customer in a reasonably short space of time that this is the most suitable product for them. Never try and skip from rapport to presentation, missing out questioning. If you don't have any clear idea of what the customer is looking for or what their personal tastes are, finding a suitable product will be based largely on guesswork.

Commitment

This is the final stage of the sales conversation, and often the one which sales people find the most difficult. At this stage you should aim to obtain the customer's commitment to buy. Even if you are not able to make the customer part with any money, at least try and obtain some level of commitment of the customer's intentions.

Each stage of the sales conversation is of equal importance, and in order to be proactive in your selling, you will need to be fully skilled in each area. The first stage, rapport, has already been covered in some depth in Chapter 1, but the other stages, questioning, presentation and commitment are covered in detail in the following pages.

EFFECTIVE QUESTIONING TECHNIQUES

As we have discussed, questioning is a vital part of the sales conversation, but it also has many other uses too. Good questioning skills are necessary when taking telephone messages or taking a request for a colleague, or even when asking your manager to explain something to you. By using effective questioning techniques you will be able to obtain the information you need in a variety of situations, quickly and efficiently.

Questioning can also be used to great effect to clarify your understanding of information or of a request made of you, and when used properly, this should limit any errors or misunderstandings in your day-to-day work. The ability to ask questions effectively is a fundamental part of our daily communication skills, but for the purposes of this section of the book, all of the examples given will be related to a sales situation. However, the techniques given can be used in a variety of other situations as well.

Types of questions

There are two main types of question, these are **open** questions and **closed** questions. A closed question is a question which invites a 'Yes' or 'No' answer but does not restrict the person answering the question to using only these responses – in fact they will very often go on to give you much more, nevertheless, it is still a closed question, e.g. 'Did you want a return ticket?' An open question is a question to which the person responding cannot answer 'Yes' or 'No', e.g. 'What date will you be travelling?'

Both open and closed questions have their place in the sales conversation, but as a rule you should be using mostly open questions in the initial stages of the investigation to elicit as much information as possible from the customer. While it is possible to do a complete investigation with closed questions, it would probably take twice the time and you may miss some important information. Closed questions are better suited to checking information, e.g. 'That was for two weeks?' or 'Would you like a private balcony?'

Construction of questions

For a question to be an open question it must start with one of the following words: **who, when, where, how, which, what** or **why**. These are known as the seven W's as they all contain the letter W. Any question which does not begin with one of the seven W's is a closed question. For example, 'What date will you be travelling?' is an open question, but 'Do you know what date you will be travelling?' is a closed question as 'Yes' or 'No' could be given in answer.

....

Exercise

Below is a list of questions, some of which are open questions and some of which are closed. Read through each one and indicate by ticking the appropriate description whether you think the question is an open or a closed one.

	Open	*Closed*
1 Is it just for two people?	____	____
2 How long will you be staying?	____	____
3 Are you paying by cheque?	____	____
4 Where will you be travelling from?	____	____
5 Do you have a resort in mind?	____	____
6 Do you want the hotel to be close to the beach?	____	____
7 Is it from Gatwick?	____	____
8 What passport do you currently hold?	____	____

You can check your answers with those below.

....

Assignment

Before continuing with the text, practise your questioning skills on a friend or colleague.

Ask them to think of a holiday or a trip they would like to go on. They should not disclose anything about it to you at this stage. Your task is to use open questions to establish as much as you can about the proposed trip. Your partner's role is simply to answer your questions, but they should answer only 'Yes' or 'No' whenever you ask a closed question. Time yourself and see how long it takes you to obtain all of the information. As you become more practised at asking questions you will find that you will be able to establish the customer's needs in a very short space of time.

Having established that there are two main types of question, open and closed, we need to look a little more closely at different types of questions and their uses.

....

(1) Closed, (2) Open, (3) Closed, (4) Open, (5) Closed, (6) Closed, (7) Closed, (8) Open.

CASE
STUDY

Mr Smith is looking for a holiday for his family and has visited his local travel agent for some advice. Mr Smith is served by Tony, who tries to establish Mr Smith's needs and then find a suitable holiday for him. Here is the part of the conversation where Tony investigates Mr Smith's requirements.

TONY: Who will be travelling?

MR SMITH: My wife and I and our five year old daughter.

TONY: When would you like to travel?

MR SMITH: Around the second week of June.

TONY: And how long would that be for?

MR SMITH: A week.

TONY: Where would you like to travel to?

MR SMITH: Well we haven't made any firm decisions, but probably Ibiza, Majorca, somewhere like that. We don't want a very long flight because it's the first time our daughter will have flown.

TONY: So something in Ibiza or Majorca. And which airport did you want to fly from?

MR SMITH: Luton.

TONY: Right then, Mr Smith, I'll have a look on the computer and see what's available for you.

Tony started to search through the various computer systems for availability to Ibiza and Majorca for Mr Smith for the dates he wanted. There was, in fact, quite a lot of availability, but each time Tony showed the relevant brochure to Mr Smith, he didn't seem very interested. Tony's apparent fruitless search continued for another twenty minutes, but still nothing he found seemed to satisfy Mr Smith. Tony began to get impatient with the customer. The man was obviously a time waster and had no intention of making a booking.

Eventually he turned to Mr Smith and said, 'Well the companies that I've checked so far seem to have quite a lot of availability, so I suggest the best thing would be if you were to take those brochures away with you, have a look through them, and if there's anything in there which appeals to you, give me a call and I'll gladly see if it's available.'

Mr Smith thanked Tony for his help and left. Tony never heard from him again, and assumed that his assumption of Mr Smith being a time waster had been correct.

Why was Tony unable to find anything that interested Mr Smith? Read through the dialogue again. Do you agree with Tony that Mr Smith really was a time waster?

Although Tony used good open questions to establish Mr Smith's basic requirements, he doesn't have a full profile of Mr Smith's personal tastes and preferences. All Tony really knows is: who is travelling; when they are travelling; how long they are travelling for; a vague indication of where they would like to travel; where they would like to depart from. While it is necessary to obtain this information from a customer in order to find them a holiday, this does not provide enough information on which to select a product which matches the customer's needs. The information that Tony has obtained are called **material needs**. The missing part of the customer's profile are the **human** needs.

In an order-taking situation, i.e. a situation where the customer has already chosen the product they want to book, it may only be necessary to establish the material needs in order to make the reservation. But in a selling situation, such as the one outlined above, it is vital that human needs are established so that a full customer profile is obtained and a product then matched with it. In Mr Smith's case he had not made a choice on either the destination or the accommodation.

What else could Tony have found which would have helped him to choose a suitable product for Mr Smith?

Human needs questions which may have helped Tony are:

- What sort of holiday are you looking for?
- What standard or type of accommodation would you like?
- What facilities do you require?
- What kind of a resort would you be interested in?
- What are your pastimes and leisure activities?

If Tony had asked Mr Smith some questions like the ones above, he would have had a much clearer picture of the type of holiday that would have been suitable, and would probably have been more successful in finding something which interested Mr Smith.

Human needs questions are an essential part of the sales investigation process. They should always be included as part of your questioning in a situation where the customer has not made a choice of destination or accommodation.

Assignment   Practise your ability to ask human needs questions with a friend or colleague. Assume that your partner has not chosen a destination for their holiday. Your task is to ask them all about their pastimes and preferred activities on holiday, and the type of resort and accommodation they would prefer. Use the types of human needs questions given above. Try and use open questions all of the time.

Establishing priorities

Most customers consider at least one aspect of their travel requirements to be a priority, and this should be established when the customer's needs are investigated. Priorities fall into four main categories. These are:

- **People** – Establish whether any of the party have special needs which must be catered for. If a large group is travelling, their priority may be that they all stay in the same accommodation.

- **Place** – It may be a priority that a customer goes to a particular destination, even if that means a change in dates.
- **Price** – For some customers the price may be more important than anything else, and their date of travel and destination may be entirely governed by that.
- **Period** – Most people are restricted in some way in the dates they can travel. It is advisable to find out just how restricted they are before you start checking for availability.

In a situation where a customer has not made a specific choice, it is very important that you find out exactly what the priorities are to ensure that these are catered for when you present them with a possible solution to their holiday requirements. For example, if a customer's priority is that the hotel must provide vegetarian food, then this will rule out any hotel which is not able to make such a provision.

The question of price

This can be quite a difficult area to investigate, but it is nevertheless an important one. Since very few people will be in a position to say that money is no object, you need to establish the price range that the customer would be interested in. On the whole, people will want to feel that they are getting value for money, but do bear in mind that the value they are talking of is relative to their income and standard of living – a family of four on an income of £800 per month will probably be more interested in a lower price range than a couple who's joint monthly income is £2500 per month. However, you should never judge a customer's financial standing by appearance alone as you could very easily be caught out.

The way you word any question about price is important. Avoid at all cost, 'Do you have a budget?' as the answer will undoubtedly be 'Yes' leaving you none the wiser. The dictionary definition of budget is not only 'inexpensive' but also 'an amount of money set aside'. Therefore the word budget does not necessarily mean in the lowest price bracket, and you should be very careful that you do not misinterpret what the customer means. The best way to establish what price range the customer is interested in is to ask first, 'What standard of accommodation are you looking for?' and then 'What price range do you have in mind?' This will soon tell you how realistic the customer is being and you can advise them accordingly.

The question of why?

You will have noticed that as yet we have not covered how and when to use the last of the seven W's, why. This question is not normally used in an investigation unless it is in connection with a switch selling situation. Switch selling will be covered in some depth in later pages.

The only other circumstance in which you might use this question is if you are unsure that the customer has chosen something with which they will be entirely happy, e.g. if a customer has elected to stay in an hotel in San Antonio in Ibiza, and you believe that they are looking for a quiet holiday in an uncommercialised area, you might ask, 'Why did you choose this particular resort?' You can then judge whether or not they have made the correct choice, by the answer they give.

Summarising

Once you have come to the end of your investigation it is always a good idea to summarise your findings before you begin to look for a suitable product for your customer. Try and get into the habit of summarising at the end of your investigation before you move on to the next part of the sales conversation. Summarising enables you to:

- check that you have not forgotten anything
- check that you have correctly understood the customer
- check if there is anything else the customer would like to add.

When you are dealing with a telephone enquiry, or a customer who you will contact later in the day with a suitable holiday choice, it is very important that you summarise. The customer won't be pleased with you if you speak to them later in the day and give them information which is not suitable to their needs. A summary will safeguard against any misunderstandings before you put in a lot of time and effort which may be wasted.

Summary

To summarise the main points of questioning skills:

1 There are two main types of question, open questions and closed questions. Closed questions are questions which invite a 'Yes' or 'No' answer. Open questions cannot receive a 'Yes' or 'No' answer and must begin with one of the seven W's – who, where, when, how, which, what or why.
2 Open questions can be subdivided again into human and material needs, e.g. 'What sort of facilities would you like in the hotel?'
3 Always establish the customer's priorities, i.e. people, price, place or period.
4 Always summarise your findings at the end of your investigation before you move on to the next stage of the sales conversation.

PRESENTING THE PRODUCT

In a selling situation, once you have established the customer's needs and found a suitable product which matches those needs, you then present the product to the customer. This is a very important part of the sales conversation, as you will have to convince the customer in a relatively short space of time that the product you have selected is the most suitable for them. If we refer back to the energy of selling, you will recall that the customer who contributed most of the energy to the sale had spent a considerable amount of time researching the various options open to her and had sold the product to herself and to her husband. But when a customer comes to the travel agent and has no clear idea of the product they want, the agent needs to condense all of the necessary knowledge and skill required to sell the holiday into a very short space of time in order to achieve the same effect. It is for this reason that a high degree of skill is required to present the product to the customer in a manner which will create a high level of desire and persuade the customer to commit themselves to making a purchase.

One of the most important things to remember when presenting the product is that the customer is not buying 'the product', but what the product will do for them. A customer may elect to stay in a particular hotel, not because he or she has a particular desire to spend the duration of the holiday looking at the interior of it, but because it is located near to places of particular interest, or because they want to use the facilities it has to offer to help them to relax. So instead of buying a hotel bedroom for two weeks, the customer is buying the opportunity to relax and do some sightseeing.

Matching the product to the customer's needs

Different people have different needs and requirements for their holiday and it is important that you establish exactly what these are before you try to select a suitable product. In the previous pages we looked in great detail at how to establish customer needs, and in order to make a professional job of presenting a suitable product to the customer, it is essential that information relating to the customer's human needs is obtained, i.e. what facilities the customer wants in the resort and accommodation, and what interests and activities they wish to pursue. Once you have this information, it will then be possible to select a product which matches the needs of the customer, and present the relevant aspects of it to them in a manner which creates the desire to buy.

CASE STUDY

A travel agent has established the following needs for a customer who wishes to book a holiday:

- two adults and one child of nine years
- travelling from Gatwick during the first two weeks of July
- require self catering accommodation in Ibiza
- accommodation facilities to include: full kitchen facilities, separate sleeping area for child, swimming pool, something to keep the child occupied
- resort facilities to include: sandy beach, watersports, supermarket within walking distance of the apartment.

The travel agent has found the following apartment available and believes that it matches the customer's requirements:

Apartments Rossa
Set right beside the beach, we believe these apartments to be ideal for families. The apartments are set in their own gardens within easy walking distance of a sandy

beach which provides safe bathing in a gently sloping, shallow bay. For those wishing to partake in watersports, sailing, windsurfing and waterskiing are available on the beach for a small charge. The apartments are only a five-minute walk away from the centre of the resort, where an extensive range of bars, restaurants and shops can be found.

Facilities include:

- children's pool
- playground
- babysitting
- table tennis
- supermarket
- pool table

- playroom
- children's club
- full-sized freshwater pool
- bar serving snacks
- bakery
- tennis.

All apartments are one bedroomed and sleep up to four adults. Bedroom has twin beds, with a double bed-settee in the lounge area. All apartments have private bathrooms and fully equipped kitchens which include microwave and dishwasher. All apartments have private balcony. Sea-view rooms available at a supplement.

....

Assignment

1 Before continuing with the text, compare the accommodation description with the customer needs that have been identified.

2 Which of the facilities and aspects of this holiday do you think would be of interest to the customer?

....

CASE
STUDY
continued

When presenting the product, the travel agent should select only those elements of the holiday which would be of interest to the customer. This means that it is not always necessary to list every single facility available at the resort or accommodation, but just the specific things that match the customer's needs. In this particular case the elements which are relevant to the customer are:

- one bedroomed apartment with double bed-settee in the lounge
- full kitchen facilities, including microwave and dishwasher
- a sandy beach with safe, shallow bathing
- children's pool
- children's club
- playground and playroom
- supermarket and bakery
- watersports.

They may also be interested to know that babysitting facilities are available and that the resort centre is only five minutes' walk away. If there is anything else which you think the customer might be interested in, it is better to ask them, e.g. 'Would you be interested in tennis facilities?' rather than to list everything which the holiday has to offer.

It is far better to be selective in the information that is presented to the customer in order to make it sound more attractive and ideally suited to their requirements. Providing them with a lot of information about the holiday which is not relevant to their needs may make them feel that the product is not so suitable for them after all.

Assignment

1 Conduct a pole amongst your friends, colleagues and family and establish what these individuals like to do on their holidays. Make brief notes on your findings.

2 Below is a description of the hotel which you have elected to present to everyone that took part in your poll. Which elements of the description would be of interest to each individual and why?

Hotel Los Almontes

Situated on a long stretch of sandy beach, this hotel is ideally located for those who wish to relax and enjoy the beautiful surroundings and facilities of this hotel. For those who wish to explore, there are some lovely coastal walks to deserted coves along the bay, and for the more energetic, the hotel offers bicycles for hire. For good shopping and a variety of restaurants and evening entertainment the town is five minutes away by complimentary hotel bus service.

Facilities include:

- Olympic-sized swimming pool
- free watersports on beach
- squash courts
- horse riding
- bar
- coffee shop
- à la carte grill room
- soundproofed discothèque
- childrens club five days a week.

- children's pool
- four tennis courts, one floodlit
- table tennis
- reduced green fees at nearby golf course
- poolside bar
- pizzeria
- terrace dining-room with buffet service
- babysitting service

You probably found from the results of your poll, that although everyone involved had different needs, there was something in the hotel description which was suitable for everyone. However, had you read out the complete description to everyone involved, they may not have felt the property quite as suitable.

Selling the product

Having selected the relevant parts of the hotel or holiday description that match up with the customer's needs, the next stage in the presentation is to phrase each of these elements in a way which creates a desire in the customer to buy the product.

So how do you create a desire in the customer to buy?

....

CASE STUDY

Andrew and Janine both work in a high street travel agency. Both have a similar amount of experience and both spend most of their day dealing with customers in face-to-face sales situations.

When Andrew sells a holiday to a customer he does a full investigation of both human and material needs, selects a suitable product, and then tells the customer what the hotel has to offer. A typical presentation from Andrew may sound something like this:

'The hotel's next to the beach. It's got two swimming pools, one freshwater, the other saltwater. There's also a children's pool. Sports facilities include tennis, mini-golf and basketball. The hotel has two restaurants, and it says here that the Pearl Room is "renowned for its high standard of service and excellent choice of menu". There's also a poolside snack bar which is open during the day.'

Janine, like Andrew, also fully investigates the customer's human and material needs, but when she selects a suitable product for the customer she tries to present it to them in a way which makes it sound interesting and appealing, and personalises the description to meet their needs. Janine's presentation might sound something like this;

'I think you might be interested in this hotel. It's right on the beach, so you can just stroll out from your veranda on to the sand. There are two pools, one freshwater, the other seawater, and also a children's pool, so you won't need to worry about your son's safety. If you do want to spend the day by the pool, there's a poolside snack bar, so you'll be able to get lunch and any drinks you want during the day without having to get dressed and go into the hotel.

For your husband, the hotel has its own tennis courts, so if he wanted to play, the hotel will make arrangements to hire out equipment. I know you prefer to be booked under a bed-and-breakfast arrangement so that you can eat out, but on the occasions when it may be more convenient to stay at the hotel for the evening, there are two restaurants available, and one of them, the Pearl Room, has a very good reputation for providing good service and choice of menu, so it might be worth giving that a try.'

In this case study you can see that Janine has a much more expressive way of presenting the product to the customer than Andrew has. Although Andrew had selected a holiday which was suitable to the customer's requirements he failed to present the product in a way which was at all inspiring. Even though he has selected the information which would be of particular interest to the customer, simply reading out the details straight from the brochure does not make the product sound of any particular interest to the customer. Janine, however, first selected the elements of the holiday which most closely matched the customer's needs, and then explained them to the customer in a way which made them sound interesting and relevant to their own particular requirements. Janine personalised the product, and was able to draw a mental picture for the customer of what they could be doing on holiday. Janine was making use of the information she had already obtained about the customer's human needs and was using **benefit statements** to create a desire in the customer to buy the product.

Benefit statements

A benefit statement is a phrase or sentence which describes to the customer how the product will benefit them, rather than just telling them what the product is. While Andrew listed all of the aspects of the holiday which might be of interest to the customer, he just stated them as facts or features about the holiday. Janine however, explained the benefit of each of the relevant elements of the holiday. She was using benefit statements to create a desire in the customer to buy the product.

A **feature** is a fact about the product. A **benefit** is what the product will do for the customer. For example, if a customer wishing to go to Orlando has mentioned that they do not wish to drive to the attractions each day, an accommodation which has a complimentary bus service may be of interest to them. When the product is presented, it could either be presented as a feature, 'The hotel runs a complimentary bus service to the attractions', or as a benefit, 'This hotel has a complimentary bus running to the attractions, which means that you won't have to drive every day if you prefer not to'.

The feature tells the customer what the accommodation can offer, the benefit tells the customer how that particular feature will be of a benefit to them. Once you know what the customer is looking for in their holiday, and you have found something suitable, you can quickly create a desire in the customer to buy the product by personalising the product to them and by using benefits to describe the product.

When constructing benefit statements you need to include each of the following:

1 the fact or feature of the product which is suitable to the customer's requirements
2 a personalising word or phrase, such as 'you' or 'your son/daughter/husband'
3 A benefit phrase which explains what the product will do for the customer.

An example of the construction of a benefit statement is:

The apartment has a swimming pool – feature
... so you ...   – personalise
... can swim every day.   – benefit

A true benefit must contain all of these elements, but it does not necessarily matter in which order. In this example, the benefit statement was constructed as feature + personalisation + benefit, but equally it could have been constructed as personalisation + benefit + feature, e.g. 'You (personalisation) can swim every day (benefit) as the hotel has its own pool (feature)'.

Here are a few more examples of features which have been turned into benefit statements:

Feature	*Benefit statement*
There is a supermarket on the apartment complex.	You can do all of your food shopping in the complex supermarket, so you won't need to carry heavy bags for any distance.
Shops and bars are situated 100 metres away from the hotel.	If you would prefer a little variety, there are a range of shops and bars a short walk from the hotel.
There is a babysitting service.	The hotel offers a babysitting service, so if you and your husband would like to spend an evening out, the hotel will look after your son.

Using benefit statements in this way is a very effective way of making the product sound attractive to the customer, and once you become proficient you will greatly increase the number of enquiries that you are able to convert into sales.

....

Assignment   Using the information below, present the relevant aspects of the holiday to a friend or colleague using benefit statements.

Customer needs:

- two adults
- departing any time in June
- two weeks duration
- departing from Manchester airport
- price range between £400 and £500 per person.
- travelling to a Greek island
- accommodation requirements – twin room with private bath, shower and WC; balcony with sea view.
- accommodation facilities – swimming pool, good restaurant for occasional evening meals, gymnasium or fitness suite, tennis
- resort requirements – sandy beach nearby, tavernas and restaurants within walking distance, local historic sights, sea fishing, local shopping, walking, visiting local villages.

Hotel Olympia

This luxury four-star hotel is situated on its own sandy beach on the northern coast of Crete. For those who prefer to relax in pleasant surroundings, this hotel has a good range of sport and entertainment facilities, and for the more adventurous, there are good coastal walks from the hotel. The hotel is able to offer its guests a good range of watersports from the beach including waterskiing and windsurfing. In the summer months the hotel is able to arrange diving and fishing trips.

Local interest – The picturesque village of Aghia Peraklia is a five-minute walk from the hotel. The village is set around a pretty harbour which is surrounded by shops, restaurants and tavernas. Other local villages are easily reached by the local bus service. The ancient historic sight of Knossos is only twelve miles away and well worth a visit.

Facilities:

- freshwater heated outdoor pool
- children's section of the pool
- squash courts
- table tennis
- hairdressers
- poolside snack bar
- indoor pool
- gymnasium
- 2 tennis courts
- shop
- cocktail lounge
- Apollo Restaurant

All rooms are twin bedded with private bath, shower and WC and have a private balcony, some with a sea view.

Cost:	£
2 adults basic cost of £400.00	800.00
2 flight supplements of £22.00	44.00
Sea-view supplement, £3.50 per person × 14 nights	98.00
2 × insurance at £29.50	59.00
Total cost	1001.00

The brochure as a selling aid

If you work in an environment where you have direct face-to-face contact with the customer, then you can make good use of the brochure as a selling aid. Brochures contain a lot of information, and this can be used to your advantage. Certain aspects of the holiday can be pointed out, and the customer can be shown photographs, maps and charts, etc. While a good verbal presentation using benefit statements will help to create a mental image for the customer, using visual aids will greatly enhance that image and will help you to sell the product.

Before reading any further, just stop to think how important the sense of sight is to us. Consider the five senses that each of us would normally have: smell, taste, touch, hearing and sight. Assuming that everything we know from the day we were born until this very moment has come in through one or a variety of these five senses, how much do you think has come through each one? Do each of our senses play an equal role, or do we use some more than others?

You might be surprised by the following figures. Three per cent of everything we know we learn through our sense of smell; another 3 per cent we learn through our sense of taste; 6 per cent of our learning is through our sense of touch; 13 per cent of our learning comes from our sense of hearing. This leaves the remaining 75 per cent which we learn through our sense of sight.

You can see from these figures that our sense of sight is very important in our learning and understanding of things, and this should be remembered when selling a product to the customer. Make use of the brochure as much as possible to reinforce your sales presentation. Photographs, maps and temperature charts are obvious items to point out to your customer, but you may also wish to show the customer the price grid, or flight timings or even highlight important aspects of the text. When using the brochure in this way, do remember that it is a selling aid, and should be used to accompany your sales pitch, and not as a substitute for it. Never fall into the trap of reading out brochure descriptions to the customer and never hand them the brochure to read themselves. This is not selling!

If possible, try to ensure that the customer is easily able to view the brochure. People who work in travel, very quickly learn to read text upside down and if you can already do this, then you can have the brochure facing the customer and point out the relevant parts of it in your presentation. If you are not yet able to read upside down, then let the customer have their own brochure, so that you have one to refer to. However, if you do this, do ensure that you point out things on the customer's brochure and not on your own! Whenever anything is pointed out, try and do it with the tip of a pen or pencil as this focuses the customer's eye on what you want them to see and looks far more professional than using a finger.

To summarise, the key learning points of presenting the product are:

- Find a product which matches the customer's requirements.
- Select the elements of the holiday which are appropriate to the customer's needs.
- Use good benefit statements to create a desire in the customer to buy the product.
- Use the brochure to help to visually reinforce your sales pitch.

CLOSING THE SALE

Actively closing the sale fills some people with apprehension. Perhaps they feel that trying to close the sale is putting too much pressure on the customer, or that it should be left up to the customer to say whether or not they want to buy, or most commonly of all, that when they ask the customer for the booking, the customer will say no.

There will of course be situations where the customer is not in a position to make up their minds there and then. Perhaps there are other members of the party who are travelling that need to be consulted before a decision can be made, or perhaps, due to lack of availability, the customer may need to consider travelling on a different date to their original choice and therefore need to confirm this with their employer. But when you have the party with you and there is no change in date involved there is no reason why you can't close the sale there and then. One thing is for certain though, most customers will need a little gentle persuasion to help them make their decision to buy.

An annual holiday is probably one of the single most expensive items that a family will make in the year, and they need to feel comfortable that they will be happy with their purchase. Unlike other consumer items of similar value, the customer cannot bring the holiday back for a refund if, once they have experienced it, it is not what they had hoped for.

During the sales conversation, the customer makes a conscious transition from listening to the sales pitch to deciding that they will probably consider making a purchase, and they will show this through a variety of subtle body movements, by asking a certain type of question, or by the use of verbal mannerisms. Once you are able to recognise these signals that the customer is sending out, you will know that you have reached the point at which you are able to stop selling the product, and move on to close the sale.

....

CASE STUDY

The following are three examples of sales people trying to close the sale.

Miles uses benefits to present the product to his customer and shows the relevant points in the brochure to support his presentation. After he has stated the final benefit, he looks at the customer and waits for a reaction. None is forthcoming, the customer looks rather nonplussed by the whole thing. Miles feels he must do something as he knows that as the salesperson, he should take the lead in trying to close the sale.

'Would you like to book this holiday?' he asks.

'No I don't think so,' replies the customer.

Abigail presents a holiday to her customer in a very enthusiastic manner. She thinks this holiday sounds really exciting and would like to go on it herself. She hopes the customer will be impressed as well and will make a booking today.

'It sounds a really good holiday, and there's plenty for all of you to do.'

'Yes that sounds fine,' says the customer. 'How much is the deposit?'

'It's seventy-five pounds per person,' says Abigail. 'And look here, it says that they have a disco every night and there are film shows . . .'

'I don't think that's quite our thing,' says the customer. 'Do you take Access?'

'Yes, we do,' says Abigail. 'I'd love to go to this hotel. Sounds as if they go on until all hours.'

The customer thinks, 'Mmm. I wonder if it might perhaps be a little too lively for our liking.'

Matthew presents his product to the customer and has used several strong benefit statements. The customer has been nodding for the last few minutes and then says, 'Sounds absolutely ideal.'

Matthew still has a few more points he would like to make, but he knows the danger of overselling the product, and besides, the customer has already decided he wants to buy the holiday. Matthew can always make his other points while he is processing the booking.

This case study demonstrates how important it is for you to recognise buying signals, however subtle, once the customer gives them. In the first example, there were no buying signals as the customer was not ready to buy. This could have been for a number of reasons, perhaps the product wasn't suitable or the sales presentation had not been thorough enough. Whatever the case, the agent tried to close the sale before the customer was ready to make a commitment and lost the sale. Customers dislike being pushed into making a decision, and if they feel pressurised they will probably back out of the sales situation altogether.

In the second example, we saw that although the customer was ready to buy and showed definite buying signals, the agent failed to recognise them and continued with the sales pitch. In this situation, the agent runs the risk of 'overselling' the product. The danger here is that once you pass the point at which the customer is satisfied that this is the right product for them, overselling can sometimes have the opposite effect and talk the customer out of buying the product. Once the customer indicates that they are ready to buy, stop selling. If there is something really important that you feel you must tell the customer, you can bring it into the conversation later on as you complete the transaction. In the final example, the agent recognised the buying signals when the customer gave them and was able to move smoothly into the final stage of the sales conversation and close the sale.

. . . .

Recognising buying signals and then acting on them at the appropriate time is a very important part of the sales conversation and may take some practice. You need to strike exactly the right balance at this point in the sale to ensure that you move at the pace at which the customer is happy. Even though you should be in control of the sales conversation, you must also ensure that you are not going too fast or too slowly for the customer.

Common buying signals are:

- asking questions about ancillary services, such as car hire, getting to and from the airport, or the cost of insurance – if the customer had no interest in the product they would not be interested in this kind of information
- asking about methods of payment, or how much the deposit is or when the balance is due
- if you are serving a couple, they may start to discuss the product, or ask one another what they think
- agreeing with you, and making positive comments such as 'That sounds fine' or 'That looks lovely'.

Occasionally you may come to the end of your presentation and receive no reaction at all from the customer, as in the first example in the case study. If this is the case, you must take the lead and find out what the customer is thinking in order for you to take the appropriate action. Perhaps the best way to do this is simply to ask the customer what they think of the product by asking them something like, 'How does that holiday sound to you?'

The answer you receive to this question will provide you with a good indication of what to do next. If the customer says, 'Yes that sounds fine' you can then move on to closing the sale. If the response you receive indicates that the customer just needs a little extra convincing, e.g. 'Mmm . . . I think that sounds OK. What do you think?' then you can summarise the main benefits again. However, you may receive a response which indicates that there is something with which the customer is not happy, e.g. 'Well I'm not too sure really, perhaps I'll leave it'. If this is the case, you will need to find out what the problem is, and then overcome the objection in whatever way is appropriate.

HANDLING OBJECTIONS

If the customer is going to raise an objection about the holiday, it will usually be at this stage in the sales conversation, and the way that the objection is dealt with could mean the difference between making or losing the sale. Some customers will be entirely honest and tell you exactly the reason why they are not happy with the holiday, you can then either try and overcome the objection or, if this is not possible, find a suitable alternative. However, it is often the case that the customer will object, but will not disclose the real reason for the objection, and may give a false reason why they are not happy with the product. This is a false objection. You may not always be able to tell the difference between a true or a false objection, so before you try to do anything about it, you need first to establish what kind of objection it is. The following conversation demonstrates how this can be done.

> AGENT: So what do you think about this holiday Mr Jones?
> MR JONES: Well, I'm not so sure about this hotel.
> AGENT: What exactly is the problem?
> MR JONES: Well, it sounds as though it might be a little noisy.
> AGENT: Would you prefer something a little quieter?
> MR JONES: Yes.
> AGENT: Leaving aside the noise levels, is this the sort of holiday you are looking for?
> MR JONES: Yes, everything else is fine, I would just like something a little quieter.
> AGENT: So if I found you something of a similar standard and price range, with the same facilities, but in a quieter location, would that be alright?
> MR JONES: Yes, that would be fine.

In this conversation, the agent was able to identify exactly what the problem was by isolating the issue of the noise factor from everything else about the product by using the 'Leaving that aside . . .' technique. Once the customer had agreed that apart from the noise, he was quite happy with the product, the agent then double-checked this statement by asking if the customer would be in agreement to a holiday that had the same facilities and was in the same price range but quieter. The customer agreed, indicating that price was not an issue, and therefore the objection of noise was a true objection.

Sometimes, it will not be necessary to go as far as looking for an alternative product, as you may be able to overcome an objection by using a benefit statement. For example:

MR JONES: I'm not happy about these flight timings. We'll have to be at the airport at five o'clock in the morning.

AGENT: Yes, it is an early start, but it does mean that you will be at your hotel by lunchtime, so you'll have the afternoon to relax and settle in. And your return timings are very good. You'll be leaving your hotel at about half past ten in the morning, so you won't be waiting around all day, and you'll be back in the UK by early evening, so it won't be too long a day for you.

In this case the agent was able to turn a customer objection into a benefit. This can be an effective way of handling true objections, as you may be able to put a different, more positive light on something which the customer initially sees as a negative issue.

However, some customers will raise false objections, and this is usually when they consider the price to be more than they want to spend. The technique for identifying whether or not an objection is a true or false one should be employed in this situation, but you may find that you need to repeat the process a number of times before you get to the real reason for the objection.

AGENT: So what do you think about this holiday Mr Jones?

MR JONES: Well, I'm not so sure about this hotel.

AGENT: What exactly is the problem?

MR JONES: Well, it sounds as though it might be a little noisy.

AGENT: Would you prefer something a little quieter?

MR JONES : Yes.

AGENT: Leaving aside, the noise levels, is this the sort of holiday you are looking for?

MR JONES: Well the pool looks a bit on the small side.

AGENT: So if I found you a similar hotel, same price range, but a little quieter and with a larger pool, would that be alright for you?

MR JONES: Um. Well perhaps we could find something a little less expensive than this one.

AGENT: What sort of price would you be prepared to go up to?

MR JONES: We really didn't want to go over £400 each.

The agent has now identified the real problem and can now address it by trying to overcome the objection with a benefit statement such as, 'Well this is a very good hotel, Mr Jones, and all of the sports facilities you wanted are included in the price. If we were to look at an alternative hotel where the price was lower but you paid for your watersports locally, the overall cost of your holiday probably wouldn't be much different.'

If this option was not open to the agent, or the customer was not swayed in his decision by this benefit, then the agent should renegotiate with the customer exactly what his requirements are before starting to look for an alternative product, e.g. 'So we're looking for something around the £400 per person mark, with all of the same facilities. Now how important is it to you that the hotel has a larger pool than this one?'

If the agent continues in this way, it will eventually be possible to distinguish between the true and false objections raised. It is quite possible that none of the objections except the final one about price are real objections, but if the agent finds that they were all true objections, then this would indicate that the investigation of the customer's needs was not as thorough as it might have been.

If you find yourself in this situation, persevere until you are able to establish the real reason for the objection, and then gain the customer's agreement that they are happy with what you will do next before you spend time on finding another more suitable product. Very few customers are time wasters, but if you are not able to identify and overcome true objections, you may well loose their custom to a competitor.

Asking for the booking

Once buying signals have been identified and any customer objections overcome, the final part of closing the sale is to actually ask for the booking. There are a number of different ways this can be done, and which way you choose will very much depend on the situation and the preceding conversation you have had with the customer. Here are a few examples of the way in which you could ask for the booking:

'Would you like to book that?' This is the most commonly used form of close, and requires a simple 'Yes' or 'No' answer from the customer.

'How will you be paying?' A less direct way of asking for the booking, but a good way of moving into the commitment stage of the sales conversation. This form of close should only be used when you are very sure of your ground and the customer has made it clear through buying signals that they will be buying the product.

'I'll go ahead and book that for you then.' A strong and direct way of closing the sale. Again, only to be used when you are very sure that the customer has made a firm decision to buy.

'Which of these would you like?' To be used when the customer has a choice of products.

If you know that you normally use the same form of closing phrase or question, practise using some of these suggestions and see how you get along.

Levels of commitment

Wherever possible, it is preferable to aim for the highest level of commitment (see Fig. 3.3), a definite booking, rather than an option (a provisional booking usually held for twenty-four hours at which time it will expire without penalty). If you ask for a definite booking and the customer is not in a position to commit fully to buying the product at the time, you can always offer to hold the

Highest level

Firm booking with full payment

Firm booking with deposit

Option, agent agrees to contact customer for further instructions

Option, customer wishes to make contact to instruct agent on further action

Nothing held, but agent agrees to contact customer for further instruction or with further information

Nothing held, customer states that if further help is required they will contact the agent

No agreement is made, customer leaves

Lowest level

Fig 3.3 Commitment levels

reservation for twenty-four hours until a decision can be reached. When this is done, be sure to take the customer's telephone number before the conversation ends so that if you do not hear from them by the end of the following day, you can contact them to find out what they would like to do. You should always try and ensure that you continue with the enquiry until the customer finally makes a booking. Even if you were not able to take the customer as far as holding an option, and they instead indicate that they would like to go away and think about what they have been offered, try and contact them within a couple of days to see if there is anything else you can do.

To summarise, the key learning points of closing a sale are:

- Identify the buying signals and then stop selling.
- Ask the customer what they think of the product if buying signals are not forthcoming.
- Identify true and false objections and overcome them in an appropriate manner.
- Ask for the booking.
- Aim for the highest level of commitment.

Assignment Refer back to the customer and holiday details given on pages 104–5 and role-play the following situation, preferably with the same person who helped you for the previous assignment on presentation skills.

1 Ask your partner to object to something about the holiday, they can decide whether or not the objection is true. Your task is to establish the validity of the objection and try to overcome it with a benefit statement.

2 If you are successful, try and identify any buying signals that are given to you and then try and aim for the highest level of commitment.

3 If you are not successful in closing the sale, discuss the reasons why your partner felt unable to make a firm commitment to buy the product.

SELLING EXTRAS

Once you have successfully closed the sale, your sales pitch need not end there. As well as the basic package that the customer has purchased, you probably have access to a whole range of 'extras' that may be of interest to the customer. In many cases, the customer may not even be aware that you are able to offer this extra service, but by doing so, you will be providing the customer with 'one-stop shopping' and thus increasing the level of customer satisfaction.

Some extras may be a little cheaper if bought from you rather than from other sources. But even if they are not, it is often a lot more convenient for the customer to have everything packaged together and paid for as one balance before the date of travel, rather than having to spend time shopping around before they travel, or needing to find additional spending money once they are abroad.

CASE STUDY

Ben always makes a point of offering additional services to any customer who makes a purchase from him. He prefers not to adopt a hard sell approach, but finds that if he suggests an extra to the customer, they are usually surprised that he is able to offer such a service, and impressed by his efficiency. Ben is by no means always successful in his attempts to sell extras, but a good 50 per cent of his customers will make additional purchases once the idea has been put to them. Ben's advice to his colleagues?

'It's always worth offering an extra to the customer, and over half of them will take it. Don't be afraid to ask – the worst that can happen is that the customer will say "No". If you never ask, you'll never receive a "Yes" '.

Ben believes that it is very easy to offer extra services to the customer once they have made the decision to purchase their holiday. Not only does it create a good impression with the customer, but it will also increase your profit margins.

Depending on the sector of the industry that you work in, there are a number of additional items you could offer the customer. Here are a few suggestions for you.

Transport to the point of departure

The customer will usually have to make their way to the point of departure for their holiday. Obviously if they are taking their own car abroad with them on a ferry, then they will have their own transport, but for other types of trip and holiday, you could offer the following:

- Coach or rail ticket – Even if you are not a licence holder yourself, many tour operators offer this service as an extra in their brochure.
- Taxi service – If you don't already have an arrangement, most taxi firms will agree a set rate and pay you a commission on every group of passengers you refer to them.

Airport parking

If the customer decides to drive themselves to their point of departure, they will need to park their car. Many off-airport, car parking sites allow customers to book ahead and will pay a commission to you for promoting their service.

Overnight hotel accommodation

If the customer has a long journey to the departure point, or is travelling very early in the morning or returning late at night, they may prefer to stay in a hotel near to the departure point before they make their onward journey. Many airport hotels offer free parking for the customer for the duration of their trip if they stay the night before they travel, and will arrange a courtesy transfer to the airport for them in the morning and collect them when they return.

Currency and traveller's cheques

The customer will need to obtain foreign currency and traveller's cheques from somewhere, and if you are able to offer this service to the customer, it will be much more convenient for them to purchase these from you and collect them with their tickets, than have to deal with a bank or a bureau de change.

Passport and visa service

As a matter of course, you should always check whether the customer holds the valid passport and visa necessary for their trip. If the customer requires these documents and you are able to offer a passport and visa service, the customer will almost certainly prefer to pay you a handling fee than spend time and effort arranging the documents themselves.

Car rental

Many customers book and pay for car rental once they arrive at their overseas destination, and this is revenue that could easily have been earned by you if you had offered them this service at the time of booking. A frequent objection raised by the customer when they are offered the option of pre-purchasing car hire before they travel is that they believe it to be cheaper to book in the overseas country. This is very rarely the case, and there is no guarantee that the size of car they want will be available. If it is not, they will have no alternative but to book and pay for an alternative size of car.

If a customer does raise an objection about pre-booking car hire, you may be able to use one of the following advantages to help persuade them:

- The customer is guaranteed at least the standard of car they booked and paid for. If the size they wanted is not available, they will receive an automatic upgrade to a larger car at no additional charge.
- As the payment has already been made in the UK, there is no need for the customer to find payment for the car rental out of their spending money.
- If payment is made in the UK before travel, then the customer will have paid in sterling and will know exactly how much the bill will be for. If an overseas payment is made by credit card, it will be in a foreign currency, and sometimes the exchange rate will work against the customer, causing the bill to be higher than they had expected.
- Pre-purchasing car rental in the UK means that the customer will be using a reputable company. Small overseas offices do not necessarily operate to the same standards as companies represented in the UK.
- Insurances can usually be prepaid in this country.
- Companies represented in the UK generally offer a twenty-four hour breakdown and recovery service. This is not always available from smaller overseas-based companies.

If the customer has not considered car hire as an option, it is worth comparing the cost of a few excursions with the cost of two or three days' car rental. The comparison is usually quite favourable, and will allow the customer more freedom to explore on their own.

Insurance

Every passenger travelling overseas should be covered by insurance of some kind. Always ask the customer if they would like to take out insurance. If they tell you that they already have cover, do check that it provides sufficient cover for medical bills and cancellation, etc.

Whenever you make a sale, always try and offer the customer an additional extra. You may not always be successful, but if you don't offer the service, the customer may not realise that it is available from you.

SWITCH SELLING

At certain busy times of the year, a customer's choice of holiday may not be available, and an alternative will have to be sought. If this happens to a travel agent, then the first course of action may be to find another operator who provides the same hotel. However, this is not always possible, and in the case of a tour operator trying to sell an alternative, this option will not be open. The customer has already made a decision to make the booking, and will obviously still want to travel, so it is important that a suitable alternative is found and sold to the customer without delay.

So what is the best way of selling an alternative? The one thing which certainly should not be done is to send the customer away to make another choice. This is not being very helpful to the customer and it defers nearly all of the energy of selling back to them. In a switch-selling situation, unless the customer specifically states that they want to make another choice themselves, the onus is on the salesperson to find a suitable alternative.

A professional approach to this type of situation is first to find out why the customer chose this particular holiday. This information, should provide you with the customer's human needs which, as was discussed earlier in this chapter, are vital if you are to find a product which is suitable to the customer's specific requirements. If the customer does not initially provide you with as much information as you would like, there is nothing to stop you doing a small investigation to obtain a full picture of what the customer is looking for in their holiday. Once you have this information, you can then set about finding a suitable alternative.

CASE STUDY

The following conversation demonstrates how to investigate the customer's human needs in order to find a suitable alternative holiday:

AGENT: I'm sorry, Mr Brown, I've checked all of the operators who feature this holiday and there is nothing available for the dates that you wanted. Did you have a second choice I could check for you?

MR BROWN : No, we'd really set our hearts on this one.

AGENT: Well, perhaps I might be able to find you a suitable alternative.

MR BROWN: I'd be grateful if you could.

AGENT: Perhaps first, you could tell me why you chose this particular holiday.

MR BROWN: Well, my wife and I lead very busy lives and we wanted to relax and have a few weeks away from it all. This hotel was ideal because it is set on the beach, away from the main resort and looks very quiet. Another attraction of this particular hotel was that it had tennis courts. We both enjoy a game now and then.

AGENT: So ideally, you're looking for something that is quiet and with a tennis court. Is there anything else that is important to you in your holiday?

MR BROWN: A good restaurant in the hotel, and a good-sized pool. We're not too keen on a very large hotel though, this one only has one hundred rooms.

AGENT: Did you still want to stay at this resort?

MR BROWN: Not necessarily. We would like to go to Menorca, but it doesn't have to be this resort.

AGENT: So if we need to look at an alternative resort, what sort of thing would you be looking for?

MR BROWN: Nothing too big or commercialised. My wife likes to do a little shopping and sightseeing, and we'll probably want to eat out a few evenings. Above all, something with a bit of local character and some nice scenery.

AGENT: You had chosen a twin room with balcony and sea view at the original hotel, at a cost of £475 for the two weeks. Shall I look for something in the same price range?

MR BROWN: We're not too concerned about the price, more with finding the right holiday. We'd be prepared to go up to around £550, as long as the hotel has all of the facilities we want and it's in the right sort of area.

AGENT: OK then, Mr Brown. I'll see what I can find for you.

The agent now has all of the customer's requirements: the departure date, the duration, the hotel facilities, the resort facilities, the activities the couple want to pursue, the type of room and the price range. It will now be possible to look for an alternative to match all of those requirements.

Presenting the alternative

Once a suitable alternative has been found, the agent can begin to sell it to Mr Brown. But to be really effective, presenting an alternative has to be done in a special way. The customer had set his heart on the original choice, so the agent needs to convince him that the new choice is at least comparable, if not better, and the most effective way to do this is to sell by comparison. This means that the presentation is made by selling the benefits of the new holiday as a comparison to the original.

When a presentation of this sort is to be made, the first thing to do is to look for all of the aspects of the new holiday which are the same as the original choice, then the things which are better than the original, and finally, you may find some aspects of the holiday which are worse than the original choice. If there are things about the new holiday which are worse than the old, you will have to tell the customer, but the impact of this will depend on how this is put and how well you have presented the other aspects of the holiday.

CASE STUDY continued

Let's see how the agent dealt with Mr Brown. First, the comparison between the original hotel and the alternative:

Original choice, Playa Blanca
4-star hotel, 110 bedrooms
Large freshwater pool
Sun terrace

Alternative, Santa Marina
4-star hotel, 200 bedrooms
Large freshwater pool and an indoor pool
Sun terrace

Poolside bar	Poolside bar
Coffee shop	Coffee shop
3 tennis courts	2 tennis courts, one floodlit (equipment for hire)
Waiter service restaurant with table d'hôte menu	Buffet service for breakfast and lunch. À la carte and table d'hôte menu for evening meal

Location:

Quiet location	Quiet location
Sandy beach across the road	Built on a sandy beach
Set amid pine trees	Set amid lawns
A few local shops and restaurants within walking distance	Local beachside restaurant
Resort five minutes away by taxi	Resort ten minutes walk away

Resort:

South-west coast of Menorca	South coast of Menorca
1½ hour transfer from airport	1¼ hour transfer from airport
Quaint whitewashed buildings	Charming unspoilt village
Shops, restaurants and discos	Shops and restaurants
Set around a picturesque cove	Set around a pretty harbour with village fishing fleet

Accommodation:

Twin room with WC, bath, shower and balcony with sea view	Twin room with WC, bath, shower and balcony with sea view
£475 per person	£520 per person

Having made all of the necessary comparisons, the agent will now present the new holiday to Mr Brown. The best way for the agent to do this is to begin the presentation by telling Mr Brown of the features which are the same as his original choice, followed by anything which might be worse than the original and finally with any aspects of the new holiday which are better than the original. If the alternative costs less money, this could be mentioned early on in the presentation, but if the cost of the alternative is higher than the original, then leave this until the end, to ensure that the customer is sold on the idea of the new holiday, before they hear how much extra it is going to cost.

The agent's presentation to Mr Brown is as follows:

'This looks like a suitable alternative for you Mr Brown. It's the Santa Marina Hotel which is set on the south coast of the island. The holiday still departs on the fifteenth of September for two weeks and it's still a four-star hotel which features all of the facilities you wanted in your original hotel.

It is a slightly larger hotel, but it does have a few extra facilities which may be of interest to you. The restaurant at the new hotel is better than the one at the Playa Blanca. The restaurant there had a table d'hôte menu, the Santa Marina has a choice of table d'hôte or à la carte in the evening, so you have a good choice of menu. The Santa Marina has tennis courts, which I know are important to you, and their facilities are a little better as they have a floodlit court, so you'll be able to play in the evening when it's a little cooler if you prefer. The Santa Marina has the facility to hire tennis racquets and balls, whereas you would have had to take your own equipment to the Playa Blanca. The Santa Marina has a good-sized swimming pool and also an indoor pool if you would like to make use of that during the evenings.

The location of the hotel is better, it is right on the beach – you would have had to cross over the road to get to the beach at the Playa Blanca. You mentioned that you wanted the resort to have local character, well, the centre of the resort is set around a natural harbour which has its own working fishing fleet. There are still plenty of shops and restaurants for you to visit in the village, and it looks as though the resort may be a little quieter than your original choice as there are no discos or nightclubs – your first choice of resort had two.

The cost of this holiday is a little more than your original choice, the two week price is £520 per person, but it is a much better standard of hotel and I'm sure that you will agree, that for a little over an extra £3 per person per night it's well worth the additional cost.'

You'll notice that the agent made comparisons between the two hotels as much as possible and was even able to counter the issue of the size of the hotel by balancing it with the fact that as a larger hotel, the Santa Marina had more facilities that the customer might find of interest. As to the additional cost of the hotel, this was put to the customer as something that was worth paying to stay in a the better standard of hotel, ' . . . and at a little over £3 per person per night . . . ' doesn't sound too much extra to pay. It most certainly sounds more appealing than, 'It's a total of £90 more than your original holiday'.

....

This principle of switch selling is quite effective, but does need a little preparation beforehand. However, this needn't take you very long, and once you become practised and confident with it, you will find it quite straightforward.

To summarise, the main points of switch selling are:

- Establish why the customer chose the original holiday.
- Find an alternative holiday based on those needs.
- Compare the two holidays.
- Present the new holiday, using a comparison of features that are the same as, better than, or worse than the original choice.
- Discuss any increase in price at the end of your presentation in terms of a small amount per person per night, rather than a total additional figure.

NOTIFYING CUSTOMERS OF A CHANGE

From time to time it may be necessary for customers' holidays or travel arrangements to be changed after they have been booked. This may be done for a number of reasons, and it is never a pleasant task to have to inform customers of changes.

Suppliers always do their best to avoid making material changes to the holiday, as it usually involves a lot of extra work and can cost the tour operator money, either in the form of compensation or in the cost of the new service or contract, leaving them with a reduced profit margin. Everyone in the travel industry wishes to safeguard their reputations for providing a reliable and high-quality service and making a large number of material changes may damage this.

Why changes are made

Material changes to a holiday can be made for many reasons. Here are a few of the most common reasons.

Consolidation

This is the term given to the process of merging two flights or departures into one. At the beginning of every season suppliers have to estimate the numbers of passengers they believe they will be able to book on each departure. As the season progresses and bookings increase, the supplier is able to see where the forward slack periods are likely to be, and will again estimate how likely it is that they will be able to carry sufficient passengers to reach a point at which they are able to make a profit or, at least, break even. If a particular departure does not have sufficient passengers to break even – in other words, the operator stands to lose money – they may decide to combine two separate flights into one, and therefore prevent a loss. For example, a supplier may have booked passengers on the following flights:

> Newcastle to Malaga   Sunday 25 March   dep. 09.00
> Glasgow to Malaga   Sunday 25 March   dep. 10.00

If neither departure has sufficient passengers to reach the necessary break-even point, the supplier may decide to combine these two flights by cancelling the Newcastle departure and transferring passengers on to the Glasgow flight, or vice versa.

This situation may also arise with escorted tours, whereby the supplier does not have enough bookings to make the running of a specific tour financially viable. He may then transfer booked passengers to the same tour, but on a different date, or offer an alternative tour for passengers booked on the original departure date.

Change of hotel

This does not happen very often, but when it does it is usually because the supplier has felt it necessary to withdraw all customers from the hotel, perhaps due to poor service or complaints, or even because of a closure of an important facility at the hotel, which the supplier believes will affect customers' enjoyment of their stay. On rare occasions the supplier may cancel due to contractual problems, but this is a very unusual occurrence.

Act of God

This includes any natural disasters, such as earthquakes, volcanic eruptions and hurricane damage, or war or civil unrest likely to cause danger to foreign tourists and holidaymakers. In cases of extreme political disturbance the British Government may advise holidaymakers not to travel to a certain country or part of the world. Similarly, whenever an epidemic, or outbreak of disease occurs, the World Health Organisation in Geneva will issue notices to warn travellers of possible danger. In all cases where there is a possible danger to travellers, tour operators will make a collective decision to suspend departures in the interests of safety.

Informing the customer of changes

It is never a pleasant task to have to inform customers of changes, but those necessary due to an 'Act of God' are probably the easiest to deal with. Customers will obviously be disappointed, but they are probably already aware of events and will almost certainly not wish to travel to that part of the world. At such times, cancellations are usually expected and customers are pleased to know that the tour operator has made the decision not to operate, and that they will automatically be offered a full refund.

Informing the customer of a material change to a holiday can be a little less straightforward. Full cancellations are rarely made, but the tour operator may have to make alterations to arrangements. These may include a change of flight departure or arrival time, a change of airline, a change of departure or arrival airport, changes to the resort, changes to the accommodation or an alteration to a published itinerary. Although some of these alterations may be considered minor changes by insurance companies or suppliers, the inconvenience which such rearrangements bring are often the cause of some distress to customers.

Think about this from the customer's point of view. They have probably had their holiday booked for some time and have no reason to doubt that they will be travelling on the service they have booked and staying at the destination they have chosen. The customer will have been making plans for some time about how they will get to the airport, and what they will do when they arrive at their destination. They have imagined themselves lying by the pool or looking out to sea from their balcony, and have pictured themselves visiting all the places they want to see. To the customer, their carefully chosen holiday represents far more than just a flight number and a hotel name, and any changes to these arrangements will almost certainly be regarded as untimely and unwelcome. For the customer this will often mean a major personal adjustment to the picture of the holiday already drawn in their mind. Even if the changes do not appear particularly major to you, it may completely upset the customer's plans, so try always to be sympathetic and understanding and expect that the customer may not welcome these changes.

CASE STUDY

Mr and Mrs Blackmore are an elderly couple who have booked flight seats from Gatwick to Malaga for their annual holiday. They booked the flights through their local travel agent who has also arranged a rental car for the duration of their stay, to be collected at Malaga airport. Mr Blackmore has made private accommodation arrangements and is booked to stay for two weeks at a villa in a quiet country location about two hours drive from the airport.

In the post this morning, Mr Blackmore received a copy of a letter from the tour operator with whom the flights are booked, attached to a compliment slip from the travel agent. The letter from the tour operator simply states that it has been necessary to change the flight on which the Blackmores have been booked, to a later flight which now arrives in Malaga at 20.30. Mr Blackmore is upset. His original flight was due to arrive into Malaga at 15.30, giving him plenty of time to collect the hire car and drive to the villa in daylight. A flight arriving at 20.30 would mean that it will be dark before he and his wife have left the airport and, as Mr Blackmore has never visited the area before and does not like driving at night, he feels that these alterations are quite unacceptable. He is equally annoyed at the way in which he has been informed of these changes. There is no accompanying letter of explanation from the travel agent or information regarding what he can do about the change to his holiday.

Mr Blackmore telephones the agency to make enquiries. When he gets through he explains the situation and how unhappy he feels about the alternative arrangements. The young travel agent who answers his call is not exactly helpful, and is only able to tell Mr Blackmore that the changes to his holiday have been made by the tour operator and that, sadly, there is nothing that can be done about it.

Mr Blackmore decides to go into the agency himself in order to speak to the manager. He recounts his conversation with the young clerk and tells the manager that, given that the change was very disruptive, he did not consider their attitude to have been very helpful. The manager listens sympathetically and asks Mr Blackmore to explain why these alternative arrangements are unacceptable. He then telephones the tour operator to see if they can help, and learns that the reason for the change is that the original flight has been consolidated with the later flight to make the operation more profitable. He explains the customer's problem with regard to the late arrival time, and the operator consults the supervisor to see if a more suitable alternative can be found. The manager explains the situation to Mr Blackmore, who is then satisfied that everything is being done to help resolve the situation. Finally, the tour operator returns, offering a Luton departure on the same day, arriving in Malaga at 14.00. Mr Blackmore is happy that this is a much better alternative which will enable him to reach his holiday villa in the daylight, and tells the manager that he will accept the Luton flight.

In this case study, you can see both the correct and incorrect way to advise customers of changes to flight arrangements. In the first instance it may have been better for the travel agent to telephone Mr Blackmore directly to let him know of his flight change. This would have enabled Mr Blackmore to discuss the changes immediately and directly with the agent. In the event, the young clerk was worried about the customer's reaction, and thought that any unpleasantness would be avoided if Mr Blackmore was contacted indirectly, by post. However, it was also clear that the customer received little sympathy when he did telephone the agency. The point here is not who was to blame for the flight change, but the effect that this change was to have on the customer's arrangements. Although it may be a natural reaction to make the customer aware that the changes were not the fault of the agent, it is nevertheless the responsibility of the agent to ensure that customer goodwill is maintained. By simply deferring the blame, the agent was actually saying, 'This is not our fault, and there's nothing I can do about it'.

When Mr Blackmore saw the manager and was given the opportunity to state why the alternative was inconvenient, the manager listened sympathetically and was able to find a suitable solution. Even if the operator had been unable to help with an alternative flight, Mr Blackmore would, at least have been satisfied that the manager had tried to help.

If you have to notify a customer of a change to their flight arrangements:

- try to contact the customer by phone to advise the changes
- be prepared for an initial unfavourable reaction
- sympathise with the customer and explain the reason for the changes
- if the customer has very strong reasons for not accepting the change, investigate other possible alternatives.

Notifying the customer of a change to resort or hotel

When a hotel or resort change is made to a customer's holiday arrangements, this is often more difficult to deal with than changes to flight arrangements. Whilst a change in flight may cause inconvenience, a change in hotel or resort may cause a major upset because, in the mind of your customers, they are no longer having the holiday they had planned and looked forward to.

When a change of this nature is made the tour operator will always try to provide a comparable alternative, or sometimes something a little better than the original booking. In putting alternatives of this kind to the customer, the same techniques are used as for switch selling, but you must be prepared for the customer's initial reaction to the news and be able to deal constructively with the objections that will undoubtedly be raised. This is the responsibility of either the tour operator dealing with the matter through the agent or directly with the customer, or the travel agent dealing with the matter direct with the customer.

CASE STUDY

Jane works in the administration department of a tour operator and, when necessary, it is her responsibility to notify travel agents or customers of changes to their holidays. This is not a part of her job that she particularly enjoys but, since she has learned how to handle the situation properly, the task has not been quite so unpleasant. Dealing with travel agents has never caused too much of a problem, although one or two have made a fuss, but it is always those customers who book direct that Jane really dislikes dealing with. In the past she has had a number of unpleasant conversations which she has found upsetting. At her last appraisal, Jane discussed this with her supervisor and between them they analysed how Jane was dealing with these calls and why they caused her such a problem. Through their discussions, Jane realised several things about herself:

- She always worries about the reaction she would receive from the customer which undermined her own confidence before she even picked up the telephone.
- She tends to take the customer's natural reaction of anger and disappointment personally and becomes defensive, which makes the situation even worse.
- She does not prepare for the call by comparing the facilities of the original choice with the new one.
- She does not know how to deal with customers' objections, so tends to dismiss them altogether.

Once Jane realised these things about herself she and her supervisor worked together to help her become more effective in this situation. Now Jane gives herself time to prepare before she makes the call and makes a list of all the things in the new holiday which are the same, or better than the original. When she makes the call she tries to do it in an environment where she will not be disturbed, and puts herself in a clear and positive frame of mind before she does so. When she speaks to the customer she tries to sound pleasant and understanding, and allows the customer time to express their immediate anger and disappointment before she continues. She sympathises with how the customer must feel but, at the same time, remains positive about the possible alternatives. She explains the benefits of the new holiday and reassures the customer that all of the aspects and facilities of the alternative are the same as the original choice. Jane now expects the customer to raise an objection at some point during the conversation and accepts this as a normal reaction but, instead of dismissing the objections, she acknowledges what the customer has said and tries to balance or overcome these with a benefit.

Now Jane does not mind dealing with this type of call and rarely ends the call without a satisfactory result. Her advice to her colleagues is: 'Think about how you would feel if you were the customer. It's only natural for customers to be angry and upset, and the best thing we can do is to be sympathetic, but positive about any change. Above all, you should prepare before you make the call and make sure you have all the facts. If you don't do this you can't respond properly when customers object.'

Assignment   Role-play the following situation:

You work for a travel agent and have received notification that one of your customer's holidays has been changed. Your task is to deliver this news to the customer in a manner which is positive and professional, and which maintains the customer's goodwill. The information you have received from the tour operator is as follows:

> *Due to extensive building work in the area, which is causing some disruption to our clients during their holidays, all passengers booked to stay at the Los Alimos Hotel have been transferred to the Los Gigantes Hotel in the same resort. We apologise for the inconvenience this may cause and offer compensatory payments of £30 per person.*

Using the descriptions outlined below, compare the original holiday with the new one, and make some brief notes about what you will say to the customer. Then explain to the customer the change and the reason for the change to the holiday. Allow the customer time to express their immediate reaction, show empathy with the customer and deal effectively with any objections raised.

Los Alimos

In a central position overlooking the sandy beach, which is accessible across a busy road, only 200 metres walk from the town centre, a comfortable hotel with friendly staff, in a good position close to all the resort facilities.

Facilities – swimming pool, sun terrace, sun beds payable locally, games room, table tennis, volley ball, two lounges, two bars, restaurant and shops.

Entertainment – live music five days a week, free disco, weekly folklore shows.

Meals – all meals buffet style.

Price – based on half board in a twin room with bath, shower and balcony, with radio, telephone and satellite TV.

Official rating – 4 stars.

Los Gigantes

30 metres away from a sandy beach, a fifteen-minute walk from the resort centre, the hotel is right on the seafront and offers very comfortable accommodation in a quiet and relaxing location.

Facilities – swimming pool, sun terrace and garden, free sunbeds and umbrellas, lounge, coffee shop, two bars, restaurant with buffet and waiter service, pool table.

Entertainment – weekly flamenco show, entertainment programme, daily happy hour.

Meals – buffet-style breakfast, dinner – first course buffet style and main course with waiter service.

Price – based on half board in a twin room with bath, shower, balcony and sea view.

Official rating – 4 stars.

4

....

Handling customer complaints

The previous chapters of this book have outlined the guidelines for creating a professional relationship with the customer – providing a good standard of service and identifying customer needs in order to sell them a suitable product. However, even with this expertise there will still be occasions when the customer is not happy, either with the service provided, or with the product that was sold. In either of these cases, the customer may feel the desire to lodge a complaint. As part of your NVQ assessment, you will be expected to demonstrate an ability to handle customer complaints effectively and reach a satisfactory conclusion for all parties. This chapter aims to provide you with some practical guidelines for dealing with customer complaints and maintaining customer goodwill.

Objectives

Once you have read this chapter of the book you should be able to:
- identify the true nature of a complaint
- identify whether a complaint is valid
- act on behalf of the customer if the complaint is against a supplier
- negotiate with the customer and supplier to reach a satisfactory conclusion.

WHAT IS A COMPLAINT?

Before discussing the best way to handle a complaint, we must first consider exactly what a complaint is. Is it a casual comment made by the customer indicating dissatisfaction with an aspect of the way their enquiry was handled, or an adverse comment about the layout of the shop, or the way the telephone was answered? Or is a complaint more formal than this? Perhaps a complaint should be classified as a formal letter of complaint, or an irate customer who is very vocal in expressing their dissatisfaction. But if we only view a complaint as a complaint when it gets to this stage, then how proactive have we been in ensuring that a good standard of service has been provided at all times? If a customer has reason to make an adverse comment, however minor, then this must indicate that there is room for improvement in the service that was provided.

If you refer back to the statistics, given in Chapter 1, regarding the number of dissatisfied customers who actually make a point of complaining, you will see that they are actually very few. Only 5 per cent of dissatisfied customers complain, the other 95 per cent will not complain directly to the provider of the service, but they will tell other people about it. It is for this reason, that every adverse comment should be treated as a complaint, and appropriate action to placate the customer should be taken.

....

Assignment   1 From your own experience at work, make a list of the following:
  (a) customers that have made a formal complaint about a product or the service they have received
  (b) customers who have passed an adverse comment or seemed dissatisfied.

2 Now ask your colleagues to tell you about their own experiences.

....

It is very likely that you will only remember the customers who made formal complaints. Most people have a tendency to disregard passing comments of dissatisfaction and only consider them to be a complaint when either the customer becomes very angry or writes a formal letter expressing their dissatisfaction. But consider this: if you had just 10 people in the whole year who expressed some dissatisfaction, but did not formally complain, and therefore their comments were not followed up, statistically, they will between them have told at least 90 other people about the poor standard of service they have received. This means that in one year at least 100 people would have a low opinion of the standard of service that your company provides, and you won't even realise it. This provides a very strong argument for acknowledging any comment of customer dissatisfaction, however minor, as a complaint. Prompt action to rectify the situation, even if only by way of an apology, will go a long way to enhance the reputation your company has of looking after its customers and listening to what they have to say about the service that you provide.

WHY IS IT IMPORTANT THAT COMPLAINTS ARE HANDLED EFFECTIVELY?

When a customer makes a complaint, they are doing so because they are unhappy with the service or product they have received and wish further action to be taken. This action need not be compensation, in fact if it is a complaint about service, it is more likely that the customer wants their rights to be acknowledged and an assurance made that action will be taken to prevent a reoccurrence of the situation in the future. Whatever the nature of the complaint, the one thing the customer will always expect is some form of action, whether it be an apology or an explanation, and will be most dissatisfied if this does not happen. A customer who complains and receives prompt action and is quickly able to reach a satisfactory conclusion will usually praise the way that the complaint was handled, and this will negate any ill-feeling that was caused by the issue which initiated the customer's complaint. However, when a customer has cause for complaint, and is then dissatisfied with the way the complaint was dealt with, they then have two causes for complaint – the issue which caused the initial dissatisfaction and the poor response they received subsequently.

CASE STUDY

Mark works in a travel agency which deals with both commercial and retail travel. The office is usually very busy and the staff are expected to deal with a variety of enquiries and are usually under some pressure to complete their work on time. One morning Mark is busy at his desk, when a customer approaches him. Mark does not recall having seen him before, but the customer's body language and facial expressions indicate that he is very angry. He throws down an airline ticket on Mark's desk.

'I tried to come back from Paris with this yesterday, but the flight times written on it are wrong, and I missed my flight. I had to buy another ticket to come home. What are you going to do about it?'

Mark looks at the ticket and sees, with some relief, that the ticket was issued by his colleague. 'Well, this isn't my booking,' he replies. 'You need to speak to Jane.'

'I don't care who made the booking,' retorts the customer, 'I just want to know what you are going to do about it!'

Mark is beginning to look uncomfortable and is looking for a way out of this increasingly unpleasant situation. 'Well, you really need to speak to Jane,' he says, 'I can't comment on what she has done. Did you reconfirm your return flight with the airline?'

'Why should I do that?' asks the customer. 'As I far as I was aware the flight was confirmed.'

Mark looks somewhat relieved. 'Ah, but that's not the point,' he says. 'You're supposed to reconfirm your flight timings with the airline. If you had done that, you would have been aware of the change in flight times.'

The customer looks ready to explode. 'This flight didn't change, it didn't exist. How dare you try to blame me for your own incompetence. Who's in charge here? I want to speak to the manager.'

In this situation, a customer who was already angry at an error which appeared to have been made by the travel agent was made even more angry by Mark's attitude towards him. First, Mark tried to avoid becoming involved with the problem by suggesting to the customer that he needed to speak to his colleague who had made the booking. When the customer refused, he then tried to blame the customer for not checking his return flight times. Mark has exacerbated the problem and now the customer has two causes for complaint. Even if the manager is able to resolve the problem, he may not be able to convince the customer that he should continue to use the services of the agency.

What should Mark have done?

Initially Mark should have apologised for the inconvenience caused to the customer. Note 'inconvenience'. It would not be appropriate at this stage to apologise for any error, since it may not be apparent where the error lies. Mark should have shown a willingness to assist the customer even though he had not been involved in the booking himself. As far as the customer was concerned, the error was made by the company, and any representative of that company should act on its behalf to help solve the problem. Mark should have asked the customer to explain exactly what happened, and then acted accordingly. Under no circumstances should he have blamed the customer for any of his actions.

Let the customer have their say

If you had been the customer in the case study, think about how you would have felt at the airport when you realised that an error had been made, and the emotions you would have experienced when you discovered that the only way you would be able to get home would be to purchase another ticket. You would have probably felt extreme anger at the apparent incompetence of the travel agent who made your booking for you. You would have rehearsed in your mind the tirade you intended to launch on the travel agent the next morning. On your way to the agency the following day, your adrenalin would have increased as you rehearsed once again what you would say and by the time you are actually standing in front of the travel agent's desk, you will be at boiling point. All of the anger and frustration at the previous day's events are pent up inside you and you have to let go. Once the agent acknowledges you, an overwhelming urge to let out all of your emotions takes over any normal rational approach you might adopt in this situation, and all of the emotion comes rushing out.

This is a perfectly normal reaction to this kind of situation. If you are faced with an angry customer with a complaint, then the best thing to do is to let them vent their anger. The customer needs to let go of all of the pent up emotion before they will be able to discuss the matter rationally. Sometimes this may be a little frightening, but if it does happen to you, just try to remember that it is a natural reaction, and that you might have behaved in exactly the same way if you had been the customer. If you try and stop the customer by interrupting or disagreeing with what is being said, this will only make matters worse.

Assignment   Think about situations where you have had cause to make a complaint. How did the person you spoke to respond to your comments? What action was taken to resolve the problem. How satisfied were you with the outcome? In view of the way your complaint was dealt with, would you recommend the company to any of your friends or family?

ESTABLISHING THE NATURE OF THE COMPLAINT

In the earlier case study, the travel agent made no attempt to question the customer about the incident and did not locate the file or analyse the facts available. Had he done so, the customer would probably have considered the agent's approach more acceptable, and the reason for the error may have been identified. It may even have transpired that the travel agent had acted in good faith on the information given by the airline, thus exonerating them from any blame. Whenever a complaint is received, the first step in trying to resolve the matter is to establish the facts.

Assignment   1 If you had been in Mark's position, what questions might you have asked the customer to establish the facts?

2 What other information might have been available to you, to help clarify exactly what happened?

Questioning skills are a very important part of the fact-finding process at this stage of a complaint. You need to be absolutely clear in your own mind exactly what the complaint is about and what happened at each stage. Skilful questioning will also help the customer to focus on the issue and may relieve some of the tension of the situation. There will of course be the occasional customer who may take exception to being questioned in this way, but they are a rarity, and most people, once they realise that you are trying to help, will be cooperative.

As you are discussing the problem with the customer you should maintain good eye contact and positive body language. Leaning slightly towards the customer and nodding at appropriate points will show that you are listening and that you are concerned about the customer's problem. When appropriate, it is a good idea to make some notes. These can be referred to later on and will help to ensure that there was no misunderstanding between you and the customer – it will also demonstrate to the customer that you intend to do something about the problem. Once you feel that you have all of the information you need from the customer, you should then explain what will happen next. This may be that you need to investigate the matter further with other parties, or refer the complaint to a higher authority who will then contact the customer direct.

Some customers choose not to visit you in person, but instead will write a letter of complaint. A letter of complaint will usually catalogue the series of events that have led up to the complaint, but even so, you may need to do some further investigation to obtain the full story.

CASE STUDY

Elaine arrived at work looking forward to the day ahead. She was hoping to confirm a large group booking that she had spent a considerable amount of time working on. She sorted through her mail which contained invoices and travel tickets, but at the bottom of the pile, was the following letter:

Dear Miss Jenkins

I am writing to complain about the recent holiday that you arranged for me to Rhodes, which was far from your recommendation of a relaxing holiday.

Our outward flight was delayed by seven hours which meant that we completely lost the first day of our holiday, and when we did finally board the aircraft, there was no apology for delay, and the staff were extremely rude and unhelpful. When we did eventually arrive at our hotel, there was a noisy party going on in the bar next door which made it impossible for us to sleep.

The hotel was situated on the beach, as the brochure describes, but we were unable to swim, as the sea was full of jellyfish. This was not stated in the brochure, and rather defeated the object of choosing a beachside hotel. We were therefore forced to use the hotel pool which, although of a good size, was in shade after about eleven o'clock in the morning, except for one small area which seemed to have been claimed by people who were up before sunrise every morning.

The resort was not what we expected either. Good food was very difficult to find, the shops were very expensive, and an area to the west of the harbour had a great deal of building work going on which was very noisy and unattractive.

We had looked forward to this holiday for some time, and both my wife and I needed to relax, as I believe we made quite clear to you at the time of booking. Instead we spent a miserable two weeks which caused my wife considerable stress and I am therefore looking for recompense for this disastrous so-called holiday.

Yours faithfully

Mr M Banks

Elaine felt hot and flustered. She had obviously sold Mr Banks a totally unsuitable holiday. She pushed the letter to one side to give herself a little time to calm down.

She would have to speak to her manager about this, and it looked as though it might cost the company a great deal of money.

Receiving a letter written in an accusatory manner such as this one, is never pleasant, and it is understandable that Elaine felt badly when she read it. But if we take a closer look at the content of the letter, we can see that it is very subjective in its tone and actually states very few facts about the problems experienced by the customer which were within either the travel agent's or the operator's control.

Read through the letter again, and make a note of each of the issues about which Mr Banks complains. Based purely on the information contained in the letter, which of the issues he raises do you feel are a genuine case for compensation?

Later on that morning Elaine took the letter to her manager. As he read through the letter, he didn't become angry as Elaine had expected, but instead a smile passed over his face.

'Let's take a look at the file, Elaine.'

Elaine handed it to him.

'Do you remember this customer?' he asks.

Elaine replied that she did.

'Did you recommend this holiday to him, or was it his own choice?'

Elaine thought for a moment and then replied that the customer had come into the agency having already made the choice.

'Well, I don't think you have anything to worry about, Elaine. You're not responsible for anything that's in this letter. There may be one or two points that we could take up with the operator, but I don't think he'll get much from them. Leave it with me, Elaine. I'll phone the operator later on today and ask them if they've had any other complaints about the hotel, and then I'll contact Mr Banks myself.'

Elaine's manager was able to view the complaint in a calm and objective manner, which enabled him to separate the facts from subjective views about the holiday over which neither the operator nor the travel agent had any control. This does not mean to say that the manager will dismiss the complaint entirely, but he will be able to calmly analyse any further information he receives from the tour operator, before he makes contact with the customer. The way the complaint proceeds from there on will very much depend on what further information comes to light.

RESPONDING TO THE COMPLAINT

All staff who have contact with the customer have a responsibility to deal effectively with the first stage of the complaint, i.e. either to placate the angry customer in front of them and to obtain some background information as to the nature of the complaint, or to receive written complaints and gather relevant information from customer files and records. From this point on, the way in which the response to the complaint is handled is very much dependent on company policy for dealing with complaints.

Assignment for non-supervisory staff

1 What is your company policy on dealing with customer complaints?

2 What type of complaint or customer dissatisfaction is it within your authority to deal with on your own?

3 If you receive a complaint from a customer regarding the quality of the product purchased, at what stage should you hand the complaint over to a supervisor or manager?

4 Make a few notes of your own if you are able to, and then discuss each point with your manager. Ensure that you are both quite clear on the parameters of your responsibility when dealing with any type of complaint.

Assignment for supervisors and managers

1 What is your company policy for dealing with complaints?

2 What is your company procedure for recording complaints and monitoring their progress?

3 Which types of complaint or customer dissatisfaction would you expect your staff to deal with without reference to you?

4 Which types of complaint would you wish your staff to transfer to you to deal with personally?

5 Discuss each of the above points with your staff to ensure that your company's complaints policy is understood by all concerned. If no written document to this effect exists within your company, you may like to discuss its formulation with a person of authority within the company.

It is assumed that in most cases, company policy will dictate that it is the responsibility of the manager, supervisor or some other person of authority to deal with any formal complaints beyond the initial contact with the customer. The following pages are therefore aimed at managers and supervisors, but non-supervisory staff may also find the information of interest.

COMPLAINTS AGAINST A PROVIDER

Many of the complaints you receive will probably be against a provider of travel services, this may be an airline, a tour operator, hotel, etc. Whichever it is, the following is a suggestion for dealing with this type of complaint in a professional manner which maintains the goodwill of the customer.

As was discussed earlier, the first course of action should be to gather some basic information from the customer as to the nature of the complaint. Once it has been established that there is a genuine case for lodging a complaint against the provider, the customer should then be asked to write a factual account of the complaint and any action which was taken by the customer or the provider at the time to try and resolve the issue. For example, if the complaint was against the standard of hotel accommodation, what was done in the resort to try and rectify the problem. Once the formal letter of complaint has been received, the manager should acknowledge this in writing to the customer and explain what will happen next, e.g.

Dear Mr Jackson

Re: Car hire from Malaga Airport 22 June

Thank you for your letter regarding your difficulties with the above car rental reservation. I have passed a copy of your letter, together with my own to the customer services department of . . . Car Rentals of which a copy is enclosed.

I expect to receive a reply from the company within the next fourteen days at which time I will contact you with whatever information I have available.

If you wish to discuss the matter further, please do not hesitate to contact me.

Yours sincerely

Helen Stanton
Manager

Once this letter has been sent to the customer, then a note should be made to check on the progress of the complaint within the time-scale stated. If no reply has been received, then further communication with the provider will be necessary and the customer informed of the progress so far, even if this is only to say that no reply has yet been received.

When a reply has been received, it should be passed on to the customer. If the provider has made an offer of compensation, then it is up to the customer to decide whether or not this is acceptable. If it is not, you may either ask the customer to write a letter to this effect or take up the negotiations on the customer's behalf. The action you choose at this stage will depend very much on your own company policy on dealing with customer complaints. If you or the customer are unable to come to a satisfactory agreement with the operator, then you may advise the customer to take the matter to the appropriate industry body.

COMPLAINTS AGAINST A MEMBER OF STAFF

When you receive a complaint of this nature, a careful balance needs to be achieved between maintaining customer goodwill and maintaining a loyalty to one's own staff. While it would be inappropriate to tell a customer that no member of staff of yours would behave in such a way as they have described, or would not have made such an error as they claim, it would be equally inappropriate to criticise or condemn your member of staff. A manager who states, 'Well, that's Mary for you. She can't ever be trusted to pass on messages' only serves to demonstrate that he has failed to train his or her staff and ensure that minimum standards of performance are achieved. This will give the aggrieved customer a very poor impression of the way that the company is run.

If you do receive a complaint against a member of staff, you should try and remain as objective as possible and question the customer to obtain the true facts of what happened. Once you have done this, you need to speak to the member of staff concerned to hear their side of the story. You will not be in a position to comment or take any further action until this is done. Even if you have strong suspicions of your own as to what actually happened, in fairness to both parties, you should follow this process.

Once you have obtained the facts from your member of staff, you need to respond to the customer. Depending on your company policy, you may choose to write or to telephone or to do both. When you do respond, choose your words carefully. Remember that your objective, whether the complaint was valid or not, is to maintain customer goodwill. A poorly worded response will not achieve this objective.

....

CASE STUDY

Mrs Leonard called into her travel agent, complaining that when she had booked her airline ticket to Madrid, she had asked if it was possible to alter her return date as she would not be sure of her plans until after she had travelled. She says that the clerk who served her, Julia Barrett, had assured her that it was in order to change the ticket without penalty. She made her booking, collected her tickets and travelled to Madrid the following month. Three days before her booked return journey, she telephoned the airline to change her flight to the following week. The airline told her that the ticket she was holding did not permit a change of travel date, and that the only way to alter her arrangements was to buy another ticket. Mrs Leonard was anxious not to incur any further expenses, so returned on her originally booked flight.

The complaint was passed to the manager of the agency, who spoke to Julia about the booking. Julia was quite adamant that Mrs Leonard made no such request. Below is the letter that the manager wrote to Mrs Leonard in response to her complaint.

Dear Mrs Leonard

I am writing to you regarding your complaint against my member of staff, Julia Barrett.

I have discussed your accusations with Julia, who assures me that at no time during her discussions with you, was any reference made to the possibility of changing the return date of travel.

The ticket which Julia issued to you, clearly states that reservations cannot be changed and refunds cannot be made. I therefore fail to see why this did not come to your notice until after you had made your outbound journey.

I am sorry that you were not happy with the service that you received in your dealings with our company, but I can assure you that I am confident that all of my staff provide a professional service to our customers at all times.

Yours sincerely

Malcolm Black
Manager

When Mrs Leonard received this letter she was very angry. She had not expected to get very far with her complaint as she was well aware that it was her word against the travel clerk's. Her objective in complaining was to express her dissatisfaction and to ensure that no misunderstandings of this type occurred again. She was not expecting any recompense, and an apology for any misunderstanding would have been quite sufficient. However, the tone of the letter from the manager was rather provocative, and she felt that it was attacking her right as a customer to express dissatisfaction. Mrs Leonard was in fact more angry with the response to her complaint than she was about the complaint itself, and decided that she would contact the Managing Director of the company and complain about the tone of the letter she had received.

....

A complaint of this nature is very difficult to investigate since it is the word of a customer against the word of an employee. If there are no notes to the contrary on the file and no other member of staff was involved in the booking or recalls anything about it, there is little more the manager can do than to take what his member of staff says at face value. However, in the case study, while it would have been incorrect of the manager to admit liability, the letter should have been written in a more sympathetic manner explaining that there must have been some misunderstanding between the customer and the member of staff, and offering an apology for the inconvenience suffered by the customer. This shows the manager's intention to maintain customer goodwill and admits that perhaps communication was not as good as it might have been, but it accepts no responsibility for a mistake. Once this matter is settled, it would be wise for the manager to review the accepted procedure of ensuring that customers are advised clearly and fully of all restrictions that apply to airline tickets purchased and to note on the customer file that this has been done. A check of this kind will help to ensure that customers are informed of such restrictions and will serve to clarify the history of the booking.

NEGOTIATING WITH THE CUSTOMER

In the previous case there was some doubt over whether an error had been made or not, but there may be occasions where there is no doubt at all that a member of your staff has made a mistake. In this instance it will be necessary to admit liability and to negotiate compensatory payment as appropriate.

Depending on the seriousness of the error, you may choose either to write to the customer stating your offer of compensation, or you may choose to telephone and discuss the matter in person. Dealing with the customer over the phone requires a greater degree of negotiating skills as you may need to bargain with the customer to reach a satisfactory outcome. That said, if you feel confident enough to negotiate in this way, it will create a more professional image to the customer, than receiving an offer by letter.

Basic guidelines for negotiation

1 Decide in what form the compensation is to be. Is it an *ex gratia* payment, a reduction on the price of the product, a free extra to go with the product, i.e. free car hire for the duration, or an amount off the customer's next purchase. Examine each of these alternatives carefully. It obviously makes more business sense to offset the compensation against something else than to actually pay out an amount of money.
2 Before you negotiate, decide what is the most you are prepared to offer.
3 Decide what is the least you could reasonably offer the customer without being insulting.
4 When you make your initial offer, do so confidently. If the customer detects any hesitance in your voice, they may realise that there is more on offer.
5 If the customer tries to negotiate a higher amount and you feel it necessary to comply in order to maintain customer goodwill, be careful of the way in which you increase the offer, e.g. if you have offered £50 off the cost of their next holiday and you are in fact prepared to go up to £100, your increasing offers should diminish in value. So if you start with an offer of £50, your next offer should be say for £75, then if necessary, £85, followed by £90. The customer will realise that the increase is diminishing and will probably stop negotiating before you reach your ceiling. If you steadily increase your offer by ten pounds each time, the customer is more inclined to keep going, since every time he rejects your offer, it increases by the same amount, giving no indication what your ceiling is.
6 Once you have reached a satisfactory compensatory arrangement, you should write to the customer stating what has been agreed.

Summary of the main points of this section

- Any comment of customer dissatisfaction should be treated as a complaint.
- Customers are just as concerned with the way the complaint is dealt with as they are with the outcome of the complaint itself.
- If the customer is angry, let them have their say.
- Investigate the full facts of the complaints.
- Respond to the customer in an appropriate manner.
- When appropriate, negotiate a settlement.

5

....

Written communication

In the travel industry, written communication is as important as telephone and face-to-face conversation. Many people find that writing what they mean is very much more difficult than saying what they mean and, just like the spoken word, there is an art in choosing the correct written word. As part of your NVQ assessment you will be expected to demonstrate your competence at writing business letters and memorandums. This chapter aims to provide you with the necessary skills to meet this requirement.

OBJECTIVES

Once you have read this chapter of the book you should be able to:
- **write business letters using appropriate business language**
- **use appropriate grammar and punctuation in a business letter**
- **present written communication in a professional manner**
- **make your message clear through written communication**
- **use memorandums as an effective form of internal communication.**

WHEN SHOULD YOU USE WRITTEN COMMUNICATION?

In business, written communication should be used whenever it is necessary that information is recorded, rather than just communicated verbally. Booking confirmations are a good example: even though the details of the reservation have been discussed and agreed verbally, the purpose of the booking confirmation is to give the customer written details of what has been agreed. This provides a written record for future reference and gives the opportunity for any misunderstandings or errors to be identified and then rectified. If no written confirmation was received by the customer, and a misunderstanding, such as date of travel, had occurred, it would be very difficult to prove any error. It is also very necessary in order to keep full records and documentation of transactions and agreements.

Internal memorandums are used extensively in business to advise employees of various pieces of information. By having the information presented to them in writing, there is less likelihood of a misunderstanding, providing the memo is well written, and all recipients have something which they can refer to in the future should they need to. Sometimes complex information is presented in written form, because it is easier to read and comprehend such information than it is to decipher a message given verbally. Imagine trying to make sense of your job description if it had been presented to you verbally instead of in writing; it would have been very difficult to understand, and almost impossible to remember. Messages of this type are often clearer when in writing rather than in the spoken word. The more complex the message, the greater the need to put it in writing.

Finally, do remember that some documents need to be in writing as a legal requirement. A signed booking form, for example, is a written contract between the customer and the provider. Without it there is no proof that the customer agreed to the terms and conditions stated by that provider.

HOW IS WRITTEN COMMUNICATION DIFFERENT FROM VERBAL COMMUNICATION?

While the same request or item of information could be conveyed either verbally or in writing, the language of the communication is quite different. Although some verbal communication is very formal, as a rule it is never as structured as the content of written communication – verbal communication is usually quite spontaneous. For example, if a customer was to telephone you and ask for some information about a certain destination, the request might be: 'We were thinking of going to Canada next year, I was wondering if you had any brochures? We were thinking of starting the holiday in Toronto and making our way across country, probably finishing up somewhere like Calgary. Do you have anything that would cover that sort of thing, or is it too far to drive?'

This request is quite acceptable in a verbal form, but imagine what you would think if you had received the request by letter, which used the same words as had been used in the verbal request.

10th October 1994

Dear Sirs,

We were thinking of going to Canada next year, I was wondering if you had any brochures? We were thinking of starting the holiday in Toronto and making our way across country, probably finishing up somewhere like Calgary.

Do you have anything that would cover that sort of thing, or is it too far to drive?

Yours faithfully

S. C. Graham

If you had received this through the post, you would probably consider it a very poorly written letter. The manner is inappropriate to written communication, and the instructions are not clear. Does the writer want a reply stating whether or not you have this information, or is a request for the information to be sent? If Mr Graham had decided to write to you asking for this information, a more appropriate tone may have been as follows:

10th October 1994

Dear Sirs,

I am considering planning a trip to Canada in the spring of next year and was wondering if you could provide me with some information.

My intention is to fly from London to Toronto and to spend four weeks travelling across Canada, ending in Calgary. I had considered the possibility of taking a fly-drive holiday, and wondered if any company was able to provide a holiday of this sort. If this is not possible, perhaps you would advise me what alternative arrangements I could make.

I would be very grateful if you would send me whatever information you have to my business address.

Yours faithfully

S. C. Graham

The language used in this letter is much more appropriate to written communication. It is more formal, and makes it quite clear what the customer is asking for, and provides specific instructions as to what action he would like you to take. To respond properly to the first letter, you would have needed more information. The first letter is inappropriate because the language is meant for the ear and lends itself to conversation where one person is listening and is expected to answer immediately. The second letter, however, is more appropriate because it is written for the eye, i.e. to read. Written communication is strictly one way and there will be a delay in the reply. This means that unlike verbal communication, the recipient cannot clarify any points which have been made, unless they make the effort to contact you in person, and sometimes poorly written communication can be misinterpreted with disastrous consequences.

Assignment Imagine that you need to write to a friend giving them instructions on how to drive from your house to your office.

Assume that they do not know the area, and compile a set of written instructions, which will ensure they make the journey without getting lost. You may not include any maps or drawings in your instructions, but you will need to ensure that your instructions enable the reader to visualise the journey.

THE LAYOUT OF A LETTER

When writing business letters, you need to adopt an accepted format. Some companies have a house style in which all letters are to be addressed. If no house style exists, individuals may adopt the layout they learnt as part of a typing or word-processing course. The precise layout of your letter is not that important providing that it is acceptable to your company and promotes a businesslike image, but whatever particular layout you choose, the following should be included in a business letter as appropriate:

1 The date
2 A reference
3 The address of the person to whom you are writing
4 The address of the person sending the letter
5 The salutation
6 The heading
7 The body of the letter
8 The close
9 The signatory
10 The position the signatory holds within the company
11 Notification of an enclosed document.

An example layout of a letter is shown in Fig. 5.1, and a description of each numbered item thereon is given below:

1 *The date*
   In this letter the date is placed at the very top of the letter, but it could also be placed underneath the address of the person to whom the letter is addressed. In this case the date is expressed as 3rd February 1994. It could also be expressed as 3 February 1994. Letters originating from other countries sometimes express their dates with the month first, February 3rd 1994. Never express a date in a letter numerically, 03/02/94.

2 *The reference*
   This is not always necessary to include in a letter, but will often appear at the top of a business communication where a secretary has typed the letter. In this case the reference PS/ft indicates that the letter was typed for Pat Sayer (PS) by Fiona Thomson (ft) the secretary. Other forms of reference may be reference numbers as appropriate.

① 3rd February 1994

② Ref: PS/ft

③ Mr J Knowles
Ashbrook
Holly Lane
Epsom
Surrey

④ T&E Tours Ltd
151 High Street
Croydon
Surrey
CR0 27Y

⑤ Dear Mr Knowles

⑥ Re: GROUP BOOKING TO LIVIGNO, 22nd MARCH 1994

⑦ With reference to the above booking, I am happy to enclose your revised confirmation which confirms the name changes effected on 22nd January. All other details remain the same.

I am expecting to receive tickets for the group within the next two weeks, and will forward these on to you once they have been checked.

If you have any queries regarding the confirmation, please do not hesitate to contact me.

⑧ Yours sincerely

Fiona Thomson
⑨ (pp. signature of Fiona Thomson)

Patricia Sayer
⑩ Travel Consultant

⑪ Enc.

Fig. 5.1   An example layout of a letter

3 *The address of the person to whom you are writing*
This should always appear on the left-hand side of the letter. If you are using a window envelope, ensure that the address is lined up correctly so that all of it appears through the envelope. Where this is common practice, business-headed paper often has four dots printed on it as a guideline within which the address should be typed.
4 *The address of the person or company sending the letter*
If you are using headed notepaper, this should be printed at the top of the paper in any case. In any other form of letter, where headed notepaper is not

used, such as a letter of acceptance of a job, the name and address of the respondent should appear on the right-hand side of the letter at about the same level as that of the address of the person to whom the letter is being sent.

5 *The salutation*

In this letter, the salutation is 'Dear Mr Knowles'. This is the appropriate salutation when the letter is addressed to a specific person. When the letter is addressed to a company or a department, and the name of the person who will receive the letter is not known, e.g. addressing a letter to the accounts department of a company, then the correct salutation would be 'Dear Sirs'. This is more acceptable than the salutation 'Dear Sir or Madam'.

6 *The heading of the letter*

It is common in a business letter to include a heading which indicates what the letter is about, in this case the heading is about a group booking to Livigno. The example layout given shows the heading typed in upper case, it is also acceptable to type the heading in upper and lower case providing it is underlined.

7 *The body of the letter*

The body of the letter should contain all of the information that the recipient requires. Your first line or paragraph should indicate in as short a space as possible the reason for writing the letter, e.g. 'I am writing to inform you of our acceptance of the change in our hotel accommodation'. If there has been previous correspondence, then refer to it in the first paragraph, e.g. 'Further to our letter dated 25th April . . . ' or if the letter is a follow-up to a telephone conversation, 'Further to our conversation this morning . . . '. If you have included a heading in your letter, then a good start to the letter is, 'With reference to the above . . . '.

Break up the letter into paragraphs. Each new subject or topic should be covered in a new paragraph. In the example letter, a line space is given between each paragraph. In this case, the start of each new paragraph is flush with the left-hand margin, but it is acceptable to indent the first word of each new paragraph, although this is now a less common form.

If a word processor is used to type the letter, there is a facility to 'right hand justify' the text. This means that the words on the right-hand margin line up so that the text is a block, as in the example letter. If 'right hand justify' is not used, then the text will appear with 'ragged ends'. This means that the words on the right hand margin do not line up. Some people consider that this does not look as tidy as right-hand justified work.

The last paragraph of your letter should bring the letter to a close. In the example letter the writer invites the respondent to contact her if there are any further queries. Other suitable closes may be 'I look forward to receiving your reply/confirmation/cheque' or 'I hope this answers all of your queries' or 'I would be grateful if you could contact me as soon as you have any further information' or 'Thank you for your interest in our company/product, etc.'.

8 *The close*

The close that is used in a letter is dependent on the salutation. In this case the salutation of 'Dear Mr Knowles' requires the close of 'Yours sincerely'. If the salutation had been 'Dear Sir or Sirs' the close would be 'Yours faithfully'.

9 *The signatory*

This letter states the signatory, the person who is signing the letter, as Patricia Sayer. Even when the signature is easy to read, it is good practice to also type the name of the signatory below the signature. There may be occasions when the person who has written the letter is not able to sign it themselves, perhaps they have dictated the letter, or have left a message for their secretary to send the letter in their absence. In this case, the person who typed the letter will sign on behalf of the person who it is from, putting 'pp' before their signature.

10 *The position of the signatory*

It is good practice to state your title after your name when signing a letter.

11 *Notice of an enclosed document*

Whenever you enclose another document with a letter the abbreviation, 'Enc.' should be added at the bottom of the letter to indicate to the recipient that they should expect to find another document enclosed.

PUNCTUATION

When writing a business letter, it is important that it is punctuated properly. Poor punctuation, or punctuation that is missing altogether, makes reading the letter difficult, and can sometimes change the meaning of a letter completely.

Here is a list of the most commonly used forms of punctuation and their uses:

- Full stop (.) – To be used at the end of every sentence or paragraph, and at the end of an abbreviated word. For example, cont., the abbreviation of continued.
- Comma (,) – To be used at the end of a phrase within a sentence, or at a point where it would be appropriate to take a natural pause: e.g. 'While every effort has been made to help with your enquiry, we feel your best course of action may be to contact the insurance company direct.' or 'Weekend departures, whether they are from Gatwick or Heathrow, carry a supplement of £20 per person.' Commas should also be used when writing a list of more than two items: e.g. 'You will need to attach luggage labels to your suitcases, golf clubs, and hand luggage.'
- Apostrophe (') – To indicate ownership, e.g., if Mary has her own desk, it is 'Mary's desk', the date of today is 'Today's date'. In both of these examples a possessive singular 's is used. A possessive plural, the apostrophe only, is used when added to a word which is a plural ending in an s, e.g. notice that requires seven days, is 'seven days' notice'. Possessive words which do not require an apostrophe are; his, hers, theirs, ours, yours and its. Apostrophes should also be used to indicate the omission of letters, e.g. shouldn't, wouldn't, can't and it's. 'It's' in this case indicates an abbreviation of 'It is', and is not the possessive form of 'it' which is expressed as 'its', e.g. 'The train makes its first stop at Clapham Junction'.
- Colon (:) – Are commonly used to introduce a list: e.g. 'Below are the items of clothing which you will need to take on a ski holiday: thick ski jacket, salopettes, T-shirts, thick socks, scarf, thick gloves.'
- Semi-colon (;) – Used to separate clauses in a sentence, e.g. European depar-

tures are from terminal two; international departures are from terminal three.
- Question mark (?) – Used at the end of a sentence which is a question: e.g. 'What is the cost of a return ticket from London to Aberdeen?' A question mark is not necessary after a request which is made in writing: e.g. 'Would you please telephone me on Thursday.'
- Inverted commas (' or ") – Used as speech marks, although it is extremely unlikely that a business letter would contain direct speech: e.g. He said, 'I'll post your cheque on Monday.' The other use for inverted commas, is to mark the importance of a special word or title: e.g. 'The information you require can be found in 'The ABC Guide to International Travel', under the section appertaining to that destination.' or 'I am not able to comment on whether this particular part of the resort is 'safe', but I can confirm that we have not received any notification of passengers who have experienced any difficulties in the area.'

Assignment   Punctuate and capitalise where required the following letter:

Dear Sirs

I am writing to you in connection with the advertisement you carried in the local paper the Herald dated 22nd April regarding your proposed trip to Eurodisney my wife and I would be very interested in the trip and have the following questions are the entrance fees into Disney included if not what is the cost per person what standard of hotel is the one featured in your tour and how far away is it from the Disney complex we intend to travel with our two sons aged ten and twelve can you please advise me of the reductions whilst we are in France we would also like to spend a few days in Paris would it be possible for you to send me details of any hotels that you would recommend in the Opera region ideally we are looking for a three-star hotel.

Yours faithfully

Mr K Longman

CREATING A PROFESSIONAL IMAGE

It is important that any business correspondence projects a professional image of your company. A customer who receives a well-written business letter from you, which is well laid out and properly punctuated without any spelling mistakes will probably think nothing of it. But if they notice anything wrong in the letter, they may consider that if you can make simple errors like this in a letter, you would probably not be too careful in your attention to detail in your other work.

CASE STUDY

Mrs Giles had been dealing with her local travel agent for a number of years and had made at least one booking with them every summer. She had, on occasion, felt that perhaps they were not as diligent as they might be, and one or two minor errors had been made over the years, but nevertheless they were the only travel company in the area, and on the whole the service was not too bad.

This morning a letter arrived for Mrs Giles from the agency (see Fig. 5.2). Mrs Giles was not impressed to receive this letter and felt that as a 'valued customer' who had been booking with the company for a considerable amount of time, they could at least have taken the trouble to spell her name correctly. It would appear that someone had glanced through the letter, by the fact that the spelling of her address had been altered, but Mrs Giles felt that having noticed an error like that, the letter should have been retyped. Altering a letter by hand in this way was most unprofessional.

Mrs Giles read through the rest of the letter, and noticed with some irritation, that there was a spelling mistake. The company had booked her 'two paces' instead of 'two places'. She was hardly surprised. Mrs Giles threw the letter away. She had no intention of attending the presentation on Sri Lanka. If the standard of the letter was anything to go by, she didn't hold out too much hope for a well-planned,

---

22 April 1994

Mrs D Gill
~~24 Kollard Road~~   24 Kollard Road
LONDON
SW12 9AQ

Dear Mrs Gill

As a much valued customer, we would like to invite you to our special evening presentation on holidays to Sri Lanka.

Sri Lanka is an exciting destination, and we feel sure that you would be interested to learn more about it.

The presentation will be held at our offices on Tuesday the 17th May at seven thirty in the evening. We have reserved two paces for you and your husband, and very much look forward to seeing you then.

Yours sincerely

Mrs J Barrett
Manager

Fig. 5.2   Case study letter

professional presentation. But more importantly, the letter served to confirm Mrs Giles's feelings about the company's lack of attention to detail. If they couldn't even write a letter without several careless errors in it, how did that reflect on the way they conducted their business? Mrs Giles decided that she wouldn't be using Intatravel again.

Mrs Giles's reaction to the letter is not untypical, especially if the recipient is in business themselves and is used to writing and receiving business letters.

- Always read through a letter *thoroughly* after it has been typed, and if there are any errors in it, they need to be corrected – but not by hand.
- Always check against your records that names and addresses are correctly spelt.
- Double check your spelling – never guess. If in doubt, look it up in the dictionary. If you are using a word processor which has an automatic spell-check on it, read the letter through anyway, as the spell-check will not pick up incorrect words, e.g. in the letter to Mrs Giles, a spell-check would not recognise 'paces' as a misspelling as 'paces' is a word in the dictionary.
- Always check and double check any letters before they leave your office. A badly written and presented letter says more about the company than the words written on the page.

MAIN TYPES OF LETTERS USED IN BUSINESS COMMUNICATION

Although there are many types of different letters which you may be required to write, for the purposes of the book these could be broken down into four main categories: a request, a response, a notification and an itinerary. As part of your NVQ assessment you will be expected to provide a number of examples of different types of letters that you have written on a variety of topics. On the next few pages, you will be given some examples of the layout and content of each of these types of letter and an opportunity to construct your own letters.

Letter of request. The letter in Fig. 5.3 clearly states what the request is and how the writer wishes the recipient to respond to the request. Clear indication is given as to the subject of the request. When writing a letter of this type, ensure that all the information the recipient needs is included in the letter and the request is self-explanatory. Always bear in mind the needs of the recipient when writing any letter.

Letter of response. In Fig. 5.4 the letter states at the beginning that it is in response to a request which has been received. It then sets out the response to the request. You will see that in this example the response has been set out under numeric headings. This is an acceptable way to present information and will help the recipient to clarify the information contained in the accompanying brochures.

Ref: MB/hr

2nd June 1994

Sunbright Holidays
Unit 3
North Park Industrial Estate
Crawley
West Sussex
RH10 5TE

Alton Travel
15 Lower Road
Bradford
BRA 7HG

Dear Sirs

Re: JACKSON × 4 DEPARTING 09 AUGUST 1994. Booking Ref GH5437S

With reference to the above booking, we would like to request a bouquet of flowers
to be placed in the client's room on the day of their arrival, accompanied by a note
reading 'With best wishes from all at Alton Travel'.

We understand that the cost of arranging flowers is £22.00 and would be grateful if
you could send us an invoice separate from the customer's invoice as they are to
know nothing of these arrangements.

For your information, this is the customers' honeymoon. We would therefore be
grateful if you would make every effort to ensure that their holiday is special.

Yours faithfully

Mike Bullen
Travel Consultant

Fig. 5.3   A request letter

Notification of change. The letter in Fig. 5.5, notifying a change to the
customer's holiday plans, goes into some detail to explain exactly what has
happened and how it will affect the customer's plans. It then goes on to explain
what options are open to the customers and what action they need to take and
when by. Note that no negative words are used in the letter such as
'unfortunately' or 'I'm afraid that . . . ' and no reference is made to a 'problem'.
When writing a letter like this, try to be factual and provide the customer with
as much information as possible on which they may base their decision.

An itinerary. When typing out an itinerary (see Fig. 5.6), it is important that
it is clear to the customer. Using headings for each column, as in this example,
makes the information clearer and easier to read. Setting out the details in
columns makes it appear tidy and well presented. By stating the arrival date and

Ref MB/hr

22 June 1994

Mr H Kettering
Rippon House
22 Martin Hill
Bradford
BRA 9GS

Alton Travel
15 Lower Road
Bradford
BRA 7HG

Dear Mr Kettering

In response to your recent request regarding information on cruises from Southampton, I am happy to enclose two brochures which you may find of some interest, each containing a suitable cruise.

1. Carousel Cruises. Cruise no. 423 which appears on page 24 of the brochure departs from Southampton on the 1st and 15th of September and visits the Canary Islands and Madeira. There is currently availability for all categories of cabin except court cabins on Marine Deck.

2. Estos Cruises. Cruise no. M34 on page 15 of the brochure. This cruise departs from Southampton on the 3rd and 18th of September and visits; Gibraltar, Majorca, Alicante, Corsica and Estoril. All cabin categories are available, and Estos are currently offering up to £200 off brochure price for cruises booked and paid for in full before the end of this month.

Alton Travel are agents for both of these companies and we would be more than happy to make all the necessary arrangements for your holiday. If you require any further assistance please do not hesitate to contact us.

Yours sincerely

Mike Bullen
Travel Consultant

Enc.

Fig. 5.4 A response letter

the number of nights accommodation booked, there is less room for misunderstanding when giving information regarding hotel accommodation. If the information was given as 04–06 April, this could be interpreted as arriving on the 4th and departing on the 6th, or for the nights of the 4th, 5th and 6th. Do take care when writing itineraries so that there can be no room for information being misinterpreted.

Ref MB/hr

15th May 1994

Mr and Mrs K Chester
45 Sandy Lane
Bradford
BRA 7JG

Alton Travel
15 Lower Road
Bradford
BRA 7HG

Dear Mr and Mrs Chester

Re: GOLDEN BAY HOTEL, MALTA

With reference to the above hotel, we have received notification from the tour operator with whom your holiday is booked, that the hotel has found it necessary to close the swimming pool for immediate repairs. The pool is not expected to re-open until December 1994.

The operator proposes to continue using the hotel, but we feel we must point out to you that as well as the obvious inconvenience of not being able to use the pool facilities, the building work is likely to cause a considerable amount of noise and possibly dust. As you have elected to have a sea-view room, which also overlooks the pool at the hotel, you may experience some inconvenience if using your balcony.

We have discussed the matter with the tour operator, who have agreed that under the circumstances they would be prepared to transfer you to another hotel of your choice which is featured in the brochure, at no additional charge to yourselves. I have checked availability for the dates you wish to travel and there are two very good four-star hotels in the area which currently have availability, The Atlantis and The Dolphin.

You are of course welcome to continue with your holiday at the Golden Bay if you so wish, but if you would prefer to transfer to another hotel then I would advise that we make the necessary arrangements as soon as possible.

I would be grateful if you would contact me by the end of this week to notify me of the decision you have reached.

Yours sincerely

Mike Bullen
Travel Consultant

Fig. 5.5   A notification of change letter

MB/hr

10th March 1994

Mr H Burke
DMS Printing Ltd
12a Buckland Avenue
Bradford
BRA WDE

Alton Travel
15 Lower Road
Bradford
BRA 7HG

Dear Mr Burke

Re: BUSINESS TRIP DEPARTING 30TH MARCH 1994

With reference to the above, I have pleasure in enclosing your travel documents together with invoice no 12/302.

All of your reservations have been confirmed and your itinerary is as follows:

Date	From/To	Flight no	Check in	Departs/Arrives
31/03/94	Heathrow/Milan	AZ342	09.20	10.20/13.00
01/04/94	Milan/Rome	AZ098	17.50	18.30/19.15
04/04/94	Rome/Turin	AZ221	15.10	15.50/16.30
06/04/94	Turin/Heathrow	AZ301	16.05	17.05/18.45

Hotel accommodation:

Date	Duration	Hotel	Address
31/03/94	1 night	Raffaello	Viale Raffaello, Viale Certosa 108 20156, Milano
01/04/94	3 nights	Visconti	Via Federico Cesi, 37 (Piazza Cavour) 00193 Rome
04/04/94	2 nights	Ambasciatori	104 Corso Vittorio Emanuele 54 10121 Turin

If you have any queries regarding the above, please do not hesitate to contact me.

Yours sincerely

Mike Bullen
Travel Consultant

Enc.

Fig. 5.6   An itinerary

Assignment   Now put your letter-writing skills into practice. Choose at least two of the following:

1 A letter to a customer stating that a coach tour of the Scottish Highlands is no longer stopping at Gairloch, but an extra two days will be spent on the Isle of Skye. Total duration of the holiday remains the same. No additional cost will be incurred by the customer. Holiday no. SH512 departing 14th May. If the change is not acceptable to the customer, the operator will refund all monies paid in full.

2 Responding to a request from a customer regarding apartment holidays in Orlando for the summer of 1994. Include details of the type of accommodation available, its location and the cost.

3 A request to a hotel, tour operator, or overseas ground handling agent, requesting that customers are upgraded to a superior room at their hotel. Arrange for new invoices to be sent as confirmation.

4 An itinerary showing a proposed trip of your choice. The itinerary should include at least four different flights and three lots of hotel accommodation.

Write your letters in the style and format that have been explained in the previous pages, paying special attention to punctuation, spelling and layout of the letter. Once you have typed your letters out, ask your manager to check them through for you.

WRITING MEMORANDUMS

Memorandums, or memos, are a commonly used form of communication within organisations. They are an ideal way to ensure that the message has reached everyone concerned and that the staff have a written document to refer to in the future. Sometimes, companies can become top heavy with memos, with too much information communicated to the staff in this way. Memos are a good reference point and often back up verbally communicated information, but they should never replace the spoken word entirely. Sometimes the tone of a memo can be somewhat offensive if poorly written, giving the reader the impression that the memo has been written by way of a reprimand or, even worse, as a way of avoiding talking to the person concerned about a specific point, and instead issuing a dictat to all employees.

How would you feel if you received this memo?

INTERNAL MEMORANDUM

To: All Staff

From: David McAlpine

It has come to my notice that certain members of staff have been making a considerable number of personal calls during peak periods. This must stop.

Not only does this increase the company's phone bill by quite a considerable amount, but the time that is spent on idle chatter is time which would be better spent in doing the work that you are paid to do.

You are all aware of the slim margins that the company is working to, and every effort must be made to reduce our overheads. If this is not done, there may be some question over the level of salary increases this year, if indeed there are to be any increases at all.

Anyone found to be making personal calls without the express permission of their immediate supervisor will be severely reprimanded.

A memo of this kind is never pleasant to receive, especially if you were not a party to the conduct described in the memo. The tone of this memo is also very inappropriate, and will undoubtedly upset a few people and could be considered to be a demotivating factor. The writer obviously feels very strongly about the points he is making, but on this occasion has chosen the wrong method of communication. The memo states that 'certain individuals' have been guilty of making personal calls, so it would have been far better to have spoken to them individually about the problem. Then, if the writer still felt it necessary to send out a general memo, it should have been by way of an instruction rather than an order.

A more appropriate memo might have been:

INTERNAL MEMORANDUM

To: All Staff

From: David McAlpine

In an effort to reduce our overheads for the coming quarter, it has been necessary to review areas where staff could assist in bringing our spending in line with our income. One area which has been highlighted as a possible area where costs could be reduced is our telephone bill. I would therefore request that staff try to keep business calls made during peak time to a minimum, and refrain from making personal calls in peak time unless it is an emergency. With regards to personal calls, please try and keep these to as few as possible. If we all make an effort, it should be possible to reduce our bills quite considerably. I do not intend to pose any stringent regulations regarding personal calls, but if this initial drive fails to reduce our costs, I may have to consider further measures.

Guidelines for writing a memo

1 Use a standard format. Most companies have a standard format for writing memos. If no standard format exists within your company, then an accepted format is as shown in Fig. 5.7. An example memo is provided in Fig. 5.8.
2 If the information in this memo supersedes information in previous memos, this should be noted in the body of the memo with instructions to destroy previous memos as appropriate
3 Depending on your company policy, you may or may not wish to sign the memo.

INTERNAL MEMORANDUM

To: (State either the names of all the staff or departments who are to receive the memo.)

From: (The person who has issued the memo.)

Date: (The date the memo was issued.)

CC: (The names of any additional staff who are to receive copies.)

THE HEADING

(It will help staff to file memos if the heading makes it obvious what the memo refers to.)

. . . . **the subject-matter of the memo** . . . .

Fig. 5.7 An example format of a memo

> **To:**   All staff in reservations   **Date:** 7th December 1994
>   operations and administration.
>
> **From:** Debbie, Flight Controller   **CC:** RF, HJ.MN and GH
>
> ---
>
> ### RE: CHRISTMAS FLIGHTS TO TENERIFE
>
> Due to the usually high demand for seats over the Christmas period, our allocation to Tenerife is now full. However, due to the high number of requests that we are still receiving for Christmas availability, we have decided to charter an additional aircraft to meet these needs.
>
> From today, the new flight is available on our system and is as follows:
>
> 15 December 1994 LGW/TFS Dep 12.45 Arr 17.30 Flight no KT321
> 29 December 1994 TFS/LGW Dep 18.45 Arr 21.45 Flight no KT322
>
> This flight can be sold with any hotel accommodation still on allocation. Normal booking procedures apply.

Fig. 5.8 An example memo

....

Assignment   Issue an internal memo to your colleagues stating a new procedure in your office. You may choose what that procedure is. Follow the format for memos given above.

....

SUMMARY OF THE MAIN POINTS OF THIS CHAPTER

- Use appropriate business language when preparing written documentation.

When writing letters:
- Use a standard format for letter writing which should include the following as appropriate:
    1 The reference
    2 The date
    3 The address of the person to whom the letter is being sent
    4 The address of the person who is sending the letter
    5 The correct salutation, e.g. Dear Mr Jones, Dear Sirs
    6 The heading, i.e. to what the letter refers
    7 The body of the letter, separated into appropriate paragraphs
    8 The close, e.g. Yours faithfully or Yours sincerely

9 The name of the person who is sending the letter
10 The position held by that person
11 Notification of any enclosures.

- Use correct punctuation in the letter
- Ensure the presentation of the letter creates a professional image of the company.
- Check and double-check the spelling.

When writing memos:

- Use a standard format indicating: who the memo is to; the date of issue; who the memo is from; who else is to receive copies of the memo.
- Give the memo a heading indicating what the contents refer to.
- Ensure that the information contained in the memo is factual.

6

....

Making a public presentation

Standing up in front of a group to deliver a speech, or make a presentation, has long been considered one of the most stressful situations to be in. On a list of the most feared human predicaments, public speaking comes second only to the fear of dying. With this in mind, this chapter aims to provide you with practical tips and guidelines which will enable you to deliver a public presentation which is sharp, interesting and professional.

OBJECTIVES

Once you have read this chapter of the book you should be able to:
- **identify how nerves can effect the presentation**
- **use the voice to maximum effect during the presentation**
- **use body language to enhance your presentation**
- **make effective use of microphones**
- **plan and structure your presentation**
- **make effective use of visual aids**
- **state guidelines for effectively handling questions from the audience.**

So what is it about public speaking which not only robs us of our dignity, but turns normal, rational human beings into quaking, disorientated wrecks? Most participants on presentation skills training courses would say that the first manifestation of fear is the unavoidable attack of nerves which comes over them as they stand up in front of the group. Nearly every course participant feels this, whether or not the other group members are friends and colleagues, or completely unknown to them prior to the training course. Being nervous, though, is a necessary and very natural reaction; as you will learn in this section, a degree of nervousness is essential in any public speaking situation. Let's look closer at the reasons behind those initial nervous reactions.

There are many psychological fears which underscore the way we feel about getting up in front of a group. The greatest, and probably the most disturbing of these is one of the basic fears of life – the fear of failure. As you will learn in the next chapter of the book, which introduces you to assertiveness, this is one of a number of powerful emotions which follow us from early childhood all the way through our adult life, and which maintains a very strong grip on the predict-ability of the way we react to similar given situations. There is nothing new or radical in this view – we have felt the effects of these pressures for a very long time.

An interesting tale about a young David Livingstone demonstrates well the fear of speaking in public. Livingstone, before he became famous as an explorer, was invited to deliver a sermon to a large and select local church gathering. He duly accepted, and spent a worthy amount of his time preparing his speech and making himself ready for the big day. When the time came for him to take the pulpit and give his sermon, he walked slowly from his seat, climbed the little winding staircase which brought him to the lectern and looked out to face the entire church audience seated before him. His calm outward appearance, though, belied the panic he felt within, and Livingstone froze in absolute terror before the assembly. Agonising seconds ticked by as the audience stared up in antici-pation, until he realised that the sermon he had rehearsed so carefully was completely lost to his memory. Finally, he stood upright in the pulpit, looked out to the back of the church and said in a dignified voice, 'I am so sorry, ladies and gentlemen. I have forgotten everything that I wanted to say.' He then turned, left the pulpit, and walked from the church.

Thankfully, very few people experience the drastic effects of totally freezing before an audience as did the young David Livingstone. But, the one fear which confronts most of us in similar situations, and which is largely responsible for our nervousness, is the fear of failure – of saying the wrong thing, of doing the wrong thing, and of making fools of ourselves. This, then, is the most common trigger for our initial nervousness.

OVERCOMING THE FEAR OF PUBLIC SPEAKING

First, it is important to stress that not everyone feels all of the symptoms of general nervousness in a public speaking situation. Some of us will usually experience one or two of the effects of an attack of nerves at the outset but, happily, most speakers slip very quickly into a routine, and normal composure returns within a matter of seconds of standing up to speak. Having pre-presen-tation nerves is perfectly natural, but it is essential to have an understanding of why this happens in order to overcome the initial effects. Let's consider the outward effects of the inner nervousness we so often experience.

These effects can be divided up into body, voice and co-ordination, as follows:

Body
- perspiration, especially forehead and hands
- shaking, mainly of hands and knees
- shuffling of hands or feet
- constant fiddling with hair, jewellery and clothing

- avoiding eye contact with the audience
- set features and lack of smile

Voice
- drying out of throat and inside of the mouth
- rise in natural pitch
- quavering of voice
- gasping and breathlessness
- stuttering and stammering
- verbal mannerisms

Co-ordination
- rigidity and static stance
- uncontrollable swaying movements
- involuntary hand gestures
- dropping things and clumsiness
- drying up or grinding to a halt.

HANDLING NERVES

CASE STUDY

At an important industry training seminar a few years ago, I watched a presentation on car rental from a woman who represented a major car hire company. The venue was a rather large and imposing room, containing approximately 300 travel industry managers and owners, and speakers addressed the audience from a rostrum on the stage.

The speaker was introduced, she walked on to the rostrum and stood just about centre stage, having elected to wear a lapel-microphone which would enable freedom to move around and freedom of hand movement. It was an important meeting and, with so many important industry managers, the occasion gave a golden opportunity for principals to present and sell the benefits of their particular products. The woman was extremely nervous and, from her introduction, it became clear that she had either had no training, or that she was doing this for the very first time. She spoke, using cue cards (key words written on small cards) to guide her speech. This is one of the most useful methods of self-prompting, but it does require the speaker to follow the cards in a logical sequence. Anyway, our speaker had one very quick-forming habit during her presentation, and that was that she could not help herself playing with the cards, at first just fingering them, but then beginning to twist them and grip them as she began to transfer her nervousness to this convenient diversion.

Before long, it became obvious to the more experienced presenters in the audience that this nervous mannerism was beginning to take over and that, because the speaker was unaware that it was happening, she was unable to stop herself from twisting the cards more and more. All of a sudden, there was an audible crack, and the cards sprayed into the air and fell to the ground all around the speaker. In playing constantly with the cards, she had bent them back into a spring-coil, so that when she lost grip with one hand, the cards had shot into the air. She now had a real problem. Not only had she lost her flow and lost her place, but because she was now on the floor trying desperately to gather the cards together, the audience had a distraction.

All eyes in the room were now on this unfortunate person who had lost complete control of her presentation. And, when she had gathered up the cue cards, her problems were not over, as she had obviously forgotten to number the cards and was now unable to put them into order again. Not surprisingly, the presentation was not a great success though, for many in the audience, it was certainly a memorable one.

The case study shows just what can happen when nerves remain uncontrolled, when a nervous habit goes unrecognised by the speaker and how its effects can completely destroy an otherwise very good presentation. Nervousness is perfectly controllable once the nervous habits have been identified. On the best practical training courses this is normally achieved by the use of video recording facilities, where the speakers are able to see themselves on playback, and given the opportunity to pick up on any verbal or – as in this case – physical mannerisms which may be distracting.

....

Every speaker suffers initial nervousness. It is quite natural, in fact, essential to giving a good performance as it is this nervousness which enables the body's adrenalin to start pumping. Adrenalin is one of the important hormones of the body which is pumped rapidly into the system whenever we are faced with a potentially frightening situation. In the days of our prehistoric ancestors, when they were suddenly confronted by some wild animal, the rush of adrenalin enabled them to make a rapid choice between 'fight or flight' – they could either stand and face the danger head-on, or they could turn and run for their lives. Adrenalin pumps energy to the muscles, where it is urgently required to enable a lightening response. Today, we rarely have to face wild animals, but we still make full use of our ancient fight or flight facility and the adrenalin which makes our nerve ends supercharged and our reflexes razor sharp.

USE OF THE VOICE

....

CASE STUDY

On a practical presentations training course some years ago, I had in my group a rather quiet, middle-aged travel agent who had chosen as his first subject, the topic of brass bands, in which, as it turned out, he was passionately interested. Each speaker had to talk for just five minutes on a favourite subject – no visual aids and no help other than a set of cue cards. On each occasion, the rest of the group of seven became, along with myself, the selected audience, making notes on specific aspects of the speakers style and delivery.

This particular talk on brass bands turned out to be five minutes of incredible boredom, not from the content of the speech, which was very informative and interesting, but from the absolute monotone in which the talk was delivered. The speaker's voice remained on precisely the same pitch throughout the entire five minutes and, with the staccato delivery, the outcome was devastating. The audience struggled to keep themselves awake, so powerful were the effects of this man's monotonous voice. The subject-matter and the storyline of his speech were sadly lost. The voice development exercises turned out to be an essential part of the course for this man.

This case study clearly demonstrates how important it is to make full use of the voice in a presentation. Even if you have a very expansive knowledge of the subject, a well-structured presentation and good visuals, you will quickly lose the attention and interest of your audience if they find you dull and uninspiring, or difficult to listen to.

....

Most really good public speakers have usually undergone some form of voice development in order to tone up and enhance the quality of their speaking voices. Everyone's speaking voice is composed of five separate elements which make up the overall effect of the voice. Each of these elements can be used to great effect, and most can be further developed to enhance the quality of the voice. The five elements are volume, pace, pitch, clarity and emphasis, so let's take a look at these and see how each one affects our speaking voices.

Volume

The volume of your voice needs to be raised to a level which will reach every member of the audience. Many find that they need to practise voice projection in order to do this, so try this exercise.

....

Exercise   Stand facing a wall in a suitable room. Take a deep breath and then, with your chest out and pulling the muscles of your stomach in, let out your breath slowly. Do this a few times to focus on expanding the chest and holding in the stomach. It will enable you to breathe out, using the muscles of your stomach to control the expulsion of air.

Now try the same exercise, but this time softly make the sound of the five vowels as you breathe out – A . . . E . . . I . . . O . . . U.

The voice is projected, not by shouting, but by controlling the diaphragm through the stomach muscles. As you progress with this exercise, make each vowel sound louder until you can hear the strength of your voice projected against the wall. You will find that regular exercises of this kind help you to develop your voice and make it stronger.

Once you get used to projecting your voice, you can use the variability of the volume to good effect. You will find that your are able to get the audience's attention by using volume, and not simply by raising your voice. If you wish to make the audience more attentive in order to make a specific point, try dropping your voice and speaking more quietly. This has the dramatic effect of drawing audience attention in towards you as the speaker and, if you lower your voice slightly at the same time, this will focus their listening directly on to the words you are saying. Volume, therefore, is not simply about speaking louder – it is about using the voice to best effect.

Exercise

Try reading the piece below out loud to a friend or colleague, using the volume instructions, and see just how much more effective this can be than simply saying the piece at the same volume. First, say the following sentence out loud, at the same volume throughout:

'If you're thinking that this tour must be extremely expensive, let me tell you that we have arranged a special price of just £285.'

Now try the sentence once more, but this time, lower your voice over the last few words, '. . . of just £285.'

Did your friend or colleague notice the difference in the effect? If you also managed to slow down the words at the same time (see Pace below), the enhancement to the central message should have been quite obvious. This is a very effective means of bringing audience attention to a particular point, so try it in your own presentations.

Pace (and pause)

Regardless of the pace of your normal speaking voice, in a public speaking situation that pace needs to be moderately slow so that the audience can take in all that you are saying. Listening over prolonged periods can be very difficult, so you will have to find a pace that is neither too slow nor too fast. One point about nervousness is that it makes many people talk faster than they normally would. Those who are untrained in public speaking will often say that they simply wanted to get their speech over as fast as possible. Remember, too, that you can slow down the pace of your words just as you can decrease their volume – it has precisely the same effect when you have a particular point to make.

The need to pause is very often forgotten by presenters. This usually adds to the general effect, so that fast speakers are apt to charge straight through their talk without pausing to take breath. Pauses need to be emphasised dramatically in order to give the audience time to hear the words and to focus on a particular point.

Exercise

Read the following two sentences out loud and listen to the difference in this dramatic effect.

'So remember that if you book now, you'll receive twenty pounds off the normal selling price.'

'So remember . . . (pause) . . . if you book now . . . (pause) . . . you'll receive (slowly) twenty pounds off (normal pace) the normal selling price.'

Did you notice the difference? Pace and pause are two of the most useful aspects of the speaking voice particularly when you wish to emphasise a special point, highlight a feature or stress a particular benefit.

Pitch

Everyone has a natural register of pitch. Some of us have naturally deep voices and others fairly high-pitched ones but, no matter what your natural register, using the other aspect of pitch – the voice's wonderful variability – is what makes the human voice so interesting. If there is no pitch within the voice, then we end up with the sort of monotone highlighted in the previous case study. Monotonous voices stay at the same pitch throughout, and it is this lack of variation in the voice which makes such a voice outstandingly boring. So, while there's not always a lot which can be done about our natural pitch, and the range within which we would normally speak, there is much which can be done to enhance the 'interestability' of the voice to make it more interesting.

Exercise

Try saying the short sentence below out loud as instructed, and get someone else to listen and tell you what different effects they hear.

'Everyone who goes to Florida goes to Disneyworld.'

Try saying this sentence, raising the pitch of the voice over the words 'Florida' and 'Disneyworld', then say the sentence once more, lowering the pitch of your voice over these words.

Did it make a difference in any way? You will find that most people listening to the first sentence will see it as a positive statement, suggesting that visiting Disneyworld is a natural part of any visit to Florida. It is said almost by way of invitation – perhaps as a suggestion of a 'must' to be included in the itinerary. The raising of the voice for the word 'Florida' sounds approval, and raising the voice again for the word 'Disneyworld' makes the positive link.

People listening to the second sentence will regard it as a negative statement, suggesting that the speaker disapproves, and that it is entirely predictable that everyone who visits the one, automatically visits the other. The lowering of the voice for the word 'Florida' sounds disapproval, and lowering the voice again for the word 'Disneyworld' makes the negative link.

Clarity

Clarity of voice is essential whenever you are addressing an audience, and your success in being clear will depend very much upon the audibility of your voice and the pace at which you speak. Words which are amplified through a microphone may certainly be louder, but not always quite so clear and crisp, so good sound-balance of any equipment is important. In any public speaking situation words need to be clearly and precisely enunciated. If your normal speed of delivery is rapid, then you will need to concentrate on slowing down to a more moderate pace. Audibility is often impaired unwittingly by the speaker, especially when various presentation aids are employed. Do not turn towards a visual display during your presentation and talking upstage. Many a speaker's voice has been lost to the audience as they turn their head to talk to the projection screen. Speak moderately slowly and clearly, and face the audience at all times – that way, you can be sure that your message will be heard.

Emphasis

This is the stressing of certain words in order to emphasise their strength and importance. The richness of the English language means that the meaning of entire sentences can be altered just by emphasising one word within the sentence. If we take the simple sentence 'Don't walk on the grass', it is clear that the message can be changed simply by stressing, in turn, each of the first two words – 'don't' and 'walk'. '*Don't* walk on the grass!' is an imperative – a directive not to walk on the grass – which is obviously said as a warning. 'Don't *walk* on the grass!' is also an imperative, but it is a little more confusing. Because the emphasis is on the word 'walk', it seems to imply that it may be in order to 'hop', 'skip', 'jump' or 'run' over the grass.

Exercise

Try this exercise in emphasis on a friend or colleague, and get them to write down what each repetition of the following sentence conveys. Say the sentence out loud, emphasising in turn the word which is italicised:

'*He* says this restaurant is the best in town.'
'He *says* this restaurant is the best in town.'
'He says *this* restaurant is the best in town.'
'He says this *restaurant* is the best in town.'
'He says this restaurant is the *best* in town.'
'He says this restaurant is the best in *town*.'

Using an appropriate voice register

Register refers to the style or form of language customarily used in specific circumstances. One of the very first lessons for those entering the world of business is that everyday, casual conversation is largely inappropriate in the workplace. We learn quickly to adopt a 'business' register, and this is reflected in both the language we use and the deference we show to customers. When we greet customers, we tend to say, 'Good-morning, how can I help you?', whereas in a social situation, meeting friends, we would be far more likely to say, 'Hi! How are things?', something you would only say in the workplace to someone who was a friend or well known to you.

We tend to adopt an even more formal language over the telephone, mainly because we are not in a face-to-face situation and therefore unable to see each other's reactions. The contrast between the business register and the social register may often be heard over the telephone where the caller turns out to be someone we know. The opening register is quickly altered to reflect the relationship between the speakers. So, we hear, 'Good-morning, ABC Travel. How can I help you? . . . Oh, Hi! It's you. How're things with you, then?' The speaker answers in the normal business register, then quickly changes to a social register when the caller has been identified as a friend. Any attempt to continue in the business register would cause the friend to question such behaviour. We do not talk to friends in such a formal way.

In a public speaking situation, different rules of register usually apply. The nature of the situation, the degree of formality and distance between speaker and audience normally dictate the use of a recognisable public speaking register. We would normally begin by saying, 'Good evening, ladies and gentlemen. Welcome to our cruise presentation.' and continue in a similar fashion, using a formal or semi-formal business language.

There are times, however, when you may be asked to give a presentation or talk to a specifically targeted audience, and where you would need to adopt a slightly less formal approach. A school careers talk is a typical example, where you would normally be addressing both parent and students and the aim of selling the idea of a career in travel would be reflected in the language you use. The guiding rule in such a case is to be friendly but never familiar.

Humour may be included in all but the most formal of presentations, and helps to lighten the situation and put everybody at ease. Jokes, however, should always be avoided, as they invariably offend someone, and never, ever start a presentation by telling a joke. If the audience doesn't appreciate your joke, you may find yourself working twice as hard to try to regain their respect. Finally, pitch the level of your talk according to your audience, and try to avoid travel jargon and slang words and phrases.

BODY LANGUAGE

CASE STUDY

I was engaged in the training of tourist guides during the early 1980s and took out a group around a historic city in the West Country to give them some instruction on presenting themselves in the open air to a group of tourists. They had all made a very comprehensive study of the history and background to their city, and were well able to talk at length about those sights worth seeing.

I asked each in turn to make a short presentation to the rest of the group (who doubled as tourists). They were to introduce themselves as if they were just commencing a tour, and then give a short presentation on the immediate surrounding area. One of the group, a retired gentleman whom we shall call Peter, obviously knew his stuff and, as a Dartmoor walking guide, had no qualms about addressing an audience. Peter, though, was not so used to presenting himself to a static, listening audience – his forte was talking 'on the hoof' as he led his parties over the moors.

His standing presentation turned out to be most amusing. As he began to talk to his audience, he leaned forward somewhat, took a step forward, then a small step to the left, then a step backwards and to the right, from where he repeated the process again. Each time he made a particular point, he would go through the same little 'dance' again, and each time he did this, the circle he was describing with his feet got wider and wider, and the group had to respond by moving further and further away from him. His talk, though informative, was now largely irrelevant as the group concentrated on moving out of his way. He, amusingly, was concentrating so hard on his speech, that he was completely unaware of the rolling and dancing movement of his body.

I finally stopped him, and we took a look at the relative positions of himself and the group – he was now standing alone in the middle of an enlarged circle of fellow guides. The point was made instantly, and there was much good humour between Peter and the rest of the group as he realised what his body had been doing involuntarily while his mind had been concentrating on the all-consuming message he was so keen to put across. The cure for his unwitting antics was as immediate as it was complete.

As we have seen from the last case study, the way you present yourself before an audience is important to the success of your message. Learn to use your body as a form of personal expression to enhance your message. Audiences will obviously be conscious of you as a person, and will also become conscious of your technique in making good use of movement. So with this in mind, let's take a closer look at how body language can be used to best effect.

Stance

If you are standing behind a lectern, your lower body will be hidden from the audience's view. If your knees are knocking together, they will not be able to see it. However, where you have to address an audience from the floor, or up on a stage in full frontal view, stance becomes an important part of your personal presentation. Men should try not to stand with feet together, as if standing to attention, and neither should they stand with legs spread apart and hands clasped behind the back, as this is redolent of a sergeant-major on the parade-ground shouting at the troops. Stand upright and keep your legs slightly apart, but remember not to be too stiff or formal. Women always look best standing with one foot slightly in front of the other, and should certainly avoid the sergeant-major position. If you have a tendency to transfer weight from one foot to another, this is perfectly OK, provided that you do it naturally and in a gentle, relaxed manner. Avoid any tendency to swap legs like a clockwork toy, or the audience will begin to notice that you are doing it and will turn their concentration to waiting for your next move.

If you feel comfortable doing so, there is nothing to stop you moving around a little during the presentation, providing it is purposeful and achieves the purpose of 'changing the scene'. A presenter who paces up and down can be most distracting to the audience, but someone who uses the stage area to shift positions will create a more interesting scene.

Hand and arm movements

Many speakers find great difficulty in knowing just what to do with their hands once they become conscious of the dangers of involuntary movement under stress. The lesson is quite simple – movement is permissible, but it is the involuntary movements which cause audience distraction. It is also perfectly OK to express yourself with arm movements, though not entirely advisable to describe enormous circles in the air. If you feel comfortable, then arm and hand movements can be used to very good effect to add emphasis and to convey a strong message.

Eye contact

Try always to look at the whole audience, which will mean casting your gaze around the room to those seated at the front, back and to the sides. Nervous, or untrained speakers generally concentrate their gaze on some distant object, or on one particular person in the audience. This serves no other purpose than alienating the audience from the speaker, so you must ensure that you look at and smile to your audience and welcome them into your presentation. If you are worried about being put off by catching someone's eye, you can always direct your gaze on to people's foreheads. From several feet away, it is impossible for the audience to realise the difference.

MICROPHONE TECHNIQUE

A microphone is an extension of your voice, serving the purpose of amplifying the voice to give it sufficient volume. Microphones are normally fixed or free-standing, but there is an art to using them properly. Speakers who have had no training in microphone techniques usually find themselves distracted from their central task, and often spend valuable time wrestling and struggling to contain a piece of equipment which seems to have a mind and a life of its own.

Microphones are of two types – unidirectional and multidirectional. The multidirectional has a gauze-covered, rounded end which contains the tiny electronic pick-up – the unit which receives the sounds from your voice. Because of its rounded shape, this type of microphone is able to pick up your voice from a variety of different angles. You are safe to speak into the end of this microphone from the front or from the side, provided of course that you do actually speak into it. The second type of microphone, the unidirectional type, has a flat gauze end, and must always be positioned so that it is pointed directly at your mouth. These microphones are normally tubular in shape, with the pick-up positioned inside, which means that you have to talk down into it, just as you would if you were talking into a piece of pipe. If you are unsure which type of microphone you have in front of you, ask the person in charge of the public-address system.

The first point of importance, then, is to make absolutely sure that you are talking into the microphone. If you are not, then you will not be heard. Ideally, the end of the microphone should be a couple of inches away from your mouth. Any closer, and you run the risk of voice distortion. Just how you arrange the microphone will depend upon the means by which it is mounted, i.e. the type of stand which is used.

Fixed microphones are mounted on a variety of stands, both short and long. The stand most commonly used on lecterns is the 'gooseneck'. Here, the micro-phone is mounted at the end of a long bendy pipe, which can be moved by the speaker in any direction. The most comfortable working angle for most speakers is to have the microphone pointing up towards the face at an angle of about forty-five degrees.

Microphones mounted on a straight stand are a particular problem. The microphone itself sits in a small holder, which can only be moved through an angle of ninety degrees, from the horizontal to the vertical. It is the stand which causes so many problems, as this has to be adjusted to suit the height of the speaker, and very few people know how to make this adjustment. The stem of the stand comes in two parts, joined by a knurled grip, which is turned clockwise or anti-clockwise to tighten and loosen it. You will need to grasp the stem of the stand with one hand, then turn the knurled grip with the other, pulling out or pushing in the upper stem according to your height. If you adjust the microphone first to an angle of forty-five degrees, you can then higher or lower the stand to the appropriate height. Make quite sure that you retighten the knurled grip to avoid the stem slipping back down.

One of the difficulties of the upright stand – that it stands very close to your body – is often overcome by making use of a boom, as pianists and drummers use to sweep over their instruments. The boom, when angled up towards the speaker, allows far more freedom of movement. Whatever type of stand has been provided for you, try to give yourself time before your presentation to address the microphone, so that you know exactly how to make the necessary adjustments.

Sometimes you may be offered a 'roving' microphone, either one which can be hand held or one which is mounted on your lapel. Both are extremely useful in allowing the speaker freedom to walk around. For the untrained user, though, the cautionary note is to watch out for the trailing microphone lead. It is very easy to step on the lead and tug the tiny microphone from your lapel, or trip over the lead and find yourself addressing your audience from the floor, so be warned – don't step on the lead!

Finally, remember that microphones are a very useful part of the presenter's tool kit and, used properly and effectively, they will enhance your presentation and allow you to speak more easily to your audience.

DELIVERING YOUR MESSAGE

Many first-time speakers feel self-conscious or frightened that they will succeed only in making a fool of themselves in front of the public, or that the audience won't find their talk very interesting. The key to making the best presentation can be summarised by the two words – 'planning' and 'preparation'. With this in mind, this section of the book has been written to provide you with some practical guidelines for making a slick, professional public presentation.

CASE STUDY

Tony is the manager of a local travel agency. He has been in the travel business for many years, has a very sound product knowledge and is well thought of by his clients. Tony is an outgoing, sociable type who loves meeting people and who is able to talk very articulately about virtually any travel topic, especially cruising, of which he has considerable personal experience. He has kept his agency a top cruise sales agency for the past twelve years, and manages to maintain his position as a top commission earner for several cruise lines.

Tonight, he and his staff are giving a cruise presentation to sell a completely new concept in cruising to a specially invited audience. A lot of thought has gone into preparing the venue, arranging the seating and organising the drinks and refreshments. Tony is to give the main talk on the new product, and feels that with his many years of experience selling cruises to his clients, he will be able to talk quite freely and informally to the audience.

However, when Tony gets up to talk, he quickly realises that he seems to have left his normally articulate, bubbly personality behind in the agency. He starts off briskly enough, introducing himself and his staff to the audience and explaining how the evening will unfold. However, when he glances up at the clock after his introduction, he realises that his off-the-cuff, chatty style has used up precious minutes and that he is left with only fifteen minutes of his allocated slot of thirty minutes. Faced with the prospect of delivering his whole thirty minute talk in half the time, he finds himself gabbling through the speech as fast as he can go. He fumbles for the right words and struggles to put his selling points across to the audience and, when he finally walks off, he knows that he has failed to live up to his reputation as a professional salesman.

So what really went wrong for Tony and why did he lose his self-confidence in front of so many of his own customers?

The answer is very fundamental: Tony failed to realise (until it was too late) that the skills he needed for his public presentation were quite different from those he would normally use in private consultations with his customers. First, Tony made the mistake of believing that he could talk to a large audience just as he would talk to individual customers who came into his agency. Second, he lost all sense of time, and realised that he had spent so much time introducing himself and staff that he was left with virtually no time to put across his sales talk. Third, he lost his way and, in so doing, lost his usual articulate and smooth delivery with which he would normally win over his customers. Let's look in more detail at these points and see where Tony might be able to put things right for his next presentation.

The first lesson is clear – you cannot talk to a large group of people in the same way you would if you were sitting with a customer in your agency. A homely, person-to-person style reserved for talking with one or two close customers rarely has the same effect when used in a large, open conference room. Your style of delivery must be altogether more formal and rehearsed. Only very accomplished speakers are able to get up and speak straight off the cuff to an audience, and seldom does this happen in a sales situation unless the speaker is thoroughly conversant with his subject *and* makes the same sort of speech on a regular basis.

The second lesson concerns time, or rather the lack of time, necessary to deliver your talk. Tony failed to plan ahead, and then fell into the trap of grossly underestimating the amount of time he needed in order to be able to say what he wanted, in the way he wanted to say it. You will need to rehearse your speech carefully beforehand so that you know exactly how long you will need in front of the audience.

The third lesson is, perhaps, the hardest of all to experience – when you fail to plan your presentation thoroughly, you will inevitably miss out many of the important selling points that you want to make. Tony failed to plan properly because he believed that all that was necessary was to stand up and articulate in his usual fashion. He discovered that speaking in public is not the same as talking in private.

TARGET AUDIENCE

One of the first considerations for anyone planning a presentation must be the target audience. This is normally not a problem when you are able to choose your audience but, if you are an invited speaker at someone else's venue, find out exactly who your audience is before you write your speech. Some things you will need to consider are: the type of group you are meeting; the age range of the group; whether single-sex or mixed; and the special interest which has brought the group together. This is very important, as there is little point in talking to the local Townswomen's Guild about a rugby tour to France. You can only be sure of your subject when you are sure of your audience.

CASE STUDY

Julie is the manager of a small travel agency. She is an expert skier and has travelled all over Europe and other parts of the world in pursuit of her hobby during the last eight years. She decides to give a presentation on skiing to an invited audience, and arranges a special tour departure to one of the best beginner and intermediate skiing resorts in Austria. With assistance from her staff of five, Julie sets out to invite to the event as wide an audience as possible.

On the evening of the presentation, the hall is full to capacity and the audience is seated and waiting. Julie and her staff are on hand during the early part of the evening to answer questions, then, after a short break, Julie steps forward to give a presentation on their special ski departure.

As she begins to settle into her talk, Julie realises that there are a number of very experienced skiers in the audience who obviously share her love for the sport. She breaks away from her scripted speech to say a little about the opportunities for experienced skiers and, seeing that some of her audience are obviously able to relate to her experiences, she begins to talk more and more enthusiastically about advanced skiing. She talks about the complexities of the lift systems, describes some of the best red and black runs to be found throughout the ski area and talks about the challenges of skiing over the mogul fields. Julie concludes her evening by reminding her audience that learning to ski is great fun and that this is a particularly good resort for all grades of skiers.

After the evening's presentation, Julie and her team monitor the number of bookings they receive in the agency. They discover, after about a month, that only two people – both experienced skiers – have actually booked for their special ski departure. They begin to analyse the presentation to try to find reasons for such a poor response, and send out a questionnaire to try to find out why people were not interested in the special ski departure. By the time of their special departure date just two more skiers have booked and paid their money.

The returned questionnaires indicate that, contrary to expectations, there were three different common interest groups in attendance at their ski presentation. First, there were the experienced skiers, to whom Julie ended up directing most of her talk. Second, there were those who had skied before, but who considered themselves far from experienced, and third, there were the customers who had never skied before.

So, where had Julie gone wrong with her presentation and why did she end up with so few bookings?

The lesson to be learnt from Julie's presentation is that audiences must be properly targeted if one single message is to be put across effectively. The target audience was dictated by the product, i.e. a special departure to an Austrian resort ideal for beginners to intermediate skiers. Julie should have directed her talk to these potential customers, concentrating on facts which were relevant to their lack of experience – equipment hire, ski school, *après-ski* and other activities available at the resort. As she got into her presentation, though, Julie began to alienate herself from her target audience by addressing only those more advanced skiers, who were able to relate to her own skiing experiences. Julie should have targeted her audience more carefully from the outset.

When you plan a presentation, think carefully about your target audience. A skiing holiday for beginners will probably not be of great interest to more advanced skiers, unless they can be attracted by some unique selling point (USP). Similarly, a coach tour through Italy, visiting museums and art galleries will hardly be of interest to young families or the young singles market.

The obvious starting point is to make a list of existing customers who have booked similar tours/holidays, and then to consider the potential customers, bearing in mind:

- common interest grouping
- ideal socio-economic grouping
- status: single, married or family
- expected age range
- possible spending power.

Once you have a profile of the type of audience you wish to attract, your next step is to set an objective for your presentation.

YOUR PRESENTATION OBJECTIVE

Many presentations lack real success because no clear objective has been set by the organiser. They may have a subject in mind, but without a precise objective there will be no clear direction for the presentation, and the essential message of the presentation will be muddled. Presentations are used primarily as a vehicle to sell something, whether a product or an idea, and you should be clear in your mind about what you expect as a result of your presentation. If your intention is to sell a particular product, you will need to identify precisely what that product is, and what it is you wish to achieve, i.e. your exact target.

Objectives have to be realistic, which means that they must always be:

- measurable
- achievable
- specific.

So, if you wished to give a presentation on a safari holiday to Kenya to an invited audience of one hundred, you might set an objective to 'book at least 10 places on a special departure to Kenya with Crown Safari Holidays'. This objective is very precisely written. It is measurable – you are aiming for 10 booked passengers; it is achievable – you are looking for a 10 per cent take-up from the targeted audience; it is specific – a special departure with Crown Safaris. It is also a realistic objective in that it is linked directly to your target audience, and that you are looking to sell to just a small percentage of that audience.

Having a clear and concise objective is paramount to the success of your presentation, as it gives you a precise path to follow and enables you to measure the exact outcome of your event. The question you should always be able to ask at the end of your presentation is, 'Did we achieve what we set out to achieve?'

CHOOSING A VENUE

The venue you choose for your presentation should be in keeping with your budget and the type of product you are trying to promote. Most large or medium-sized hotel rooms are suitable, as are local halls or even sports clubs. Some promoters even make their presentation at a factory or company premises where they have an audience *in situ*. Be careful, though, as product and audience may not be well matched. You may like to consider a venue which has close links with your product, such as a tennis club for a promotion on tennis holidays in Portugal, or a golf club for a promotion on golfing holidays. Remember, too, that you should check out the venue well before you intend to use it, looking at overall size and accessibility, the facilities it offers and the suitability of the seating arrangements. Check also that the date you have chosen for your presentation does not clash with any other national or local event, or coincide with popular TV viewing times if you believe that your target audience is likely to be watching.

Assignment   Select a topic on which to give a presentation, and make notes on the following:

1 the possible target audience most suited to the promotion topic

2 the exact objective of your presentation, using the framework of measureable, achieveable and specific

3 the type of venue which would be most suited to both presentation topic and target audience.

STRUCTURING YOUR PRESENTATION

Unless you are promoting a product on a regular basis, you will probably lack the fluency and spontaneity to be able to talk from memory, and you will almost certainly need to plan your presentation with care. All the best talks or presentations have one thing in common – they each have a recognisable structure. In its simplest form, the structure will consist of:

- the beginning, or introduction
- the middle, or main message
- the end, or conclusion.

Such a structure, though, is rather too simplistic for most sales presentations. A much better approach is afforded by the AIDA (Attention, Interest, Desire, Action) principle, which is borrowed from marketing. The simple public speaking model can be overlaid on the AIDA model:

Attention	
	introduction
Interest	
Desire	main message
Action	conclusion

Now let's see how the model can be used to provide a solid working structure for your presentation.

Attention

Before you start to speak to your audience, you will need their undivided attention or you will find that you are speaking to yourself. An audience needs time to get seated and settle down. People invariably chat to each other or to friends and acquaintances and, whilst they are busy talking amongst themselves, they cannot be listening to you.

Few people, unless they are extremely well known and awaited by an expectant audience, can walk out on stage and command instant attention. It takes a big personality to silence an audience just by appearing on stage before them. So, the trick is to get the audience settled as soon as possible so that the evening can commence in an orderly and planned fashion. Perhaps the simplest and most effective way is for someone with a stentorian voice to announce, 'La-dies and gen-tle-men', followed by a welcome and an outline of the agenda for the evening.

There are, however, more dramatic ways to gain the audience's attention, and few things are more dramatic than light and sound. In the theatre, when the play or show is about to begin, the house lights fade and every one knows immediately that the curtain is about to rise. Note that the lights are not simply doused – they fade gradually to allow the audience time to adjust, to stop talking and to settle down in expectation. Try to look on your opening as the switching of focus from the audience to you, and give them time to quieten down and transfer their attention from each other to you. Some of the best audio-visual displays commence after the lights have been faded, as a low introductory note, surging dramatically to a crescendo. Audience attention is equally dramatic.

The rules, then are simple; if the house lights are up, dim them; if the house lights are subdued, bring them up, and similarly with music. Once you have your audience's attention, you are ready to maintain their interest.

Interest

Attention focuses your audience on you. Interest maintains that attention and whets the audience's appetite for what is to come, i.e. your principal message. At this stage, then, you are still in the process of introducing yourself and your presentation.

....

CASE STUDY

As a college student, studying travel and tourism, I looked forward to the regular Wednesday afternoon sessions on travel-related topics given by guest speakers. One particular week we assembled to listen to a talk on effective use of the telephone, given by a representative from the GPO, in those days a nationalised company responsible for both mail and telephones. By two o'clock that afternoon some 60 students were gathered in one of the lecture rooms to hear what we believed would be a very informative talk.

After being introduced, our speaker rose to speak. He looked straight to the back of the room, pointed to the telephone he held in his hand, and said in a staccato voice, 'Most people don't realise that when they pick up the telephone, they're holding in their hands public property.'

Eyebrows were raised as students glanced around at each other. One or two suppressed a snigger. I reflected on the speaker's first words, and the talk continued in exactly the same vein as it had begun.

How do you think the talk continued after the speaker's introduction?
In fact, the talk continued precisely as it had begun – a lecture on the rules and regulations laid down by the GPO for their subscribers. The expected advice on telephone-speaking skills and effective communication was never given. Instead, our speaker continued exactly as he had begun, and we listened to an hour of rather humourless and dry talk about the importance of keeping to the official rule-book. The speaker's opening line certainly drew our attention – for all the wrong reasons – but failed miserably to maintain our interest.

What our speaker omitted completely was both his initial welcome, and an introduction, which needs to cover the following:

- your name, position, and the name of your company
- names of all your staff
- names and companies of invited speakers or presenters
- title you have given to your presentation evening
- agenda and timetable for the evening.

....

One of the most effective ways of introducing your topic and maintaining the interest of your audience is to start with a rhetorical opening question, 'How would you like to be lying in the sun on a deserted tropical beach whilst it's snowing back in England?' or perhaps, 'How would you like to visit ten different countries in three weeks and do it all from the same luxury hotel? Come aboard our beautiful cruise liner, and we'll show you how!'

Put this way, a rhetorical question makes an immediate impact, fires the audience's imagination and prepares them for the principal message of your presentation. Impact is extremely important in any stage presentation, so don't forget, your audience will be attentive and listening, and they will quickly make a judgement on the way your presentation is likely to unfold, based on the manner in which you introduce your talk. Your 'interest' line should always whet the audience's appetite for more, and don't forget that when you have finished . . . pause for effect.

Assignment Refer back to the topic you chose in the previous assignment, and make a few notes for your own introduction and 'interest' statement. Try to find a short and snappy introduction which will gain the immediate attention and interest of your audience.

Desire

Desire is the main body, or central message of your presentation. It is the 'sales pitch' where you lay out your wares and invite the audience to buy. It is here that you need to paint a picture for your audience, certainly with the use of visual aids, but also by using descriptive and imaginative language. If you are selling a product, though, it is now that you will need to give a full description of what you are offering, including any unique selling points. In any case, you will need to make sure that you cover the following points:

- type of tour or holiday you are selling
- mode or modes of transport involved
- full details of times and duration
- description of the accommodation
- full description of the board arrangements
- prearranged and optional excursions
- free-time activities
- cost, together with discounts/supplements.

Try to pace your speech as if you were unfolding a story, making sure that your timing, pace and pause allows the audience to take in all the important details of your main sales message. Illustrate your talk where appropriate by making good use of pre-prepared maps, diagrams and pictures of every important descriptive detail. Remember to personalise your tour or holiday by using possessive pronouns, 'Your hotel is located at . . .', 'Our coach will then depart for . . .'. In this way, you transport the audience to that situation so that they really feel as if they are taking part. Once they become interested in the product, they will then begin to see themselves in their hotel room or sitting on the coach. Personalising the product is a way of taking the audience on an imaginary trip. It is far easier to see the enjoyment of a holiday if you can see yourself there, at the resort.

This is also where you can make good use of benefit statements to support your message and help to personalise the product: 'Your flight departs at 07.00, so by lunchtime you can be relaxing by the hotel pool' or 'Our reps will be on hand to help you in any way they can. They'll even arrange babysitting for you if you have children, and want to spend an evening on your own.'

Once you have fully covered the main points of your presentation, you should make quite sure that your message stays with the audience by summarising the main points again, using visuals to highlight the key points if you feel that this will help to emphasize your message. When you come to the summary, remember to let the audience know by using link-phrases such as: 'So let me just remind you once more about our special offer . . .', 'Before I go, then, let me just remind you . . .', 'So finally, please remember those three main points . . .' or 'Let's just look again at the main details of . . .'. And you can then reiterate the main points of your presentation. The summary will need to be crisp and sharp – there's no point in boring the audience with another speech – just make your point, and stop.

Action

Just as impact is vital to the start of your presentation, so a gradual winding up of your speech is essential at the finish. The trick is to ensure that your listening and attentive audience are not suddenly tipped off the end of your presentation. It happens more often than not.

CASE
STUDY

At a company presentation once, I listened to a speech from the company treasurer, reporting – with the help of an overhead projector – on the reorganisation of the company. For the last part of his speech he had been talking, not to the audience, but to the screen behind him. What struck me most, however, was the way he suddenly stopped his speech to announce, by way of question time, that he had finished his talk. The audience had been engrossed in the details of the reorganisation chart, and were still following his commentary, when the whole presentation suddenly came to an abrupt end with the words, '. . . and so the full reorganisation of the company should be completed by the end of the year – any questions?'

After this sudden announcement, there was a pause as the audience began to realise that the presentation had actually finished, then a further pause as they considered whether there were any questions they could ask. In the event, no one did put a question and, after a little shuffling at the front, our presenter sat down.

The case study above demonstrates how important it is to prepare your audience for the end of your presentation; in fact, as important as introducing your talk when you first stand up. The speaker in this case suddenly realised that he had said all there was to say, and simply came to a halt, throwing in the call for questions by way of saying 'Thank you and goodbye'.

If the end of your presentation is to be as slick as the beginning, you should consider exactly what you are going to say at the end. If you are selling a product or service, you must let the audience know exactly what action they need to take with regard to booking or reserving a place; in other words, they need to know:

- what they have to do next
- how they go about it
- when they must do it
- where they can do it.

Asking a rhetorical question is often the best way of introducing these details. You might like to outline your 'action' with: 'So, now that you've heard all about our special ski departure, you will want to know what you need to do. We shall be taking bookings tonight, at the end of our presentation. Just see Joanne who's standing over there, and don't forget the special reduction for booking on the night. For those who need more time, remember that you can come into the agency right up until the departure date. All you need to do is pay the deposit of £x and complete a booking form. We do the rest – it's as simple as that.'

Closing the presentation

After your 'action' statement, you need a short, sharp closing line to round off your presentation in a positive and confident way. You have summarised the main selling points of your talk and you have told your audience what they need to do about it. Now you just need to wrap up the presentation with a one-line reminder and a thank-you: 'So ladies and gentlemen, if you've never skied before, this is a wonderful first opportunity. Let me just say thank you to you all for coming along tonight. It's been a pleasure to see you. Thank you.' Your audience is now in no doubt that your presentation has finished and, if they have enjoyed your talk and you have finished on a positive note, they will normally always respond by applauding.

We should conclude this section by just taking another look at the AIDA model:

- Attention – attracting the audience's attention to ensure that they are ready to listen, and introducing yourself and your talk.

- Interest – making a short statement or posing a question to arouse the audience's interest.
- Desire – the main message of your talk which outlines the product, service or subject, and a summary to reiterate the primary points.
- Action – telling your audience what they have to do next and concluding your talk.

WRITING YOUR SPEECH

Some of the best presentations are given by speakers who have given themselves time to practise and rehearse their talk. Notes are important, but the emphasis should always be on 'notes', and not on a speech written verbatim on to pieces of paper. If you write your speech, the odds are you will end up reading your speech and, unless you are very well practised at reading an Autocue, you will always sound as if your are reading. Every public speaker strives to sound natural, and the only reliable way to achieve a natural flow is to allow yourself to speak as freely as possible. The less you write down, the less you will have to read out.

....

CASE STUDY

I attended a sales presentation a little while ago which had been arranged at a large local hotel. A quick glance around from the back of the room suggested an audience of well over 200 people – a very good turnout indeed. I came in part way through the evening, and did not hear the first part of the presentation. When the short travelog had finished and the lights had gone back up, the speaker, a local travel agency manager, stood up at the lectern at the front of the room and began to summarise the presentation.

'So – in – conclusion – ladies – and – gentlemen – let – me – just – say – that – it – has – been – nice – to – see – you – all – here – and – we – hope – that – you – can – travel – with – ABC – Travel – this – year.'

It was quite the dullest delivery I had ever heard, and the main reason was obviously the fact that the speaker was reading his speech straight from the A4 cards on which every word had been written. The voice was a dreary monotone – the voice of someone who was unrehearsed and quite unprepared to let go and speak from the heart. Yet I knew the speaker as someone who, in the agency at least, was a knowledgeable and articulate speaker. The person standing at the front did not appear to be the same man.

....

This little story is typical of the way some untrained presenters tackle the problem of delivering a message, and the fact that this very articulate salesman could sound so different in the agency on a one-to-one basis made it particularly disappointing. There is, though, one very noticeable point at which virtually every dreary public speaker regains their composure and reverts to normal fluent speech, and that is at the point of question time. Where the speaker knows the answer to a question, and can give an off-the-cuff answer, they invariably return to speaking in a natural manner.

Why, then, should any speaker wish to employ methods which serve only to hinder the natural flow of speech? The answer is quite simple: most people unused to public speaking do not trust themselves to remember their 'lines' unless every word is scripted. It is first a matter of confidence, and second a matter of practise.

Once you overcome the initial objection, however, the prospect of speaking from pre-prepared notes is a challenge. It will free you up and allow you to use natural words. The problem with scripts is that they are written for the eye, not for the ear. Speaking from notes will not only enable you to speak more freely, it will also enable your personality to shine through.

One very effective way of structuring your speech is to use a technique called 'mind-mapping'. This is a method of brain-storming which enables you to list headings and subheadings, and then add the key points which you want to cover. For example, a tour operator giving a presentation to a group of travel agents promoting Crete as a new destination may have prepared a mind-map like the one in Fig. 6.1. Once you have mapped out your headings and subheadings, you can decide on the order in which to present them.

A word of warning. Prices and costings should never be mentioned too early

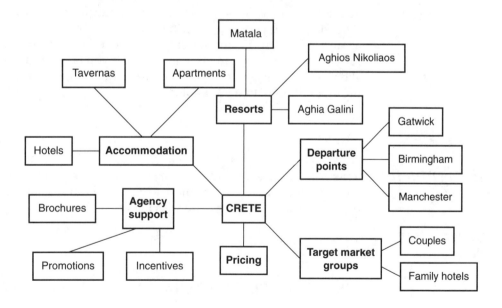

6.1 An example of a mind-map

Resort – Aghia Galini   ③

Natural harbour
Mountains
Good variety of local cuisine
Fishing trips
Accommodation/tavernas + hotels

6.2 An example of a cue card

in your speech. Leave these until later so that your audience is given time to absorb some of the other benefits of the holiday. If you mention price too early in your presentation, some may lose interest if they are unable to relate the price to other benefits. The relative value of the cost of your product will normally only be realised once the audience is able to relate price to real benefits.

The key points of your presentation can very easily be written down on cue cards, and the most effective size is usually that of a postcard. This is a comfortable size to hold in one hand. Number your cards and, on each one, write a subheading, and then a few key phrases and words to prompt you as you speak (see Fig. 6.2). Use light-coloured card and a heavy felt-tip pen as this is easier to see when you need to glance quickly at your notes.

By preparing your cards in this way, they will not be a distraction to your audience, and will leave you entirely free to express yourself in your own way. If possible, bind your cue cards together with a ring or treasury tag to safeguard against losing any. Finally, consider whether or not the lighting will be adequate for you to be able to read your cue cards. If you are commentating to projected slides, remember that the room will be darkened and that you will need some means of illuminating your notes.

Assignment   Refer back to the topic you chose in your earlier assignment. Make a mind map of the key points that you wish to make in the main body of your speech. Now number each key point in the order you wish to present them.

USING VISUAL AIDS IN YOUR PRESENTATION

The inclusion and effective use of visual aids can do much to enhance your presentation and ensure that the audience remembers much more of the content. It is a fact that our sense of sight plays a very major part in the learning process, and visuals aid general understanding. Good visual aids, then, are important to your presentation, but if careful preparation and rehearsal are ignored, the results can be disastrous.

....

CASE STUDY

I attended a managers' conference once, at which two area managers gave a talk on 'The Art of Giving a Presentation' which became a most useful lesson in how not to conduct a presentation. The talk was scheduled as a serious demonstration of the use of cue cards and visual aids, but soon degenerated into comic display, to disintegrate later into a highly embarrassing and unrehearsed farce.

The first signs of disaster showed as the principal speaker outlined his model for running a neat and professional presentation. As we, the audience, had already been given the notes from which he was reading, we quickly became bored with having to listen to what we were perfectly able to read in about half the time. Each point was laboriously read out by the presenter to an audience whose attention was not directed at him, but at the notes they held in their hands.

Once this part of the presentation had been completed, we were promised a short film by way of a diversion. The film had no particular message for the audience, but was intended simply as a light-hearted piece of fun to round off the presentation. There was a long silence as the two area managers struggled to come to terms with the back projector, which quite simply refused to function. We looked on, rather puzzled to understand the cause for the delay. Then suddenly the film began to roll, not on to the screen as intended, but through the opaque curtains which covered the screen at the back of the stage, and which one of the two presenters was hurriedly trying to open. Amid the feverish activity, it was realised that the house lights were still up.

The scene descended from farce to chaos as the film was now running, sound full on, through the curtains which refused to open and in competition with the house lights which refused to dim. By this time the audience had begun to realise that this was no carefully rehearsed demonstration, but rather a frantic attempt to salvage something from a disastrously inept piece of theatre. In the end, further embarrassment was saved only by the appearance of the house janitor, who was called hastily to locate the lights and curtain switch, and to control the booming noise of the video.

The lesson had been a salutary one, though it has always been difficult to know just who profited most by this inept performance – the presenters or the audience.

....

Planning of the use of visual aids is vital if you are to guarantee the minimum of disruption to your presentation. Consider first exactly how many different visual aids may be at your disposal:

- pre-prepared flip chart
- overhead projector and screen
- slide projector
- back projected video
- video and monitor
- cine-film
- posters and displays.

Then think about one or two visuals which will make the maximum impact, and consider how they will match the size of your audience and furthest distance from the front of the stage. Any more than two types of visuals can be considered confusing to your audience, and will certainly present you with a lot of work. The rule is to keep it simple.

Types of visual aid

Flip chart

Easy to pre-prepare and use, and available at most venues.
Watch-points: Only suitable for smaller groups, where the audience is able to read the script on the flip chart. If referring back to pages, do ensure that you can easily locate them by turning back the corner of the page. Writing will need to be neat, legible and level and spelling must always be checked carefully. Avoid talking to the flip chart.

Overhead projector (OHP)

A particularly useful piece of equipment which can be used to project images on to a screen, even under normal lighting conditions. Transparencies are prepared either by hand or by putting heat-resistant acetates through a photocopier. These can be used effectively to build up pictures by simply overlaying them.
Watch-points: Always switch off the OHP when not in use as bright lights and the noise from the fan can be a great distraction to your audience and to you. Always switch off the OHP before removing one transparency and placing the next on the screen or your audience will see them sliding on and off. The OHP needs careful positioning to ensure that the light mechanism does not block the audience view or cause a keystone effect, or distortion of the image. Do not move the OHP once the unit is switched on as the (expensive) bulb may blow. Make sure you know how to change a bulb if this should happen.

Slide projector

A good method of illustrating talks and a particularly effective way of combining good quality colour images with narrative. Can be operated by remote control.
Watch-points: Ensure that slides are correctly located in the carousel, and that they are in the correct order. Rehearsal is essential to ensure that your slides appear at the precise moment they are timed to do so. You will be in the dark, so you will need to make arrangements, or to have lighting to enable you to read

your notes. The projector needs careful positioning to ensure that nothing obstructs the images it projects.

Back projector

A modern video, projected on to a large screen which is either curved or split-screen. Still pictures are normally projected on to the split-screen and moving pictures on to the curved screen.

Watch-points: The only real problem with the curved back projector is that it needs to be viewed as near to ninety degrees as possible because picture definition is lost around the edges of the screen for those who are sitting at an oblique angle to the screen.

Video

An easy to use visual which, though having a much smaller screen size than the back projector, uses the same neat and compact VHS tapes. Many different companies sell or rent travelogs, and you should be able to find a video on practically any destination.

Watch-points: The size of your audience dictates the size of the screen. The rule of thumb is 1 inch of screen per 1 foot away from the audience, so a 20 inch screen can normally be seen from 20 feet away. Check the tracking on the video player to ensure it is synchronised and make sure you test-run the film before you start.

Cine-film

A reel-to-reel film which is fed through a film projector and forward projected on to a big screen. Not very widely used today due to the enormous popularity of the video, but you can still find some very good quality films on cine-film.

Watch-points: Cine-films are not the easiest to set up and operate, and they run with a constant whirr. They need to be operated in total darkness which can cause difficulties if you are giving a commentary at the same time. Old films are apt to break, so make sure you know how to rethread a broken film.

Posters and displays

Cheap and colourful. You can position these at any convenient point around the room. Most national tourist boards are happy to supply you with high-quality posters if you are having a presentation on their country. Displays can be placed where they make maximum impact.

Watch-points: Posters need to be firmly fixed to a flat surface. Their flimsiness does not lend itself to being held up by hand and moved around. Be careful that displays are not likely to be knocked over when you announce that the drinks are ready.

Preparing your visual aids

If you decide to create your own material for slides or OHP, or you intend to use a pre-prepared flip chart, here are some useful tips:

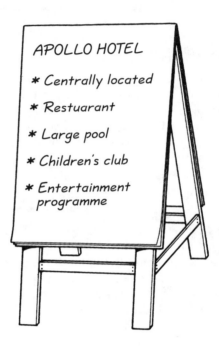

6.3 An example of a pre-prepared page of a flip chart

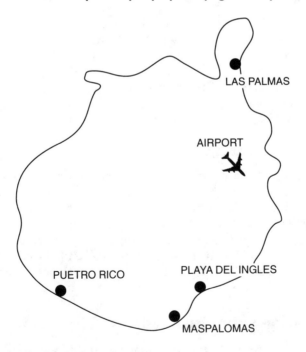

6.4 Map of Gran Canaria

1 Avoid putting too much information on to the paper or transparency. Key words and short statements are better than a page of text (see Fig. 6.3).
2 Keep strictly to one topic per frame or sheet to avoid mixed or confusing messages, i.e. you should not list the facilities of a hotel next to the price, but use one frame for each topic.
3 Be careful of the colours that you use. Some light colours cannot be seen easily from a distance, others do not mix readily. Use dark colours such as black or blue for text, and lighter colours as highlighters.
4 Where you create your own maps, use different shaped symbols – squares, triangles, circles, etc. – to denote the various features such as airport, resorts, etc. (see Fig. 6.4).

HANDLING AUDIENCE QUESTIONS

Why should you allow for audience questions?

Audience questions serve several purposes. First, they allow you to gauge the effectiveness of your presentation. If the audience asks lots of qualifying questions, your presentation has obviously stimulated much thought and interest. If, however, the questions are simply to clarify points you have already made, then perhaps you need to consider whether you might have put things across more clearly. Question time also gives the audience the opportunity to participate, and allows you to expand on specific points which have been raised.

Audience questions should come at the end of the presentation, after you have covered action. In your introduction you should always make a point of forewarning your audience that question time has been allocated.

How do you get audience question time started?

CASE STUDY

Sharon had just finished a very good presentation on a tour to China. She gave an excellent summary of the main points of her talk and wound up her presentation with a good selling statement. She paused, and then turned to the audience.

'So, ladies and gentlemen, I'm sure you've got lots of questions to ask me.'

There was only silence, as everybody looked around to see who would ask the first question. Sharon became more and more uneasy. She looked out at the audience and then said rather cautiously, 'Well, it doesn't look as if anyone wants to ask a question, so I'll just remind you that . . .', and Sharon continued to wrap up her talk and direct people to the drinks and refreshments provided. To her surprise, though, no sooner was the formal part of the evening's presentation concluded, than she became inundated by questions asked by members of the audience who had slipped up to the front of the hall to see her privately.

So, why did the audience fail to take the opportunity to put questions when they were invited?

The answer is that, very often, no one wants to be the first to speak up. This may be because of general embarrassment, or perhaps because people feel that their question will be ridiculously simple, and that they will look foolish for asking it. At such times, the audience may look for a natural leader – someone who is not embarrassed to put the first question. The fact that members of the audience rushed up to Sharon at the end of her presentation was proof that they really did want to ask questions. Sharon can now only give individual answers, and will not have the advantage of making replies to the whole audience. Could she have handled the situation any differently?

Like Sharon, you should always be prepared for a situation where the audience is reluctant to ask questions, and remember that their lack of response is not necessarily a reflection on your presentation. It may be that things were outlined so well in the presentation that nothing needs further clarification. More often than not, though, you will find success with one of the following suggestions:

1   Pose your own question and then answer it:
    'Something I'm often asked is whether it's best to pre-purchase Disney passes, or better to buy them at the gate. (pause) Well, our resort reps hold supplies of Disney passes, so if you intend to visit a number of attractions and make use of a five-day pass, you'll make a considerable saving by buying them in this way. However, if you only intend to visit the Magic Kingdom, it is probably better to buy a pass on the gate. Our resort rep will be able to give you all the up-to-date information. (pause) Now, are there any other questions?'
    If you intend to use this ploy, think about your question and answer when you plan your presentation.
2   Another method of getting questions started is to arrange for someone in the audience to put the first question should there be no response. If you choose this option, ensure that the 'audience plant' is not known as one of your associates, and make sure that you have previously agreed what the question will be.

Dealing effectively with questions

CASE STUDY

I once attended a very enlightening talk by a professor of history who had just given a socialist's view of a particular historic event. During question time I watched with interest the interaction between the speaker and a member of the audience who held very opposing views, and who was determined to 'hog' the floor. The speaker listened carefully to the first question and then gave his answer. As he did so, he looked at, and spoke only to the questioner. Members of the audience seated immediately behind and in front of the questioner began to shift themselves to try to catch the speaker's eye and, as time went by, more remote members of the audience began to shuffle in their seats – at this point still very interested in what the speaker had to say by means of reply.

When the questioner asked a further question, and the speaker again addressed himself solely to her, the audience began to look increasingly disinterested. This quickly turned to frustration and irritation when the questioner was allowed to put a third question and as the audience realised that this had become a two-way conversation between speaker and questioner. I could sense the increasing frustration of the audience, and finally stepped in to say, 'Excuse me, but would it not be a good idea to open this debate to others in the audience?' This was greeted by nods of agreement from the rest of the audience, and the debate was finally opened up.

This incident demonstrates how easy it is to lose the respect of your audience, first by addressing only the questioner and alienating others in the hall, and second, by losing control of the situation and allowing one person to hog the floor. The audience was soon disenchanted with the speaker and, in becoming increasingly angered by the situation, had stopped listening to the debate. In continuing to answer questions put by only one member of the audience, the speaker had shown himself incapable of controlling his own presentation.

What could and should the speaker have done to ensure that he maintained control?

Here are some guidelines to help you handle matters more professionally:

1 First, repeat the question. You can paraphrase or reword this, but there are important reasons for repeating the question: it double checks that you have understood the question; it gives you thinking time before you have to answer; it ensures that the audience has also heard the question; it therefore, means that they will understand the answer.

2 When you give your answer, make it a full and informative one which will be of general interest to other members of the audience. Emphasise important points, but don't allow yourself to wander into other subjects unless they have a direct bearing on the original question. If, as often happens, the question reminds you of another point you want to make, then answer the original question before making your own point.

3 Make sure that you answer the whole audience and not just the person who asked the question. If the rest of the audience is not included then, as the case study showed, question time becomes no more than a private conversation, especially where the questioner goes on to ask further questions.

4 Once you have given your answer to the whole audience, go back to the person who put the question and ask if you have fully answered it.

5 If the questioner then asks a further question, you should answer it briefly and then move on, especially where you can see that others wish to ask a question.

6   Never put a questioner down by saying, 'I thought everyone would know that' or 'I did actually make that point in my talk'. Answer every question politely, and don't allow your irritation to show, even if you and the rest of the audience regard the question as facile or inappropriate. If your audience suspects a 'put-down', then they will almost certainly take the questioner's side. If you alienate the audience, then you will certainly destroy the good impression you have made.

Handling difficult situations during question time

What should you do if someone in the audience asks a question to which you do not know the answer?

Questions of this kind are usually of two types: those asking for very specific data which you can only answer by reference to other sources, and those of a factual nature, where you really do not know the answer. If you really do not know the answer, say so, but do it in such a way that it does not destroy your credibility as a travel expert. You should say, 'I'll need to get the latest information on that' or 'Yes, that's a changing picture, and I'd like to see you when I have the latest information'.

If you don't know the answer, though, never throw the question open to your audience. If someone else knows, or thinks that they know the answer you will lose control and undermine your credibility. Neither should you be tempted to lie.

Here are some guidelines to help you with this situation:

1   Promise to see the person privately afterwards, then make arrangements to provide them with the answer at a convenient time.

2   Ask a knowledgeable colleague to handle the question. If you know you are likely to be asked questions of a specialised nature, discuss which areas you are likely to pass over to them. If you have made a joint presentation with another speaker, you might invite them to answer the question. If you do, make sure that you retain control of the situation by taking the lead again when the question has been answered.

What should you do if a member of the audience uses question time as an opportunity to make a complaint or a statement?

This can cause a certain amount of embarrassment, especially where the complainant believes they have a valid case. Obviously, there is no point in becoming embroiled in an open debate, neither is it worth entering into any form of discussion. You may need to adopt a fairly assertive approach if you wish to avoid things getting out of hand, but your presentation is not the place for this sort of discussion. Tell the complainant quite firmly, but politely, that you will gladly take up their complaint, but that it must be done through the normal channels. If the complaint is about the tour operator, and their representative is present, the same action should be taken. Above all, you should guard against being drawn into any argument which may harm the credibility of you and your company.

As soon as you realise that you are listening to a complaint, the best approach is to say,

'Right, sir (or madam). We obviously need to look into this matter. Perhaps you will see me directly we have finished?' This is normally sufficient to placate the genuine complainant, but if you have someone who is determined to make a stand, you will need to repeat your message and be firm. Complaints made in this way are very rare. Some people like to make a big show and maximise your embarrassment, but it is more likely to be a genuine grievance and, if it is, you may need to consider how things got this far and why the matter wasn't dealt with through the normal channels.

Ending the question session

When you see that you are coming to the end of your allocated question time, you should tell your audience. Do this by stating that you have time to take two further questions, then point out those from whom you will take a question, give your answers and close the session. If there are still people keen to ask further questions, you may need to offer them an opportunity to speak to you privately afterwards.

Question time is often a good opportunity to reflect on your performance and on the balance of your presentation. Too few questions may indicate that the points were well covered, but may also point to audience fatigue or general disinterest. Too many questions might suggest that the subject was not covered sufficiently well, but it might also indicate that the audience was keen to learn more. Whatever your findings, remember that the real test of success is how your presentation shapes up to the aims and objectives, and the target you set before you started.

SUMMARY

Let's just recap on the main points from this chapter on presentations:

- Identify your target audience and set an objective.
- Structure your talk or presentation, making sure you have a good beginning, middle and end.
- Use the marketing principle called AIDA – Attention, Interest, Desire and Action.
- Use a mind-map to focus on the important issues.
- Use cue cards, but write only the key points.
- Highlight all key points by using visuals.
- Use a register appropriate to your audience.
- Make full use of voice and body language.
- Summarise the key points of your presentation.
- Close in a positive way.
- Allocate a specified amount of time for questions.
- Sum up when you have finished.

7

Basics of assertiveness

No book on interpersonal skills would be complete without a section on assertiveness. This is the art of stating your case clearly, concisely and respectfully to others. Assertiveness is a form of behaviour which is used to communicate to others when we speak or when we use body language. Each of us is capable of adopting different styles of behaviour – aggressive, non-assertive or assertive – depending on the situation and our own internal feelings about such matters. Good communication skills often require a high degree of assertiveness to enable us to say what we think, want and feel in a way which is honest but, at the same time, respects the feelings of others. Assertiveness does not come naturally to all of us; it is necessary to learn the underlying influences which cause us to behave in a certain way, and then to develop assertiveness techniques to deal with situations which might previously have been handled in a less appropriate manner. This chapter aims to provide you with an insight into the different styles of behaviour, and guidelines to develop a more assertive approach to communication in certain important situations.

OBJECTIVES

Once you have read this chapter of the book you will be able to:
- **identify the verbal and non-verbal characteristics of the states of assertiveness**
- **identify situations in which you find difficulty in adopting an assertive approach**
- **use assertiveness techniques to decline offers and refuse requests**
- **deal effectively with anger and criticism**
- **deal effectively with potential confrontation.**

TRANSACTIONAL ANALYSIS

Before covering specific aspects of assertiveness, we first need to look at a theory of communication developed in the 1950s by Canadian-born Eric Berne, called 'transactional analysis'. This theory was originally developed for use in psychology, but is now often incorporated in training and development programmes on communication and interpersonal skills.

Berne's theory was that in each of us as adults, there exists three states of mind called 'ego states'. These are **Parent**, **Adult** and **Child** and, although most of us have one predominant state which is evident in our usual method of communication, we are all able to switch from one ego state to another depending on the situation and our feelings towards it.

The three ego states

Parent

Parent represents most of the things we learned up to the age of five from our parents and other figures of authority. Beyond this age, the learning is merely reinforced. As parents have two main functions in life – caring, and teaching and discipline – the Parent state is divided into two categories; nurturing parent and critical parent.

How to recognise the Parent ego state in communication The nurturing parent is caring and sympathetic, and uses phrases like 'poor thing', 'how sweet', 'never mind', and is generally concerned about humanity. Body language used in this ego state may include: a pat on the arm, a sympathetic smile, or a gentle look of understanding. The critical parent is controlling and limiting, and makes pronouncements such as, 'the young of today don't know they're born', 'that's typical!', 'it shouldn't be allowed', 'you can't do that'. Other critical parent clues are; 'don't', 'always', 'never', or anything judgemental which is an automatic reaction. Such pronouncements are never based on analysis or consideration of the real facts. Critical parent body language includes; frowning, pursed lips, finger-wagging, tutting and sighing, and is usually accompanied by a stern look. The critical parent does not smile.

Child

The child in us represents what we felt and the way we behaved as very young children. The Child state, like the Parent state, stays with us throughout our lives and is about feelings and emotions, elation, laughter, anger, play, frustration and creativity. The Child state, like the Parent state, is divisible into a number of substates; the natural child, the rebellious child and the adapted child.

How to recognise the Child ego state in communication The natural child is simply that – natural, fun, full of laughter, noisy and uninhibited. Typical natural child statements are: 'sounds great', 'look what I've done', 'let's do it'. The rebellious child can be subtle or more obvious. The obvious state is one of temper tantrums and rages, and a typical statement would be, 'I won't do it!' or 'I don't care'. The subtle state is a far more devious state, often inciting others to be the rebels. Typically, people using this ego state will say, 'don't take any notice of him' or 'you don't want to be bothered with that'.

The adapted child is an adult state which looks back to childhood and the helplessness and hopelessness of being an infant. The adapted child uses phrases like: 'I can't', 'It's no good', 'Sorry', and looks downcast and uncomfortable, pouts and often looks on the verge of tears. This is the grown up saying, as a child would, 'I can't cope . . . I can't manage'.

Adult

The adult is the thinking, rational and reasoning part of us which is not emotional. The Adult state represents maturity. This is the calm and collected person who is able to analyse facts and thoughts, and able to make a sound, rational decision.

How to recognise the Adult state in communication The adult may use words and phrases such as, 'I believe we should . . .', 'comparatively speaking . . .', or will ask open questions such as, 'why', 'what', 'when'. Adult body language is always open, expressive and meaningful.

Transactional analysis in communication

The importance of transactional analysis (TA) in communication is that we respond to a given situation in a like manner, that is, in the same ego state. As we have just outlined, people have three different ego states – Child, Parent and Adult – and certain actions trigger off a corresponding reaction in us; e.g. certain things will always trigger the anger response and certain situations will always trigger a laughter response.

You will remember that these behavioural patterns are experienced and learned during childhood and are heavily influenced by those closest to us, and their own response to given situations. However, we do not simply respond to an action. It is actually more complex than this in that there is usually an expected type of response from the other person, called 'the pay-off'. So, on a miserable, cold November day, if I were to meet someone at the bus-stop and pass the remark, 'Raining again! It never seems to stop', I am doing so in the expectation that the other person will pass a similar remark in agreement, 'Typical British weather'. This is the pay-off. I complain about the weather, the other person supports my complaint, and I feel that my complaint has been justified.

In a similar way, two people may be talking about the state of modern youth.

'Children today', says one, 'get everything they want. We never did.'

'They don't know they're born,' says the other. 'We didn't have half of what they have – and the money that's spent on them!'

And so the conversation continues, each one receiving a pay-off in the form of a validating comment from the other.

This kind of conversation, perhaps meaningless in its way, is nevertheless, very commonly heard. You will notice in this example that neither person is discussing an actual incident, although it is fair to say that something has either been seen, heard or read to trigger off such a response. Both parties were actually using the Parent state to communicate, and you will remember that this is characterised by pronouncements which demand no analysis of the facts, no in-depth discussion of data and no examination of the particular issues. These are simply triggered responses which fit the form of conversation in an ideal way.

Each separate interaction, the pronouncement made by that person, is called 'a transaction'. Transactional analysis is the study of Child, Parent and Adult interactions between two people. The case above is a Parent transaction. The analysis of transaction between two people shows that these can be either a complementary transaction, or a crossed transaction. Let's see how these work in practice.

Complementary transaction

In the following example, both people are using Parent to speak to each other.

    A: Well! Isn't that just a typical reaction from Barbara.
    B: I know, but that's about all you can expect from her.
    A: She should look to her own department before she criticises me.
    B: Exactly. People in glass houses shouldn't throw stones.

Both parties in this transaction are communicating at Parent level and are being judgemental about Barbara. This is a complementary transaction because both are receiving the response they are looking for and in so doing are triggering off a further Parent response of the same kind which serves the purpose of confirming each one's prejudices against Barbara. In this example both parties are communicating in the same ego state, Parent. A's Parent is talking to B's Parent and B's Parent is responding back to A's Parent. This is why the transaction is complementary.

Complimentary transactions do not necessarily need both parties to be using the same ego state. Let's say that instead of Critical Parent (CP) talking to Critical Parent as in the previous example, instead A's Critical Parent spoke to B's Adapted Child (AC). In order for this transaction to remain complementary, B's Adapted Child would have to respond to A's Critical Parent. So A plays the part of Critical Parent throughout, and B responds as Adapted Child throughout, e.g.:

    DAVID: Sharon, how many times have I told you not to let tickets go out until I've checked them? (CP)
    SHARON: Sorry, David. [*Shrinking a little*] I forgot. (AC)
    DAVID: Well make sure you don't do it again or there will be trouble. (CP)
    SHARON: I'll try, David. Sorry, David. (AC)
    DAVID: Well, I get fed up with telling you. (CP)
    SHARON: Yes, I am sorry, David. [*Looks on the verge of tears*] I'll try and remember in future. (AC)

This is perhaps a not untypical scenario in any travel agency where the manager is dissatisfied with the standard of work delivered by a member of staff. The way in which the situation was dealt with, however, was not so typical. In this case, the manager is using Critical Parent to admonish Sharon's Adapted

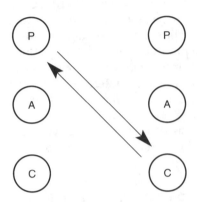

Fig. 7.1 Model of a complementary transaction between Parent and Child states

Child (see Fig. 7.1). It is Sharon's Adapted Child which replies – you will remember that typical Child responses are: 'Sorry', 'I can't manage', 'I never seem to get it right', 'I can't cope'. The conversation will remain complementary as long as Sharon's Adapted Child continues to respond in the expected way to David's Critical Parent. David's first remark was a reaction triggered by the situation, and Sharon's first apology, given in response to David's Critical Parent, confirms his Parent status. Each time these two speak to each other, they are simply reconfirming their status as Parent and Child and providing that each responds in a similar vein the conversation will continue in exactly the same manner.

This does not necessarily mean that both parties are happy with the outcome of the conversation, in fact far from it. Although it is likely that David feels satisfied that he has properly dealt with the situation by behaving in this way, probably in the same way that his own parents spoke to him when he was a small child, Sharon probably feels very upset and humiliated by the whole incident. She will be experiencing all of the feelings of a small child which has been told off by its parents. It is because she subconsciously recognised David's tone as Critical Parent, that she automatically responded as she would have, to one of her own parents when she was told off. Simply because the transaction is complementary does not mean that both parties are happy with the outcome.

David may think that in acting in the way in which he did, he had solved the problem, especially as Sharon was so apologetic and has promised not to do it again. If she responds in true Adapted Child fashion, she will ensure that she doesn't make the same mistake again so as to avoid incurring David's wrath in the future. However, the problem is not always solved by such a transaction. David has singularly failed to act in an adult manner, i.e. to find out the root of the problem by simple examination of the facts. One thing you may notice about this transaction is the complete lack of attention to factual information, unless, of course, David saw his previous reprimand as a matter of fact. In this event, the complementary transaction of Critical Parent to Adapted Child may have solved the problem, but very importantly it is worth noting that David has failed to establish the underlying reasons for Sharon's lack of attention to detail.

One other very dominant ego state adopted by people in a superior position, is Nurturing Parent, and is more likely to be used by women than by men. This is the mode of the caring sympathetic parent figure removing the troubles of the worried child. Nurturing Parent (NP) works best with Adapted Child (AP). This is a true complementary transaction which satisfies both the need of the Parent state to nurse and give comfort, and the needs of the Adapted Child which asks for security, love and understanding. Nurturing Parent is inappropriate to any state other than Adapted Child, and can be regarded by others as a tendency to interfere or be suppressive.

> JOYCE: I think we've got a little bit of a problem here. Would you like to discuss it now, or shall we have a little chat later? (NP)
> SHARON: Oh, those tickets! I'm sorry, I forgot to ask you to check them. (AC)
> JOYCE: Not to worry, I'm sure they were alright. (NP)
> SHARON: I'm sorry, I've got so much to do, I just forgot. (AC)
> JOYCE: Don't worry about it. Are you under too much pressure? You haven't been looking very well. (NP)

In this example, Joyce's Nurturing Parent is just what Sharon's Adapted Child responds best to. Joyce has soothed Sharon's worries about being told off and is showing concern about her general well-being. Although this is a true complementary transaction in which both parties are satisfied with the pay-off they are receiving, the satisfactory outcome to the issue of unchecked tickets is doubtful, since Joyce appears to be more interested in Sharon's welfare than the original issue. In cases where staff recognise and manipulate such behaviour in a manager, the situation could arise where staff are allowed to be a little lax in their approach, and consider the manager to be a little soft and easy to get round.

Crossed transaction

We have already said that complementary transactions are, in their way, harmonious responses from each individual. But what might have happened in the case of David and Sharon's conversation if Sharon's Critical Parent had responded to David's Child? The result, as you will see, is that both parties adopt a superior attitude and talk down to one another.

> DAVID: How many times have I told you not to send tickets out until after I've checked them? (CP)
> SHARON: You've never said that. (CP)
> DAVID: Don't take that tone of voice with me young lady – yes I have. (CP)
> Sharon: Oh no you haven't! And how am I supposed to get them checked when you're never here? (CP)
> DAVID: How dare you talk to me like that. Just who do you think you are? (CP)
> SHARON: [*Throws down files and stalks off*] (Rebellious Child)

This is a crossed transaction (see Fig. 7.2) because Sharon does not respond in the manner which David's initial reaction demands. Instead Sharon turns her Critical Parent on David's Child which causes David to respond with double ferocity, i.e. David's Critical Parent now tries to control Sharon's Rebellious Child

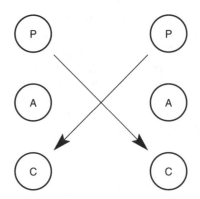

Fig. 7.2 Model of a crossed transaction showing each person's Critical Parent addressing the other's Adapted Child

– an indignant manager talking to an aggressive subordinate. As you can see though, this fails to move Sharon and her Critical Parent turns the blame on to David's Child. This then turns into a 'strongest wins, weakest loses' contest, with David's Critical Parent using the full force of his managerial authority to shout down Sharon's Rebellious Child. Finally the show down ends with Sharon making a last rebellious gesture by stalking off. The crossed transaction ends with David believing that he has asserted his authority and Sharon in return disregarding it by turning her back on him. As you can see, this type of crossed transaction always turns into a conflict because the Adult ego state is totally missing.

Using the adult

The Adult ego state is one of analytical and reasoned argument. This is the rational, inquisitive, thinking and reasoning person. The Adult ego state offers an opportunity for discussion of the facts and generally leads to an amicable and satisfactory solution.

Let's look at the scene once more, and see how an initially crossed transaction turns quickly into a complementary Adult transaction (see Fig. 7.3) and an amicable solution.

> DAVID: Sharon, I noticed that you sent some tickets to Mr Jenson yesterday. Was there any reason why you didn't ask me to check them? (Adult)
> SHARON: I'm sorry, David. [*Shrinking a little*] I forgot. (AC)
> DAVID: We have discussed this before, Sharon, and it is important that tickets are double checked to ensure that any errors are picked up. So how can we make sure that you remember to get them checked in the future? (Adult)
> SHARON: Well . . . [*Hesitates*] (AC)
> DAVID: [*Waits patiently*] (Adult)

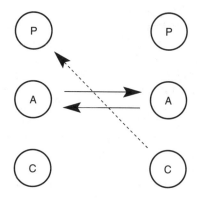

Fig. 7.3 Model of a crossed transaction which becomes complementary through the use of the Adult ego state

SHARON: Well, I could put an extra column in the ticket stock book to say who checked the tickets. (Adult)

DAVID: Alright, we'll give that a try and see how we get along. Have you got any more tickets to issue today? (Adult)

SHARON: Yes, there are some for Mrs Moore, I'll show them to you when they're finished.

David's Adult enquiry after the facts received a very childlike apology from Sharon, not perhaps the response he was expecting. However, his patience with Sharon is rewarded when she realises that such an apology is inappropriate and begins to change her ego state to Adult. At the point where Sharon begins to change her ego state, i.e. 'Well . . .', had David lost patience and switched to Critical Parent with the typical remark, 'Well come on – out with it!', Sharon would have reverted to Adapted Child (AC). By continuing in the Adult state, David encouraged Sharon's Adult to respond and together they work out a solution in true Adult fashion.

Assignment   Think about situations at home or at work where you have communicated in a way which was perhaps not entirely appropriate.

1 Which ego state did you use?

2 What were your internal feelings when you used this state? (anger, rejection?)

3 What kind of response did you receive from the other person?

4 Had you communicated in an Adult state, how might this have affected the outcome of the conversation?

The first and very important stage of ensuring that you communicate in an appropriate manner is to identify exactly what triggers off your emotions and tunes you into a particular ego state. Dr Berne refers to this as 'hooking'. For example, you may be behaving in a perfectly adult and rational manner until some poor unsuspecting soul makes a comment similar to a pronouncement your own father continually made when you were a small child. Subconsciously, you tune into all of the bad feelings you experienced then, and have an uncontrollable urge to behave in the same way now as you did then. This could be to express anger and frustration, or to withdraw and sulk. The person who made the comment won't understand why you have behaved in this way, and will probably consider that you are overreacting, or are simply in a bad mood. What they won't know is that they have inadvertently 'hooked' your Child and that is what they are now experiencing. This doesn't mean that your behaviour is 'childish', it just means that all of the emotions described in the previous pages have been unleashed.

To behave in an assertive manner, you need to be able to understand what causes these, perhaps temporary, lapses in personality and try to overcome your natural internal feelings and deal with the situation in a calmer, more adult manner. This can't be done overnight, but with thought and practice can be achieved.

THE FOUR STATES OF ASSERTIVE BEHAVIOUR

To examine the art of assertiveness more closely, we need to understand the characteristics of the four states of assertive behaviour. The states are; Aggressive, Indirectly Aggressive, Non-assertive and Assertive.

Aggressive behaviour

Aggressive behaviour is characterised by an angry and forceful manner which is sometimes aimed at belittling others, attacking their ideas or personalities, and generally ensuring that any potentially threatening situation is knocked down or removed. The aggressor always sets out to win any situation which is seen as potentially threatening. Aggressive types have a tendency to 'fly off the handle' at the slightest thing and have a reputation of being very prickly characters, whom most people seek to avoid. If a person lacks self-esteem, they may use aggressive behaviour as a way of keeping others at a safe distance lest they should discover their vulnerability and use it against them. Being on the receiving end of aggressive behaviour can be unpleasant and often provokes an equally aggressive response. Alternatively, well-aimed attacks from the aggressor may make the recipient feel very hurt and upset. Either way, aggressive behaviour does nothing to cement good working relationships – it usually drives people apart or puts others immediately on the defence.

In a work situation, this can make communication very difficult, especially if it is the manager who is the aggressor. Staff will keep their distance and will often be afraid of the repercussions from saying what they feel or asking for help with a problem. Although the aggressive manager may feel it necessary to ensure that staff toe the line, such behaviour usually results in low staff morale. Aggressive behaviour is more commonly seen in those holding a superior position, simply because their authority makes it safe for them to act in this way. If aggressive superiors were to relax more, and develop an assertive approach, staff would almost certainly have greater respect and morale would benefit.

Non-verbal signs of aggressive behaviour

Impatient sighs, hands on hips, pursed lips, chin thrust forward, finger pointing, foot tapping, stalking about, door slamming, drawer banging, etc.

Verbal signs of aggressive behaviour

'Rubbish!' 'You don't know what you're talking about', 'If you think you're so clever, you do it', 'Who asked you?', 'Only an idiot would think of that'.

Indirectly aggressive behaviour

People who are indirectly aggressive have most of the same internal feelings that an aggressive person has, but the outward expression of their emotion is quite different. The indirect aggressor will show few outward signs of aggression other than through their body language, but this is rather more subtle than the direct aggressor. The indirect aggressor never launches into a full-frontal verbal attack, but instead will look to operate undercover, though still aiming at the vulnerability and sensitivity of others. Attacks by directly aggressive people, whilst unpleasant, are at least straightforward and open. Open aggressors rarely disguise their intentions. The more subtle indirect aggressor will aim with as much precision, but will then often smile sweetly and deny any intention of malice. Indirect aggressors are usually capable of harbouring deep grudges. Staff working for an indirectly aggressive manager never feel entirely at ease with them, but can never quite put a finger on just what it is that makes them uncomfortable. The normal sense is one of being manipulated, and this can make staff very wary.

Stronger characters may try to outmanoeuvre the indirectly aggressive manager, but once their actions or intentions are detected, it is likely to become a cold and steely battle for supremacy. What appears as friendly rivalry on the surface may often conceal earnest and deadly intent.

Signs of indirectly aggressive behaviour

It is very difficult to categorise the specific signs which give someone away as an indirect aggressor. These people usually project an exterior quite different from the way they are truly feeling. They are well able to hide their real intentions and aims, and often have the ability to change colour (and sides!) like a chameleon. When in a high state of anxiety, the indirect aggressor may unintentionally let their mask drop by showing some of the non-verbal behaviour more characteristic of the direct aggressor. However, body language is more likely to be subtle and the indirect aggressor's real feelings may be betrayed only by a flash of the eye or tensing of the facial muscles. Recognising the indirect aggressor is often more a matter of intuition than observation.

If you cross swords with an indirect aggressor, you may just feel a sense of discomfort, or an underlying feeling of insincerity, guardedness or over secretiveness. Indirect aggressors are closed books, and the unwary seldom realise this until they are unfortunate enough to be just another casualty.

Non-assertive behaviour

The non-assertive, or passive person, avoids any kind of confrontation. Their way is usually to give in to others. They find it difficult to make painful decisions and will generally avoid taking responsibility, often manipulating others to make decisions and do the unpleasant bidding for them. Non-assertive people are usually put upon, sometimes even inviting this, but they also have a need to let others know how much they are asked to do and that they always get the most dull and uninteresting tasks. Non-assertive people tend to have a fairly negative and fatalistic outlook on life, but seem to lack the willpower to do anything about it. Instead they sit back and wait for the world to change, and for change to force itself on them. The usual cry is, 'Well, there was nothing I could do about it'.

Non-assertive people have a tendency to put themselves down. They invariably refuse to accept any responsibility for what befalls them, and often try to attach themselves to a stronger, more assertive person, who will give them a helping hand through life. Sometimes these partnerships work well, but more often than not the stronger character becomes irritated or frustrated at the other's lack of drive and will-power, and resentful at having the burden of this dependency.

In the case of a non-assertive manager, many problems will arise. The manager will be unable to make the decisions or take on the responsibility that the position demands, and any problems with the staff are likely to be ignored in the hope that they will sort themselves out, and save the manager from confrontation or from having to make an unpleasant decision. The non-assertive manager will find it difficult to take the lead in any interview and will almost certainly be unable to exercise any discipline or control on the occasions when this is necessary. Staff may well take advantage of this situation, work the system and do as much or as little as they please. They may also become frustrated at the manager's apparent lack of ability to take the lead, and may feel demotivated as a result.

Non-verbal signs of non-assertive behaviour

Shifting of weight from one foot to the other, avoidance of eye contact, head down, slumped shoulders, nervous movements, closed body and hand gestures.

Verbal signs of non-assertive behaviour

'There's nothing I can do about it', 'Well you know how it is . . .', 'It's out of my hands', 'I'm not very good at this sort of thing'.

Assertive behaviour

Assertive people are generally open and honest, and find no difficulty in saying what they want and how they feel, while at the same time respecting the feelings of others. They take responsibility for their actions and will usually think things through if they are angry, rather than storming into a situation in a rage. Assertive people will negotiate and work towards a satisfactory solution to a problem which is acceptable to both parties. This is a 'win–win' situation. The assertive person has self-confidence and personal security and therefore has no need to put others down. Instead they are able to recognise the strengths of others and use them in a productive way. They will not feel threatened by the abilities, opinions or positions of others, and although they may feel a little angry or upset if their own ideas are rejected, they will try to view the situation as objectively as possible and try not to take the rejection personally.

An assertive manager usually possesses very good communication skills and is seen by their staff as fair and approachable, yet able to be firm and exercise strong leadership skills where necessary. The assertive manager will be very good in any situation which requires negotiation skills in order to reach a satisfactory outcome and will probably be effective at solving day-to-day staff issues and conflict. They can usually be relied upon to take up an issue on behalf of their staff and speak rationally about it to an authority figure in order to reach a satisfactory outcome.

Non-verbal signs of assertive behaviour

Open hand gestures, relaxed upright position, good eye contact, genuine smile, head upright.

Verbal signs of assertive behaviour

'I see your point of view, but explain how this affects our product', 'I've noticed that you've been late a few mornings this week and I feel that we need to discuss this', 'That sounds a great idea. Where do we go from here?', 'Thanks for asking me, but it's really not my sort of thing. I appreciate the thought though'.

....

Exercise

Read through each of the four scenarios below and identify which state of assertiveness is being used in each case.

1 Mandy wants the day off next Tuesday to see her grandmother on her seventieth birthday. She has already been allocated next Thursday and would like to swap this with another member of staff. She approaches her manager, but stands some distance away until her presence is noticed. Her manager looks up and smiles.

'Yes Mandy.' says her manager.

Mandy chews her lower lip and then says haltingly, 'You know that I wouldn't normally ask . . . um . . . well I was wondering. I've got Thursday off, and well, could I have Tuesday off instead? I know it might be a bit of a problem. It doesn't matter if I can't, but I just thought I'd ask . . . that's it really.'

2 Janice storms through the office door and heads straight for her desk. She slams down her briefcase and glares at a note that has been left in the top of her tray.

'What's this?' she blasts. 'How many times have I told you, I don't deal with accounts queries any more?'

Janice's assistant manager approaches.

'Janice?' she says.

Janice purses her lips, exhales deeply and says, 'Not now, Helen. Can't you see I'm up to my eyes?'

3 Martin needs to speak to a member of his staff, Jenny, about an error in her work. He calls Jenny into his office.

'Jenny. We've had a call from Mr Blake complaining that you gave him a wrong departure time. I've checked the file and there does appear to be an error. Can you throw any light on this?'

4 Susan has heard that a member of her staff, Sandra, has complained that she doesn't get the opportunity to do any of the interesting work in the office. Susan calls Sandra into her office to discuss the matter. 'I understand that you're not happy working with us, Sandra.'

Sandra is completely taken aback by this statement and is immediately worried. Susan continues, 'I've heard that you've complained that I'm not giving you enough interesting work. I was rather surprised at that.'

Sandra feels that she has been cornered and is desperately looking for a way out.

'No,' she says, 'it's just that I'm keen to get on and learn new things, that's all.'

Susan offers a condescending smile.

'Well, we all have to start somewhere, my dear. Once you've proved to me that I can trust you to get on with the tasks that you're given without making any more fuss, then we'll see what else you might be able to do.'

Sandra feels rather uncomfortable about the conversation, but isn't really sure why.

'OK,' she says.

'Good,' says Susan. 'Well, we'll say no more about it.' She shows Sandra out and makes a mental note to keep an eye on the girl in future. Sandra feels that she has been manipulated in some way, but isn't quite sure how. Somehow, she doesn't feel that Susan has been entirely straight with her.

Answers

1 Mandy is being non-assertive and is positively inviting a refusal to her request.

2 Janice is very aggressive. She is obviously in a bad temper, and doesn't appear to feel the need to modify her behaviour towards her staff. In fact she probably feels justified in being angry with them too.

3 Martin is being assertive. He has stated the facts without any accusation or display of anger and invites Jenny to give her side of the story.

4 Susan is being indirectly aggressive. She feels threatened by Sandra and wants to quash any challenge to her decisions. Her attack on Sandra is not direct, but

manipulative. Her smile is not sincere or friendly, but expresses an 'I've won' type of attitude. Susan will probably make life very difficult for Sandra if she feels that Sandra raises any further challenges in the future.

Assignment

1 Read through the following scenario:

You are the supervisor of the accounts department. Your Managing Director has just stopped you in the corridor and informed you that a young lady by the name of Tracey Hodges is to be transferred to the accounts department from another office where she has fallen out with the manager.

'She's starting next week. Hope that's alright with you,' he says as he walks away.

You've heard all about Tracey Hodges and the disruptive influence that she has. You know instinctively that your own staff will be very unhappy about her arrival.

2 Make some notes on a sheet of paper about how you would react to this news in each of the behavioural states: aggressive, indirectly aggressive, non-assertive and assertive.

HOW BEHAVIOUR CHANGES IN DIFFERENT SITUATIONS

Everyone has a dominant behavioural state which is used in most communication. However, you may be aware that certain situations, or perhaps, certain people cause you to behave in a totally different manner.

CASE STUDY

Jerry was appointed to the position of Operations Manager of a medium-sized tour operator three months ago. He has a reputation of being outgoing and friendly and is considered fair and a good leader by his staff. Jerry has no problems with communicating in an assertive manner with his staff, with travel agents and with direct customers who telephone the department, and is usually able to settle any disputes or disagreements in an amicable way.

Once a month Jerry is called to attend a manager's meeting at which the Managing Director and the other four department heads are present. Prior to the first meeting Jerry was a little apprehensive, and was conscious that he wanted to make a good impression on the other managers who were to be present. To this end, he spent a good deal of time in preparation for the meeting and made a list of the points he wanted to raise. However, when he got to the meeting, his confidence evaporated and he found he was subordinating himself to the other managers. When asked for his comments on specific issues he declined to comment, stating that the others were in a far better position than he to make such a judgement. When agreements were sought, he found himself going along with what the others had said, even though inside, he did not agree. Jerry was appalled at his behaviour, but put it down to nerves and assumed that the next meeting would be much better. However, at the next meeting his behaviour was little altered, and, try as he might, Jerry was unable to communicate in the assertive manner which came so naturally to him when he talked with his staff. After the third meeting Jerry began to notice that the others didn't ask for his opinions and had a tendency to conduct the business of the meeting without any acknowledgment or referral to him. Jerry knew that to succeed in his new role and to earn the respect of his fellow managers, he needed to change his behaviour. But how? What was it that caused him to behave in this way?

Here, Jerry is a manager who is able to adopt an assertive manner with his subordinates, but finds it very difficult to be assertive with his colleagues and superiors. When faced with this situation he becomes non-assertive, and is perhaps considered rather weak by the other managers. It's not that Jerry lacks ideas and managerial skill, it's just that something inside of him makes him adopt a passive and subordinate role when communicating with people who he considers to be superior to him. If we refer back to Transactional Analysis, Jerry subconsciously recognises the other people at the management meeting to be parental figures of authority. He allows his Child to be hooked and adopts a Child to Parent, or non-assertive role of communication. In order to overcome this problem, Jerry needs first to recognise what is happening to him internally. Once he understands the reason for this switch in behavioural state, he will then be more able to make the changes he needs in order to become more assertive in this particular situation.

Once he has done this, Jerry needs to visualise himself being assertive at these meetings, and perhaps the easiest way for him to do this is to recall an incident during a meeting in which he would have liked to have behaved in a more assertive manner. He should then rehearse in his mind what he would have said or done if he were to be given the opportunity all over again. Having done this a few times, Jerry should now prepare himself for the next meeting. He should think about the issues which are likely to be discussed and imagine himself at the meeting making his points in an assertive manner. He may even find it useful to practise in front of a mirror so that he can observe his body language and ensure that this, too, is conveying an assertive message. Visualising the scene in this way will not necessarily mean that Jerry will become assertive with his colleagues overnight, and he will need to review his progress after each meeting and repeat the visualisation process. With patience and determination, he will begin to change his behaviour, and this will soon become evident to his colleagues, who may then invite him to contribute to the meetings and value his thoughts and opinions.

Assignment   1 Think about how you respond to different people and situations. Using the grid
in Fig. 7.4, identify which state of assertiveness you would normally use in each
of the situations with the person indicated at the top, e.g. you may behave in
assertive manner when you make requests of co-workers, but adopt a non-assertive manner when making requests of a friend.

2 In the situations where you have identified a behavioural state other than
assertiveness, try and identify what it is about the situation that makes you behave
in this way.

3 If you would like to change your behaviour to be more assertive in any specific
situation identified above, then you can start by practising the visualisation
techniques described in the previous pages.

....

ASSERTIVENESS TECHNIQUES

Once you have identified specific situations in which you find difficulty in
behaving in an assertive manner, you may need to employ more specific assertiveness techniques to overcome this behaviour. The remainder of this chapter provides
guidelines for adopting specific assertiveness techniques, including: refusing a
request, handling criticism, dealing with anger and dealing with confrontation.

Make requests	Friend	Spouse/ partner	Family	Authority figures	Co-workers and subordinates
Initiate and maintain conversation					
Stand up for your legitimate rights					
Refuse requests and invitations					

Fig. 7.4 State of assertiveness grid

Refusing a request

How good are you at saying 'No'? Some people find this a very hard thing to do and find themselves in all sorts of unwelcome and unintended situations as a result – accepting unwanted invitations, agreeing to things they would not normally agree to, or taking on work they really don't have time or the capacity to do. Unfortunately, in both the business and the leisure environment, such people are quickly recognised as a 'soft touch' and may find others taking advantage of their passive nature.

What is it that makes us feel so badly about saying 'No'? People who find difficulty in refusing requests usually feel ill at ease for one of the following reasons:

- they might hurt the other person's feelings
- they consider that saying 'No' is quite selfish
- they find it far easier to say 'Yes' than to say 'No'.

If you ever experience any of these feelings, you need to examine the methods by which you refuse, or even accept requests from other people.

Do you try to make excuses? 'Thursday? Oh, if it had been any other day I would have come, but I'm busy I'm afraid.' Or do you defer the decision to someone else? 'Well, if it were up to me I'd say yes, but I think you had better ask Malcolm.' Or do you find yourself saying 'Yes' when you really mean 'No'? You say, 'Yes, of course I'll do those returns for you'. You think, 'I hate doing returns and I haven't got the time. Why do I always let myself be persuaded so easily?'

In none of these situations are you being very honest with yourself, and being honest with yourself is one of the fundamentals of assertiveness. If you simply put up an excuse, the person making the request will almost certainly recognise it as an excuse, and may be more put out than if you had originally been straightforward in your refusal.

....

CASE STUDY

Anabelle has been asked by a friend to go along to a social event organised by the local Travel Trades Club and join a panel to debate the issues of personal safety when travelling abroad. Anabelle is reluctant to become involved, but doesn't like to let her friend down, so she agrees. As the date draws nearer, Anabelle becomes increasingly uncomfortable about the debate and tries to think of ways to get out of it. She discusses it with a friend at work to see if there is someone else who might go in her place, but no one is interested. She asks her husband for advice, but he only concludes, 'Well, you did agree to do it, you can't let her down now.'

Anabelle can see no easy way out and eventually decides to phone her friend and explain that she made a mistake in agreeing to be part of the debate, to apologise, and to withdraw gracefully. She dials her friend's number.

'Hello, Kate, it's Anabelle. I was just ringing about the debate on Thursday.'

'Oh hi, Anabelle,' says her friend, 'I was just going to ring you. We've got an excellent team together for the debate and we've decided to allocate the various topics before we start. We'd like you to take "Looking after your valuables". Is that OK?'

Anabelle's heart sinks, she can't possibly withdraw now.

'Yes, that's fine,' she says and terminates the conversation.

Thursday morning arrives and Anabelle still can't find a way out of attending the debate. Eventually she makes a decision and phones her friend at work. A secretary answers the call and informs Anabelle that Kate is in a meeting and offers to take a message. Anabelle is relieved at not having to speak to Kate herself.

'Could you tell Kate that Anabelle Johnson rang. I'm supposed to be attending a debate this evening, but I've developed the most awful migraine and I'm just off home to bed. So please tell here that I'm very sorry, but I won't be there tonight.'

Anabelle puts the phone down filled with relief that she doesn't have to go, but feeling a strong sense of guilt about what she has just done.

When Kate comes out of her meeting, her secretary gives her the message. Kate feels slightly annoyed. She had a feeling that Anabelle would drop out at the last moment, and recalls that this is not the first time that Anabelle has withdrawn from an arrangement on the day. Last time it was a migraine, too. Kate feels very hurt that her friend should lie to her in this way.

'I didn't force her into it,' she thinks. 'If she didn't want to be involved I'd rather she had just been honest with me and said so.'

By behaving in this way, Anabelle has made the situation far worse than if she had been honest with her friend in the first place, and had refused the request. Now she feels guilty about what she has done. She has let Kate down at the last minute, and Kate is understandably annoyed at the way Anabelle has behaved.

Let's examine the ways that Anabelle could, and should have dealt with the situation. She could have refused the request outright.

'Thank you for thinking of me, Kate, but I'd be terrified. I really don't think I would do a very good job.'

If Kate had been persistent, then Anabelle should have remained firm.

'No, Kate, really. I'll have to say No!'

If Anabelle really couldn't find it within herself to refuse the request outright, then she could have bought herself a little time.

'I'm really not sure, Kate. Can I think about it and let you know tomorrow?'

By doing this, Anabelle is allowing herself some breathing space to ensure that she makes the right decision, and so that she can rehearse a refusal if that is what she decides to do.

'Kate, I've thought about your request, and I'd really rather not be involved in the debate, but I'm happy to help in any other way I can.'

....

When you find yourself in the awkward position of having to refuse a request, there are a few useful guidelines which may help you to be more objective:

1 Be straightforward and honest.
2 Give a factual reason why you are saying no.
3 Offer an alternative course of action if this is appropriate.
4 If you find yourself unable to say 'No' at the time, give yourself some breathing space, and then rehearse your refusal.
5 Don't allow your emotions to interfere with rational decisions. Listen to your internal voice. If it says 'No', then so must you.

Assignment   Role-play the following situation.

A member of your staff has left the company, leaving a desk unoccupied. A lively girl, Sarah, has asked if she can move to the empty desk saying that it's a nicer position by the window. You suspect the real reason is because the empty desk is next to her friend, Chloe. You're not happy about the move because you believe that if Chloe and Sarah sit together, there will be constant noise and chatter, and very little work will get done. Sarah is standing in front of you now waiting for an answer. What will you say?

Rehearse the dialogue in your mind before you give her your answer. Ask the person who is playing the part of Sarah to be very persistent with her request, and to try to make you change your mind.

Dealing with criticism

There will be occasions in your career where you will receive criticism for your actions or behaviour. This criticism may be valid or invalid, and presented to you in a constructive or a destructive way. While you can do little about the manner in which the criticism is delivered, or the attitude of the criticiser, you are responsible for your personal reaction to the criticism. To most of us, criticism is unpleasant under any circumstances, but learning to accept that some criticism may be valid, and being able to deal with it in an appropriate and positive manner, makes the whole process much easier for you and for those around you.

You may know some people 'who just can't take criticism'. Why are they labelled in this way? And how do they internalise criticism or adverse comment to make them react as they do? Our general reaction to criticism usually has its foundations in our earliest memories of childhood. If as a child someone receives constant criticism for their actions, they may react in either of two ways in adulthood – first, in the Adapted Child ego state, by withdrawing into themself, becoming depressed and feeling hopeless at their apparent ineptitude, or second, in the Rebellious Child ego state, by flaring up at the criticiser and becoming angry and aggressive.

Some people may find that they react unfavourably to particular types of criticism. These are usually related to past experiences which invoke unpleasant emotions, and it is because of such unpredictable reaction that someone may be seen as always overreacting to unintended criticism or the casual comment. Do you have any particular sensitivity to criticism of a specific action or personal attribute? Can you identify why you react so strongly?

Reaction to criticism is quite different in each of the four assertive states:

- The aggressive person will flare up and deliver an immediate counter-attack on the person who gave the criticism.
- The indirectly aggressive person probably won't retaliate openly, but will find another way to 'get back at the critic' for what they have said.
- The non-assertive person will accept the criticism even if it is not justified, and will immerse themselves in self-pity and negative feelings.
- The assertive person will judge the validity of the criticism, perhaps by seeking further specific information, and will respond accordingly. If the criticism is invalid, they will state their own case, but if the criticism is fair, they will accept it and will usually look to remedy the situation.

The assertive person will use a technique called **Negative Assertion**. This entails agreeing with the basic tenet of the criticism, a technique which often takes the heat out of the situation, especially if the criticism is delivered as an attack or as a hostile response, e.g.

> JACK: 'You know your trouble, Alan. You're just too quick to jump to conclusions.'
>
> ALAN: 'Yes, I do rely on my intuition a lot, and I agree that sometimes I can be wrong. But my own intuition is something I value, and it's served me well in the past.'

Alan has 'rolled with the blow', but has not lost face. He has admitted that sometimes his intuition can lead him to make a wrong decision, but he has not dismissed his instinct as a flaw in his character. Jack can of course respond to Alan's reply, but it will be very difficult for him to maintain a hostile manner. Jack's initial attack invited an aggressive response, but Alan defused the situation with his assertive response, which rather cancelled out the intended exchange.

Criticism, when handled well, can provide a valuable opportunity for learning. If someone makes a criticism of the way that you are, or the way that you handled a situation, you may be able to gain a valuable insight into how people feel about you, what you do, and the way you do it. Any feedback of this kind is important to help you modify your behaviour and enhance the quality of your working relationships, e.g.

> MARIA: 'I hope you don't mind my saying, but this does seem a rather long-winded approach.'
>
> RACHEL: 'You could be right. I like to do things this way, but do you have an idea of how it could be done more quickly?'

Rachel's response is accepting of the criticism, and offers an invitation to Maria to express her thoughts on how the task could be more streamlined. If Maria were just looking to provoke a reaction, Rachel would have found her out in asking for further ideas. If it is genuinely meant, then Maria's alternative suggestion might offer a good, alternative approach. If Rachel had reacted in an aggressive manner, however, Maria would probably have decided to keep her ideas to her herself in future.

Another technique to help you deal effectively with criticism is **Negative Enquiry**. This is most useful when a criticism is hostile or given as a 'put down'. Negative enquiry means taking the subject-matter of the criticism and asking a direct question about it. This forces the critic to be more specific, and therefore, more objective, e.g.

> CAROLINE: 'Why is it always you who goes on the good educationals? You're so selfish.'
>
> JENNY: 'Do you think that I'm not being fair in the way I allocate the educationals?'

By using negative enquiry, Jenny is asking Caroline to be specific about her feelings that Jenny is being selfish. If Caroline really does have cause for complaint, this gives her the opportunity to say something.

Invalid criticism

There may be the odd occasion when you receive criticism for something you know to be completely untrue. Let's say that you are meticulous in your completion of documents, and that you take the time and trouble to be thorough and accurate. If someone then criticises you, by saying, 'You never do any of your own paperwork' then you have very good grounds for denying the accusation. If you do receive invalid criticism, you should always state your case immediately, 'That's completely untrue. I always make a point of completing my own paperwork.'

If you have a tendency to discount your own efforts, you may be drawn into the trap of trying to think of an occasion when you might not have been as thorough as you usually are. This is a difficult situation which tends to add some validity to the claim of the critic, though, if you have been brought up to think that you are often in the wrong, it is sometimes hard to remain objective when someone makes a direct accusation like the example given above. One way round this difficulty is to answer the critic with a slow and reflective observation on their statement, e.g. 'I don't think you have any grounds to say that. Would you like to explain?'

···

Assignment

1 Think about criticisms you have received in the past and make a note of at least three. Do you feel that the criticism in each case was fully justified? How did you behave at the time? Make a note of what you said if anything, and what you felt inside. If you responded, which behavioural state did you use. Having learnt assertiveness techniques to handle criticism, how might you have responded differently now?

2 Ask a person you trust and feel comfortable with to help you with the next part of the assignment. Role-play the following situation:

Your brief: You manage a team of six staff and you have been called in to see the managing director because one of them has made an accusation that you have behaved unreasonably on a number of occasions. You may embellish your side of the story during the role-play.

Your partner's brief: You are the managing director of a travel company and have two managers working for you. One of the manager's is a personal friend who you see socially. The other manager is not your type at all and you do not like him/her. You have just received a complaint from a member of the second manager's team stating that the manager has been treating the staff unreasonably. This is just the sort of information you like to hear. Now you can have things out with this manager once and for all. You intend to adopt an aggressive manner with the manager and hope to be able to put him/her on the spot. You may embellish your version of the story during the role-play.

The objective of this role-play is to present the person playing the part of the manager with the opportunity of dealing with both valid and invalid criticisms in an assertive manner. The role-play should last at least twenty minutes and, if done properly, should prove hard work for both parties. Discuss the outcomes once you have finished.

....

Dealing with anger

Anger is a natural human reaction, yet many of us feel a desire to suppress any display of anger or even to pretend that we are not angry at all. The reasons for this are many: it may be that as a child you were taught that displays of anger were a bad thing, for which you received punishment; it may be a fear that as adults we will offend others by showing anger; it could be that we are frightened of losing control in the face of anger by doing or saying something which we would later regret. If you are one of the many people who suppresses anger, you should remember that pent up emotion will come out somewhere, sometime, and it may not be entirely appropriate when it does.

....

CASE STUDY

Mary is a junior partner in a small travel agency. She has a 20 per cent share in the company, and works closely with Janet, who is the major shareholder. Janet and Mary do not always see eye to eye, but Mary finds it very difficult to say what she feels about the decisions that Janet makes, and the way that she behaves towards the staff and to Mary herself. Mary believes that it would be very remiss to express her anger and frustration to Janet when the staff might overhear, so she puts on a brave smile and bottles up all of her feelings of anger.

However, she needs to find an outlet for her bad feelings, and the target is usually her husband. Mary often returns home in a state of extreme anger and frustration, bangs doors and picks a fight with her husband. When this first happened, Mary's husband was rather taken aback at Mary's behaviour, but as time passes, he feels a certain amount of resentment that he should suffer the effects of Mary's frustration with this impasse. Home life is now somewhat strained, and both feel that they need to take stock of the matter in order to restore harmony to their marriage.

In this case study, it is clear that Mary is suppressing the anger brought about by one situation, and transferring her frustration to another, unconnected situation. Mary still needs an outlet for her anger, and is releasing this at home. Her husband is, not surprisingly, at a loss to understand why he must bear the brunt of this frustration. He is not the cause of Mary's anger, yet he is certainly on the receiving end of her pent-up emotions. The truth is that Mary is seeking the easiest way out – refusing to show in the work situation a side of her nature she would rather keep hidden, while releasing her feelings and emotions on someone who probably knows and understands her personality, and from whom she has nothing to hide.

There is no doubt that the different personality types deal with anger in different ways:

- The aggressive type will always explode when they feel angry and the ground may be felt to shake for a few miles around them. Truly aggressive types find it almost impossible to contain their anger and need to find a very fast outlet for it. However, these people seldom stop to consider whether they actually upset or offend anyone by their behaviour. They are normally quite oblivious to innocent parties who inadvertently wander into their line of fire. Aggressive people are very quick to flare up, but will usually settle down equally quickly.
- The indirectly aggressive type may show a flash of anger, but they are more likely to retaliate when the offending person is off guard. Some indirectly aggressive types may store up anger and harbour grudges for a very long time, and be constantly on the look out for ways to get even with the person who made them angry. An indirectly aggressive manager who is angry with a member of staff is less likely to make a direct display of anger, and more likely to get even by exercising their superior authority, e.g. by withdrawing privileges or exercising tighter control over the 'offender'.
- The non-assertive timid type never show that they are angry in any way. They will most probably grit their teeth, swallow hard and attempt to smile. Non-assertive people are more likely to internalise their feelings, and sometimes resort to tears and/or withdrawal. These people often develop headaches and other physical symptoms due to stress which is a form of internalised anger and frustration. In extreme cases this may lead to clinical depression.

You may remember from previous talking points that you do not always adopt the same behavioural state when facing anger. Refer back to your notes on the earlier assignment where you drew up a list of the behavioural states you use on the different people with whom you communicate. You should have concluded that you tend to deal with anger in different ways with different people, i.e. you may internalise the feelings of anger you have for your mother, while being quite happy to explode at your secretary. Let's review how anger should be handled most appropriately.

Handling anger in an assertive manner

To handle anger assertively does not mean that you have to hide the fact that you get angry. What it does mean is that you harness the energy created by your anger and use it to deal constructively with the source of that anger. Some people find it necessary to seek a harmless outlet for their anger before they can face their tormentor in a rational way. This might be achieved by going for a walk, digging the garden, playing at sport or punching a cushion. It really doesn't matter what you do, so long as you can express your anger in a harmless way – some form of physical release is usually best.

However, there will be occasions when you are unable to find an alternative outlet, and you will have to deal effectively with your anger at the time. If you really feel that you cannot think clearly, or say what you need to say without flying into a rage, then buy yourself a little time. Explain that you are angry, but state that you would prefer to discuss the issue another time, e.g. 'I'm very angry about this. I would like to discuss it later when I've had time to think about it.' This is also a useful tactic if you prefer to be left alone and cannot trust yourself to be civil to a member of staff who may call in, e.g. 'I'm feeling rather angry about something at the moment. Can I come and see you a little later?' Most people will be happy to give you the space you need.

There may, of course, be occasions when you prefer to give an immediate explanation for the reasons for your anger. This is fine provided you can keep your anger under a measure of control. You can express anger assertively through body language and a show of determination, but be careful that you do not tip the balance into aggression by pointing your finger or banging the desk. Try to keep your voice steady and calm. People who are most effective in handling anger tend to speak in a measured, quieter tone, and this can be very effective, as those who have ever been on the receiving end know. If you are careful to control your anger, the situation should not escalate and get out of hand.

Dealing with anger in other people

If someone else is angry in an assertive way, it should not be a problem to deal with, but if you suffer a blast of anger from an aggressive person, it can be quite frightening and you may feel powerless to do anything about it. If it's an angry customer that you have to face, then unless they become totally unreasonable, the best way is to let them have their say and allow them to run out of steam of their own accord. If you are dealing with a colleague or a member of staff who has lost their temper and is shouting in anger, then here are a few suggestions for taking a little of the heat out of the situation.

1 Never shout back, make a sarcastic comment or allow yourself to be drawn into an argument. Avoid any actions which only 'add fuel to the fire' or which have a tendency to prolong or exacerbate the situation.
2 If you are not already standing, then do so. Once you are on the same level as the aggressor you may feel less intimidated. You should not, however, attempt to move in on the other person, but rather simply stand your ground and keep calm.

3 Don't be tempted to say things like, 'Calm down' as this often has the opposite effect on someone who is really angry.

4 If you want to stop the flow of angry words, then try repeating the person's name until you have their attention. Try to maintain eye contact whilst you are doing this.

5 Once you have the attention of the other person, you need to speak straight away, but don't be tempted to start by putting your side of the story. If you do this, you are likely to trigger off another angry response. Just what you do say will depend very much on the relationship you have with the other person, the circumstances that cause the anger and the environment in which it happens. You may say, 'I know you're angry, but we really need to discuss this rationally' or, 'I'm sorry you feel so angry about this. Let's discuss it when we've had a little time to think' or, if you are not already there, 'I think it may be better if we discuss this in my office.' Under no circumstances should any angry scenes take place out in the open. A manager who conducts an angry exchange in front of his staff will quickly lose their respect.

Assignment

1 Think about an occasion when someone has shown their anger to you, and you were unable to handle the situation properly. What happened? How did you behave? How would you rather have behaved?

2 Role-play the following situation. The objective of this role-play is to provide you with an opportunity to practise dealing with another person's anger. Ask a friend or colleague to vent their anger on you in an aggressive manner, and ask them to keep going as long as they can. Your role is to use the tactics described in the preceding pages to try to stem the anger. If you are not successful the first time, discuss what happened and try the exercise again.

Don't be afraid of the power of your own emotions. If you are successful in stopping anger which seems real, you may experience a surge of adrenalin during the role-play. This is natural and helps you to deal with the situation. Once a really angry exchange is over, you may feel a little shaky. Some women feel the need to cry, but none of this means that you are weak – it's just nature's way of finding an outlet for your nervous energy. This 'recovery' time is best spent on your own, away from other people.

Confronting other people

Confronting another person with a grievance or problem is perhaps one of the most daunting prospects in interpersonal relationships, and it is here more than in any other situation that you will find an assertive approach valuable. If you have delayed discussing something because you felt too angry to deal with it at that time, you will need to return to the situation at the soonest opportunity to confront the issue. Cool confrontation is always preferable to heated anger. By all means go back to confront the issue, but do so cooly and collectedly.

For the non-assertive person, the problem is one of getting round to dealing with the situation. The tendency with non-assertive types is to delay in the hope of avoiding any kind of confrontation. Walking away from the problem will not make it go away – it will simply delay the inevitable. The issue will eventually have to be confronted, or there is a danger that the non-assertive person will harbour a grudge or feel awkward about the relationship. This person then begins to build up inner resentment against everything the other says or does, whether insignificant or not. In the end, this build up of resentment will cause an explosion – usually over some fairly minor issue.

Whether you are aggressive, assertive or non-assertive, you will need to think very carefully about what you want to say and what you hope to achieve. Don't think of confrontation as an opportunity to win the case. If your whole aim is to beat the other person, you will most likely succeed, but you will be so intent on scoring enough points to win the contest that you will lose sight of the fact that you need to discuss the issue in an adult fashion in order to reach a win–win solution.

....

CASE STUDY

Marjory manages a small high street travel agency and has a staff of four. She has been at the shop for many years and prides herself on her experience and sales and management skills. Lucy is the assistant manager of the shop. She joined the company a few months ago and is bright and very go-ahead. She is enthusiastic and has lots of new ideas, but Marjory feels the need to restrain her on occasions as her enthusiasm has a tendency to run away with itself. Marjory recently had two weeks' leave, and returned to find that in her absence Lucy had made a number of changes. The brochures were racked differently and the brochure store had been reorganised. When she looked in the stock cupboard, although it had been tidied, everything seemed to have a new place. Marjory felt a flush of anger: as soon as she was out of the office, Lucy had tried to take over and Marjory wasn't going to stand for this sort of behaviour.

Shortly after Lucy arrived, Marjory called her into her office. Lucy asked if she had had a good holiday. 'Very nice, thank you,' said Marjory through tight lips. Lucy guessed there must be something wrong and said no more. Marjory glared at Lucy and then asked how things had been during her leave. Lucy cheerfully explained all the things that had happened and outlined the bookings that had been taken. She looked at Marjory, waiting for praise, but none came. Marjory remained stony-faced. 'And what about your little reorganisation?' she asked. Lucy looked puzzled and Marjory continued, 'When I came in this morning, the first thing I noticed was that the racks had been reorganised. Then I looked in the brochure store, and found that that's all been changed, too. You have even reorganised the stock cupboard.'

Lucy could see that for some reason Marjory was displeased with what she had done. 'We thought we'd tidy up a bit, and make things easier to find. We thought you'd be pleased.'

Marjory's face flushed with anger. 'Pleased that you chose to do this behind my back? I've been running this office for twenty years without your help. If it needed any reorganisation, then it's my decision to make.'

Lucy began to feel angry, but tried to maintain a calm exterior. 'I'm sorry if you feel offended, Marjory. No malice was intended, but the girls and I discussed it, and this is what we felt would be easier for us to work with.'

Marjory looked ready to explode. 'How dare you! Who do you think you are to discuss things like this the minute my back is turned?'

Lucy fixed her with a steady gaze. 'As I've already said to you, Marjory, this was not intended to offend you. The reorganisation seemed a good idea and we thought you'd be pleased. I'm sorry that you aren't.'

'I'm getting very tired of your attitude, young lady,' blazed Marjory. 'It doesn't seem to have occurred to you how I might feel about this. I'm the manager around here, not you, and you'd do well to remember that. Don't think I haven't noticed the way you keep pushing yourself forward. I won't have it.'

Lucy looked wearily at Marjory. 'I'm sorry you feel this way, Marjory. I don't think we're achieving anything here. Perhaps it would be better if we discussed this another time.'

'Now, you listen to me, young lady. You can't just walk out of here. We're going to sit here and go on until this is sorted out. You'd better start behaving in a more civil manner to me if you want to carry on working here.'

Lucy stood up. 'I am being civil with you, Marjory, but you appear to want to fight. May I suggest that you examine your own behaviour before you criticise the behaviour of others.'

The manager in this case study failed. She started off the conversation in a hostile manner and became increasingly angry that Lucy was not responding to the attacks she was making. She became more and more frustrated with the situation and lost sight of the real issue, resorting to a personal attack which, when challenged, had no substance. She lost the case altogether when she criticised Lucy's responses, to which Lucy pointed out that she was being more civil than the manager. The end result of this particular situation was that although Lucy knew she had won this particular battle, she had lost all respect for her manager, and started to look for work elsewhere.

Guidelines for successfully handling confrontation

1 Set aside enough time to deal with the issue. If this is likely to take the whole afternoon, then be prepared. Once you start to confront the issue, you must see it through to the end.

2 Be specific about the issue, and don't start the conversation with an attack. Instead of behaving as Marjory did, a more appropriate start to the discussion

might have been, 'I see you've had a reorganisation while I've been away, can you tell me exactly what you have done?'

3 Be specific about your feelings, e.g. 'I was a little upset that you felt you needed to do this while I was away.'

4 Don't make any judgemental statements, such as, 'You're selfish' or 'You just don't think'. Making general statements like this serves no purpose except to antagonise the other person.

5 Try and use 'I' statements rather than 'You' statements, e.g., 'I was rather surprised at the decision you made' rather than, 'You made the wrong decision' or, 'I would prefer it if you didn't interrupt me' rather than, 'You always interrupt'.

6 Don't blame other people for your own emotions, e.g. 'You make me so cross'. A more assertive comment would be 'I get very cross when you do that'.

7 Be specific about the behaviour you wish to discuss. Rather than, 'You always look so untidy' say, 'I feel that your uniform would look better if you gave it a good press'.

8 Use the 'broken record' technique. Broken record enables you to avoid being sidetracked on to other issues by continuing to state your point or request, e.g.

> RICHARD: I know the busses are infrequent, but we expect you to be here at nine o'clock.
>
> CATHERINE: But the bus often comes early, and if I miss it, it takes me half an hour to walk.
>
> RICHARD: I realise that, but that doesn't alter the fact that we expect you to be here at nine o'clock.
>
> CATHERINE: It's not only me. Sally gets in late sometimes.
>
> RICHARD: And I shall be speaking to her too. But the purpose of this discussion is to ensure that you are here by nine o'clock.

9 Come to an agreement about what will happen in the future. Whenever possible, you should try and reach a 'win–win' solution. This means a solution which leaves both parties with some dignity. In the previous case study, the parties may have been able to come to an agreement that Lucy should discuss with Marjory any future changes she wishes to make before she makes them.

10 Try to end on a positive note, e.g. 'I'm glad we've been able to discuss this'.

CASE STUDY

The following is a transcript of a conversation between a manager and a member of staff, which demonstrates how a sensitive matter can be discussed and resolved in an assertive manner.

> ALAN: Becky, I wanted to talk to you about your sick days last week.
>
> BECKY: What about them?
>
> ALAN: Well perhaps you could explain to me again what was the matter.
>
> BECKY: I told you before. I had an upset stomach. I think it was food poisoning.
>
> ALAN: And you say that you were in bed for the two days that you were off.

BECKY: Are you accusing me of something?

ALAN: No. I just wanted to get it straight in my own mind what you told me, that's all. (Avoiding being drawn into an argument)

BECKY: Well now I've told you again.

ALAN: Are you sure that you have told me everything Becky?

BECKY: Are you calling me a liar? (Inviting an attack)

ALAN: Should I have any reason to consider that you have lied to me? (Negative enquiry)

Becky remains silent.

ALAN: I had the day off on Wednesday, and I saw you working on your uncle's market stall. (Specific and factual account of the issue.)

BECKY: I wasn't. I told you, I was ill.

ALAN: Are you saying that I was mistaken? (Negative enquiry)

BECKY: [*floundering*] Well . . . you must have been.

ALAN: I don't think so, Becky. If you need to help your uncle, then we'll see what we can do to enable you to take market day as your day off. But I'm rather upset to think that on this occasion the day was taken as sick leave. ('I' statement)

BECKY: Well, I didn't feel well.

ALAN: But you felt well enough to work for someone else.

BECKY: It was only in the morning.

ALAN: But nevertheless, you were working for someone else. (Broken record)

BECKY: Well alright I was. I need the money. This wouldn't have happened if you hadn't stopped everyone's overtime.

ALAN: I accept that loss of overtime pay could be a problem for you, (Negative assertion) but it is still not acceptable for you to take sick leave in order to work for someone else. (Broken record) We need to come to a more satisfactory solution in the future. What do you suggest?

BECKY: Oh, I don't know. [*pauses*] It would help if I could take my day off on market days.

ALAN: Well, I can't promise that you can have every Wednesday off. The others may want Wednesdays from time to time as well. How about if we say that you can have every other Wednesday off, and you can work out with the girls which day you can have for the other weeks?

BECKY: Thank you, Alan. I'm very grateful. I promise I won't let you down like that again.

ALAN: I'm glad that we've been able to discuss this, Becky. I hope that we won't need to discuss this again. (Positive ending)

BECKY: No, we won't. Thanks, Alan.

Alan handled the situation very well and employed a number of assertive techniques: negative enquiry, negative assertion and broken record. He was specific in the points he wished to make and refused to be drawn into an argument. He reached a conclusion which was satisfactory to both parties.

Assignment Now practise dealing with a confrontation in the following role-play. You will need the help of a friend or colleague to play the part of the accounts manager.

Scenario: You attended a manager's meeting yesterday afternoon at which there was a disagreement between yourself and the accounts manager. You felt that you remained factual and concentrated on the case in point, but the manager retaliated by saying, 'Well your expenses are a work of art. You don't seriously expect me to believe that everything you claim for is a legitimate business expense?'

The other managers looked very embarrassed and quickly changed the subject. You were furious at the time, but did not feel the meeting an appropriate forum to deal with the situation. However, you intend to speak to the accounts manager today.

Using the guidelines given in the previous pages:

1 Confront the accounts manager with your grievance.

2 Maintain an assertive manner throughout the discussion.

3 Don't allow yourself to be sidetracked or drawn into an argument.

4 Try and reach an agreement at the end of the discussion as to what will happen in the future.

DEVELOPING ASSERTIVENESS SKILLS

Refer back to the list of difficult situations that you wrote down in an earlier assignment. How confident would you now feel about dealing with each of these situations? If some of those situations still seem a little daunting, don't despair, developing assertiveness skills and having the confidence to use them takes a little practice. To help you on your way to successfully changing your behaviour, here are some guidelines for you to follow:

1 Start in a safe environment. Try out your assertiveness techniques in a situation which you have already identified as being fairly easy to deal with. You may prefer to practise outside of the work environment, so that it is less important if things don't initially go entirely to plan, e.g. try asking the milkman if he would close the gate in future.

2 Set yourself some goals. If it helps, you might like to make a note of what you want to achieve, e.g. 'I won't allow Malcolm to bully me', 'If I'm too busy to take on extra work, I will say so', 'When I get angry, I'll try and give myself some thinking time before I do or say anything'. Repeat your goals over and over to yourself, especially if you know that you are likely to be faced with a situation which you have found difficult to deal with in the past.

3 Think positively. Try to remove any negative thoughts about yourself. If you tell yourself enough times that you can't do something, you won't be able to. This is called a 'self-fulfilling prophecy'. The positive side to this phenomenon

is that it also works in the reverse. If you tell yourself often enough that you can do something, the chances are you will be successful. This is known as positive self-suggestion.

4 Practise visualising yourself handling situations assertively. Go over in your mind what you will say and how you will deal with the responses and reactions that you may receive. Try to examine the situation from a number of different angles. This way, you are less likely to be taken by surprise if the other person behaves in an uncharacteristic way.

5 Allow yourself time to develop. Don't expect overnight success. Accept that it may take you some time to develop your assertiveness skills, perhaps a few months.

6 Monitor your progress. You may find it helpful to make notes on how you have dealt with certain situations. This will give you something by which to measure your progress. Being able to see how far along the road you have travelled will motivate you to continue to the end.

7 Review each situation as you deal with it. Try to replay the conversation in your mind as accurately as possible. Assess what you said and how you behaved. If the outcome of the situation was not what you had hoped for, then identify the reasons and decide how you would deal with the situation in the future. Don't be too hard on yourself. When you are not as successful as you would have liked, consider it as an opportunity to learn rather than as a failure.

8 Reward yourself for your successes. For added incentive, promise yourself a treat once you have achieved one of your goals, perhaps a meal out or a trip to the theatre. You've worked hard for it.

8

....

Interviewing

Interviewing is an important part of any manager's job, and there are many different sorts of interview that, as a manager, you may be required to conduct. An interview is essentially a conversation, though it is often the case that interviews turn out to be more like interrogations. The reason for this is that vital interpersonal skills are often forgotten during the interviewing process, only to be replaced by a range of different emotions, feelings, pre-conceptions and prejudices about both the interviewee and the outcome of the interview. The art of interviewing is, therefore, more than simply asking questions and getting answers. This chapter aims to provide you with the guidelines and general interviewing techniques required to successfully conduct any type of interview.

OBJECTIVES

Once you have read this chapter of the book you will be able to:
- **state the different types of interview and their purposes**
- **state the ground rules for interviewing**
- **state the various types of questioning techniques to be used in an interview**
- **use effective questioning techniques to elicit information from an interviewee**
- **state obstacles to effective listening**
- **use active listening skills in an interview situation**
- **state the effects of non-verbal communication during an interview.**

We have said that an interview is a type of conversation, but it is a very special one, having aspects and features which mark it out from ordinary everyday conversations with family, friends and acquaintances. If you think about the sorts of conversations which occur on, say, social occasions, then a regular pattern is usually clear. People tend to talk around a particular topic or point of view, and may even become engaged in in-depth discussions, but the conversation will quite often change direction as it progresses. A new line of conversation may be triggered off by some chance remark, or change direction with the introduction of a different point of view. During the course of the evening, a variety of different topics may have been discussed by this process of gradual change, and the only time we are conscious that this is happening is when we stop to consider how it was that we started off talking about one subject, e.g. the weather, and ended up talking about something completely different, e.g. the price of petrol. Social conversations can be lively or dull, agreeable or contentious, serious or just great fun, but at the end of evening, when it is time to go home, we are normally quite happy to break off and go our separate ways.

WHAT IS AN INTERVIEW?

Interviews – and all interviews are conversations – are quite different from social conversations. Two very important differences set them aside. First, an interview is a conversation which has a specific purpose or objective. This may be to discover the cause of a particular problem, as in a grievance interview, to select the right person for the job, as in a job interview, or to offer helpful advice, as in the case of the counselling interview. Second, because interviews have a specific purpose or objective, it follows that in order to achieve that objective, the interview must be conducted along agreed lines, and therefore, have an agreed structure. An interview which has no objective and no structure is nothing more than an ordinary conversation and, if the outcome happens to be successful, it will be purely by accident and not by design. You will find that most interviews are far too important to be left to chance.

MAIN TYPES OF INTERVIEW

The different types of interview in which you may become involved are:

- selection
- appraisal
- counselling
- disciplinary
- grievance
- termination

Each of these interviews has a different objective and the interviewer and interviewee play different roles in each.

The job selection interview

This interview is probably the most familiar in a working situation. Even if you have not yet conducted one, you will almost certainly have been in attendance at a job selection interview. The sole objective of the selection interview is to assess the candidate's suitability to perform the job. Your role as interviewer is to elicit relevant information from the candidate on which to assess their suitability. The candidate's role is to supply any relevant information which may demonstrate ability to perform the required tasks within the job.

The appraisal interview

An appraisal interview occurs as a private interview between a member of staff and their immediate supervisor. The objective of the appraisal is to review and assess a member of staff's past performance, to identify any training and development needs and agree on future projects and performance objectives. The interviewer may need to adopt a number of roles while conducting an appraisal interview, depending on the issues which may arise out of the process. Commonly, the interviewer will act as reviewer and adviser, but may also need to act as counsellor, should any problems arise during the interview. The interviewee's role is to contribute to the assessment of their personal performance and to help identify personal training and development needs.

The counselling interview

Managers will from time to time have to conduct a counselling interview. This normally occurs when a member of staff appears to be having work-related problems which might be indicated by a drop in their normal standard of performance, or a personal problem which is adversely affecting their work or the work of those around them. The objective of the counselling interview is to provide a safe platform from which staff can begin to address their problems, to facilitate further discussion of an agreed problem, and then to reach an agreement with the interviewee about how the situation can best be rectified. The role of the interviewer is as investigator to establish the nature of the problem, and then as adviser and confidant(e) to resolve the problem. The role of the interviewee is to freely discuss the problem and help in finding a mutually agreeable course of action.

The disciplinary interview

Disciplinary interviews often come most readily to mind as the sort of interview in which a manager or supervisor may be involved. Disciplinary interviews should, however, never be the first recourse when a problem is perceived, but rather be considered as the last when all other actions, such as individual counselling and performance reviews, have proved ineffectual, or in the case of gross misconduct of an employee. The objective of a disciplinary interview is to reinforce the standards which the company expects of its employees, and to issue any warnings as necessary. The role of the interviewer is to act as upholder of company standards. The role of the interviewee is to agree on how their performance can be rectified.

The grievance interview

Grievance interviews are those instigated by a member of staff when they wish to make a complaint or lodge a grievance about a working condition, practice or relationship. The objective of the grievance interview is to solve the grievance to everyone's satisfaction. It is always necessary for the interviewer to obtain all relevant information relating to the problem. The role of the interviewer is to act as mediator and, subsequently, judge. Acting too early as judge may jeopardise reaching the most sensible decision, and no decision can be made until all the facts have been gathered. The role of the member of staff is, therefore, to provide as much factual information about the issue as possible.

The termination interview

Termination interviews should always be conducted whenever a member of staff leaves the company of their own volition. It provides a useful opportunity for the employer (or manager, on behalf of the employer) to discuss with the member of staff any issues about their employment which may highlight unfavourable working experiences or difficulties in the working environment. The termination interview, properly conducted, provides a rare opportunity for an employer to establish these facts, as the departing employee is in a unique position to make adverse comment on the various aspects of the running of the company and its working practices. The role of the interviewer is to act as investigator, whilst the role of the departing member of staff is to provide relevant, factual information about their experiences as an employee of the company.

All of the types of interview mentioned above, except termination, are covered in depth in the following chapters of this book as it is a requirement of your NVQ assessment that you are able to demonstrate an ability to undertake each of these interviews.

While, as we have said, each interview has a different objective and, therefore, a largely different content and structure, there are a number of ground rules and techniques which apply to all interviewing situations. These include the interviewing environment, general questioning techniques, and the importance of non-verbal communication (NVC) or body language in interviewing situations. More specific questioning techniques are covered in the chapters dealing with each particular type of interview.

Assignment

1 Think about a conversation you have had on a topic about which you have fairly strong feelings.

2 Write down notes on: (a) someone who was in total agreement with your point of view, and (b) someone who entirely disagreed with your point of view. Try to describe how you felt about that person, their attitudes, their values and their standards.

3 How much, in each case, do these match up to your own?

4 Did you have a more favourable view of either person?

CASE STUDY

Steven had worked for the same company for nearly ten years. He was hard-working, diligent, and always turned out work of a high standard within the agreed deadline. He was skilled, knowledgeable and articulate. He was also quite outspoken, and was known as one who did not suffer fools, especially those in a position of responsibility and authority. While this endeared him to the more open and enlightened managers, some more authoritarian figures regarded his views and opinions as heretical and dangerous. Though not necessarily always in agreement with his views and ideas, there were those who were quite able to acknowledge the many good things which Steven achieved. For others, Steven's achievements remained largely unacknowledged as they failed to make up for his self-assured and outspoken nature.

Steven went for an internal interview for a new position within the company. It was a job which Steven believed would require a high degree of particular knowledge and and skill, and a job to which he thought he could bring his own considerable talents. Steven's interview, however, was not a success and he did not get the job.

The interview was conducted by a panel of senior managers: one who was largely sympathetic to Steven's straightforward approach; one who felt that his approach was a threat to managerial authority; and one who saw his role as an interviewer as setting traps for the interviewee. The success (or, rather, lack of success) of Steven's interview was totally dependent on the preconceptions and prejudices of the panelists, each of whom was conducting his own very separate interview. Steven felt obliged to defend himself from left and from right – from the one interviewer who set traps to challenge the things he had done, and from the other who dismissed as irrelevant the things he had done and who attacked him for his views and opinions.

This case study makes a number of very important points:

1 Putting interviewees in an antagonistic situation will not serve to encourage them to be open, but will only add stress to a situation which needs to be stress-free.
2 The onus of responsibility is on the interviewer to lead and direct the interview in a manner fair to both participants.
3 Any preconceived ideas the interviewer may have will always affect the manner in which the interview is conducted.
4 An interview conducted on the basis of preconception and prejudice loses sight of all objectivity, and simply ends up as a subjective exercise, designed to confirm those prejudices.
5 Interview panelists rarely pull in the same direction, and find great difficulty in speaking with a common voice and for a common aim.

Though our case study concerns a job selection interview, you can imagine how the negative approaches of two of the interviewers could adversely affect the conduct of other sensitive interviewing situations, such as a skills appraisal or a counselling interview.

The principle lesson of this case study is that you should always be aware of your own personal feelings, and how these can so easily affect the conduct and the outcome of the interview. It is clear from the example above that Steven was given no chance to demonstrate either his ability or his potential. Neither could the panel have drawn any satisfaction from Steven's defensive reactions to their questioning techniques. Putting your interviewee through hell during an interview will not give you many reliable indicators as to their likely behaviour in a real working situation. People always react best to kindness and consideration in an interview.

GROUND RULES FOR INTERVIEWING

Whatever type of interview you are conducting, the following ground rules will always apply.

Create the right environment

All interviews should be conducted in an environment which offers maximum privacy and which ensures that the interview will not be interrupted. Ideally, interviews should be held in private offices, and if you do not have an office of your own, you may need to arrange in advance to borrow a colleague's office. If no office is available in your organisation, then try to find a quiet room or area where you will not be overheard or interrupted by other members of staff.

Whichever type of interview you are conducting, make absolutely sure that staff and colleagues are aware that you should not be interrupted and, if necessary, take the telephone off the hook so that you do not receive unwanted internal calls whilst you are in conference. Remember that any interruption is an unwanted interruption. If it really is impossible to conduct the interview in any privacy, and you cannot guarantee not to be interrupted, it may be necessary to consider conducting the interview off the premises. Privacy is important to the interviewing process.

Wherever you decide to hold your interview, it is important to consider the layout of the interviewing room, and the impression it creates. If you have decided to conduct the interview in a private office, it might be considered that the room's normal layout is the most natural way to hold the interview, with the interviewer taking up a position behind the desk and the interviewee sitting opposite. However, though this might seem the most natural layout to adopt, it does set up a visible division of hierarchy between interviewer and interviewee.

If the interview is to be conducted in your office, on your territory, be aware that it will be perceived as your territory by both you and your interviewee. By remaining behind your desk, you are reinforcing the image of your superior position and authority and, if this is acknowledged by the interviewee, it will have the effect of making him or her feel in a subordinate position. This may, in turn, affect the openness of the interview and inhibit the interviewee. Remember that for most people, the situation itself will be sufficiently inhibiting. You will find also that the desk becomes an unnecessary physical barrier which not only destroys the space between you and your interviewee, but acts as a psychological

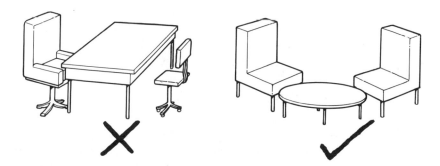

Fig. 8.1 Seating arrangement for an interview

barrier to the creation of necessary rapport. To avoid this, arrange the seating so that you and your interviewee do not face each other across a desk. The best seating arrangement is shown in Fig. 8.1.

Prepare for the interview

Whether you are conducting a job selection interview, an appraisal or a counselling interview, you should take care to prepare all information well in advance. Allow yourself time to read through all documentation – application and review forms, progress charts and action plans – which is pertinent to the interview. This preparation is to remind yourself of important details necessary to the discussion, and should be a prerequisite of every interview you undertake. It does not create a very good impression if you miss out on important details during the interview because you have failed to do the basic background work before you start.

Structure the interview

Every interview must have a clear structure – a beginning, middle and an end – though details of the structure will depend on the exact nature of the interview and its main aim and objectives. These are discussed in detail under the relevant interview headings in the following chapters, but the general guidelines below outline the importance of the introduction, the questions and the conclusion to every kind of interview.

Introduction

Take your time to ensure that both you and the interviewee settle into the situation at the commencement of all interviews. You will need to exchange normal pleasantries, and ask a few basic questions to establish the well-being of the interviewee, so try not to rush straight into things by asking searching questions at the beginning.

Questions

This is where you settle into achieving the main objective of the interview, and where you will need to begin asking those questions immediately relevant to your interviewing objective. Remember, though, that your role is to direct and lead the conversation, not to do all the talking – you will not learn much about the interviewee if you are the only one speaking.

Conclusion

The interview should always come to a gradual conclusion; you should not suddenly stop talking, jump to your feet and show the interviewee to the door. Give time for the interviewee to ask questions or query points and, if necessary to the outcome, you will also need to reach an agreement on your findings. An interview should always end with some agreed action so, before you finish completely, make sure that everyone is clear about the next step.

Encourage the interviewee to do the talking

We have already said that the interviewee should do more talking than the interviewer. As a guide, the ideal ratio of talking (or 'air time' as it is otherwise known) is 30:70; that is 30 per cent from the interviewer, to include given information and questions, and 70 per cent from the interviewee, which includes answers, explanations, expanded discussions, etc.

Close the interview

Whichever interview you conduct, it is your responsibility to bring the discussions to a decisive end, either by summarising the discussion or by stating what will happen next. In the case of a counselling interview, a summary will be necessary to outline what each party will try and do to rectify the situation, and arrangements will be need to be made for a further discussion to reassess the situation.

Assess your own performance as an interviewer

It is important to find sufficient time after every interview to assess the outcomes to see whether they match your stated objectives. Ask yourself a few basic questions:

- Did I achieve what I wanted to achieve?
- How good were my questioning techniques?
- Is there anything I would do differently next time?
- Was my approach correct?
- How much rapport did I manage to strike up with the interviewee?
- What improvements do I need to make to my interviewing techniques?

QUESTIONING SKILLS

Good questioning skills on the part of the interviewer are an essential ingredient of a good interview. As an interviewer, you will need to pitch each of your questions at a level suited to the interview, and phrase them in such a way as to elicit as much information as possible from the interviewee. There are many different questioning techniques which you can use.

Closed questions

Much has been written about 'closed' and 'open' questioning techniques, and why the latter should always be used in all interviewing situations. Recent research has proven that in selling situations it really does not matter how you ask questions. The important point is that you follow a pattern of eliciting facts in an ordered form. In many other types of interview it certainly does matter which questions you pose, and when, so the following notes are designed to help you understand the importance of the timing and effects of the questions you ask.

Closed questions include those which begin 'Did you . . . ?', 'Can you . . . ?', 'Are you . . . ?', 'Were you able to . . . ?', and which only demand a 'Yes/No' answer from the interviewee. Of course, this does not mean that the interviewee is restricted to answering 'Yes' or 'No'. Closed questions have a very specific use in an interview – for checking given information: 'So you worked in Spain for two years?' and for obtaining a direct answer: 'We need someone to start at the beginning of next month. Can you do that?'

However, whilst closed questions are useful for eliciting direct and very pointed information from the interviewee, they should be avoided at the beginning of the interview, or when you need to get the other person to talk. Remember, closed questions may limit the amount of information the interviewee will freely give, especially when he or she is nervous or reluctant to talk.

Open questions

Open questions do not allow the interviewee to reply with a simple 'Yes' or 'No', but invite the interviewee to open up. To a question such as, 'How did you feel about handling customer complaints of this type?' the interviewee cannot answer 'Yes' or 'No', as this would be inappropriate. If the interviewee is at ease, he or she should give the sort of reply which will tell you something about the way in which they work and you will have more information than you asked for. If the interviewee is reluctant to talk, though, an open question can still only result in a one-word answer such as, 'Fine' or 'OK'.

So, putting the interviewee at ease is part of the solution, and posing the right sort of questions is another. But, getting the interviewee to open up and talk at times and in situations where this is not straightforward, marks out the really practised interviewer from the beginner. People will not always talk freely just because you have asked a question in an open form, and they will not necessarily tell you all you want to know in their first reply. You will need to learn to listen out for the clues which tell you which paths to pursue with further, more probing questions, and which paths are dead ends and not worth pursuing. The art of interviewing is the art of asking the right questions, in the right order and at the right time.

You will also find that you are able to trim your questions to suit the sort of answers you are looking to receive. For example, 'How long do you spend on average with your clients?' is much narrower in scope than 'What is your opinion of the quality of service provided by our industry?'

Directive questions

Directive questions are used to expand on specific points raised by the interviewee, as in, 'You mentioned that you didn't like dealing with ski enquiries. What is it exactly that you don't like?' This is a very effective method of probing the interviewee's feelings and attitudes, and helps to avoid the sorts of misunderstandings and misinterpretations which occur when interviewees' replies are taken purely at their face value. Learn to listen out for the message from the interviewee. It is specific information you want and, if the replies are too general, you will need to probe a little further by asking more directive questions.

Leading questions

Leading questions take a theme, an idea or a situation and, by wrapping these within phrases such as, 'You don't . . . do you?' or, 'So you feel . . . don't you?', the questioner seeks to obtain a simple agreement from the interviewee. Less experienced interviewers often use this questioning technique to confirm their understanding of a particular point or aspect raised by the interviewee. Very often, though, such leading questions merely confirm the interviewer's own bias or prejudice.

Leading questions invite the interviewee to agree with, or deny the central premise or the assumption in the question. 'So, you don't find it easy to deal with Mrs Laing, do you?' Although the interviewee may try to counter this assumption, it is often very difficult without turning the questioner's assumption completely around. Unless the interviewer is very sure that they have understood the interviewee's line of thought completely, then this kind of question can often seem rather accusatory, and perhaps undermine the interviewee's confidence. The wise interviewee can quite easily read into the assumptions made by the interviewer, and may well use this to their advantage. So, if the interviewer asks the question, 'So, you think you will fit in here, then?', the interviewee would be foolish to answer anything other than 'Yes, of course.'

On the same theme, you should try not to allow your own particular thoughts or line of thinking into the conversation, or the astute interviewee may quickly realise that you are looking for an 'ideal' answer, and provide it, even if, in reality, it is not the sort of answer the interviewee would normally give.

....

Assignment   Test your own questioning skills in an interviewing situation. You will need the help of a friend or colleague for the following role-play.

1 Ask your partner to consider some aspect of their job, or a particular event in their career, which they have particularly enjoyed. Your task is to interview them to establish as much information as you possibly can about what happened, how they dealt with specific issues and what their feelings and attitudes were to the situation. Try to make full use of a wide variety of questioning techniques, and probe as deeply as you can. The interview should last at least ten minutes.

2 Once you have completed the interview, summarise the important aspects of your findings, then discuss with your partner the following:
(a) the sorts of questions you put to them
(b) their effectiveness in eliciting the required information
(c) the proportion of 'air time' they felt was given.

LISTENING SKILLS

Mastering a suitable questioning technique for the occasion is the first step to success. The second step is employing active listening skills. You will only be able to respond to information provided if you actually hear the answers and make sense of them. Listening is very hard since most people find speaking infinitely easier than listening. The difficulty is mainly one of concentration.

CASE
STUDY

I was once at a gathering of student academic awards, and was speaking with someone I had not seen for some time. She had recognised me, and had started immediately in on a conversation about the past. I smiled, and went on to ask her questions about what she had been doing, and what she planned for the future. As she was enthusiastically outlining her plans to me, I looked intently at her – not listening, but all the while searching through my mind to put a name to her face.

My lack of attention to the conversation was exposed when I later asked her a very fundamental question on the topic she had been explaining. She immediately frowned, and asked me if I had actually listened to a word she had said. My excuse was lame and, worse still, her name still would not come to me!

Common obstacles to listening

1 Your mind is on other things – while the interviewee is speaking, you allow your concentration to wander to other related matters, or perhaps even switch off entirely, because you are preoccupied with some other problem or issue

which is demanding your attention. As the interviewer, it is your responsibility to ensure that you direct all your attention to the interviewee and forget about other matters.

2 Evaluating what is being said – it is natural to human understanding that we continually evaluate what is being said to us, and we often do this in order to make a judgement about it, or the person who is saying it. As interviewer, be aware that some of your concentration is diverted in the mental process of evaluation and, as a consequence, you will not hear all of what is being said to you.

3 Rehearsing your reply – based on your evaluation of what you hear, you may then start to think about a response, whether as a reply or as a further question and, as you do this, you will listen even less. You may not realise that you are doing this as part of a normal mental process, but in the time you take to rehearse your reply you will not be fully concentrating. Once you have rehearsed your reply, you will then start to listen again, and begin to wait for a gap in the conversation.

4 The long speech – those who habitually launch into long speeches or fervent explanations, never quite getting to the point, have the effect of making most people switch off. As interviewer, you will need to learn to control the conversation and, if necessary, redirect things or politely interrupt to summarise what you think the speaker has said.

5 Message anxiety – a state of mind caused by something the interviewee has said, which causes anger or hostility in the mind of the interviewer. The interviewee is usually quite innocent of the reaction that they have aroused, speaking entirely without adverse intent, but has inadvertently triggered feelings of hostility and anger in the interviewer, who either stops listening altogether or begins to distort the meaning of the message.

6 Distortion of messages – where the interviewer has a preconceived idea at a subconscious level, of what they wish to hear, the message can often be distorted from the interviewee's intended meaning so as to fit into the interviewer's own internal dialogue. Interviewers who distort messages in this way often have a tendency to categorise interviewees into 'all bad' or 'all good' types, so as either to confirm their prejudice against the interviewee as a type, or to support the inference that that type of interviewee is basically good.

Being a good listener requires practice and concentration. It also demands that we should remain detached from our own thoughts and feelings during the course of the conversation. Intuition is quite often falsely attributed to the cause of the interviewer's response, when it is more probable that the real obstacles to good, active listening are our own prejudices and preconceptions.

....

Assignment   Practise your own listening skills in the following exercise. You will need the help of a friend or colleague.

Agree with your partner, a controversial topic such as 'A woman's place is in the home' or 'The death penalty should be reintroduced in Britain', which is to be discussed. The choice of topic is entirely your own. Once you have agreed on a topic, your partner should take a standpoint which is in direct opposition to your own. So, for example, if your topic is 'The government should divert spending on the arts to funding the further provision of nuclear arms' and this is a statement with which you fully agree, then your partner should take up the standpoint that more money should be spent on the arts, and less on nuclear arms. Agree your standpoints before you begin the discussion.

When you are ready, you may begin the exercise. Your partner should state his or her case and the reasons for it. Your task is to listen intently to what your partner is saying and then, before you reply, summarise to your partner what was said to you. Get an agreement that your summary was correct before you continue with the discussion, and follow this process through each time before giving your own response.

This is a very difficult listening exercise, as your natural reaction is to respond to your partner's argument by continually reformulating and reinforcing your own opinion. If your partner is playing a good responding role, you may experience a little anger at their argument, which may further inhibit your ability to listen. But, by summarising what has been said before you respond, you should find yourself forced to concentrate on the opposite perspective rather than reacting to your own prejudice and feelings. This exercise often has to be repeated several times before you are able to summarise correctly what has been said to you, but you will find this an excellent way to develop valuable listening skills.

NON-VERBAL COMMUNICATION

Most people refer simply to 'body language', but non-verbal communication (NVC) covers a whole range of body postures and movements associated with our emotions and the way we feel. The interviewer needs to be aware that this is a two-way process and, while he or she may be able to study the interviewee more closely, equally, the interviewee may be able to pick up any small sign of annoyance, hostility or disagreement on the part of the interviewer. Hands, feet, facial expressions and stance all tell a story about how we respond and react to situations, and those who know what to look out for are able to read and interpret even the most insignificant signals. Although in this short work it is not possible to provide an exhaustive list of body language postures and movements, there are several basic ones which will help you to recognise the signs.

As people, we are usually quite capable of expressing a range of moods and emotions when we wish to show our feelings: a beaming smile, a downhearted look, a frown, annoyance, elation – all of these emotions can be readily used to show our feelings openly and expressively. But why is it that others are also able to read our emotions even when we try hard to hide or suppress them, as in an interviewing situation? The answer is simple. So much of our body language is expressed at a subconscious level, and we often fail to realise that our gestures and postures can be interpreted by others. It is often possible to tell more about a person's attitude or state of mind from NVC than from the words they use to express themselves. Let's divide the signs into positive and negative.

Positive gestures

Generally, open gestures indicate an open and positive attitude. Typical posture is leaning slightly forward towards the other person and, if in a seated position, with open hands held apart and palms up. More serious and attentive, though still positive, is leaning to one side, usually with weight on one elbow and an attentive look. 'Echoing' is also a very positive sign, where the listener expresses accord with the speaker by adopting similar stances and copying arm and hand movements. So, if the speaker has folded arms, the listener will mirror this; if the speaker rests a hand on his chin, the listener will do the same and echo the movement.

There are one or two 'open' stances, however, which are normal signs of distance and superiority. Standing upright, with legs apart and hands behind the back is typical, as is leaning right back in the chair, especially with legs crossed and outstretched. The first of these stances is normally done with a view to looking down on someone, the other with a view to unsettling the other person. Either way, it is most difficult to talk to someone whose body language quite clearly suggests 'I'm not going to listen to you'.

Negative gestures

Displeasure and disagreement are usually quite easy to spot. Often this is shown when a person shifts suddenly and uneasily, or by a long stare, or even when a person looks away from the speaker and stares. There are a number of little distracting movements which also show detachment and distance, especially where a person turns attention to the adjustment of some item of clothing, such as a shoe or button, or inspects hands and fingernails. Finger-drumming is a well-known sign of impatience, as are deep sighs and long, deep breaths with lips tightened. People who become impatient with a situation often tend to lean back in the chair, drawing the head back and looking at the speaker as if through a telescope.

Anxiety shows itself in many different ways. The first sign is often the wringing of hands, and some people will also begin to break out in a sweat. Trembling is not uncommon, often accompanied by rapid and darting eye movements, or avoidance of any eye contact. Shuffling movements also show signs of anxiety though, when a person goes into a more withdrawn state, there is a tendency to look down to the ground, tighten the muscles and bring arms and legs up to the body in a closed position. For the most part, then, the more negative signs of body language are those which close down the person's contact with the interviewer and hold off any sign of physical proximity.

9

....

Recruitment

At some point in your career you will need to be involved in the recruitment of new staff, and as part of your NVQ assessment you will be required to demonstrate your knowledge and understanding of the recruitment process and be able to conduct selection interviews. This chapter aims to provide you with the knowledge and skills necessary to help you to recruit the right person for the job.

OBJECTIVES

Once you have read this chapter of the book, you should be able to:
- **devise a job specification**
- **devise a person specification**
- **conduct a selection interview**
- **assess the suitability of candidates.**

Reasons for the recruitment of a new member of staff will vary. It could be that an existing position has become vacant due to the original jobholder leaving, or being promoted or transferred, it could be a new position that has been created due to company expansion, or perhaps additional staff are required due to the increased volume of work. Whatever the reason for recruitment, it is absolutely necessary to be clear about what the job holder will be expected to do. You will also need to consider the type of person who would be most suited to the job, and the sort of personality, previous experience and qualifications you are seeking. As part of your recruitment process, you will need to draw up two separate specifications, one for the job and one for the person. These specifications are a very necessary part of job selection – whether you are seeking an internal or external candidate.

THE JOB SPECIFICATION

A job specification is similar to a job description, and describes the precise responsibilities and parameters of the job. It should include a list of all of the tasks to be undertaken by the new job holder, and the exact parameters of those tasks.

Job specification for the position of Senior Counter Clerk

Duties:

Dealing with a variety of retail customers, both face to face and over the telephone

Selling a wide range of products including: package holidays for both European and worldwide destinations; cruising; independent itineraries; scheduled and charter flights, rail, ferries, car hire and ancillary services

Use Travicom, (airline computer reservation system) to book and issue scheduled airline tickets

Service commercial travel accounts as required

Maintain customer files and records

Complete sales returns for air and rail tickets

Provide basic product training for trainees as required.

Responsible to:

Branch Manager and, in his absence, to the Assistant Manager.

Responsible for:

Trainees, including full-time trainees, Saturday staff, and work experience students.

Conditions of employment:

The jobholder will be expected to work a five-day week including most Saturdays. A day off will be given during the week

Hours to be worked are 09.00 to 17.30 Monday to Saturday with one hour for lunch

The jobholder is entitled to four weeks paid leave per annum

Company uniform is provided and must be worn at all times that the job holder is at the office

Salary is £11,000 per annum, reviewed annually at the end of June.

Fig 9.1 An example of a job specification

A job specification should also make clear who the job holder will report to and which staff, if any, will be responsible to the job holder. Details of the conditions of employment must also be decided, including hours of work, holiday entitlement, salary and other benefits. Once the job specification (see example in Fig.

9.1) has been drawn up, the next stage of the recruitment process is to draw up a person specification.

THE PERSON SPECIFICATION

The person specification should itemise all of the knowledge, skills, experience and qualifications that are necessary in order for the job holder to be able to perform each of the tasks to the required standard. These need to be quite specific, as they will form the basic framework for selection, and the basis on which candidates' suitability will be assessed at the interview stage.

When writing a person specification, it is important to be realistic. Of course, it is desirable to take on the best person for the job, but there is often a temptation to draw up a person specification for the 'ideal candidate', who may be far more highly skilled and developed than is demanded by the requirements of the job. Setting the person specification too high will have one of two effects; either it will be very difficult to attract candidates because the salary will not be in line with their skills, or they will quickly find they are unable to use their skills and that the job is far too limiting for them. Where this happens, it often results in early termination of employment by the new employee – a drain on resources and the time, money and effort which has gone into the recruitment process.

CASE STUDY

Beta Travel were looking to fill a vacancy for an administration clerk. The manager, Bob Palmer, sat down to consider the sort of qualifications and skills he would need for the position, and decided that with the job market as it was, there was a good chance of getting a well-qualified person to take on the job at a fairly low salary. The job was advertised in the trade press, and a number of highly qualified candidates applied for the job. Interviews were held, and a suitable applicant was chosen. Bob Palmer was pleased to think that he had managed to take on someone with such good qualifications and experience. However, his joy was rather short-lived. The new employee came to terms with the job in a very short time, but quickly realised that she was overqualified, and that the job would offer insufficient challenge. She quickly became disillusioned and, after considerable frustration, she left to go to another agency. Bob was surprised to see her leave so quickly and put it down to the fact that he had been unlucky in choosing the wrong person for the job. He decided to recruit once more – same advertisement, same job specification and the same person specification.

The manager was incorrect in his assumption that he had chosen the wrong person for the job. His real mistake had been in overestimating the qualifications and skills necessary to do a simple administration job and, as this case demonstrates, a person who is overqualified is unlikely to stay in a job which offers very little challenge. Successful recruitment is really not about matching the person to the job – it is about matching a person's level of skill to the demands of the job. In addition to these requirements, though, it is usually also necessary to match other details such as age range, personality, personal circumstances and appearance.

The person specification in Fig. 9.2 gives a very clear outline of the sort of personal qualities required for the vacancy, and this information can be used as a basis for the job advertisement. Notice that on this job specification, no reference is made to ideal age range. A suitable candidate could reasonably be expected to have about three years experience in retail travel, though, in reality, any qualified person up to the age of retirement could do the job. The main stipulation is that the applicant should have the necessary skills and qualifications. If you are looking for applicants of a certain age, then this should also be stipulated in the person specification and made clear in the job advertisement.

....

Assignment   Consider a new or current position within your own organisation for which it may be necessary to recruit a new member of staff. This can be either a full-time or part-time position.

1 Draw up a job specification for this position, to include all of the tasks within the job, and using the criteria from the previous model.

2 Draw up a person specification for the type of candidate that you wish to see in the job. Remember to be realistic about the degree of skill and the qualifications necessary to perform the work effectively.

....

SELECTING APPLICANTS TO INTERVIEW

Once the vacancy has been advertised, you should be ready to receive applications for the position. The first stage of the selection process is to study each application. Set aside those which fail to meet your criteria. These you will not be interviewing. Then draw up a list of all those applicants whose qualifications and experience match your specifications, and separate out those who seem, on paper, to be most suitable. These will be the applicants you will interview.

Depending on the recruitment policies of your organisation, you may require any or all of the following methods of application: CV, application form, letter of application. If it is necessary for the candidate to have good handwriting, your advertisement may state that any application should be accompanied by a handwritten letter. If a good telephone manner is essential, you might ask them to telephone for further information. If you intend to assess candidates' suitability in this way, you must ensure that they speak to you, or someone else involved in the recruitment process. This will enable you to make objective comparisons between candidates, and to rule out any who do not meet your standards. You should also be clear about any particular personal skill or ability essential to the

Person specification for a Senior Counter Clerk

Knowledge required:

Sound product knowledge of popular European and worldwide holiday resorts

Knowledge of worldwide cruising products

Knowledge of geography commensurate with COTAC Level 2

Good knowledge of reference manuals and other sources of information.

Skills required:

Selling skills

Good interpersonal skills

Highly numerate

Advanced telephone skills

Highly literate

Good communication skills

Ability to:

Operate Travicom system to book and issue scheduled airline tickets

Book and accurately process a variety of package holidays

Construct and accurately cost independent itineraries

Read and interpret information from timetables, specifically air and rail

Issue British and Continental rail tickets.

Qualifications and experience:

Minimum of five O Levels or equivalent, must include Maths and English

COTAC Level 1 or equivalent

Trained Travicom operator

Minimum three years' experience in a fully licensed retail agency.

Personal Qualities:

Smart appearance

Flexible approach to days and hours of work

Must be prepared to spend some time away from home if necessary

Ability to work on own initiative

Friendly outgoing personality.

Fig 9.2 An example of a person specification

APPLICANT ASSESSMENT FORM

Applicant: Julie Smithers

		Ideal	Adequate	Unsuitable
Qualifications:	Five O Levels or equivalent}			
	Maths}		*GCSE*	
	English}		*grades?*	
	COTAC 1 or equivalent	✓		
	Travicom trained		*?not formal*	
Experience:	Three years in retail travel	✓		
Knowledge and Skills:	European packages	✓		
	Long haul packages	✓		
	Independent itineraries	✓		
	Ground arrangements	✓		
	Air fare construction		?	
	Manual ticketing		✓	
	Air timetables		✓	
	Travicom operation		*Level of experience?*	
	Rail timetables and fares		✓	
Qualities:	Ability to work in a team			
	Flexible approach to working hours			
	Ability to work on own initiative			
	Legible handwriting	✓		
	Smart appearance			
	Selling skills			

Letter of acknowledgment sent Yes/No Date _____
Invitation to interview Yes/No Interview date _____
Rejection letter sent Yes/No Date _____

Fig 9.3 An applicant's assessment form

job, and this should be stated in the advertisement, e.g. 'fluency in French is essential'.

Applicant assessment forms

The best way to make your decisions about applicants' suitability is to use a simple assessment form. The purpose of this is to help you compare applicants' knowledge, skills and qualifications with those specified in your profile for the ideal person. The form is intended as a recruitment aid, which will help you to eliminate unsuitable applicants, and recognise those whose qualifications and qualities are closest to your requirements. Your final choice will need to be made from face-to-face interviews conducted with applicants from your short list.

A candidate assessment form need not be a very long or complicated document. Its main purpose is to separate applicants into one of three different categories, according to their overall suitability: ideal, adequate, unsuitable. Look at the assessment form (Fig. 9.3). This has been drawn up against the job specification for the position of Senior Counter Clerk, using the applicants' CVs (Fig. 9.4) to measure their personal suitability.

The applicant assessment for Julie Smithers indicates that, although she has many of the skills required for the position, her CV does not clearly indicate the level of competence she has attained in the use of Travicom, or the extent of her knowledge and ability in air fare construction. On her CV 'some experience' might be taken to indicate that no formal training has been received. Academic qualifications, with six GCSE passes, look very good, though grades have not been given and some further enquiry will need to be made to ascertain whether these can be considered of a sufficiently high level to be O Level equivalents.

Completing an assessment form makes the task of comparing the suitability of applicants a more objective exercise and, if all applications are processed in this way, the task should not take long to complete. Whether or not Julie is called for interview will also depend on how her application compares with others which have been received.

Room has been provided at the bottom of the form to indicate what action is to be taken. If you receive a large number of applications, it may take some time to assess their suitability. You will need to consider what form of acknowledgement you will use to notify applicants. Initially this should be a card or short letter to say that their application has been received and is currently being dealt with. If you are able to make a fairly quick decision as to who will be called for interview, you will then need to send out a further notification to those who have been successful. There may also be a number of applicants whose applications are not quite to the required standard and who have not been shortlisted for interview, but whom you would like to consider should your first round interviewees prove unsuitable. It is wise to hold these applications in abeyance until you have been able to make a firm decision.

CURRICULUM VITAE

Julie Smithers
Age: 21 years
Status: Single

Education

Saltash Comprehensive School, Saltash
Qualifications gained: GCSEs in English, needlework, home economics, drama, geography and maths

Further Education

One year Travel and Tourism course at Saltash College of Further Education

Course includes: use of timetables, air fare construction and ticketing, rail and coach timetables and ticketing, car hire, inclusive tours, selling skills and telephone technique

At the end of the course I was successful in passing COTAC Level 1 Air and General.

Positions held

1988–89
Saturday job at Hargreaves bookshop. Duties included serving customers, operating the till and setting out display materials.

1989–90
Saturday job at Allens Travel, Saltash. Duties included: filing; stock control of brochures including ordering, stamping and displays; issuing coach tickets and limited administration duties.

1990 to present
Full time position as Travel Clerk at Going Places, Saltash. Duties include: booking a variety of package holidays, including European and long haul destinations; independent package holidays; business travel by rail and air, including ground handling arrangements such as hotels and car hire; raising invoices; monitoring balance of customer payments; monthly returns. I have had some experience of using Travicom, including ticket issue and fare construction.

Fig 9.4 An applicant's CV

ARRANGING THE INTERVIEW

Applicants who are to be invited for interview should be notified as soon as possible to give sufficient time for them to make arrangements to attend. Depending on your company practice, you may need to write to applicants specifying a time and date for the interview, or simply contact them to arrange a mutually suitable appointment. This should always be followed up with a written notification to every applicant stating the arrangements you have agreed, and enclosing the following information where appropriate:

- a map showing how to get to the place of the interview
- details showing where to report and whom to ask for on arrival
- details of any evidence of ability or qualifications that applicants may be asked to produce.

Who should conduct the interview?

The manager to whom the job holder reports should always be the person who conducts the interview. However, this person will need to be skilled in selection interviewing techniques, and have a clear understanding of the requirements of both the job and the prospective job holder. In larger companies it is often the personnel manager who conducts the interview, but the immediate superior should be present for at least some of the time. There are still companies which separate the task of job selection interviewing from managers in this way, even though human resource practice advises strongly against this for obvious reasons:

- As the manager is given the task of managing those staff under him or her, they should be the person who makes the ultimate decision as to who is given the job.
- Only by being directly involved in the interviewing process will the manager be able to make a judgement about the suitability of the applicant's personality and character.
- A third party acting as interviewer may not be able to make the necessary judgements about the requirements of the job and expectations of the job holder.
- The manager directly responsible for the post is best suited to provide an accurate picture of the nature of the job and the sort of applicant who would be most suited to working within his or her team.
- A manager or supervisor who has not had the responsibility of choosing their own staff are likely to resent the fact that new employees are selected for them by someone else, and such resentment will usually hinder good working relationships.

Methods of selection interviewing

There are a number of ways in which selection interviews can be conducted, though these will often depend upon the nature of the job and the recruitment policy of your company. Let's look at the three different methods of selection interviewing.

One-to-one interview

Interviewing on a one-to-one basis is still the most common method of selecting people for a job vacancy. Close contact of this nature gives the ideal opportunity for in-depth discussion, and usually promotes greater rapport between interviewer and applicant.

Possible drawbacks of this type of interview: Selection of the most suitable candidate depends almost entirely upon the solo interviewing skills of the interviewer and their ability to make an objective judgement about the applicant. Unskilled solo interviewers often recruit on the basis of similarity of personal characteristics, i.e. the more like the interviewer the applicant, the more likely they are to be successful. It is a fact that we are normally more attracted to people like us, which can present difficulties where teamwork demands a balance of personality types.

Panel interview

Panel interviews are those where two or three interviewers sit together to form a bench, or panel. Panels usually consist of the supervisor or manager, the head of department and the personnel manager. Panel interviews benefit from the variety of views and opinions of those who make up the panel, and can lead to the making of a more balanced and objective final decision. This is particularly useful where the principal interested party lacks good interviewing skills and does not feel confident or cannot be relied upon to make the right decision. Interviewing panels often benefit from the separate skills and areas of expertise held by those who make up the panel.

Possible drawbacks of this type of interview: There is always the danger that the interview may become disjointed if the panel have not discussed the objective and purpose of their various roles prior to the interview. Interviewees may be overawed by the interviewing process, especially where the panel seem particularly humourless and detached. The interviewee can sometimes feel like the interrogated. Group decisions may not always be balanced and unbiased. The reason for this is that very often, either the strongest personality or the most senior panelist tends to dominate discussions on the relative merits of the interviewees.

Group interview

The purpose of the group selection interview is to place candidates in a variety of prearranged situations to observe both individual and team behaviour. Group selection requires about six to eight interviewees working in front of a small selection panel. Methods used to judge the talents and abilities of the interviewees vary, but they may include case studies or involve group discussions in which the panel observe the individual behaviour of group members. Group selection interview methods are particularly well suited to: leadership skills;

communication skills; persuasive skills; analytical processes and problem-solving skills. In group selection, the interview team usually makes a decision on those applicants who show the most promise, and these normally go forward to be interviewed on a one-to-one basis by individual members of the team.

PREPARING FOR THE INTERVIEW

When you have decided on the method of interviewing best suited to your particular needs, you should give some thought to how you will prepare for the interview. Make arrangements to conduct your interviews in friendly surroundings, preferably in an environment which provides both privacy and comfort. Make sure that other staff know you will be interviewing, and that they understand that you must not be disturbed. You will need to rearrange the furniture from formal office layout to something more conducive to putting the candidate at ease. A fuller explanation of how you can create the right interview environment is given in the previous chapter, under 'Ground rules for interviewing'.

Once you are happy with the interviewing environment, consider how the candidate is to be received when they arrive for the interview. If you, as interviewer, are unable to receive the candidate, make suitable arrangements to ensure that either a secretary or other member of staff is on hand to receive them. The person should be briefed as to whom to expect and when, and it is normal courtesy to offer interviewees either tea or coffee on arrival. If interviews are running late for any reason, interviewees should be informed of the delay and apologies should be tendered. It is a good idea to offer interviewees some relevant reading material where they have to wait for the interview.

....

CASE STUDY

A few years ago, a friend called Jayne was invited to an interview to discuss her application for the position of Assistant Branch Manager to a retail travel agency. She was looking forward to the interview and had taken time to prepare, and felt that she stood a good chance of being offered the job. When she arrived at the agency, she was greeted by a member of staff who was surprised to learn that interviews were taking place. She made a point of saying that she had not been informed of any appointments to see the managing director that day. Jayne was asked to wait until the managing director was available. She was offered no indication of how long she would have to wait, nor was she offered any kind of refreshment. She sat for twenty minutes until finally, the managing director appeared and asked her to come into his office. No apology or explanation for the delay was offered.

When Jayne entered the office, she was surprised to see that there was only one chair behind, what was obviously, the managing director's desk. She stood waiting to be offered the seat, and watched as the managing director took the seat himself, and stared incredulously as he offered her a pile of brochures to sit on. Jayne could hardly believe the way she was being treated. If this was how the managing director behaved towards applicants attending an interview, how on earth must he treat his staff? At this point she made the decision to terminate the interview, explained her reasons to the managing director. He displayed neither interest nor concern for her treatment, and she left.

The managing director in this case study was obviously unskilled and untrained in the art of interviewing. His cavalier attitude towards the interviewee was indicative of the kind of business he operated, as witnessed by the girl in the agency who had no idea that interviews were taking place. Apart from a lack of common courtesy, the interviewer failed to recognise the importance of creating a good impression of his company to prospective employees. Anyone who has such little regard for another human being is hardly going to present a favourable picture of himself as an employer who is caring and respectful of his staff. What this managing director evidently had never considered was that an interview is not a one-way process in which the employer has sole rights of decision. Jayne, as prospective employee, would also be making a decision about the company, and her decision was not very difficult to make.

Preparation for the interview is most important. The first thing is to put yourself in the position of the interviewee and to ask a few basic questions such as, 'What will a prospective employee think when they walk in?', 'Am I creating the right sort of impression?' and 'Would a really first-class applicant want to work here?'

If you are satisfied that the interviewing environment is right, consider how you might prepare for the interview itself. Allow yourself some time to read through the application and the candidate assessment form. You can then make a note of any specific questions you wish to ask or points you wish to discuss during the interview. Lack of preparation is not only unprofessional, it creates a poor impression, and good interviewees will probably look on it as a reflection on your management style. As we have seen, this will often influence their decision as to whether or not they wish to work for you.

STRUCTURING THE INTERVIEW

CASE STUDY

Bill is the manager of a small, but busy retail outlet. He prefers the steady life, and becomes quite stressed when under pressure. At such times he removes himself to his office and closes the door. Stress comes in many different guises for Bill, and he is certainly not the cool and collected type. His current problem is that he has to conduct a series of interviews to select a new member of staff. He dislikes the thought of interviewing, especially as he never really knows what questions to ask, and rarely finds his interviewing notes much help when it comes to having to make a decision. At the last interviews Bill conducted he lost one of the applications and became confused about which interviewee was which. This did little for his confidence, and he got the impression that the interviewees were judging him. Bill feels no more confident on this occasion, and will be very relieved when his ordeal is over.

The reason that Bill finds interviewing such an ordeal is that he never gives sufficient time and thought to preparation.

Let's consider the sort of structure which is necessary in an interviewing situation. First, a selection interview should not be considered as an informal chat about the vacancy. The real purpose of the interview is to obtain and evaluate information about the candidate which will enable an assessment to be made about the candidate's level of competence and ability to do the job. The art of interviewing is to be as objective as possible in order to provide all candidates with the same fair opportunity to compete for the job. Interviews should be conducted in the absence of preconceived ideas about candidates or their abilities, and the same approach should be adopted at each interview. It is especially important that the interviewer remains objective in the case of applications from staff already working for the company. Prior knowledge of the candidate and their job skills should not prejudice the judgement of the interviewer. The central question must always be, 'Is this the right person for the job?' And, whether applications are received from internal applicants, external applicants or a mixture of both, interviewing techniques must be constant.

You may find the following guidelines useful when you come to think about the structure of your interviews:

1 Welcome the candidate and apologise for any delay. Offer refreshments if this has not already been done. Try and put the candidate at ease as quickly as possible before the interview begins. Find some mutual point of discussion outside of the job vacancy, such as the applicant's journey to the interview. With internal candidates, you might ask something about a current work project. Don't be in too much of a hurry to start the in-depth questioning. Your first priority should be to establish a rapport with the candidate.

2 Tell external candidates a little about the background of the company but be careful not to turn your interview into a lecture. You can also briefly outline the requirements of the job to your interviewees. This will enable interviewees to ask questions about the nature of the job or to make specific points to demonstrate their ability and suitability to the job. Above all, you should be quite clear in your mind about the job requirements. Interviewees should not have to guess at what the job is about, but remember, the objective of the interview is to get applicants to talk – not to do all the talking yourself.

3 Once the requirements of the job have been outlined, concentrate on asking

the interviewee the sort of questions which will give you as much information as possible about their current levels of knowledge, skills and attitude to the job. By the end of the interview, you should have sufficient information to be able to complete the applicant's assessment form. While you will be expected to make some notes during the interview, don't spend all of your time looking down at a piece of paper. You can always write up your notes in full once the interview is over, and while the information is still fresh in your mind.

During this part of the interview, the interviewee should be encouraged to do most of the talking. As a guideline, you should be talking yourself for only about 30 per cent of the time, leaving the interviewee to talk for about 70 per cent of the time.

4 Allow the candidate an opportunity to ask any questions they have about the job or the company, and make sure you provide them with as full and honest an answer as possible.

5 Explain to the candidate what the next stage of the recruitment process will be, e.g. that successful candidates will be recalled or contacted. Explain the likely time-scale before the applicant is advised of any decisions. Under no circumstances should you disclose your opinion or your decision on the outcome of the interview, neither should you say anything about any of the other candidates.

6 Thank the candidate for coming, thank them for their interest and show them out personally.

....

CASE STUDY

A few years ago I ran a series of counselling and interviewing techniques courses for managers and area managers who needed to acquire job selection interviewing skills. The group was a mixture of experienced and less experienced retailers and tour operators, and this provided a useful basis from which to draw on collective knowledge and skills.

At one point in the first afternoon, participants were given the opportunity to engage in 'live' interviewing situations, taking turns to be either the interviewer or the interviewee. Several of the participants showed good promise, especially with the questioning techniques. Others found this more challenging and struggled to get to grips with asking the right questions at the right time during the interview.

I was particularly interested in Tom, one of the more experienced managers on the course, who admitted in his introduction that he had had little success over the years in choosing the right staff. He put this down to a lack of suitable applicants in his area, though this theory was challenged by others who had businesses in nearby towns. Tom had made the point that in his experience staff only worked for monetary rewards, and that they tended to move on within months of taking up employment with him. He felt that young people had no dedication to the job.

However, the real reason for Tom's failure to find suitable applicants soon became clear. We were at a point where each participant took on the role of interviewer to practise their skills in questioning techniques. One or two participants had been finding difficulty with applying a proper structure to their interviews, and this seemed to be mainly confined to those who had been interviewing job applicants for a number of years. Tom struggled with the format. He tried twice to get started, but each time he quickly came to a halt, not knowing which question to ask next and quite unable to remember what he had asked. I stopped the interview temporarily. Tom looked around at the rest of the group.

'This is not the way I usually conduct interviews,' he said to me.

I looked at Tom and nodded. 'So how do you usually tackle it then, Tom?' I asked.

'Well,' he said, 'I don't ask all these questions. What I do is to make sure the applicant knows all about the company first.'

'That's a good idea, Tom,' I replied, then added, 'But how do you take it from there?'

'Well, that's the point,' said Tom. 'I don't bother with all of those questions. I tell the candidate all about the company.'

'And then you tell them all about the job,' I added.

'That's right,' said Tom.

'And then you tell them what you expect from them in the job,' I said.

'Yes,' replied Tom, 'that's right.'

'And then you tell them what sort of agency you run, and what sort of business you do, and what kind of person you are looking for in the job.'

'That's right,' said Tom. 'That's exactly what I do.'

I looked at Tom, and smiled. 'And then you take on the applicant based on what you have told them,' I concluded.

'Ahh!' reflected Tom. 'Perhaps that's why I never seem to pick the right staff.'

Hard lesson though it was for Tom, he had finally found the reason for his lack of success in choosing staff. Tom had never considered that he needed to be organised, neither had he ever considered it necessary to adopt any kind of structure for his interviews. He had never considered the sorts of questions which would give him the information about the applicant that he wanted, so he turned every interview into a lecture, telling the applicant all about the company, the business and his views on people and personalities. Over the years, Tom had developed this technique to the point where he did most of the talking. What he learned from the course was that this approach made it impossible for him to make any objective decision about job applicants. Tom realised, after all those years, that he judged the ability of his interviewees solely on their reaction to his little talks.

QUESTIONING TECHNIQUES FOR SELECTION INTERVIEWS

Good questioning techniques are as essential in selection interviewing as they are in any other interviewing situation. Questions are essential to enable you to obtain sufficient information about the candidate and, from the answers you get, you must be able to make your final decision about the suitability of the applicant. You will find that the Chapter 8 will provide you with information on most of the questioning techniques you need for conducting job selection interviews, but there are also some more specific questioning techniques which need to be covered here.

You may find that your are able to assess an applicant's performance and relative experience from work that they already do in another sphere, e.g. if the job requires someone to perform a telesales role, and your interviewee is already performing that function in another organisation, you may only need to ascertain the candidate's current level of competence in that role. In cases where you are able to compare generic skills, it is a fairly simple task to ask questions which prove the applicant's current level of competence. However, sometimes you need to look more closely at an applicant's skills. Let's take, for example, an instance where the candidate is applying for a job involving a task in which they have no experience. Here, it will not be possible to refer to some other generic skill, so you will need to ask questions which establish the applicant's potential to perform the task.

The following case study is an actual account of an interview conducted by the director of a small retail outlet. The interviewing techniques he used during the interview demonstrate exactly how he used questioning techniques to establish the managerial potential of a young senior travel clerk whom he decided to take on as his manager.

CASE STUDY

Dawn wished to advance her travel career, and decided to apply for an interview for a retail manager's job. She had no previous managerial experience and had not even been responsible for looking after more junior members of staff. She was somewhat apprehensive about how she could realistically prove her potential during the interview since she had no direct experience by which she could demonstrate this. Brian, the managing director, was equally aware of Dawn's predicament, but being a skilled interviewer, was nevertheless able to question Dawn to establish her potential.

He started off by asking her to talk about managers she had worked for in the past, and to identify specific strengths which she recognised as being important to the managerial role. He then asked her to identify any managerial weaknesses she had recognised, and to explain how she would have handled the situation differently, had she been the manager herself. Dawn found that she was able to relate quickly to this line of questioning and felt confident that her answers reflected her beliefs and attitudes towards management.

Brian was equally satisfied that Dawn did indeed have the right attitude towards management, and was impressed by her answers. However, he felt that he needed to explore exactly how she would take to the responsibilities of the job, as the new manager of the shop would often be the most senior member of staff on the premises and would be expected to work on her own initiative and should have the confidence to make important decisions within the job. To establish her competence in this area, he asked her to outline the details of an emergency she had dealt with, and to explain the actions she took in response to the situation. Dawn was able to offer an impressive account of how she had handled an incident in which customers who were overseas had been mugged, and had lost their valuables, including tickets and passports.

Brian was satisfied that Dawn's account of the actions she had taken had provided sufficient evidence of her likely behaviour in similar stressful situations where she would be called upon to respond quickly and efficiently. He was happy that these actions demonstrated Dawn's ability to remain calm and collected in an emergency, and deduced (quite rightly as it turned out) that she would not be afraid to take managerial responsibilities. Dawn was given the job. In the first year she increased the business some 20 per cent over her target, and went on to build up the agency into a top retail outlet in the town.

In this case, the interviewer was able to establish the candidate's potential to take on the role of manager by asking questions about her current position as senior clerk. The interviewer also examined her attitudes towards management, and from this he was able to infer how the candidate would behave towards staff working under her. The managing director was satisfied with the potential he saw, and realised that any significant gaps in the applicant's managerial knowledge and skills could easily be remedied after the appointment. The interviewer's decision was based on the applicant's potential to make something of this new role, and proves that if you ask the right questions, you will obtain the right answers. Interviewing is very much the art of questioning.

You may not need to interview a potential applicant for the position of manager, but there is perhaps another more common situation where the candidate is applying for a job for which they have no previous experience – the job of trainee.

CASE STUDY

James has just left school and wishes to go into travel. He has no knowledge of the business, and has never worked in a travel agency, but he is quite clear about travel as a career. He has been called for two interviews with local companies, and has spent some time preparing himself for these. Part way into the first interview the local manager begins to ask James a few questions about his interest in the travel business.

'So you say you like travel, then James?'

'Yes, for a long time I didn't really know what I wanted to do, and . . .'

'And you thought you'd better make a start.'

'Yes, it was after we'd done a travel project at school. I quite liked the idea of working in an agency.'

'How do you think you'll get on with having to deal with customers, then?'

'Well, I get on with everybody at the old peoples' home I do some work for.'

'Yes, well, it's not quite the same as dealing with customers, you know. I see you did well in geography at school. Geography's very important in our business – I assume you know your European geography.'

'I study as much as I can.'

'Good, good. And how do you think you'll get on having to answer the phone?'

'Quite well, I suppose. I've never had to speak to anyone about travel arrangements, but I sometimes answer the phone for my dad when his customers ring up.'

'Right, well you'll know all about using the telephone then, won't you.'

And so James' interview continued. On the following day, he had another interview, but this time with a travel company in the next town. James had spent a little time talking about himself, when the conversation opened up into talk about the travel industry. The interviewer, manager of the agency, asked James a few questions.

'Tell me something about working at the old peoples' home. What sort of things do you talk to them about?'

'Well, they like to talk about the past quite a lot, and I always find that interesting. We have one old guy there who fought in the First World War . . .' And James describes his friend at the home.

'Are they always glad to see you when you go over there?'

'Yes, nearly always. Sometimes one or two get a bit grumpy, though, and then they tend to have a moan at you, you know.'

'And what do you say if they're not very friendly to you, James?'

'Oh, well, if they're moaning about the food, or complaining about what's on the TV, I usually get them to tell me what their favourite programme is, or get them to talk about the things they used to eat in the war.'

'And how do they respond?'

'Usually they're OK. Sometimes they go on complaining, but if you keep talking about positive things, and take their minds off worrying, they nearly always come round, and very soon they've forgotten all about it.'

'You were saying earlier that you sometimes answer the phone for your father. What sort of phone calls do you get?'

'Oh, all sorts. People phone up to get an estimate, some phone about an enquiry about getting work done. I had to deal with one person who phoned up to complain, once.'

'So, tell me what you did?'

'Well, she was expecting my dad to come that morning, but I could see from his diary that he'd arranged to go to her house in the afternoon. So she was wrong, really.'

'And so what did you say to her.'

'Well, she was quite angry at the time, so I just let her go on a bit, then I apologised that she was kept waiting, and asked her if she'd got one of my dad's calling cards. I got her to look at the details on the card, and then she realised she'd made a mistake, and . . . ' James continued to describe what had happened.

What is clear about these two interviews is that the manager has a different approach in each case. Although, unlike in the previous case study, James has had no travel experience, the two interviewers face a similar problem – judging the interviewee's potential. Again, the interviewer can only draw obliquely on the interviewee's direct past experience in making a judgement about his potential to do the job.

Which of the two interviewers seemed to be making a better job?

The answer will be clearer as we look at some of the differences, so let's review the first interview. Interviewer No. 1 asks a series of what we call 'leading' questions: 'So you say you like travel?', 'And you thought you'd better make a start?', 'I assume you know your European geography?', 'You know all about using the telephone?' These questions are not probing, they are confirming, that is, confirming the interviewer's assumptions of what he believes. However, you will have noticed that James is not invited to do much of the talking – in fact, he was stopped in the middle of giving his first answer. The interviewer also made various assumptions about James's potential to deal with customers, his geographical knowledge and his telephone skills. If we take account of the 'air-time' (the time each person spends talking) the interviewer has as much to say in the interview as James does.

Contrast the second interview. Here, the interviewer's approach is to ask more open questions – those which get James to do the talking. He also invites James to talk about himself and his experiences, by using phrases such as, 'Tell me about . . .' and 'So, tell me what you did'. This questioning line is designed to get the interviewee to open up and relate his experiences about past events. Notice that Interviewer No. 2 does not jump to conclusions or make assumptions – he probes more deeply to pursue a particular point.

The second interviewer also asks open questions: 'What sort of . . .?', 'What do you say if . . .?', 'And how do they respond?', 'What sort of phone calls . . .?', 'And so what did you say to her?', in order to find out how James reacted in past situations. The implication is plain – if James responded positively in the past, he is likely to respond well to similar situations in the future. If he manages to placate one of his father's angry customers, then he is likely to adopt the same positive approach to other customers, and if he can handle a difficult person in one situation, he will be able to do so in another. You will also have noticed the difference in air-time. The second interviewer restricts any tendency to jump to conclusions by prompting James to do the talking. Here the ratio of interviewer to interviewee is 25:75.

Of the two interviews, then, the second was more successful in discovering the interviewee's potential to do the job. The first manager was unable to resist the usual temptation which faces the interviewer – talking too much and listening too little. If he did agree to give James the job, his decision would certainly not have been based on any logical analysis, but on emotion and prejudice. The second manager did things correctly. He asked the right questions, and listened to the answers. That is the art of job selection interviewing.

Guidelines for questioning in a selection interview

1 Ask the candidate about actual experiences rather than those of some hypothetical future situation. To gauge the candidate's likely behaviour in a future role, questions should centre on concrete experience. This means either probing how they have handled a particular situation, or asking their opinion on what they have observed in others. So, if they have not worked in a retail environment before, ask them how they felt about the service they received as a customer.

2 Ask the candidate to identify their own strengths and weaknesses. This need not be limited to a work situation since many candidates have personal strengths in life skills which could be used at work, e.g. a woman returner may regard one of her strengths as being able to deal with family crises in a calm manner which minimises the anxiety of her children. Transferred to a work situation, she would probably adopt a similarly calm approach in emergencies, and deal quite rationally with any problem arising during the working day. The purpose of asking someone to state a personal weakness is not to identify unacceptable flaws in that person's character, but to assess their level of introspection, and their ability to be objective about personal performance and attitudes. Beware of anyone who is unwilling or unable to identify any personal weakness, as this may indicate a reluctance to examine and evaluate personal performance, and may well point to a strongly defensive attitude towards criticism.

3 Ask the candidate about future personal ambitions. Their response to this question usually provides a good insight into how they see themselves developing in the job, or indeed whether the job is likely to provide them with sufficient scope for personal development. If an applicant for a secretarial job with limited responsibilities and little scope for further advancement discloses an ambition to run a secretarial or administration team, it should be plain to the interviewer that, if the job were offered, the applicant would find the scope too limiting and would probably look to move on in a comparatively short time. While the interviewer may be very impressed with the applicant's future potential, caution should be exercised in appointing that person to a role which would clearly prove to be too limiting.

4 Ask about hobbies and pastimes. Whether the candidate has previous work experience or not, the way they spend their leisure time may give you an insight into their preferred roles and responsibilities, e.g. someone who, in their social life, acts as committee chairman and organises local charity events is likely to prove useful in most leading or organizing roles. A person who plays a lot of team sports is more likely to be a good team player in the workplace than someone who prefers more solitary pursuits in their free time. However, an applicant should never be recruited solely on the basis of how they spend their leisure time. A good interviewer will often infer an applicant's potential from the way in which they spend their leisure time, but will not make assumptions about current skills or competence, e.g. 'He's chairman of the local Round Table, therefore he will be an excellent manager of the sales department.' The skilled interviewer will explore the applicant's free-time role

and responsibilities, and their handling of people and different situations in order to establish how they may function in a similar situation.

5 Find out something about personal circumstances. Some care does need to be taken as to exactly what sort of information is requested, as there is a matter of personal privacy. Some highly personal matters, such as personal relationships, certain matters of finance or, in the case of female candidates, their intention to start a family, are off limits. However, questions about other important information may be asked, such as the short-term likelihood of moving house, the interviewee's current state of health, whether or not they hold a current driving license, and the arrangements they intend to make to get to their place of work.

CASE STUDY

Shankhill Travel needed to employ a part-time secretary to work for three mornings a week. The job responsibilities were limited, and included taking dictation from the managing director, typing various letters and memos, and doing basic bookkeeping. Joy, the managing director, interviewed six applicants for the job.

Hazel, the lady she was most impressed with, had a number of years of experience as a personal secretary, and was very outgoing and sociable. During the interview, Joy built up a good rapport with Hazel, and was most impressed with her many personal qualities. When Hazel was asked what she wanted in a job, she said that it was important for her to be able to get out and meet people, and that she was hoping to take on a marketing role in the future. She discussed with Joy the potential she saw for marketing a company such as hers, and suggested ways in which she might be able to help. Joy was most impressed, and decided that she could offer Hazel the job and develop her in a marketing role.

However, in discussing the matter with her husband, Joy was surprised to learn that he did not share her optimism. In fact, he cautioned strongly against taking on someone as talented and ambitious as Hazel for what was essentially a part-time administration role. 'What is your main requirement in the job?' he asked Joy.

'Well, I suppose it's really the secretarial function,' replied Joy. 'But I don't want to let someone as talented as Hazel take her skills elsewhere.'

'And you think you will be able to offer her both roles?' he asked.

'Yes, I do.'

'And which of the two roles do you think Hazel will be motivated to do?'

'Look!' said Joy. 'I believe she will be happy to do the more mundane office work if she knows there'll be something more challenging coming along.'

'And have you thought about a time-scale?' her husband asked.

But Joy had made up her mind and was determined not to let Hazel go. Hazel accepted the job offer willingly, and immediately started to draw up plans for marketing the company. However, after a month in the job, Hazel found herself becoming increasingly bored and restless. The job turned out to be little more than administration work, with no sign of the marketing role she had been promised. Hazel mentioned this to Joy several times, and was reassured that as soon as Joy had the time, they would start to plan Hazel's marketing activities. Another month went by, and still nothing happened. Eventually Hazel became so disillusioned that she left the company.

It was obvious, in this case study, that the applicant's abilities far exceeded what the primary job could offer, and the interviewer made the mistake of appointing her in the belief that she could offer something rather more challenging than the administration and secretarial job which was really on offer. Joy's real problem was her inability to match the right applicant with her own job specification. Hazel's promise as a marketeer rather blinded Joy's perception of what she most needed for the company, i.e. a secretary and administration clerk – and a part-time one, at that.

Whilst Hazel had undoubted potential in marketing, Joy failed to see that she would not be able to mix the two roles. She wanted both Hazel's secretarial skills and her marketing potential, but was clearly unable to accommodate Hazel in both. Despite promises of how the job might be developed, her overriding need for a secretary was always in conflict with her desire to keep Hazel's marketing skills to herself. In the end, of course, Hazel became disillusioned, and left. You will have noticed that Joy's husband foresaw the danger of this situation when he asked his wife to consider what she saw as Hazel's primary function and what Hazel would consider it to be.

Joy had drawn up a job and person specification, and was quite clear in her mind about the job vacancy she wished to fill, but very quickly discarded this useful framework in favour of Hazel's personality and potential. This case study demonstrates that no matter how rigorous the process of drawing up the specifications has been, the real key to choosing the right person for the job is the interviewer's ability to remain strictly objective at the interview stage.

MAKING YOUR SELECTION

Once the interviews are over, you will need to make a decision about the most suitable candidate for the job vacancy. No doubt, you will have formed impressions of those who came for an interview – their attitudes, knowledge, skills and personalities – and weighing up this information will play an important part in your final choice. This is the point where an objective overview is essential. You will probably have had some intuitive sense about the right sort of personality you want, but consider carefully the notes you made at the time. Consider some of the influences which colour the choice and decision we are likely to make, and which were discussed earlier in the chapter on interviewing. You will need to take special account of organisational and team needs, and to be conscious of personal preferences and prejudices. Think about the job, think about the person, and think about the person who would be best suited to that job.

CASE STUDY

Katie is the manager of a busy reservations office. She urgently needs another member of staff for the coming season, and will be looking to take on someone who is very capable, very reliable and who would be willing to stay for several years within the job. Lack of permanence in staff is a problem for this kind of work, and Katie has found that many of her staff leave within two years. Training and development of reservations staff in this busy environment is costly and time-consuming.

Katie has interviewed four people for the post. Two have some experience, one is just out of college and the other is a mature returner. Katie has looked carefully at their qualifications, their personality and their potential and has decided, with reservations, that a mature woman is the most suitable candidate for the job. However, Katie is concerned about her feelings for mature women. She had problems as a young manager in another company, where a mature female member of staff tended to undermine her position, and was a tremendous influence on her younger members of staff. Since then, Katie has never employed anyone she regarded as mature and motherly, and has always been able to maintain control and authority over her staff. This time, though, she has a tough decision to make, as the mature applicant has the right experience and potential she is looking for. Katie compares herself now as an experienced manager and then, as a young manager.

Now, Katie decides, she is much more mature. She has confidence in herself and regards herself as a good leader. When staff have problems, they come to her, not only because she is the manager, but also because she has the maturity to listen to their problems with sympathy, and to make the right decision afterwards. Katie knows that she is seen as the boss. Previously, Katie reflects, she was very new to the job. She lacked confidence in herself and in her ability to do the job. She always felt that she should know more than her staff, be more skilled than her staff and do more than her staff and, in order to maintain this position, she felt the need to be rigid with authority. Katie felt that then, her insecurity had led her to operate a fairly repressive regime. She was very much task driven at that time. She drove her staff hard, partly in order to maintain her dominant position as manager, and realises, in retrospect, that she had paid little attention to their spiritual needs and personal well-being. It was in this climate that one of the more mature members of staff became a focus for their problems – tensions within the office, lack of managerial recognition, little sense of belonging – most of which, Katie had to admit, was a direct result of her obsession with the job, and constant need to prove herself.

Katie knew that she had come a long way since then, but also understood in that minute why she had never contemplated employing an older woman. In her never ending quest to stay on top of her staff, she had forgotten in those early days their need for praise, recognition and encouragement. She ignored their spiritual needs and discounted their contribution and effort in achieving the very goals and targets which had secured her position. This they got from the mature lady who worked in the office, and who was always there to listen sympathetically to their problems and guide them with words of encouragement. But for her . . ., Katie thought. And she knew the decision she would now have to make.

Katie is now, of course, sufficiently mature herself, to be able to take on a mature person in the job. She is also able to recognise why she has never employed mature women to work with her.

This case study, like the others in this book, is a true account of a personal experience. Katie had spent many years discounting the possible potential of one particular group, solely for reasons which had their roots in her early life as a manager. It was only now, upon reflection, that Katie was able to face the past and come to terms with her feelings.

....

It is certainly true that some interviewers seek out particular traits or characteristics in people as a guide to whether or not they are to be considered for employment. There is the case of the manager who only ever employs brunettes. He knows that he does it. There is another case of a female manager who never employs males and, no doubt, plenty of cases of those who only ever give employment to males. A skilled, objective approach is essential when choosing the right people for the job but, for some, job selection will always be a subjective exercise.

To summarise the key points of job selection, always:

- draw up a job specification
- draw up a person specification
- make use of an applicant assessment form
- arrange interviews for the most suitable applicants
- decide on the method and conduct of the interview
- arrange a venue which has a suitable environment
- use appropriate questioning techniques to establish the interviewees' ability and/or potential
- assess interviewees' suitability against job and person specifications
- compare the relative merits of all applicants.

....

Assignment You have decided to interview Julie Smithers for the position of Senior Counter Clerk and your tasks are as follows:

1 Assuming the interview is to be conducted on your own business premises, decide on where the interview is to take place and how the furniture will be arranged. State the reasons for your choice.

2 Decide on the arrangements to be made for Julie's reception when she arrives.

3 Prepare a list of questions you wish to put to Julie during the interview.

4 Role-play the interview with Julie (you will need to enlist the help of a colleague to play the part of Julie). Her application is printed in Figs. 9.3 and 9.4 on pages 242–3.

5 Once the interview is complete, make a decision on Julie's suitability for the job.

10

....

Appraisals

As part of your NVQ, you will need to demonstrate an ability to provide feedback on staff performance and to be able to identify training and development needs. The performance appraisal interview is a valuable management tool which fulfils both of these functions, and in addition to this, provides a valuable opportunity for communication between managers and staff. Appraisals, if properly conducted, will increase motivation, communication and the quality of staff work performance. This chapter deals with the appraisal interview and all that it entails, and will help you to conduct effective appraisals.

OBJECTIVES

Once you have read this chapter of the book you will be able to:
- **state the objective of an appraisal interview**
- **state the structure of an appraisal interview**
- **discuss the appraisee's level of performance**
- **identify training and development needs**
- **agree future work objectives**
- **complete the relevant appraisal documents.**

WHAT IS AN APPRAISAL?

An appraisal is a formal interview between a manager and member of staff. During the appraisal, both parties have an opportunity to discuss the appraisee's performance, past achievements, and any problems arising out of their work or relationships with colleagues and supervisors. The appraisal should also include a discussion on the appraisee's training and development needs and all future projects and performance objectives.

An appraisal should not be viewed as an opportunity for the manager to launch any kind of personal attack on the appraisee, or provide a list of criticisms which have been saved up over a period of time. Instead, the appraisal should be viewed as a positive means of open communication to discuss all matters relating to the employee's work. This should be a two-way process, and the appraisee should be just as able to comment on the way they have been managed, as the manager is able to comment on the appraisee's performance.

CASE STUDY

Sales manager, Chris, doesn't understand the purpose of an appraisal. Her boss, area sales manager, Nigel, doesn't understand what an appraisal is either. Both have attended a compulsory one-day course on appraising staff, and both have had the opportunity to test their learning in the role-plays set up by the trainer. The problem which Nigel and Chris have is that they see the appraisal as a stick with which to discipline those staff who, perhaps, do not conform wholly to their particular management gospel. The fact that the company has just spent considerable time and resources introducing the appraisal system, gives their interpretation an official edge.

Nigel and Chris, then, see the appraisal as their opportunity to present a personal assessment to their staff. This problem is compounded because they both see this as an opportunity to judge staff according to certain subjective criteria – popularity, conformity, likeability, etc. – and someone they rate highly for these personal attributes also scores very highly on their personal assessment, i.e. nice person = competent person, likeable person = successful person. Unfortunately, the opposite is also true and, as a result, one of Chris's more senior staff receives a poor assessment, i.e. unlikeable person = incompetent and unsuccessful person.

Neither Chris nor Nigel particularly like Tom. He is seen as a loner and an outsider and, as such, he gets marked down by Chris as having a number of 'faults' which single him out for an unfair assessment. During the appraisal interview Tom's 'faults' are pointed out to him by Chris and he is given a five-point plan for the improvement of his character. He is given no opportunity to respond to Chris's adverse comments, though he is expected to sign the appraisal form afterwards to verify that he has agreed in principal to the comments and review made by his manager.

Not unnaturally, Tom is less than happy to do this as, once signed, the appraisal becomes a permanent record and is placed on his personal file. His refusal to sign is regarded by both his manager and the area manager as confirmation of his difficult and obstructive nature. More time is offered for Tom to sign the document, but he remains adamant that he will not sign an appraisal which was not negotiated. Nigel and Chris decide that more pressure should be put on Tom but, as he refuses to sign, and they find their authority is rather under threat, they make the decision to proceed with a disciplinary interview. The result of this is that Tom is given another unnecessary verbal drubbing by both managers. Finally, he signs the document under threat of further action. Tom's appraisal goes on file.

This case study, as tragic as it is true, demonstrates so well why the company appraisal has often found more critics than supporters. The appraisal process, as devised by the company, allowed maximum opportunity for fair and frank discussion between the manager and member of staff. The appraisal conducted by Chris and underwritten by Nigel was a one-way managerial assessment of the worst kind.

Every appraisal demands the guarantee of absolute freedom of expression and thought on the part of both appraiser and appraisee. Without this guarantee the appraisal process, as in Tom's case, is open to abuse by the unskilled appraiser, especially one who sees the appraisal as an opportunity to outline every negative aspect of the appraisee's character. Tom quite rightly refused to sign the document. The disciplinary interview which followed showed up both the faults in the process and the lack of managerial skills.

As you will read in this chapter, the appraisal process is designed as a means by which managers and staff can sit down on a one-to-one basis, in a non-threatening environment, to discuss any and every aspect of the subordinate's personal performance, and any subsequent training and development needs. Tom's appraisal met none of these, nor did it relate in any way to the following guidelines:

- a formal, but friendly interview between manager and staff
- an opportunity to discuss the appraisee's performance and past achievements
- a non-threatening environment where work problems can be freely discussed
- a discussion of the appraisee's training and development needs
- an agreement on all future projects/performance objectives

In the case study Chris and Nigel saw the appraisal process as being more important that the actual purpose of the appraisal – Tom refused to sign on the grounds that his review had been a one-sided assessment by his manager, and an unfair assessment, at that. Tom was obliged to sign to say that he had agreed, not with the appraisal outcomes, but with the spirit and proper conduct of his appraisal. He obviously did not and, as a result, was erroneously disciplined for failure to comply with company regulations.

No stage of the appraisal process should ever be viewed as an opportunity for the manager to exercise authority over the appraisee, launch any kind of personal attack on the appraisee, or provide a list of criticisms which have been accumulated over a period of time. Instead, the appraisal should be viewed as a positive means of open communication to discuss all matters relating to the employee's work. This should be a two-way process, and the appraisee should be just as able to comment on the way they have been managed, as the manager is able to comment on the appraisee's performance.

THE APPRAISAL PROCESS

The appraisal is essentially an interview, and should be conducted along the lines of any other interview that you undertake. Most importantly though, an appraisal needs a structure and process in order to be effective. Training should be given to all those involved – appraisers and appraisees – for while it is important to have an agreed appraisal process which every member of staff can follow, it should be stressed that the effective appraisal is never process driven.

Here are the stages we have outlined in the appraisal process:

- setting up the appraisal system
- preparing for the appraisal
- starting the interview
- discussing performance achievements
- checking performance against objectives
- discussing unsatisfactory performance
- talking over personal problems
- identifying reasons for unsatisfactory performance
- identifying training and development needs
- setting performance objectives
- agreeing the action plan
- documenting the appraisal.

Setting up the appraisal process

If your company already has an appraisal system then staff should be aware of their role within it, e.g. the format of the interview and any documents to be completed. If, however, no formal system exists, you may wish to consider the following point if you wish to introduce regular appraisals.

Who will be responsible for conducting the appraisals?

The appraisal must be conducted only by the appraisee's immediate manager or supervisor. These are the people closest to the appraisee's work outputs and who allocate work to the appraisee, check the accuracy of work and who manage the appraisee on a day-to-day basis. It is common practice in some companies for the appraisal to be conducted by a person other than the immediate manager, i.e. an appraisal for a sales clerk is conducted by the area manager, but under these circumstances, and because such managers have no day-to-day contact with the appraisee, the appraisal usually turns out to be no more than an assessment. It may be based on second-hand information which may cause a distorted view of the appraisee's performance. Worse still, an appraisal conducted by the area manager takes away the manager's authority to run their own department and take responsibility for their own training matters. Managers need to be able to interact directly with their staff, to learn about attitudes and feelings, and to cement good working relationships with staff.

PREPARING FOR THE APPRAISAL

It is essential that the appraiser prepares well for the interview and is familiar with the following:

- appraisee's responsibilities and task areas
- appraisee's recent achievements

- appraisee's current level of performance
- areas where performance is below a satisfactory standard
- possible areas of future personal development.

The appraiser should ensure that all information is factual, and not based in any way on hearsay or bias. The appraisal must concentrate on the performance *not* on the performer, and this means examining in some detail how agreed tasks were performed and what outcomes were achieved. Although the appraisee's method has a bearing on the way the task was performed, this should not be an issue unless the attitude adopted was detrimental to the outcome of the task.

The appraiser should make notes prior to the interview, ideally on a specially designed appraisal form, of the areas outlined above. Figure 10.1 is an example of a pre-interview assessment completed for a member of staff – Tracey Allen.

Member of staff: Tracey Allen   **Position**: Assistant Manager

---

Achievements in the last six months:

Secured group ski booking
Developed good relations with existing commercial account holders
Obtained three new commercial accounts
Assisted with sales presentation to local businesses
Conducted a very successful presentation on holidays to Florida
Reorganised accounts system – now a much more streamlined system
Increased business by 7 per cent – 1 per cent higher than personal target.
Passed Level Two Air exams.

Performance objectives set at last appraisal:

Level of achievement

1 = not achieved
2 = achieved in part
3 = achieved in full

Increase personal sales by 6 per cent   3
Increase general knowledge of cruising   3
Arrange cruising presentation   2

Areas of work where difficulties were experienced:

Tracey has some difficulty in delegating work to others. Has a tendency to overload herself.

Fig 10.1 An example of an appraiser's pre-interview assessment form

This form is to be used as an objective aid to the interview preparation and not as the final document of the interview. The purpose of the interview is: (a) to review the appraisee's performance in each task area, and (b) to agree on future training and development needs. The information on the final document may therefore be slightly different in view of what has been discussed and agreed between the appraiser and appraisee.

The appraisee should also be given ample opportunity to prepare for the interview. They should be given adequate notice, at least a week, and should be informed of the purpose of the interview and areas likely to be discussed. If possible, they should be invited to complete a pre-interview form covering the same areas as the one completed by the appraiser. This will enable the appraisee to make an objective assessment of their own performance and will provide common ground on which to commence the interview by making a comparison of the notes made by appraiser and appraisee. An example of a pre-interview assessment form completed by the appraisee, is shown in Fig. 10.2.

Member of staff: Tracey Allen   **Position:**   Assistant Manager

---

Achievements in the last six months:

Passed Air Level Two exams
Obtained three new commercial accounts
Assisted manager with presentation evening
Made first solo presentation
Increased personal sales by 7 per cent

Performance objectives set at last appraisal:

Level of achievement

1 = not achieved
2 = achieved in part
3 = achieved in full

Increase personal sales by 6 per cent   3
Increase general knowledge of cruising   2
Arrange cruising presentation   2

Areas of work where difficulties were experienced:

Find that work I have delegated is often not done, so end up doing it myself.
Everyone is very busy at the moment.

Fig 10.2 An example of an appraisee's pre-interview assessment form

STARTING THE INTERVIEW

Like any other interview, the appraisal should begin with the appraiser welcoming the appraisee and putting them at ease. This should take no more than a couple of minutes. An appraisee may be very nervous at the prospect of the interview, and fear that it is to be a confrontational or critical exercise. For this reason it is important that the appraiser adopts a friendly and open attitude from the outset and conveys to the appraisee that this is to be a frank and open discussion providing the appraisee with ample opportunity to express their own thoughts and views.

DISCUSSING PERFORMANCE ACHIEVEMENTS

Once the interview is under way the first topics to be discussed are those points on which both parties made notes prior to the interview. These are compared and any differences in opinion discussed to reach agreement. Whatever notes have been made, the appraiser should always start by making positive points.

When Tracey and her manager have their appraisal, the interview will start with a discussion of Tracey's achievements. If her manager is astute he may realise that Tracey plays down her achievements and is perhaps a little hard on herself. This is indicated by the fact that she has listed only five achievements whereas the manager has listed eight. The manager should make a point of stressing these achievements and use them as a tool to offer praise and build confidence. This will serve two purposes:

1 It will increase Tracey's level of motivation.
2 It will help to make her more open and receptive to any later criticism in the final stages of the interview.

The appraiser should take each issue in turn and discuss with the appraisee how the tasks were achieved, the processes used and what was learnt from each experience.

....

CASE
STUDY

Tracey and her manager are discussing her first solo presentation, and what she has learnt from this:

> ANDREW: So, Tracey. The America presentation evening went very well, and you managed to exceed your target on the number of heads booked. What did you learn from the experience?
>
> TRACEY: I was nervous at first, but then I remembered what I'd learned on that presentations course three weeks ago. I think the most useful thing was the mind-map. Once I'd written down my first thoughts and expanded on these, the rest was easy.

ANDREW: Good. What did you learn about your presentation style and delivery?

TRACEY: I was surprised at how quickly the time went. I know we practised during the course, but the first time you do it for real, you realise that the further into your speech you go, the more you relax and the less time you have. I thought the speech would take about thirty minutes, but I was talking for nearer forty-five.

ANDREW: You obviously said the right things. Anything you would change if you could do it again?

TRACEY: Oh, yes. I desperately needed a map to show where the hotel was in relation to the airport, and I thought I had too many OHPs for the length of my speech. Perhaps, next time I shall run through the talk with someone else watching, so that they can check the balance. Oh, and I lost a bit of time fumbling about with the adjustment on the OHP. It went out of focus twice.

ANDREW: Well, it may not have been a problem for the audience. What do you think you could do to make yourself a little more proficient?

TRACEY: I would welcome some further training on visual aids in the future. I don't feel I can quite get the balance yet between talking and working the OHP.

ANDREW: Well, don't be too hard on yourself. The America rep said that you really knew your stuff.

And so the discussion goes on. Andrew is giving praise, inviting Tracey to review her own performance and agreeing some further assistance to help with her development. The whole tenor of this appraisal is one of self-review and self-assessment. Notice that the manager adopts a policy of encouragement, which allows Tracey to be free to criticise herself. The secret of getting people to evaluate their performance and look at ways to improve is to give plenty of genuine praise and encouragement for what they have solidly achieved. Unlike Tom's appraisal, this manager is using a hands-off approach, and letting the appraisee do the reviewing. The result is that Tracey is able to remain objective about herself and her performance.

....

Checking performance against objectives.

The next issues to be discussed, are the personal objectives set at the last appraisal and how successful the appraisee had been in achieving them. This will serve not only to examine the appraisee's ability in achieving these objectives, but also how realistic these objectives actually were. For example, if an objective was set for Tracey which she was not able to achieve, then the issue is not *that* she failed to meet this objective, but *why* she failed, and more importantly, Tracey's view on why she failed. With free discussion, a more satisfactory outcome can often be reached in the future. Remember that in such cases, it may not be the fault of the appraisee that the objective has not been fulfilled as there may have been other influencing factors outside the appraisee's control.

DISCUSSING UNSATISFACTORY PERFORMANCE

The next issues to discuss during the appraisal are areas where the appraisee has found a particular aspect of their work difficult and where their performance has not been up to the expected standard. This is perhaps the most difficult part of the appraisal, and requires a high degree of fairness and sensitivity, combined with a firm stance on the standards of performance which are expected. If this is approached in an inappropriate manner, it is unlikely that the matter will be resolved.

....

CASE STUDY

TRUDY: Now then, Darren, let's look at the standard of your invoicing. I've got two here that you've done. They're not written out as I want them, are they?

DARREN: I don't know. I always write all the necessary information on the invoice.

TRUDY: Yes, but it's not the way I told you to do them, is it.

DARREN: I've always done them like that. I can't see anything wrong with them, at all.

TRUDY: Well, there's no cross-reference to the file for a start.

DARREN: Yes, but . . .

TRUDY: Look, Darren. All I'm saying is that you've got to complete these invoices the way I want them done. Are you clear about that, Darren.

Trudy's discussion centres on a real enough problem, but she is not handling the situation in the best way. She is concentrating on the fact that Darren does not complete his invoices in the correct way, but she has failed to establish the reason for this. If Darren is doing something incorrectly, his manager needs to find out why. There may be a very good reason, but Trudy will not know unless she asks. And unless she does ask, she will not be able to agree any solution with Darren. She could, of course, tell him outright that he must complete invoices in such-and-such a way, but this is not helpful to the process of self-assessment and improvement.

....

Unsatisfactory performance must be discussed and an agreement reached as to what can be done to bring performance up to a satisfactory level. Behaving in an authoritative or dictatorial manner is unlikely to achieve this, and will certainly do nothing to enhance working relationships. By behaving in this way, the manager is more likely to damage them, and will certainly do nothing to increase the level of motivation of the appraisee.

An appraiser who skirts around the issue, however, and fails to state directly which areas of performance are not up to standard, will equally have problems, especially where the appraisee is of a strong character. Make sure you adhere to the standards and that you make your point firmly so that the appraisee does not simply ignore your comment or dispute the facts by arguing.

To effectively discuss unsatisfactory performance, then, the appraiser should:

- outline the performance area concerned
- check the appraisee's understanding of the standard required
- discuss the appraisee's current level of performance
- identify reasons why the performance is below standard
- agree on the action to be taken.

Causes of unsatisfactory performance

A true discussion about unsatisfactory performance need not be in any way confrontational, and should always seek to disclose reasons for the drop in standards. Here are some of the more common reasons:

- The appraisee is not aware of the standards expected.
- Insufficient training has been given to enable the trainee to adequately perform the task.
- Factors outside of the appraisee's control prevent them from working to the expected standard.
- Personal problems are affecting the appraisee's ability to perform well.

Let's take each of these issues in turn and examine them more closely.

The appraisee being unaware of the standards required

This is a very common reason why performance is unsatisfactory. Quite often, a member of staff is asked to perform a task, but is not given clear guidelines or any indication of the level of performance required. Perhaps the task was learned from another member of staff, and the same mistakes and standards of performance were passed on. Whatever the reason for this ignorance of standards, the member of staff cannot be held responsible. In cases where staff are not aware of the standards, the fault lies entirely with the manager for failing to communicate them properly. Under no circumstances should a member of staff be blamed for not finding out for themselves. The onus is always on management to disclose, not on staff to discover.

Insufficient training

Where performance is below standard, the appraiser needs to establish what the appraisee's current level of knowledge and skills are, and what training has so far been received. It is likely that the appraiser will discover that a member of staff does not possess the necessary level of knowledge and skill to enable them to perform the task to the required standard. In this case, the appraiser needs to set up relevant training to address the shortfall. Whether this is done internally or externally, the appraiser should also set up a review mechanism to monitor changes in the levels of performance achieved once the training has been received.

Issues outside of the appraisee's control

This could cover a wide range. Perhaps the appraisee's performance depends upon the performance of others, especially where close teamwork involves several colleagues supporting each other. Perhaps the right information has not been forthcoming, or the equipment required to do the job is not of a satisfactory standard. If the appraisee does present these kinds of reasons in answer to unsatisfactory performance, look at each reason carefully and ask sufficient questions to establish this as the genuine cause for fall in standards.

Talking over personal problems

The appraiser may discover that a general drop in performance standard is due to a personal problem. This will obviously need to be addressed, and specific guidelines are given for helping in this type of situation in Chapter 11.

Identifying reasons for unsatisfactory performance

To identify why performance is below par, the appraiser needs to be adept at using probing questioning techniques in a sympathetic manner. If the appraisee feels at all threatened by the situation, it is unlikely that they will be particularly forthcoming with reasons for their unsatisfactory performance. The style of questioning used should be encouraging and open, and should seek to get the appraisee to assess their own performance and comment on why they believe it is not up to the standards required. For example:

'Can you explain to me what standards of dress you think we expect of you?' The appraisee's response should indicate clearly whether there is genuine ignorance of the standard or whether there is some other reason for the poor standards of dress. Another example is: 'Last time we spoke, we agreed that you would take on the responsibility of keeping the office diary up to date. How successful do you believe you have been in doing that?'

If the appraisee is sufficiently open and they are aware of unsatisfactory performance, they will more than likely admit that they haven't been doing too well. If the appraisee is able to make this sort of assessment about themselves, it makes the appraiser's task of finding a solution to the problem that much easier. However, some appraisees may not respond in a favourable manner, no matter how well the appraiser is conducting the interview. Instead, they may say quite categorically that they believe they are doing very well, or perhaps, refuse to answer the question altogether. In this case the appraiser needs to state specific evidence to the contrary and then put a further question: 'I've noticed that staff leave and days off have not always been recorded in the office diary. Can you explain why this is?' or 'I've noticed that staff leave and days off are not always entered into the office diary. What do you think you could do to ensure that you remember to do this in future?' In some cases the appraiser will need to be persistent with questioning of this kind to get the appraisee to open up and start to discuss the issue and what can be done about it, but patience is usually rewarded if the situation is approached in this way.

CASE STUDY

TRUDY: OK, Darren, let's take a look at your administration skills. Your work is always very neat and tidy. That's good. Do you find any difficulty with any aspect of documentation?

DARREN: No, I don't think so. I think I know how to complete all the documents we have.

TRUDY: How about invoicing?

DARREN: Yes, fine. I don't have any problems with invoicing.

TRUDY: Well, I'm thinking in particular about cross-reference numbers to the customer files. I notice that you don't put the reference on the invoice.

DARREN: I didn't know I had to. In the old manager's days we just used to use the file number to cross-reference. We don't have those now, so I leave that space blank.

TRUDY: OK. Well, you're right about the change, but there's still a need to cross-reference with the computer number. Did you go on the accounts course last March?

DARREN: No, they told me that as I'd been here longer than the rest of the staff, I wouldn't learn anything new from the course.

TRUDY: Well, let's talk through the other documentation processes and check out what you do. There have been a few changes since the new system was installed. If there's a need, then we can spend some time updating you. It wouldn't take very long. What do you think?

Here, Trudy's discussion focuses on facts and perceptions. It is a fact that Darren is not completing invoices as he should, but his perception is that he is doing it correctly. The fact that he was told not to bother with the accounts course has probably reinforced this perception. Trudy has been able to discover the cause of the problem without recourse to bullying tactics, and she has also come up with a simple solution to overcome the problem. Darren is generally a good worker, and it is unnecessary to adopt any other approach than discussion and reason. This way, Trudy is able to appraise his performance without destroying his confidence or risking his withdrawal from the interviewing process.

IDENTIFYING TRAINING AND DEVELOPMENT NEEDS

In a well-conducted appraisal, training needs will often become apparent during the discussion. It is then the task of the appraiser to suggest ways in which these training needs can be met, and the precise objectives of the training. If it has been decided, for instance, that an appraisee needs to develop more advanced selling skills, the question must then be asked: 'What is the training to achieve?' – better questioning skills? improved closing techniques? Once the objectives are clear, then a decision can be made as to whether it would be better to resource the training internally or externally. Should the appraisee attend a course, or would one-to-one coaching with the manager be a more appropriate course of action? The options open to the appraisee should be discussed during the interview if possible and, once the interview is over, the appraiser should look more closely at the various options, or take professional training advice on the sort of options open to them.

Development needs may also have been identified during the discussion on training, but if not, they will need to be discussed as a separate issue. Development needs relate directly to the appraisee's career progress and personal growth. Personal development may or may not include training. It is quite possible for someone to develop themselves simply by reading or further study – in fact, by any means which will broaden and develop the appraisee's knowledge and skills, and change perceptions and attitudes. Personal development is important to staff motivation. It encourages the appraisee to look at personal goals and targets and usually imbues a great sense of achievement.

The appraiser should be realistic about the extent to which personal development will assist the appraisee's career progress. Here are some useful points to consider when giving advice:

- the potential of the appraisee to learn and develop himself
- development prospects available within the company
- how newly developed skills will be used by the appraisee.

CASE STUDY

Janet, the supervisor of a small tour operations department, is appraising one of her more senior members of staff, Fiona. During the course of their discussions, Janet discovers that Fiona has good potential in a supervisory capacity, although it is clear that at present there is little possibility of a supervisor's position for Fiona. Janet does not wish to set Fiona's hopes too high, yet would like her to develop her natural ability to lead and manage others. Fiona has good communication skills, is very experienced in the job and would like to take on further responsibilities. The two spend some time discussing Fiona's personal development.

Finally, after looking at the various options, and the time-scales by which it is feasible that Fiona could take up a more formal post within the company, they agree on a solution which will ensure that she is able to develop her latent skills. It is agreed that Fiona should take on the responsibility of looking after all new trainees – their induction, initial training and personal development.

Finding solutions to these sorts of issues is an important part of the appraiser's responsibilities in the appraisal interview. It is here that good knowledge and experience can be used to help the discussions. Fiona shows promise for the future, and by offering her more responsibility, Janet is actively assisting in the development process. Taking on the new trainees will give Fiona valuable experience, and help to prepare her for any future supervisory role. Fiona will benefit now; the company will stand to benefit in the future.

SETTING PERFORMANCE OBJECTIVES

Performance objectives provide the appraisee with goals to achieve within the period leading up to the next appraisal. This is important, as the objectives will act as a yardstick by which both appraiser and appraisee can measure the appraisee's performance next time. Objectives must always be agreed with the appraisee in order to gain their commitment to try and achieve these objectives. This is especially important where targets are involved. So, if the appraisee is asked to reduce their error rate on the processing of invoices to 1 per cent, that figure must be seen as acceptable and achievable by the appraisee. Gentle persuasion through discussion is always preferable. In this way the appraisee takes responsibility for personal improvement, and will leave the interview in the knowledge that they have been set a fair and reasonable task.

The only exception to joint discussion is where the objective relates to unsatisfactory performance, and seeks to bring performance to the minimum standard required. Such performance standards may not be negotiable, but agreement on the solution is essential if the appraisee is to accept the process as fair and take personal responsibility for achieving the necessary improvements.

AGREEING THE ACTION PLAN

Once the discussions about past and present performance have been completed, a personal action plan will need to be agreed. The action plan states what has been discussed and agreed as a result of the appraisal, and what the appraisee will do during the period between now and the next appraisal.

A typical action plan will probably contain the following information:

Training to be undertaken

Company switchboard operation. Internal training to be arranged by KJ. Telephone techniques – manner, difficult calls, confidence building. KJ to investigate outside courses.

Areas of personal development

Spend a few days in administration department to learn how invoices are processed.

Take on the responsibility of checking accuracy of invoices before they are sent out.

Objectives

Reduce invoice error rate to 1 per cent.

Develop telephone techniques to create a confident and professional image over the phone.

Increase general efficiency of switchboard operation and attain a zero rate for lost and misdirected calls.

DOCUMENTING THE APPRAISAL

The main issues discussed and agreed upon during the interview should be recorded on an appraisal document (see example in Fig. 10.3) which is then signed by both parties to confirm that they both agree that this is an accurate representation of what was discussed. The document should be completed during the interview and must represent the views of both parties. An appraisal document should never be treated as a performance assessment sheet that the appraiser completes before or after the interview. The document is retained on the appraisee's file, and treated as a confidential document, though the non-confidential action plan may go forward to the Training and Personnel Department, or to whoever is responsible for the individual action plans.

ADOPTING THE RIGHT MANNER FOR THE APPRAISAL

As you will have read in Chapter 7, about assertiveness, each of us has an individual style of communication for certain situations and under given circumstances. In an appraisal it is important that the appraiser adopts a style which will encourage the appraisee to talk openly and feel able to discuss various aspects of their performance and their attitude to the job in a non-threatening environment. The way that the appraiser behaves during the interview will dictate the extent to which the appraisee feels able to do this, so the attitude of the appraiser is the key to the success or otherwise of the outcome of the appraisal interview.

The following is a description of six different attitudes that could be adopted by an appraiser, and the effects that each will have on the appraisee and the outcome of the appraisal.

The judgemental appraiser

Some less experienced or untrained managers may consider that an appraisal is a time at which the appraisee is judged and told in no uncertain terms, (a) where their performance is slipping, and (b) aspects of their character the appraiser considers unsuited to the job. Managers who approach an appraisal in this manner consider that it is necessary to 'put the appraisee in their place' and 'to put them right on a few things'. They are likely to accumulate over a period of time all the observed behaviour and comments of which they have disapproved, and present these at the appraisal as examples of unsuitable behaviour which will not be tolerated. Appraisers who adopt the judgemental approach are usually very subjective in their views and often criticise the appraisee's personality and character. This rarely leads to any true analysis of performance, nor does it allow the appraisee to state their case.

Name Of Appraisee: **Date Of Interview:**

Name Of Appraiser:

SECTION ONE

Achievements since the last appraisal:

Levels of achievement of objectives set at last appraisal:

Areas of shortfall in work:

Reasons:

Agreed action:

SECTION TWO

State of health:

Timekeeping:

Fig 10.3 An example of an appraisal document

Personal motivation levels:

SECTION THREE

ACTION PLAN

Training needs:

Personal development needs:

Work objectives for the next six months:

SECTION FOUR

a) To be completed by the appraisee.

Comments on the appraisal interview:

I have read this document and agree that it is a true representation of the issues discussed during my appraisal. I agree with the action plan above.

Signature of the appraisee: **Date:**

b) To be completed by the appraiser.

I agree that this document is a true representation of the content of the interview. This document was completed in full in the presence of the appraisee.

Signature of the appraiser: **Date:**

Fig 10.3 continued.

Emma has received her first appraisal comments from her manager, Sharlene, who does not particularly like Emma. The comments are extremely subjective and the some of the language quite emotive. Here are some of the things Sharlene had to say about Emma:

> 'Colleagues have indicated that Emma is never satisfied with the job she has currently been given.'
> 'Emma never seems to stop moaning about other people . . .'
> 'Emma thinks she is too good to be just an ordinary member of the team.'
> 'Other staff say they won't work with her because she is never happy.'

This is a typically subjective viewpoint which says far more about the appraiser than the appraisee. The language is strongly emotive – 'never satisfied', 'never seems to stop moaning', 'thinks she is too good', etc., and most of the comments are anecdotal and unsupported by fact – 'Other staff say' and 'Colleagues have indicated'.

There is little doubt that the appraiser has deliberately launched a verbal attack on the appraisee which is certainly not helpful, and is likely to make the appraisee rather defensive. Of course, this response will only serve to add to the prejudice already held by the appraiser, e.g. 'This proves my point. You just can't accept any form of criticism.' etc.

Appraisals conducted in this manner are never a two-way process, and are designed mainly to intimidate and humiliate the recipient. Unfortunately, those who adopt this mode of critical analysis very often believe that their actions are justified and that the appraisee is getting what they deserve. This is, however, one of the least helpful and least effective ways of conducting an appraisal.

The superior appraiser

Although the appraiser will hold a position of superiority within the company, addressing an appraisee in a superior manner will not create a suitable atmosphere in which to have a free and open discussion. If the appraisee is in any way nervous about the appraisal process and is worried about communicating certain issues to 'the boss', this feeling will be reinforced by a superior attitude on behalf of the appraiser and will inhibit the appraisee's willingness and ability to communicate.

Superiority can be conveyed to the appraisee both verbally and non-verbally, and is normally quite evident to the appraisee. Superiority rarely shows itself solely from a subconscious level. Appraisers who adopt this manner usually sit behind their desk for the duration of the discussion, thus reinforcing their position of authority. They will not seek to encourage the appraisee to offer his or her own opinions, and will often be dismissive of any new ideas and suggestions from the appraisee. Some will turn to a more judgemental approach where they feel their position is being threatened by someone with strong and innovative ideas.

Like the 'judgemental appraiser', the 'superior boss' will not welcome adverse comment regarding their particular management style or their working methods, no matter how constructively put by the appraisee. This is also a very unhelpful approach to the appraisal process as it is based on the premise of superiority of the appraiser and inferiority of the appraisee.

The autocratic appraiser

The autocrat, although possessing some of the characteristics of the superior appraiser, behaves in this way, not because of prejudice or a deep-seated insecurity, but simply because this is their normal way of behaving. Many organisations and departments operate quite successfully under the leadership of an autocrat and respond well to the strong direction and 'do it my way' approach. However, in an appraisal, which should be a two-way communication process, requiring the appraisee to contribute at least 70 per cent of the conversation, the autocratic approach is far from helpful. Autocrats rarely ask questions and may have difficulty in listening – a skill which is vitally important to the success of any interview. The autocrat does most of the talking simply because they would far rather give their own point of view. This sort of appraisal rarely reveals anything of substance about the appraisee, and is likely to be short on shared objectives and meaningful discussion of pertinent facts. Autocrats are never strong on open questioning techniques.

At this appraisal, the interviewee is likely to be informed rather than asked and talked at rather than listened to. Future development and work objectives will normally be set quite arbitrarily by the appraiser before the interview is terminated. Constructive criticism and objective reflection are not likely to feature in this appraisal if the autocrat really wants his or her way.

The non-assertive appraiser

The non-assertive appraiser adopts a completely opposite approach from the autocrat. As you will recall from the chapter on assertiveness, the non-assertive person finds it difficult to face up to a range of issues and to say what they really feel. In an appraisal situation, this will manifest itself as a reluctance to make any kind of criticism of the appraisee, and a tendency to back down rather than face up to any potential differences of opinion or confrontation with the appraisee.

The non-assertive appraiser will rarely address an area of unsatisfactory performance directly, and will shy away from any situation likely to be a source of argument or confrontation. Instead, it is more likely that the appraiser will avoid important issues by making oblique references to particular occurrences. The non-assertive appraiser probably dreads conducting appraisals, especially with more assertive members of staff. Discussions will neither be conclusive nor decisive as the non-assertive appraiser is always in danger of losing control of the situation. More often than not, appraisees will find themselves leading the agenda.

The frustration of having a *laissez-faire* appraiser may also lead the appraisee to question the validity of having an appraisal, since the appraisal will rarely have any concrete outcomes. In this appraisal, the onus will normally be on the appraisee to lead the way and make the suggestions, which may be good news for strong personalities, but bad news for those whose need is for guidance.

CASE STUDY

Gareth is a typical non-assertive appraiser and, as such, is regarded by most of his staff to be quite ineffectual. Gareth tends to confuse his non-assertive approach with being democratic and open-minded. What he doesn't realise is that he never contributes any original thought to the appraisal process – the thinking is always done by his staff.

Gareth never comes to terms with the real issues because he always seeks to avoid them. Unsatisfactory performance is rarely addressed by Gareth as it is a source of possible conflict. In seeking to be nice to all of his appraisees, Gareth is actually abdicating his responsibilities as manager and adviser to his staff.

Gareth's questioning technique is never truly investigative, and most of his comments and questions tend to be confirming: 'So you are happy with what you are doing, then?', 'I don't think there's anything more we need to do on this one', 'So, we're agreed on the way you'd prefer to do things?', 'Yes, I would think that that's the best way to go about it'.

The unprepared appraiser

Some appraisers begin the appraisal with little or no preparation, and have probably also failed to give the appraisee adequate notice to prepare. The unprepared appraiser sees the appraisal process as a fairly low-level or less urgent task, and is likely to conduct the appraisal as an 'off-the-record' chat.

Unless the appraiser works very closely with the appraisee, it is unlikely that they will be entirely familiar with the work that has been done, and the lack of preparation will usually demonstrate to the appraisee their lack of commitment to the appraisal process. An appraisal conducted in this manner is unlikely to achieve a satisfactory outcome, and does little to motivate the appraisee and cement better working relationships.

CASE STUDY

Miranda is never quite ready for anything she does. When it is time to conduct her team appraisals, she is usually quick with an excuse for being elsewhere at the time. Appraisees may be left waiting, but it is more likely that they will be asked to go in at very short notice. Miranda regards the appraisal as an unnecessary managerial task – she tends to regard any performance review as a slow and cumbersome process. Miranda's reactive managerial style is rather at odds with the steady interviewing technique demanded of an appraisal. She is never prepared for the interview, either physically or spiritually. Typical appraisal-related questions and statements from Miranda are: 'Oh, your appraisal, Ian. Don't think I'll be able to make it this week', 'So where would you like me to start, then?', 'I don't know if its necessary to go over that again', 'I didn't realise you knew anything about trainee assessment', 'How long since you've been involved in any sales training, now?' and 'I don't think we need to go too deeply into an action plan, today'.

The effective appraiser

The effective appraiser possesses a number of qualities which marks them out from less talented appraisers, and is able to adopt a manner suited to the needs of a particular appraisee. They will always try to create a comfortable environment for the appraisee, and seek to use questioning techniques that will encourage the appraisee to contribute as much as possible to the discussion.

Although they will have prepared well for the appraisal, they are always willing to conduct an open discussion, and will aim to bring the appraisal to a conclusion that is satisfactory to both parties. The effective appraiser will never be dismissive of suggestions for changing existing systems and working practices, but will always be prepared to explore the possibilities for new avenues. They normally encourage the appraisee to expand on their ideas, e.g. 'So if we were to adopt this method of handling customer enquiries, how do you think this would benefit the company?'

The effective appraiser will invite positive criticism of their own style of management, and will look for opportunities to learn about their own performance, with a view to developing better working relationships with the staff. The effective appraiser does not feel threatened by staff who show potential, but will seek ways in which this potential can be developed, and will look for appropriate future career development opportunities for the appraisee. Their whole approach to the appraisal is one of celebrating success, reviewing failure, exploring new avenues and of helping the appraisee to reach solutions most likely to reflect their personal development needs.

Exercise

How effective an appraiser are you? Read through the following statements and assess how well you perform in each case. Score your performance on a scale of 1 to 10, with 1 being something you never do and 10 being something you do every time without fail.

I always prepare well for the appraisal   1 2 3 4 5 6 7 8 9 10

I ensure that the appraisee has received adequate   1 2 3 4 5 6 7 8 9 10
notice of the appraisal and is aware of the need to
prepare

I create an environment conducive to putting the   1 2 3 4 5 6 7 8 9 10
appraisee at ease

I always follow a recognizable structure for the appraisal   1 2 3 4 5 6 7 8 9 10

I encourage the appraisee to contribute at least seventy   1 2 3 4 5 6 7 8 9 10
per cent of the discussion

I use open questions and probing techniques   1 2 3 4 5 6 7 8 9 10

I use specific facts to identify areas of unsatisfactory   1 2 3 4 5 6 7 8 9 10
performance

I establish the reasons for unsatisfactory performance   1 2 3 4 5 6 7 8 9 10
and act accordingly

I encourage the appraisee to offer criticism of working   1 2 3 4 5 6 7 8 9 10
procedures and the way in which I have managed them

I listen to what the appraisee has to say and encourage   1 2 3 4 5 6 7 8 9 10
them to bring forward points for further discussion

I negotiate and agree with the appraisee about their future 1 2 3 4 5 6 7 8 9 10
performance objectives.

I take steps to follow up any outstanding issues   1 2 3 4 5 6 7 8 9 10
discussed during the appraisal

....

Assignment   Role-play the following situation. You are the manager of a team of five people and
you are currently undertaking appraisals. The next interview you are to conduct is
with one of your sales staff, Mandy Cullip. Mandy has been with you for 18 months,
and on the whole her performance is satisfactory. Over the last few months you
have noticed that she is becoming increasingly restless, and you suspect that she
might be looking for another job. Mandy is a good worker and member of the team,
and you would be sorry to lose her. You hope to identify the reasons for her
restlessness and provide her with sufficiently challenging work to sustain her interest
in the job. Below is your pre-appraisal assessment of Mandy:

Achievements:
Has become expert at using computer reservations system.
Has trained new members of staff to use computer system.
Obtained NVQ Level 3.
Has increased level of independent tours booked.

Objectives set at last appraisal:

Learn new computer system	3
Finish NVQ Level 3	3
Learn how to construct and cost independent itineraries.	3

Areas where difficulties experienced:

Work is of a satisfactory standard, but Mandy appears to lack any initial personal motivation. Why?

Now conduct the appraisal interview using the structure and techniques used in the previous pages. The role-play should last for at least thirty minutes (a real appraisal may last for up to two hours). Make notes of what is agreed at each stage of the interview.

Ensure that you cover each of the following issues:

- achievements since the last appraisal
- level of achievement in personal objectives
- problem areas
- areas of unsatisfactory performance
- training needs
- areas of personal development
- future work objectives.

Once you have completed the role-play, discuss the following with your partner:

- Was the appraisee encouraged to do most of the talking?
- What manner did the appraiser adopt, and was it appropriate?
- How effective was the appraiser's questioning technique?
- How motivating did the appraisee find the interview?
- Did the appraisee feel that they were encouraged to talk openly?
- Were both appraiser and appraisee in agreement over training and development issues and future performance objectives?

11

....

Counselling skills

At some point in your career you may have a member of staff with a personal problem which is affecting their work. As a responsible manager you should be able to recognise that there is a problem, and then be able to take steps to help the member of staff resolve the problem. Though counselling is a highly skilled activity – professional counsellors undergo lengthy periods of intense training – it is possible for you, as the manager, to begin the counselling process. As part of NVQ Level 4, you will be expected to demonstrate an ability to counsel and advise staff. This chapter aims to provide you with some practical guidelines to help you to do this.

OBJECTIVES

Once you have read this section of the book you will be able to:
- **identify situations where counselling may be necessary**
- **use effective questioning techniques to establish the nature of the problem**
- **provide support as appropriate**
- **recommend outside organisations, or sources of help where the problem is beyond your personal knowledge and skill**
- **agree on any action to be taken as a result of counselling.**

WHEN IS COUNSELLING NECESSARY?

It is very rare that a member of staff with a personal problem will seek out a person of authority, such as a supervisor or manager, with whom they can discuss their problem. It is far more likely that they will try to hide the fact that they have a problem, or try to work through the problem alone, but there are usually signs that tell you that all is not well, and the astute manager should always be on the look out for them.

Typical signs which you may recognise in the workplace are:

- continual lateness, or always needing to leave early
- lack of attention to work, with its attendant errors

- unaccountable drop in performance standards
- physical symptoms such as headaches and sickness
- tearfulness or acute sensitivity
- changes in normal behaviour patterns
- tendency to become withdrawn.

Any of these symptoms will signal that your member of staff may have a personal problem which is affecting their work, or affecting their relationships with colleagues, and this should be addressed as soon as possible.

CASE STUDY

Emily is one of the senior counter-sales staff at the local travel agency. Her work is normally of a very high standard, and she has always been respected as a valued member of staff. Just recently, though, she has had to live with the fact that her parents are splitting up and home life is very traumatic. Emily feels that this is a very private matter and has not been able to say a word to any of her friends, and certainly to nobody at the agency. As a result of her problems, Emily's work rate has dropped, her usual level of concentration has gone, and her error rate has increased dramatically. Her manager has noticed some of these problems, and has become concerned to do something about it as quickly as possible.

He tells Emily that he is aware that she is not concentrating on her work and he tells her that she should concentrate more on her work, and that he expects to see an improvement. Emily felt quite depressed at this, and tried to explain to her manager that she was experiencing a number of problems in her life.

'Well, we all have problems,' said her manager, 'but we've just got to get on with life.'

Emily feels now that she has two problems – troubles at home, and lack of sympathy and support in the workplace. The stress she feels at work adds to the overall problem and Emily's work continues to suffer. Finally, she is given a written warning by her manager.

Emily's case is typical of the sorts of problems which face managers and supervisors responsible for the welfare of their staff. When the only evidence of a problem is a drop in performance standards, the manager should first treat the matter as a counselling issue, and should address this before taking any kind of disciplinary action. There is almost always an underlying reason for such unaccountable drops in performance, but staff may not necessarily be prepared to disclose their personal problems to someone at work. It may be a case that the member of staff does not know or understand how the problem is affecting their work, or it could be that they feel a great sense of loyalty to friends and family involved in the problem, and that they would rather not discuss their personal life with those at work.

It sometimes takes considerable time and effort on the part of the manager to build up sufficient trust to enable very private matters to be discussed in the workplace. Initial questioning of staff may not uncover the problem, and a degree of sympathy and patience may be required on the part of the manager in order to get to the real problem. Only once the matter has been investigated properly can the appropriate advice or action be offered by the manager.

Disciplinary action is really a last resort when problems of this sort affect work performance, and should only become part of the process once all other counselling and advisory channels have been fully explored.

ARRANGING A COUNSELLING INTERVIEW

There are a number of guidelines for interviewing which also apply to the counselling interview, and these are given in the Chapter 8. Your organisation may have special procedures for dealing with matters of this sort and, even if not, there are some simple steps which will make the delicate matter of counselling much easier.

Confidentiality is most important, and the matter must remain strictly between the manager and member of staff, unless you have a personnel department which will need to be informed. The interview should be undertaken as discreetly as possible, certainly out of sight and hearing of other members of staff and, if necessary, away from the place of work. It may be advisable not to forewarn your member of staff about what you wish to discuss, as they may find a reason not to be available or think up a quite rational excuse for their behaviour, neither of which will help to solve the problem.

QUESTIONING SKILLS

As in all other types of interview, the counselling interview demands a high degree of skill in special questioning techniques. You need to be able to put questions in a delicate and sympathetic way to encourage the member of staff to talk, but the questions need to be quite specific if you are to obtain any satisfactory response.

You may find that you need to ask the same question several times in a slightly different form in order to get any real response. Questions such as 'How are things?', 'What's the matter?' or 'Is there a problem?' are unlikely to be very effective as they are far too general, and are only likely to elicit general responses, such as 'Fine', 'Nothing's the matter' or 'There's no problem'.

Perhaps a better approach is to state your own observations about the fall in performance, and then to ask the member of staff for reasons why this might have happened. This needs to be done in a supportive manner, so that the member of staff does not feel that they are being quizzed in an authoritative way. 'Your standard of work has steadily decreased over the last few weeks. Perhaps you would care to explain to me why this is?' is a totally inappropriate start to the conversation. A much better opening remark would be: 'I have noticed that you have been finding it difficult to give your full attention to your work, and that a few errors have been made. You are normally very diligent and I can always rely on you to be very accurate in your work, so I know there must be something troubling you. What's happened in the last few weeks to upset you?'

Of course, you may not necessarily receive a direct reply even to this more sympathetic approach. It will depend upon your standing with the member of staff concerned, their willingness to open up and talk, and also the seriousness of the problem. You must be prepared to respect their privacy. If their only response is, 'I have a few problems at home', you may be able to gauge just how much your member of staff is willing to discuss the matter. In this case, a general invitation to talk would probably be the best approach: 'Would you like to tell my about it?' They may, of course, have no wish to say any more about the matter and, outside the immediate problem of the effect on work, you have no right to demand to know. If a member of staff wishes to open up and give you more details, all you need to do is listen patiently and be sympathetic.

The next step in counselling is to get the member of staff to recognise the effect that their problem may be having on both work and work relationships. Try to get the person to consider these effects by asking, 'You're bound to be upset about this, but how do you think the customers feel about your change in behaviour?', 'The staff realise that something's wrong, but how do you think they feel when you just snap at them?' or 'I can understand why you're finding it difficult to concentrate, but what effect do you think these frequent errors are having?' All of these questions are phrased in a special way. They are saying 'I understand/acknowledge your feelings, but other people may not. What effect do you think it is having on them?'

By phrasing the questions in this way, you are showing your member of staff that you sympathise with them, but you are also asking them to think carefully about the effect their behaviour is having on work and colleagues. This is a very effective questioning technique which will usually get staff to consider the consequences of their problem.

AGREEING ACTION TO BE TAKEN

The final stage of the counselling interview is to agree with the interviewee what exactly should happen next. This is unlikely to centre around how to solve the interviewee's problem, but is more likely to involve getting an agreement as to how the usual work standards can be restored. Your first responsibility is to ensure that staff work to agreed standards in a safe and happy environment. Here are some guidelines:

1 Recommend that the person takes a period of sick leave during which time it is agreed that they will take steps to resolve the problem. You will need to respect that some people may need to be at work as this provides a necessary distraction from home problems.

2 Arrange other duties for the member of staff which will keep them occupied

but remove any additional stress caused by the nature of the work itself. In this case, try to provide tasks in which margins for error are less critical.

3 Agree to allow them to arrive later or leave earlier for a set period of time to enable them to address the problem or attend appointments for counselling, etc.

4 Suggest that you notify colleagues of the problem, and ask for their sympathy and support. However, if the person does not wish this information to be disclosed to staff, you must respect their wish.

If the problem is very serious, there are a number of organisations that you could suggest your member of staff contact for further help and advice:

Relate	Marriage guidance or general relationship problems
Cruse	Bereavement counselling
Alcoholics Anonymous	Problems relating to alcoholism for self or other family members
Citizens Advice Bureau	General information on local counselling and advisory services.
Local counselling	Confidential counselling and advisory services.

Contacts for all of these organisations and other self-help groups dealing with specific problems can be found in the local telephone directory.

Reviewing the situation

Whatever action you do agree with your member of staff, you should agree a date by which you will review the situation. Set a date for this to happen before you terminate the interview. Remember that if you leave things too long (more than two weeks), the problem will stagnate and other staff may begin to feel as if nothing is being done to resolve the matter.

When you review the situation, you will need to discuss:

1 steps they have taken to help resolve the problem
2 improvements in their level of performance
3 time needed to return to a normal work pattern.

Some problems are far more long term, e.g. marriage breakdown or bereavement, and you may have to accept that not only is this likely to require a lengthy period of adjustment, but also that the member of staff will probably need considerable sympathy and support. This can be a difficult time for everyone at work who is affected by the problem. You will need to take care in striking a balance between providing the necessary support and ensuring that other members of staff are not unnecessarily inconvenienced. If staff begin to feel that the individual concerned is using the situation to their own advantage, then there will be a general feeling of discontent and a growing disaffection with that person. If this is not recognised, then you may have two problems to deal with. However difficult it may be, you should remember that you have a responsibility to keep the business running efficiently and profitably and, at some point, the member of staff must be expected to make a full contribution in helping to achieve this goal.

Assignment Role-play the following situation. A previously reliable and hard-working member of staff has been arriving late over the last few weeks and looks constantly tired. You decided to leave the matter to resolve itself until an important deadline was missed, which resulted in the loss of an important sale. No real reason could be given at the time as to why the work was incomplete, and you have decided to investigate the matter.

Show the person playing the member of staff this outline and let them decide a suitable reason for their behaviour. They should not reveal this to you before the role-play starts.

Once you have completed the role-play, discuss the following:

- Did you get to the root of the problem?
- How appropriate was the action you offered?
- How successful were you in resolving the problem?
- When will the situation be reviewed?

SUMMARY

To recap on the main points of this chapter:

- Identify situations where counselling may be necessary.
- Be discreet in conducting the counselling interview.
- Use probing questions to establish the nature of the problem.
- Show that you are sympathetic, and offer support and guidance.
- Get the individual to recognise the effect of their behaviour on their work and colleagues.
- Recommend sources of outside help as appropriate.
- Agree the action to be taken in the workplace.
- Arrange a date by which to review the situation.

12

....

Disciplinary procedure

When an employee's standard of performance drops below the minimum standard required by the employer, some course of action is usual in order to redress the balance. In many cases, the course of action taken is to conduct a disciplinary interview. Let's see why this is not always the most appropriate action to take.

There may be a number of reasons why standards have fallen below the required level. It is not simply that standards have fallen, but how soon this has been noticed that is important, and what initial action is taken to put the matter right at the earliest opportunity. Decline in standards usually occurs over a period of time and, unless it is a very serious matter, it is normal to discuss things with the person concerned by way of a work review or a counselling interview. You will find these two topics in Chapters 8, 10 and 11.

Where standards have slipped and an initial review has failed to redress the balance, it is the manager's responsibility to follow the company disciplinary code and conduct a disciplinary interview. Your understanding of the disciplinary process will be assessed as part of your NVQ qualification. This section of the book aims to provide you with sufficient information to be able to implement disciplinary procedure when necessary.

OBJECTIVES

Once you have completed this chapter of the book, you should be able to:
- **describe the objectives and structure of a disciplinary interview**
- **state the circumstances under which disciplinary action is necessary**
- **state guidelines for undertaking a disciplinary interview.**

WHAT IS A DISCIPLINARY INTERVIEW?

A disciplinary interview is a formal discussion between an employee and a manager or supervisor during which the reasons for the drop in performance standards are discussed. The aims of the interview should be to:

- establish the gap between the standard and the employee's performance
- establish the reason for the gap
- eliminate the gap or take other appropriate action.

Unfortunately, the disciplinary interview is much misunderstood, and many managers regard the disciplinary interview as an opportunity to 'read the riot act' to an employee, or merely as the formal process of issuing warnings. Although formal warnings are part of the disciplinary process, they should not be considered as the only option. It is far better to regard these as the final stage of the disciplinary action, where all other attempts to rectify the situation have failed. The situation where a formal warning should be an early course of action is in the case of gross misconduct by an employee. This may include such things as:

- theft of company property
- violence against another employee
- endangering the safety of other employees through gross neglect of recognised Health and Safety procedures

Acts considered by the company to constitute gross misconduct should be outlined either in the employee's contract of employment or in a document outlining the company's disciplinary and grievance procedures. This information should be made freely available to all staff. We now consider the guidelines for the stages of the disciplinary process.

GATHERING THE FACTS

Before you conduct a disciplinary interview, you must be aware of all of the facts concerning the matter. If the interview is as a result of a complaint lodged by one employee against another, then be sure that you have the whole story before you begin the interview. Do make sure that you are in possession of the facts and not of someone else's opinion. You should also ensure that you are fully aware of the standards of performance that are expected of your employee, and if this is documented anywhere, then you should have this to hand. If the purpose of the

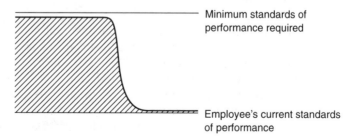

Minimum standards of performance required

Employee's current standards of performance

Fig 12.1 Identifying the standard of performance required and the level of performance that the employee is currently providing

interview is to discuss a shortfall in performance standards (see Fig. 12.1), then you will need to have specific examples to hand. It would not be fair on the employee to receive criticism of poor performance if no specific evidence can be produced to support this.

CASE STUDY

Graham has called Kirstie into his office to read her the riot act. He has received a number of complaints about Kirstie from dissatisfied customers, and intends to do something positive about it. Kirstie has been called in because she has made a number of serious errors on ferry tickets which have resulted in customers being inconvenienced. Two have since complained to the manager, Graham, who now intends to put matters right. Graham's attitude to Kirstie, though, does not help the situation. He is angry about the two complaints and, as a fairly reactive person, he has gone straight in with a rather large managerial stick. Kirstie is somewhat bruised and battered.

Graham's rhetoric may have satisfied his need to let off steam, but it has not been useful in helping him to get to the bottom of the story. As an angry boss, Graham has waded in strongly. He is not bothered with asking questions so much as letting Kirstie know that he is displeased with her performance. Typical of Graham's remarks to Kirstie are:

'Why do you do this sort of thing, Kirstie?', 'You're letting this office, this company and yourself down', 'I don't like your attitude, Kirstie', 'I don't want people who make careless mistakes working in this office', 'You'll really have to pull your socks up', 'I don't want to hear about any more problems of this kind. Is that clear?' and 'I want to see a big improvement in your work, Kirstie'.

The problem with Graham's approach is that it has not managed to disclose any of the reasons for Kirstie's fall in standards. Graham's questioning technique is not designed to probe for detailed facts, because the questions he asks are too generalised – 'Why do you do this?' Graham's normal approach is to tell his staff what he thinks of them, and in Kirstie's case, he has done just that – 'Pull your socks up', 'I don't like your attitude'. These are not statements which are helpful to the disciplinary process, and as a result, Graham is still no wiser about Kirstie's problem. One of the problems for both parties, however, is that Graham really believes that now he has given Kirstie a firm warning, the matter is over and her performance will improve.

An interview conducted in this manner will achieve nothing except to make the manager feel better. Quite possibly the manager is happy that the matter has been resolved and the employee will now become a model member of staff. The member of staff is probably very confused, angry or upset, and very demotivated. The interview did not provide any opportunity to discuss the issue, and in any case the manager appeared not to really know what the issue was. In this case it is impossible to examine the reasons for the gap in performance standards as the gap has yet to be defined.

ENSURING STAFF AWARENESS OF PERFORMANCE STANDARDS

....

CASE STUDY

Mark has taken half a day off work in order to fulfil a hospital appointment. As he did not know about the appointment until very near to the time he was due to go, he was unable to advise his manager that he would be absent. However, Mark is conscientious about his work and informs another member of staff of his appointment. His colleague assures him that she will pass the message on to the manager, and that everything will be alright if he goes off for his appointment.

The next day, however, Mark's manager calls him into her office to tell him that he has contravened the company rule on absence during working hours. Mark is somewhat puzzled, because he does not understand about the rule on absence. He tells his manager, but she is adamant that he should receive a verbal warning for being absent without permission. Mark is told that in future he must not take time off without first informing his manager and obtaining proper permission. Both Mark and other members of staff protest that they did not know about this rule, and point out to the manager that several past doctor's appointments have been kept in the same way. Nevertheless, the manager makes it clear that he has been warned.

....

Before any disciplinary action can be taken, steps must be taken to ensure that the employee is actually aware of the standards to which they are expected to work. If it has not been outlined to the employee that they must perform a task in a certain way, or there are certain working practices and procedures of which they have never been informed, then disciplinary action cannot be taken against them. However, the manager involved needs to be very sure of the facts. If an employee has acted in a way which they know to be contrary to existing working practices, their first line of defence may be to claim that they had not been made aware of this. In this case, the manager will need to establish the facts in order to prove that the employee was indeed made aware of working practices.

In the case study, it would appear that all the employees were genuinely ignorant of company procedures regarding medical appointments. They believed the accepted practice was simply to advise the manager, or some other member of staff of such appointments. In this case, the manager used her position to exert authority and issued a warning, even though no one could be absolutely sure that employees had been made aware of company procedures. Had the employees received a proper induction, and been given proper printed details of working practices and procedures, there would have been no doubt that every member of staff was aware of the accepted procedures. This is really a case of officiousness, and a more common-sense approach would have been for the manager to give the employee the benefit of the doubt on this occasion, and to have made sure that such procedures were clarified for the future.

ESTABLISH THE REASON FOR THE GAP IN PERFORMANCE

If the employee is aware of the standards of performance required, but their own level of performance has dropped, then the manager needs to examine the reasons why this has happened. This has two purposes. First, the reason identified may indicate that this is actually a counselling rather than a disciplinary matter, or that the drop in performance is not due to the employee but to faulty equipment or an error made by someone else. Second, action can only be taken to rectify the situation once the manager has identified the reason for the drop in performance standards. Even in extreme cases, where the employee has received a warning for behaving in a totally unacceptable manner, reasons for this behaviour still need to be established to ensure that there is no similar occurrence.

In this part of the interview, the manager needs to remain calm and use open questions and good listening skills. Whatever the employee says or does during the interview, the manager must not be sidetracked, and should certainly not be drawn into an argument. Once this happens the manager has lost control to the member of staff.

....

CASE STUDY

Michael, the manager of a small tour operations department, and Maggie, a long-standing member of staff, are engaged in an argument. Maggie has overstepped the line, being late more than three mornings in a row, and has been called in by her manager. Both Michael and Maggie are fully aware of the company procedures with regard to lateness, but even so, Maggie's attitude to being late is far from what her manager expects, given her position in the department. Michael reminds Maggie of the rules concerning lateness, but he is also irritated by what he perceives as a poor attitude, and allows himself to be drawn into discussion about this. Their conversation finally escalates into an argument.

Disciplinary procedures quite often centre on poor attitude, even if it does not start there. It is very easy to become sidetracked from the real issue of establishing reasons for the fall in standard, and to turn the interview into a moral debate about someone's poor attitude. Michael is now engaged in such a debate with Maggie, and the principal issue will soon be lost as the discussion goes off in another direction. Michael should stick to the known facts, i.e. Maggie is aware of the company procedures with regard to lateness, and she has been late on three successive mornings.

....

Guidelines for establishing the reasons for the performance gap

1 Ask why the employee adopted this action/behaviour.
2 Listen carefully to the answer.
3 If the answer is not satisfactory, continue to use open questions until you get to the root of the issue.
4 Clarify your understanding of what has been said. 'So you think that our policy for answering the telephone is wrong?'
5 Don't allow yourself to be sidetracked.
6 Beware of red herrings. If you believe that one has been presented to you, carefully question your employee to establish the validity of the statement.
7 Under no circumstances be drawn into an argument.
8 If you can't see a way of resolving the situation, don't resort to using your position of authority to 'win' the situation.

ELIMINATING THE GAP

Once the reason for the gap in performance standards has been identified, appropriate action needs to be taken to eliminate that gap. Even if a formal warning is to be issued, an agreement should be made as to how the employee is to modify their behaviour in the future, and if appropriate, a time by which this can reasonably be expected to be achieved.

CASE STUDY

In the case of Michael and Maggie, the conversation should have turned to ensuring that Maggie arrived at work at the appropriate time. Finding solutions to the problem is equally important. If no agreement is made between Maggie and her manager, there is no contract – other than the verbal or written warning – to ensure that she does not repeat her lateness. Michael's job, once the facts have been established, is to discuss the matter with Maggie in order to obtain an agreement for her future conduct. Conciliatory words are far better at this stage than harsh words:

'So, Maggie, what's the real reason for you being late like this?'

'I told you. I missed the bus because it went early.'

'On three consecutive mornings?'

'Yes.'

'Maggie, I'm not convinced. You've been looking pretty tired recently. Are you out quite late?'

'That's really my business.'

'Yes it is, but not when it means that you turn up late and too tired to do your job. Now, what's the problem?'

'Look, my sister's been ill recently. We're all worried about it in the family, and I've been spending a lot of time running my mother over to see her, and then I seem to spend half the night listening to my mother and her worries about what my sister will do if she can't look after the children.'

'Right. So you feel it's all on your shoulders. Is there anyone else in the family who can help?'

'Well, there's my brother nearby, but I didn't want to bother him with it. He's got his own family life.'

'But could he help. Would he be willing to lend a hand?'

'I suppose so. I just haven't really considered it. I could ask mother if she wouldn't mind if Rob takes her round to my sister's. It's just that my mother always offloads her troubles on to me.'

'And you get pretty tired in the process.'

'Yes, you're right, I suppose. I'm too soft with her, and she's keeping me up half the night. I hate being late for work. It always causes ill feeling amongst the others. Look, let me speak to my brother tonight, and I'll see if I can't sort out some kind of rota with him. That way it'll be fairer on everyone.'

'OK. Can you let me know the outcome tomorrow? We'll review the situation in the light of what you agree with your family.'

Michael's discussions with Maggie have one main purpose – to help her to come to an amicable solution to close the gap on standards. Finding suitable answers to problems often involves a degree of counselling and advisory discussion. It is usually helpful for someone not directly involved to offer friendly advice, and point the person in the right direction. Arguments only serve to waste time and energy – a solution still has to be found.

PRINTED DISCIPLINARY PROCEDURE

All companies should have a formal, printed disciplinary procedure which is available to all employees. The procedure should state:

- the managers and senior members of staff who have the authority to deal with disciplinary matters
- matters which are considered to be gross misconduct and which may result in summary dismissal
- the general approach and stages of the disciplinary procedure
- procedures for appeal against disciplinary action.

As a guideline in any disciplinary matter, employees should be given:

- clear indication of the standards of performance that they are expected to achieve and working practices and procedures with which they are expected to comply
- clear indication of where standards have dropped or which rules have been broken
- except in cases of gross misconduct, an opportunity to improve their performance before any formal disciplinary action is taken.

It is also a legal requirement that:

- individuals should be informed of the nature of any accusations made against them
- individuals should be given every opportunity to state their case
- the person in authority who is conducting the interview should do so in good faith
- the individual should have the right to appeal if they are unhappy with the outcome of the disciplinary procedure.

Disciplinary action

As well as complying with employment law and legislation, a disciplinary procedure should provide for various levels of disciplinary action, depending on the nature of the employee's conduct and whether this is a first offence. Here are those actions:

1 Informal verbal warning given by employee's immediate manager or supervisor for minor offences.
2 Formal verbal warning for a first offence.
3 Written warning stating the exact nature of the offence and the further disciplinary action that will be taken if the offence is repeated or poor levels of performance not rectified.
4 Final written warning stating that any recurrence of the offence or failure to rectify poor performance within a specified time will result in the employee's dismissal.

....

Assignment   Role-play the following situation: You have a member of staff who you consider to be a bad influence on the more junior members of the team. You have noticed on several occasions that she has told staff to ignore instructions that you have given, and has told them to disregard recognised procedures and working practices. This has caused a number of errors to be made, and you feel that staff are beginning to become confused as to what are the expected standards of performance.

You have already mentioned to the staff member concerned that you do not wish to see this type of behaviour continue, and although it seemed to stop for a little while, you know that the problem has recurred in the last few weeks. You have decided to hold a disciplinary interview.

1 Make a note of the specific issues that you wish to discuss.
2 Be sure in your own mind of the standards of performance that you expect from your member of staff.
3 Conduct a disciplinary interview using the structure and techniques described in the previous pages.
4 Agree on the action which is to be taken and a time by which the situation is to be reviewed.
5 Take whatever disciplinary action, if any, you feel is appropriate.

13

....

Grievance procedure

As a manager, you may be approached by a member of staff asking to discuss a matter over which they have a grievance. All employees should have the right to air any grievances, and all managers must take the responsibility of listening to a grievance without bias, and with a view to solving the problem – if not immediately, then at the earliest possible time after the discussion. As part of your NVQ assessment, you will be required to demonstrate a knowledge and understanding of grievance procedures. This chapter aims to provide you with the background information you will need.

OBJECTIVES

Once you have read this section of the book you should be able to:
- **state the purpose of a grievance interview**
- **state guidelines for conducting a grievance interview.**

WHAT IS A GRIEVANCE INTERVIEW?

A grievance interview is a meeting which is held at the request of the employee with the employee's immediate manager or supervisor. The only occasion where the interview may be held with someone other than the employee's immediate manager or supervisor, is where the company's written grievance procedure states that a nominated person, e.g. the personnel manager, should conduct the interview, or where the nature of the employee's grievance directly concerns the behaviour of their immediate manager or supervisor.

The purpose of the grievance interview is to allow the employee the opportunity to make a complaint, or to discuss an aspect of their job, working environment, working practices or working relationships about which they are unhappy. The aim of the interview, for both parties, should be to arrive at a workable solution to the problem.

GRIEVANCE PROCEDURE

Like the disciplinary procedure, the grievance procedure adopted by the company should be documented and be available to all staff. Although not governed by employment law and legislation, ideally the document should contain information such as that given in the following example:

COMPANY GRIEVANCE PROCEDURES

Employee rights

- Employees have the right to state their grievances.
- Managers will give the employee a fair hearing.
- Employees have the right to take the matter to a higher authority if they are not satisfied with the outcome of their initial interview.
- If no solution can be agreed upon during the interview, managers are obliged to undertake further investigations or discussions with the aggrieved employee.

Procedure

(A policy document should outline the following information.)

- How the meeting is to be documented.
- Who is able to conduct a grievance interview.
- Lines of authority in the event of the grievance going to a more senior member of staff due to an unsatisfactory outcome of the initial interview.
- Procedure if the immediate manager or supervisor is unable to resolve the problem.
- Time-scales within which managers are obliged to respond to any specific requests.

GUIDELINES FOR CONDUCTING A GRIEVANCE INTERVIEW

The interview itself may be called by either the manager or the employee. In most cases, the interview is at the request of the employee, and is quite often as a result of the employee dropping into the manager's office to discuss a problem, rather than as part of a prearranged meeting. However, in cases where the employee has written a letter of complaint to the manager, then the manager should call the meeting to discuss the issue further. Whoever instigates the meeting, the following are guidelines for the interview.

1 *Ask the employee to outline the nature of the grievance.*

At this stage the manager should listen intently and only ask questions if it is necessary to clarify what the employee is saying. The employee is probably in a state of high anxiety and may need a little time to let out their emotions and frustrations before they are able to discuss the issue in a rational way. The manager should respect this and allow the employee time to state their case.

2 *Remain neutral.*

If the grievance is against another member of staff, the manager should not disclose any personal thoughts or prejudices about the situation. Neither would it be appropriate to offer any judgement on the situation until further facts are obtained from the other party or parties involved. If the grievance is regarding working practices or procedures, then the way the manager handles this situation will largely depend on the authority of the manager to make any proposed changes and the effects such changes may have on other colleagues and members of staff. The best course of action is to investigate the various options open and have further discussions with the employee rather than making any decisions at the initial interview.

3 *Agree the next step.*

Whatever the nature of the grievance, the reason the employee felt it necessary to take the issue this far is that they wanted some action to be taken. The grievance interview would therefore be incomplete if the next stage in the procedure was not agreed. Action does not mean advising the employee that a colleague will be chastised or a working procedure changed; it means advising the employee what will happen next, e.g. 'I need to discuss this matter with Caroline' or 'I will put your views to the personnel manager'.

It should be agreed with the employee that they are happy with this course of action before it is implemented. Sometimes the mere fact of being able to discuss the matter is sufficient, and the employee may feel happier just because someone has listened. In this case the employee may not feel happy about any further action being taken, and their wishes should be respected.

4 *Follow up the issue.*

When further action is required as a result of the interview, the manager should ensure that follow-up action is taken, and agree to meet the employee again to discuss the outcome. Depending on the nature of the grievance, it may be appropriate to set a date for the next meeting before the interview is terminated. If, however, this is not practical, then the manager must ensure that a likely time-scale is indicated to the employee and that steps are taken to discuss the issue with the employee at a future date.

14

....

Handling interpersonal conflict

Conflict between employees is a major contributory factor to a drop in performance standards in the workplace. Conflict can occur between individuals, between a member of staff and a manager, within a team, or even between one team or department and another. Conflict causes low morale, a breakdown in communication and in some cases can lead to stress or even ill health. Conflict is a major causal factor of falls in quality of work and of disruptions to work, and in this respect it is important that swift action be taken to resolve the issues and resume normal, healthy working relationships. This chapter aims to provide you with some background information on the cause and effect of conflict and some guidelines to help you resolve conflict with others. Most of the information contained in this chapter is relevant to all levels of staff, but the section on mediation is aimed at managerial staff.

OBJECTIVES

Once you have read this chapter of the book, you should be able to:
- **identify reasons why conflict exists**
- **state the effects of conflicts on individuals and teams**
- **state guidelines for resolving conflict.**

WHAT CAUSES CONFLICT?

Conflict can be as a result of a disagreement, a personality clash, a power struggle, or a reaction to what one person considers to be the unreasonable behaviour of another. Rivalry is a form of conflict, and a certain measure of rivalry is considered healthy by some, and a necessary prerequisite of creative and imaginative thought.

Disagreements

As individuals, we rarely share exactly the same viewpoint and beliefs as all the people with whom we have regular or occasional contact. It is the degree of difference in our standpoints which is the usual cause of disagreement with other people. However, if we normally behave in a rational way, and appreciate and accept other people's viewpoints, the tendency to create conflict is very much reduced. If we are in dispute or disagreement about something, and have the capacity to appreciate the other person's point of view, then a rational compromise can often be reached.

In most problem-solving situations, it may be of great value to be able to discuss the problem with someone who holds a different opinion from our own. This helps us analyse the problem more objectively, and come to a more considered solution – perhaps one which we may otherwise have not considered. There are times, however, when circumstances make it impossible to discuss things rationally, and where each person becomes firmly entrenched in their views and determined not to concede their point of view. Sometimes parties simply have to agree to disagree and, provided this does not directly affect the continuation of normal work or delay important decisions, this may be considered an adult solution. Reasonable and rational discussions can then proceed. Most disagreements only become serious situations of conflict if the disagreement allows the two parties to harbour grudges and ill feelings about each other.

Personality clashes

Sometimes a clash of personalities causes conflict between two or more employees and, no matter how hard each tries, they find it impossible to learn to like the other. Personality clashes and differences, if handled in an adult way, need not lead to conflict. Many people who do not like each other are nevertheless able to work together in a professional manner, provided that they can accept each other's point of view and learn to appreciate the other's abilities and achievements. Individuals may often be able to change their methods of work, and even their attitudes, but personal characteristics are far harder to change.

Where conflict due to personalities is allowed to persist, it results in prolonged conflict with the inevitable loss of dignity and respect. Continuing conflict of this kind is sometimes very deep-rooted, and may go on for years if not checked, making working life difficult for those who are directly involved and those on the periphery.

Power struggles

Power struggles cause particular difficulties, and sometimes have quite sinister undertones. The sort of conflict which occurs between two people of equal standing is often covert, and usually ends with one clear victor, the other party normally leaving the team, the department or even the company. Power struggles are more likely to exist, though, between a manager, or other figure of authority, and a subordinate, especially where an ambitious subordinate has a strong character. It is generally the authority figure who feels threatened in this situation, and conflict normally arises out of feelings of vulnerability.

Conflicts between a strong subordinate and weak superior are rarely the result of a direct struggle to gain power. They are more likely to exist where the subordinate shows good future potential, but where this is suppressed by the superior. Conflicts also arise where the superior is more of a hands-on manager, i.e. prefers to be doing the job rather than managing others in the job, and where a promising subordinate shows considerable potential for further skills development. The perceived threat to the manager is usually that any development will give the subordinate superior knowledge and skills. The issue for the manager is not how to retain their managerial position, but how to prevent the subordinate attaining a level of competence superior to their own. Such managers are really team players, and for them, doing the job is more important than managing the job. Where conflict arises out of this situation, it is often the manager who instigates the conflict. The root cause of such conflict is usually the manager's inability or unwillingness to accept their primary function as one of managing staff and, if the problem is not recognised by a more senior person within the organisation, the conflict may go on for a very long time.

Perceived unreasonable behaviour

Where one person considers the behaviour of another to be unreasonable, the conflict arising from ill feeling often exacerbates the problem. One party normally adopts an 'aggrieved' position, feeling perhaps morally superior, and considering the other party to be a 'bad person'. Once this moral stance has been adopted, the aggrieved party will often substantiate this by continually looking for confirmation of the other's unreasonable behaviour. Situations can turn unpleasant when this goes unchecked.

The longer this kind of conflict continues, the harder the situation is to resolve, as the original cause of the conflict becomes lost in time, and the standpoint of the parties become more deeply entrenched. If things go this far, any attempt to discuss the problem without the assistance of a skilled mediator will usually result in further acrimony.

Frustration

Finally, one of the less easily identifiable causes of conflict is that which has its roots in frustration. Frustrations may be experienced by an individual or a group of people, and the most common causes are either discounting of ideas, opinions and views by management, or enforced change where the group neither has a voice nor is consulted. Such frustration may be particularly noticeable through periods of organisational change where little attempt is made to communicate with the workforce. Most people feel considerable stress whenever changes are forced upon them, or where they feel they have no part in the restructuring exercise.

WHAT IS THE EFFECT OF CONFLICT?

Unresolved conflict can have far-reaching effects, not only on those directly involved, but also on other members of the team, the department or the entire workforce. Conflict thrives on every principle of poor management – lack of communication, *laissez-faire* leadership, political in-fighting, unhealthy interdepartmental rivalry, etc. and, when left unchecked, will usually escalate into more open hostility. Most of all, therefore, conflict thrives on mismanagement.

....

CASE STUDY

Colin and Jackie both work in the reservations department of a tour operator. When they first met, they got along quite well and were both involved in the social gatherings that were arranged by various members of the department. On the whole, everyone in the team got on well, and many considered their colleagues to be friends rather than workmates. A few months ago, a bonus scheme was introduced to help stimulate bookings on certain products. Each member of staff could potentially earn up to an extra £40 a week, if they achieved additional sales on the specified products. After much discussion it was decided that the bonus would be awarded to the person who confirmed the booking, and an agreement was made, that if one member of staff had done a lot of work and had only reached option stage and the customer subsequently confirmed the booking, that the bonus would go to the person who made the option. This was easy to identify, as the reservations clerk's name was entered against the option number. This system worked well and everyone involved found the bonus system a great incentive and morale seemed high.

One day, while checking through the computer system for outstanding options, Jackie noticed that several of her bookings had been confirmed by Colin, but her name had been erased from the screen and she had not received any bonus. Jackie was furious. It appeared that Colin had deliberately taken her bookings for himself and earned bonus commission that was in fact due to her. She went straight over to Colin's desk to tackle him about it. Colin denied her accusations and said that the only reason she was behaving in this way was because she wasn't as good a salesperson as he was and if she spent more time working than chatting to her friends, then she might be a little more successful. Jackie was incensed. She knew Colin was lying, so she went to see her supervisor. Unfortunately for Jackie, her supervisor was little help, and expressed a wish not to become involved as there was no way of proving Jackie's allegations. Jackie fumed all day, and thought about ways of getting even.

Weeks passed and Jackie and Colin refused to speak to one another, but each looked for opportunities to criticise or complain about the other's behaviour. Neither would attend any social events in case they were forced to communicate, and on the occasions where they were expected to work together, the situation was so volatile, that little was achieved. Other staff began to feel uncomfortable about the situation, and felt that on some days the atmosphere could be cut with a knife.

They all felt they had to be very careful what they said to either Colin or Jackie, as Jackie had already made it plain that she considered anyone who showed friendship and support for Colin must therefore be against her. The once happy working environment had gone and was replaced by open hostility between two of the staff which affected everyone in the team.

This case study demonstrates how an incident between two people can escalate into conflict which affects everyone. Colin and Jackie behaved initially in a predictable manner – refusing to communicate. Not only did they refuse to speak to one another in the office, but they also boycotted social events as a demonstration of their determination to keep up the non-communication.

Although initially this affected no one but themselves, as time passed, other people became drawn into the situation, eventually leading to a feeling of unease within the whole team. The situation has now reached a stage at which work is affected, and morale is low. If left unresolved, it is likely that one or both of them will leave for another job. Of course, had the supervisor intervened right at the beginning, it is likely that none of this would have happened.

The main effects of conflict which is unresolved are: low morale; lack of communication; lack of cooperation; drop in performance standards.

Lack of communication

Communication is important to any organisation, and if there is a break in lines of internal communication, this can cause problems. In a situation where conflict exists, there may be a deliberate intention to withhold information from certain individuals, either because of an unwillingness to communicate with them, or as a malicious way of causing trouble, e.g. an aggrieved member of staff may 'forget' to pass on an important message to their colleague. Staff involved in conflict may choose to adopt an attitude of non-communication, i.e. refusing to speak to the other individual or individuals involved in the conflict. Not only does this restrict the flow of information within the company, but it will also make working relationships very difficult for both those directly involved in the conflict and others working around them.

Non-cooperation

Non-communication may also lead to non-cooperation. Individuals may resent situations in which they are forced to work with the other individual with whom they have a grievance. This may take a variety of forms: a point blank refusal to work with someone; total lack of cooperation with the individual, therefore making it very difficult to achieve the task in hand; actively seeking to sabotage the task in order to cease the need to work with the other individual; looking for opportunities to 'shop' the other individual for errors made or performance which is below standard in order to have them removed from the task; taking sick leave. If an employee chooses to adopt any of these courses of action, the result will inevitably be that the standards of performance will drop, and the quality of service which the customer ultimately receives will not be as high as it should be.

Drop in performance standards

Unresolved conflict will eventually affect the morale of at least one of the people involved. Once morale drops, the individual may not feel so committed to the job and performance standards may drop.

CASE STUDY

Keiron sees himself as a good manager. He is certainly a good manager of processes and systems, but his man management skills have never been developed. Keiron has taken a dislike to one of his younger members of staff, William. He wastes no opportunity to discount William's efforts and is generally unfair and unkind to the younger man. William does not understand what he has done to incur Keiron's displeasure but, because he is fairly strong willed and independent, he is able to resist Keiron's constant pressures. Keiron also does not understand the reasons for this conflict, but suspects that it might be due to the 'unreasonable' behaviour of William. In any case, the conflict has persisted for some time.

Keiron's view of subordinates is that they should have respect for management and for anyone in a managerial position. He suspects that William does not share this view, but also fails to realise that this is the primary reason for his failure to accept William as a useful member of staff. Keiron's lack of perception means that the awkwardness between himself and William goes on.

William is not entirely aware of the undercurrent and the stress which this situation is causing him. He knows that he isn't happy, but he is unable to explain exactly why this should be. He has lacked motivation for some time, and knows that his work rate and standard of work have both declined, but he is unable to give Keiron any rational reason for this.

For his part, Keiron did once try the 'nice way' with William, spending some time to give him a pep talk and encourage him to do better, but has since reverted to his more usual management methods. Keiron's style of language is mostly Critical Parent: 'You've got to get a grip of yourself, William', 'We can't have you upsetting the staff every day', 'You've got a problem' and 'Your trouble is you've no respect for authority'.

None of this is particularly helpful, and relations between manager and subordinate deteriorate – William getting increasingly frustrated as the conflict goes on and Keiron putting more pressure on William to 'buck his ideas up, and take his place in the team'. The cycle of demotivation, fall in performance, chastisement, further stress and frustration, and demotivation goes on unchecked. William is a very skilled employee, but he finds it increasingly difficult to work under these conditions. Finally, he leaves and takes his talents elsewhere.

Much has been said about the causes of conflict, but this case study shows clearly what can happen when conflict is unresolved. Keiron cannot see that the clash of personalities need not be an issue. He believes that it is William who has the problem, and William who is responsible for the increasing acrimony between them. He, Keiron, has 'bent over backwards' to resolve matters. In fact, of course, he has quite failed to resolve this unnecessary situation. It is the classic conflict spiral of tension, withdrawal, managerial inactivity, frustration, stress and needless termination of employment. For William, the unpleasantness of the past is fast becoming a distant memory. For Keiron, the problem has also gone, but he still regards it very much as 'William's problem'.

In extreme cases where conflict escalates and continues for a long period of time, those involved can suffer stress or even ill health. Stress is now a major cause for concern in many companies in Britain, as a good deal of employee sickness is due to stress or stress-related illnesses. Much of this stress is caused by unresolved conflict.

Assignment   Think about disagreements which have resulted in conflict that you have either been involved in yourself, or have witnessed between colleagues.

1 What was the initial reason which caused the conflict?

2 What effects did the conflict have over a period of time on (a) those directly involved, (b) people outside of conflict?

3 How did the conflict affect the standard of work, and/or quality of service received by the customer?

RESOLVING CONFLICT

If good working relationships are to play their part in achieving and maintaining the best business standards, then any conflict between staff must be resolved quickly and efficiently. As is already clear, conflict does not resolve itself. It is the responsibility of the supervisor or manager to bring the conflicting parties together, and help them find a solution to their problem. If the conflicting parties include the manager or supervisor and a member of their staff, then the responsibility is even greater. No dispute can begin to be resolved until someone makes the first move to break the deadlock.

Ideally, people should always try to settle their own differences and, in most cases, one or other usually decides to make peace and call a halt to hostilities. One of the problems of conflict is that, very often, the two parties take up a stance, each becoming less and less aware of the original dispute, and increasingly dependent upon reinforcement of ill feeling to keep the conflict alive. Usually, a point is reached where each of the protagonists has long forgotten what they originally fell out about. The thing that matters from now on is to fuel the general ill will and feelings of antagonism by actively seeking evidence of the other's inherently 'bad' behaviour. This shows normally in a much milder form when we say such things as, 'He never wants to listen. That's just the way he's always been', 'She's been like that for years. It's no use trying to change her' or 'I wouldn't even ask him. It's not worth wasting your breath.'

These are typically reactive statements which attribute general patterns of bad or poor behaviour to the other person, and they gradually become incontrovertible 'truths' which serve to reinforce prejudices that this person will behave in a predictably specific manner, no matter what the circumstances. This is why a mediator is useful in disputes, in being able to stand back and see a way round the otherwise intractable stances of the two parties.

CASE STUDY

A management consultant was invited to review the business of a company run jointly by two brothers. The brothers had fallen out over some long-forgotten dispute over the direction the business should take, and had never since been able to see eye to eye over any important business matter. Worse still, the business was in a state of crisis because the two brothers had ceased to talk to each other on the grounds that each one would never see the point of view of the other.

The consultant discovered this problem on arrival at the tour company and realised very quickly that he would be unable to solve anything until the two brothers began to talk to each other again. He called them together at a meeting and, turning to the elder brother, asked him to talk for about a minute on where he believed the company should be heading in the future. When he had finished, the consultant turned to the other brother and asked him to give a quick résumé of what had been said. The younger brother looked blank, and said he was unable to remember any of what had been said. 'Try!' said the consultant, and the brother began rather falteringly to relate bits and pieces of the talk.

When he stopped, the consultant told the younger brother that it was his turn to talk for a minute and outline his vision of the business and, at the end of a minute he turned to the elder brother and asked him to précis his brother's explanation. He too, found it very difficult to make a start but, after being urged by the consultant, was able to relate some of what had been said. Then, the consultant asked each brother to repeat the process again and again, each in turn saying a little more about his vision of the company, and the other giving a résumé of what had been said. Finally, the consultant got the two brothers to set out on paper all of the points on which they were in general agreement, and then all of the points over which there was general disagreement. The process of examining the business had begun.

This case study demonstrates just how conflict can get out of hand – even between two partners in a business – to a point where each has shut out the voice of the other for so long that neither is even able to listen to the other's point of view. Each time they refused to listen to the other they reinforced the conflict. The mediator was able to break down the conflict by putting each partner in a situation where they were forced to listen to the other, and therefore, finally obliged to acknowledge the other's different point of view.

Here are some useful guidelines which outline the key stages of facing up to, discussing and resolving conflict:

1 Think carefully about the consequences of not resolving the dispute, and how you might begin to approach the problem.
2 Choose the right time and place to discuss the matter – a private and non-threatening environment and adequate time to enable the discussion to go on as long as necessary.
3 Be prepared for, and open to some criticism from the other person, and accept that both parties are usually at fault in some way.
4 Concentrate on resuming normal working relationships rather than on the original causal factors.
5 Try to agree that each person will listen to the other's point of view.
6 End the conversation on a positive point by agreeing a positive action plan which depends upon the cooperation of the two disputants.

Please note that the necessary interpersonal skills required to effectively conduct a discussion of this type are covered on pp. 210–21.

THE ROLE OF THE MEDIATOR

The mediator should act as an independent person who is unbiased and who will take a neutral standpoint. The role of the mediator will need to be flexible, so that they can remain objective, encouraging rational discussion and conversation between the two parties. Where there is a reluctance to communicate, the mediator will need to take a more active role in leading the discussion, even to the point of acting as intermediary spokesperson until sufficient trust has been established. If one or other of the two parties decides to disengage from the discussion, the mediator will need to encourage continued communication or, if discussions show signs of becoming heated, the mediator will need to be a calming influence.

Quite often, the mediator's presence will allow both disputants to discuss matters in a rational manner, with minimal antagonism towards each other. If the conversation reaches stalemate, the mediator must be able to move the conversation on towards a compromise or workable solution, and make arrangements to review the effectiveness of the solution. Finally, the mediator must ensure that both parties have received a fair hearing and are satisfied with the outcome of the discussion.

In cases of conflict between a manager and subordinate, someone of higher authority should first speak to both parties separately, before they come together to discuss the main issues. The mediator will then understand how both parties feel about each other, and make it more likely that each one speaks openly about the problem in front of the other. Also, if the mediator is aware of the different perceptions of the cause of the conflict before discussions begin, it is more likely that a satisfactory solution will be achieved.

Let's now look at some guidelines for acting as mediator:

1 Make arrangements for the discussions to take place in an environment conducive to open discussion.
2 Begin the discussion by explaining the need to resolve the issues and the need for both parties to air their views openly, freely and objectively.
3 Ask questions of an open nature which get both parties to face the issues and begin to talk to each other.
4 Summarise the discussions to ensure that all points are clarified, and that both parties have a similar understanding of the facts.
5 Try to remain distant from the dispute, but remember to direct discussions towards a positive solution.
6 Outline the resolutions agreed by the two parties and set a review date as appropriate.
7 Thank both parties for being honest and cooperative.

15

Running effective meetings

As a manager one of your responsibilities may be to organise and run staff meetings. Meetings are a valuable forum for the exchange and development of ideas and well-run meetings can be both effective and stimulating for all who attend. There is an art to running effective meetings. Planning is essential as poorly organised meetings usually achieve very little and use up valuable time which might be better spent in more productive ways. As part of your NVQ assessment you will be expected to demonstrate your ability to organise and run successful meetings. This chapter aims to provide you with practical guidelines to ensure that your meetings are successful.

OBJECTIVES

Once you have read this section of the book you should be able to:
- **state the purposes of various types of meetings**
- **effectively organise meetings**
- **state guidelines for leading a meeting.**

WHY HAVE A MEETING?

Why should you choose to have a meeting? Why not simply send out a memo or have an informal discussion with staff whenever necessary? It is really a matter of effectiveness. While memos are a very useful method of communication, they should not be relied upon as a sole form of communication with staff. Written records play an important part in communication, and provide a useful reference point for the future, but written communications are strictly one-way – from sender to receiver. By allowing issues to be discussed at a meeting, communication will be two-way and will enable those present to ask further questions and clarify points and make comments and suggestions as appropriate. Staff will feel far more involved in the day-to-day decisions in their department or organisation if they are given the opportunity to enter into discussions rather than just receive a series of written communications.

Informal discussions are a much better form of communication than memos. A good manager should keep in touch with the staff and speak to them from day to day about various issues, but there will be occasions when a formal staff meeting will be a more appropriate form of communication.

Benefits of having a meeting

- Well-run meetings encourage two-way communication and open discussion.
- Meetings provide an opportunity for a number of individuals to put their views, which should enable them to come to a considered and balanced decision.
- Meetings provide a forum to update staff on important issues and developments within the department or organisation.
- Meetings provide the manager with an important insight into the way staff feel about the agenda items.
- Meetings allow staff to bring forward important issues for debate and discussion.
- Staff whose views are sought in open discussion feel more committed to any decisions which have been made.

THE PURPOSE OF A MEETING

Meetings use up valuable resources in terms of people and time, so caution is recommended in deciding when and for what purpose you will need to hold a meeting. Let's say that a meeting comprises six members of staff, each earning on average £6 an hour, a manager who earns £7 an hour and a secretary who earns £5 an hour. If the meeting runs for two hours, the cost of all those attending could be as much as £96. If the meeting achieves its objectives, then the investment is worthwhile. However, meetings which are called just for the sake of holding a meeting, often turn out to be a costly and wasteful exercise, especially if there are no objectives and the meeting is poorly organised.

Many organisations feel that they cannot function without meetings, and have a propensity to delay all decisions until a meeting can be held to discuss the issues. This is usually done in the name of democratic decision making, but is more often due to someone's unwillingness to make what may turn out to be an unpopular decision. By calling a meeting, the responsibility of the decision will be shared.

It is important to ensure that only those whose presence is genuinely required, are invited to attend your meetings. Make sure that meetings contain the right numbers and right calibre of people. Most decisions can be made without the need for close consultation with every member of staff. While it is desirable to operate in a democratic manner which consults staff at all levels, there will be times when a decisive and speedy decision needs to be made from the top. Deferring too many decisions until a meeting can be held often blocks up the company's communication system. Managers needs to strike a good balance between the need to call meetings and the need to make a lone decision.

The first consideration for managers is what the meeting seeks to achieve. You need to be clear in your own mind about this before you decide on the type of meeting you wish to run and the people who will be invited. Having an objective at the start of the meeting will also help you to focus on the important issues and measure its effectiveness. The test of effectiveness is to ask, 'Did I achieve what I set out to achieve?' Once you have decided upon the objective of the meeting, you can then decide on the type of meeting you will hold.

Team briefing

This is a most commonly used method of communicating current developments, plans and policies within the company. Its purpose is to provide information to those present and to ensure that any queries raised are clarified. The team briefing allows those present to ask questions to reinforce their understanding of the issues of which they are informed, but the purpose of a briefing is not to debate or challenge that information. The role of the leader of the team briefing is to ensure that sufficient information is provided, and to undertake to seek further information from other sources and report back as necessary.

Problem-solving meeting

The objective of this meeting is to encourage those present to put forward ideas and views to help solve a specific problem. The meeting should be encouraged to brainstorm for ideas, and the leader needs to ensure that these ideas are then properly evaluated. At a meeting of this sort, it is important that a good cross-section of people who are involved with the problem are present. If the meeting is attended by people who share a common opinion, it is unlikely that all possible solutions will be properly examined. If people with opposing viewpoints are present, this will allow the meeting to collectively examine the problem from a variety of viewpoints and thus reach a balanced solution.

Fact-finding meeting

This type of meeting should be called where it is necessary to obtain a number of viewpoints on a specific issue to provide the decision makers with enough information on which to base a sound decision. Those present will each be asked to contribute their own thoughts and feelings about a particular issue, or perhaps their own or their departments needs in a future development. For example, if a company intends to install a new computer system which is to be used by all departments, the meeting would seek to clarify the needs of each department and then base a decision on those facts.

Review meetings

The purpose of a review meeting is to discuss policies, decisions, new working practices, etc., which have recently been put into place, to discuss their effectiveness, air any problems or concerns and to make suggestions for enhancement in the future. A meeting of this type should be a learning process for all involved. Those present should be encouraged to contribute, so that a consensus can be reached on what the meeting would like to achieve. This should then be carried forward to the decision makers if they are not present.

ARRANGING THE MEETING

Once you have set your objective and decided on the type of meeting you wish to hold, you will need to give some time to organising it. Let's look at the considerations:

- What specific topics need to be discussed?
- Who needs to be present?
- When should the meeting take place?
- How long is the meeting likely to run for?
- Where should the meeting be held?
- Who will record the minutes of the meeting?

The topics to be discussed at the meeting

Careful consideration should be given to the topics which are to be discussed. Are they relevant to the meeting? Do the people attending the meeting know enough about each item for the discussion to be meaningful? If not, can background information regarding the subject be circulated beforehand? Once these issues have been considered, an agenda (see example in Fig. 15.1) for the meeting should be drawn up and circulated to all of the people who are attending the meeting.

Once the agenda has been compiled, it may become apparent that the same style of meeting will not be appropriate for all of the topics to be discussed. In Fig. 15.1, which is an agenda for a team briefing, most of the items can be approached in the style of a briefing, i.e. giving information and clarifying points. But the item regarding customer care training necessitates open discussion, feedback and suggestions from the staff. It is perfectly acceptable to include an item like this in a team briefing, but the chairman of the meeting should be aware that this particular topic will require a different style of discussion than that of the other topics and this should be made clear to the staff who are present. If the chairperson does not indicate the change of style, the staff may not be as participative as the chairperson would have liked, because they will assume that they should adopt the same role throughout the meeting, i.e. passive, and asking questions only to clarify information. This style is not suitable for reviewing.

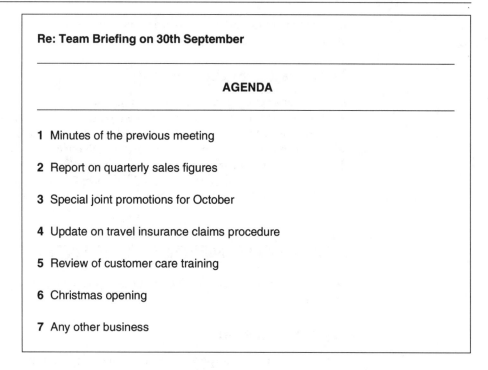

> **Re: Team Briefing on 30th September**
>
> ---
>
> **AGENDA**
>
> ---
>
> 1 Minutes of the previous meeting
>
> 2 Report on quarterly sales figures
>
> 3 Special joint promotions for October
>
> 4 Update on travel insurance claims procedure
>
> 5 Review of customer care training
>
> 6 Christmas opening
>
> 7 Any other business

Fig 15.1 An example of an agenda

Who needs to be at the meeting?

This will be very much dictated by the agenda, as it will be clear from this who needs to be involved in the discussion of the topics which have been listed. Beware of inviting more people than is necessary, and consider the relevance of the meeting to those who you do invite. If only one topic is of relevance to a particular person, is the meeting the best medium for that person to be involved? Is it possible or desirable that they are present for just that part of the meeting? Consider also the number of people who will be present. If the meeting is to be conducted solely as a team briefing, then large numbers are not necessarily a problem, but six people is more than adequate for problem solving. If numbers exceed six, the meeting is usually less effective, and the group may be unable to come to a decision.

Venue, date and duration

Once it has been decided who will attend the meeting, a mutually agreeable date should be set. If this presents a difficulty, as it sometimes does in busy organisations, the most practical time and date will need to be adopted as the best solution. Once this is arranged, a suitable venue can be sought. Make sure someone is responsible for booking the venue and that refreshments are provided where the venue is off-site. Ensure that everyone attending the meeting is aware of the venue, and how to get there.

The minutes of the meeting

As a matter of course, minutes should be taken as a record for future reference. It is the responsibility of the chairperson to arrange for someone to take minutes of the meeting, and this should be agreed beforehand. Ideally, minutes should be taken by someone who is not expected to be actively involved in the discussions, as this generally requires a good ear and a steady hand. Under no circumstances should the chairperson have to take the minutes, as this will remove him or her from the discussion and diminish their special role and function.

LEADING THE MEETING EFFECTIVELY

Leading a meeting effectively demands good leadership skills and plenty of practice.

Style of leadership

A good leader, or chairperson, needs to be able to adopt a style appropriate to the type of meeting that is being run and to the needs of the people attending. A team briefing requires the chairperson to adopt an informative style, while a problem-solving meeting requires him or her to sit back and be more of a mediator. Flexibility is always desirable.

Starting the meeting

At the start of the meeting, the chairperson should welcome the participants, outline the format and style of the meeting and state its purpose, making sure that everyone present has sufficient knowledge of the subject-matter to be involved at the desired level. Apologies for absence are tendered at this juncture, and the agenda should be laid out before those present.

Guiding the meeting

The chairperson should guide the meeting through the points on the agenda and ensure that each point is covered sufficiently to achieve the main objective. Once this stage is reached, the chairperson should summarise the main points discussed and the action which has been decided upon. If a member of the meeting has undertaken to perform a specific task related to the issue under discussion, then this should be reconfirmed. The chairperson should ensure that the meeting adheres to its agenda and to its time-scales, and keep the meeting from any tendency to sidetrack. While issues on the periphery of the topics under discussion may be relevant, the chairperson must ensure that valuable time is not wasted on a discussion which will not help to achieve objectives.

If an item is of some importance and is obviously going to take more than the scheduled amount of time to resolve, the chairperson will need to convene another meeting for further discussion. Discussions must always be directly relevant to the purpose of the meeting, or the chairperson should ask the speaker to explain its relevance.

Air time

Air time is that time which is spent in active discussion. Some people will have a tendency to say more than others, so a level of control will usually be necessary to ensure that everyone has a fair say. A good chairperson will also be aware of their own air time, and will need to ensure that they are not speaking more than is necessary. With team briefings, the need is for clear and concise information. Those who tend to ramble often lose the interest of the meeting. When the purpose of the meeting is to debate and discuss, i.e. problem-solving or review meetings, the chairperson should limit their own input, and ensure that everyone is given a fair chance to air their personal views and feelings on the subject.

Asking questions

Sometimes, the chairperson may need to stimulate discussion by opening up the meeting with questions. An effective way of controlling the meeting without too much imposition is to draw up a list of questions relevant to the various topics under discussion, and to put these to the meeting wherever and whenever the discussion needs to be opened up to other viewpoints.

Interpretation of points

Whenever necessary, it is the chairperson's job to interpret any technical points made to ensure that everyone present understands technical terms or is aware of background information which will aid understanding of specific points made. This also goes for abbreviations and jargon words which may not be understood by everyone.

Body language

Body language is often as important as spoken language during meetings. The chairperson should be quick to notice when someone's body language indicates boredom, disinterest or a wish to withdraw, and should seek to draw them back into the conversation. The chairperson should also be aware of those quieter members of staff who wish to make a point, but may be overshadowed by other more outspoken individuals. A carefully directed question is normally sufficient to elicit their thoughts and ideas, e.g. 'How will that affect the work that your department does, Mary?' or 'Perhaps James would like to expand on this from his point of view?'

Promoting interpersonal communication

The chairperson should encourage staff to talk to each other during the meeting rather than talking to the chair. At the same time, though, they must be able to regain control if the discussion becomes sidetracked or looks likely to escalate into an argument.

Closing the meeting

Once all of the items on the agenda have been covered, the chairperson should open up the meeting to 'any other business'. This is an opportunity for discussion of particular points which individual members may wish to raise. Most chairpersons usually wind up the meeting by summarising the important points, inviting suggestions for the next meeting and thanking everyone for their attendance and participation.

SUMMARY

To summarise, the main guidelines to running effective meetings are:

- Identify the aims and objectives of the meeting.
- Select the type of meeting appropriate to your objective.
- Select a venue for the meeting.
- Decide on numbers and names of those who need to be present.
- Draw up and circulate an agenda of the points to be covered.

  The key points for effective leadership of a meeting are:

- Adopt a suitable style and be prepared to be flexible.
- State the purpose and style of the meeting.
- Guide the meeting through the agenda and keep it on course.
- Make sure that air time is fairly distributed.
- Act as an interpreter whenever necessary.
- Watch for all verbal and non-verbal communication.
- Use questioning skills to stimulate discussion.
- Encourage good interpersonal communication.
- Close the meeting on a positive note.

Glossary

APEX (Advanced Purchase Excursion Fare) An economy-class, reduced price air ticket which has a number of restrictions applying to its use.

Coach class A type of economy class used by certain airlines for long-distance air routes.

Economy class A normal tourist-class seat on an aircraft. Economy-class tickets are unrestricted, and can be changed or refunded without penalty.

Independent itineraries Independent travel arrangements, comprising accommodation, transportation and ground arrangements, for individual client requirements.

Locator Computer booking reference given by airlines and tour operators.

Manual ticket issue Tickets issued by hand, as opposed to being computer generated.

Option A provisional booking, usually held for twenty-four hours, during which time the customer can decide whether or not to confirm the booking. If the booking is not confirmed within this time, the option will automatically lapse.

Sector A term used in air travel to describe part of an air journey from one point to another.

Travicom An airline computer reservations system, through which it is possible to effect bookings with most national and international airlines.

Index